Shojo Beat

ANONYMOUS NOISE

Ryoko
Fukuyama

THE ANO 6's NOISE

Anonymous Noise
Volume 6

CONTENTS

SONG 29

I WOULD HAVE BEEN ABLE TO SAY "I LOVE YOU."

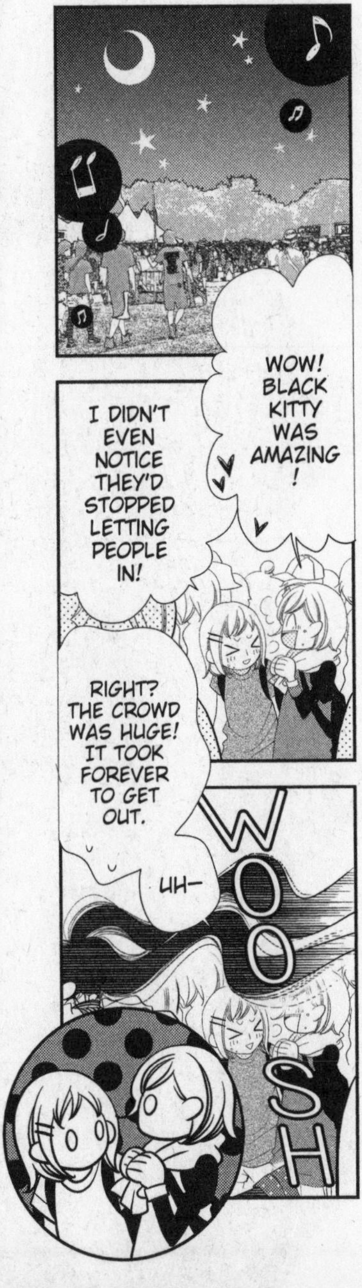

WOW! BLACK KITTY WAS AMAZING!
I DIDN'T EVEN NOTICE THEY'D STOPPED LETTING PEOPLE IN!
RIGHT? THE CROWD WAS HUGE! IT TOOK FOREVER TO GET OUT.
WOOSH
UH-

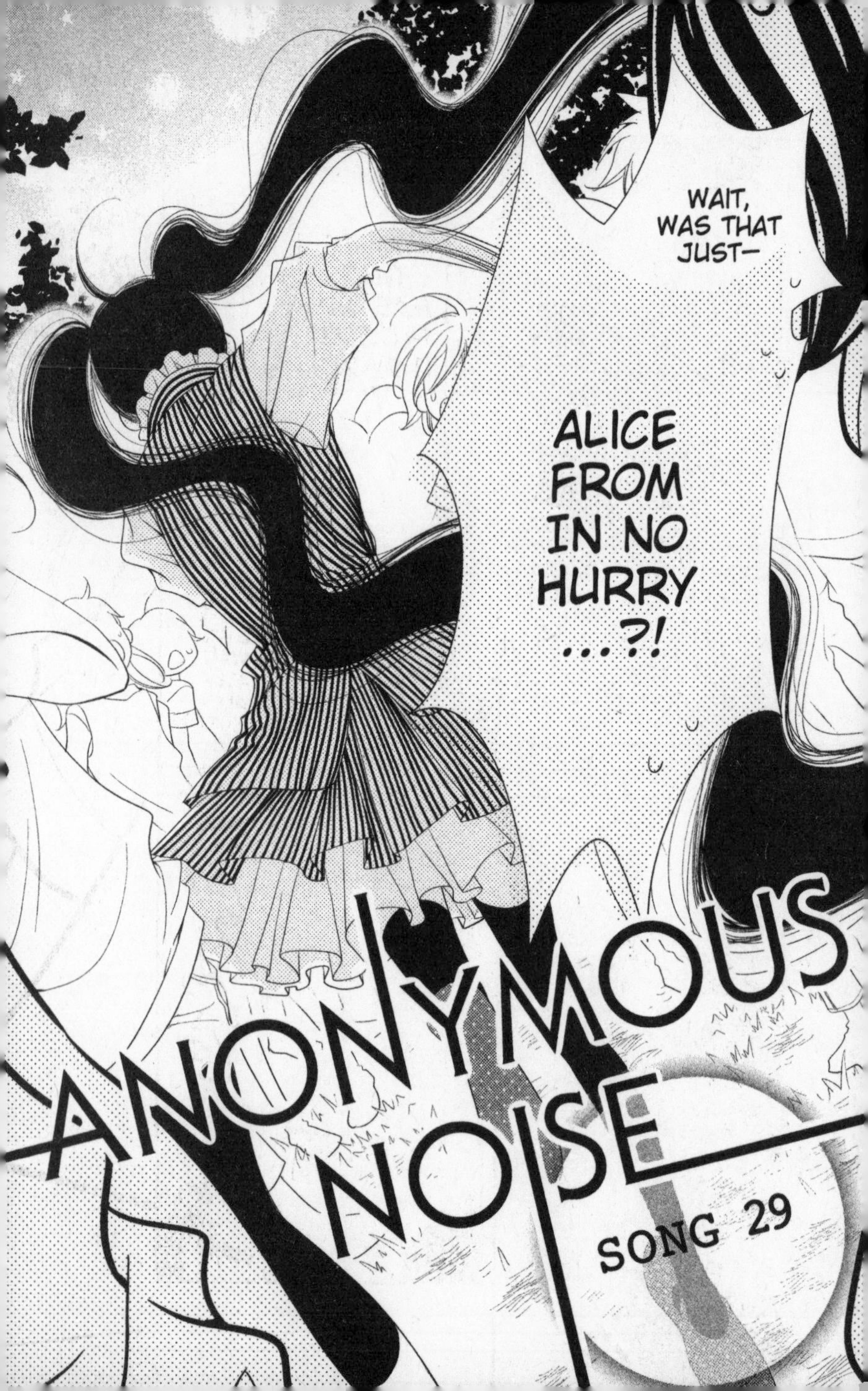
WAIT, WAS THAT JUST—
ALICE FROM IN NO HURRY ...?!
ANONYMOUS NOISE
SONG 29

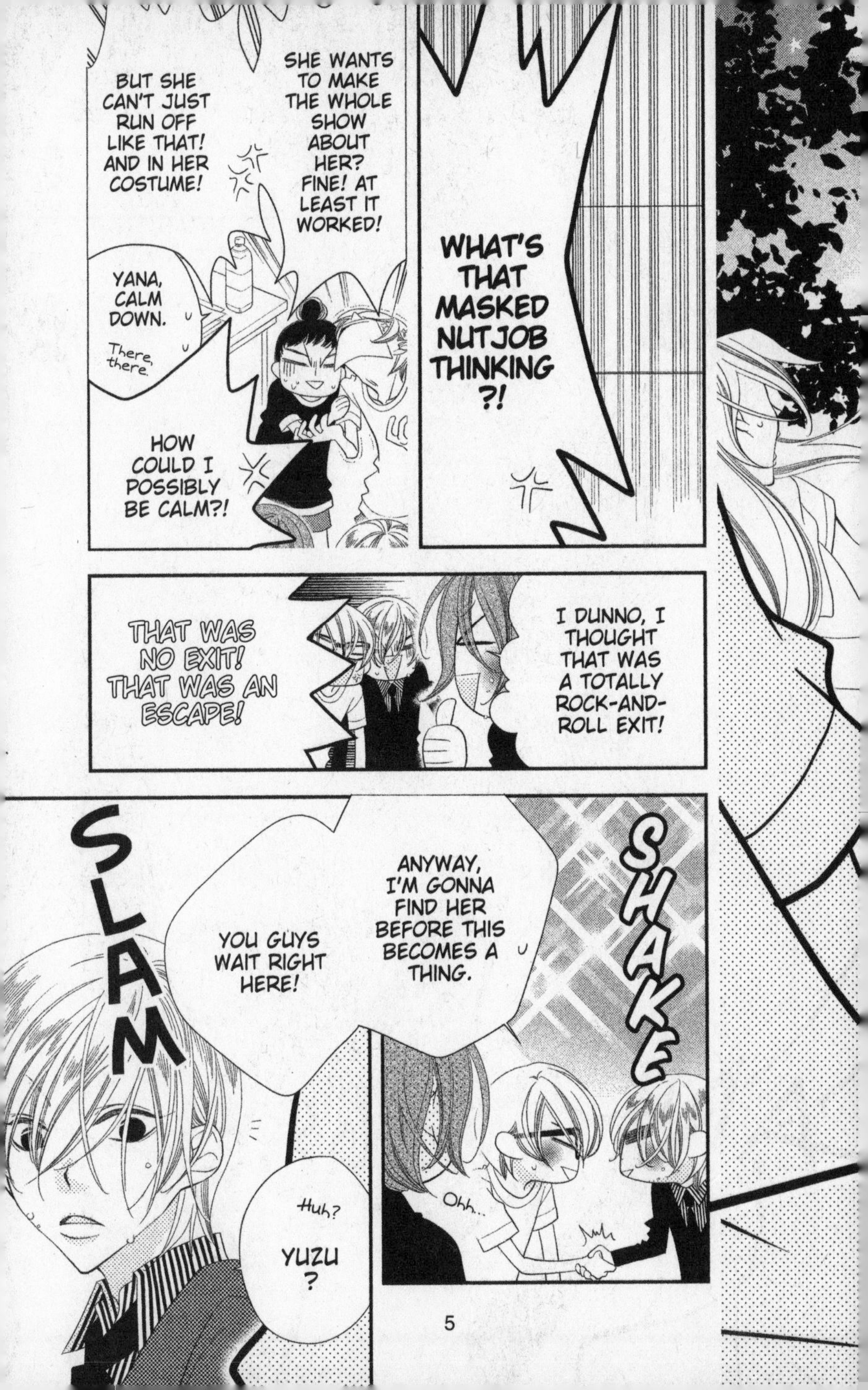
WHAT'S THAT MASKED NUTJOB THINKING?!
SHE WANTS TO MAKE THE WHOLE SHOW ABOUT HER? FINE! AT LEAST IT WORKED!
BUT SHE CAN'T JUST RUN OFF LIKE THAT! AND IN HER COSTUME!
YANA, CALM DOWN.
There, there.
HOW COULD I POSSIBLY BE CALM?!
I DUNNO, I THOUGHT THAT WAS A TOTALLY ROCK-AND-ROLL EXIT!
THAT WAS NO EXIT! THAT WAS AN ESCAPE!
SHAKE
ANYWAY, I'M GONNA FIND HER BEFORE THIS BECOMES A THING.
YOU GUYS WAIT RIGHT HERE!
Ohh...
SLAM
Huh?
YUZU?

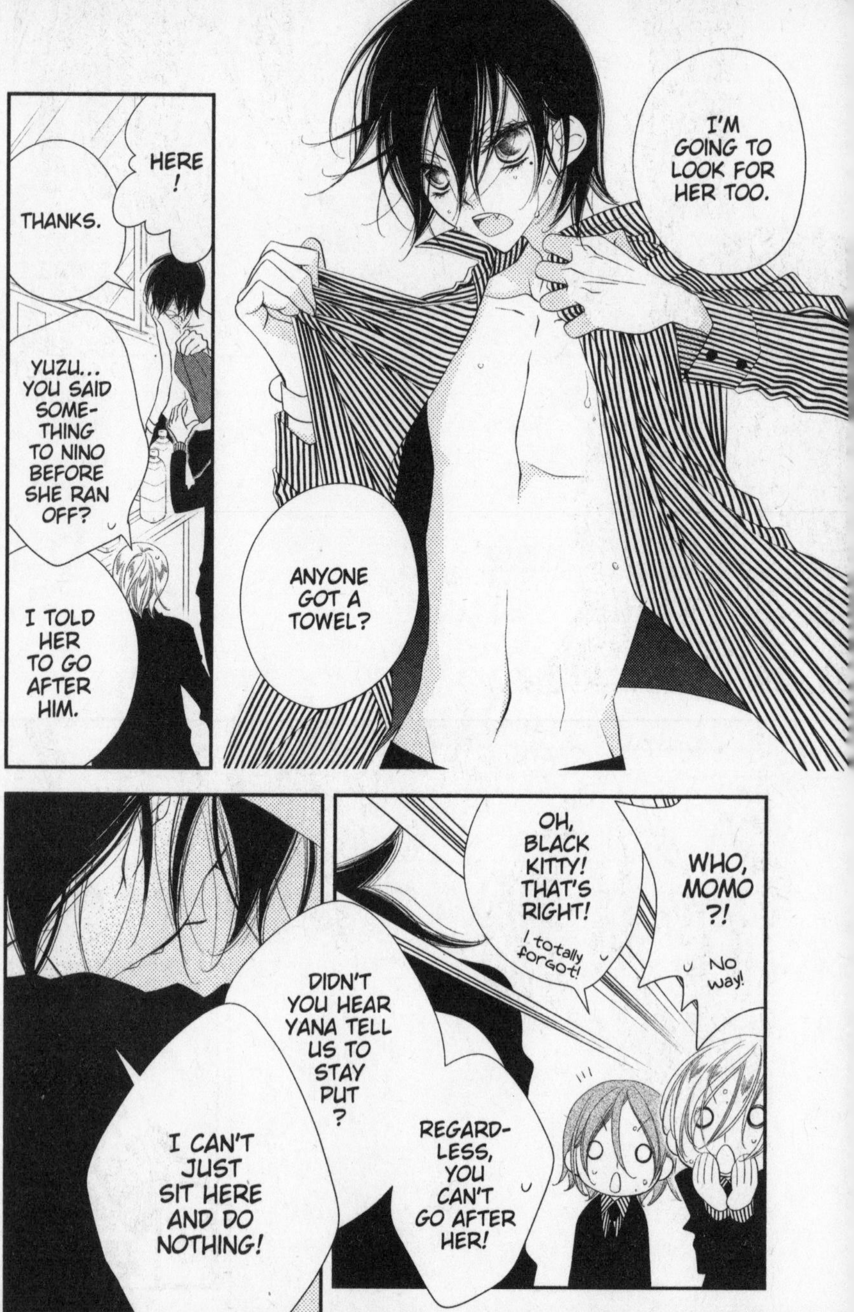
I'M GOING TO LOOK FOR HER TOO.
ANYONE GOT A TOWEL?
HERE!
THANKS.
YUZU... YOU SAID SOME-THING TO NINO BEFORE SHE RAN OFF?
I TOLD HER TO GO AFTER HIM.
WHO, MOMO?!
No way!
OH, BLACK KITTY! THAT'S RIGHT!
I totally forgot!
DIDN'T YOU HEAR YANA TELL US TO STAY PUT?
REGARD-LESS, YOU CAN'T GO AFTER HER!
I CAN'T JUST SIT HERE AND DO NOTHING!

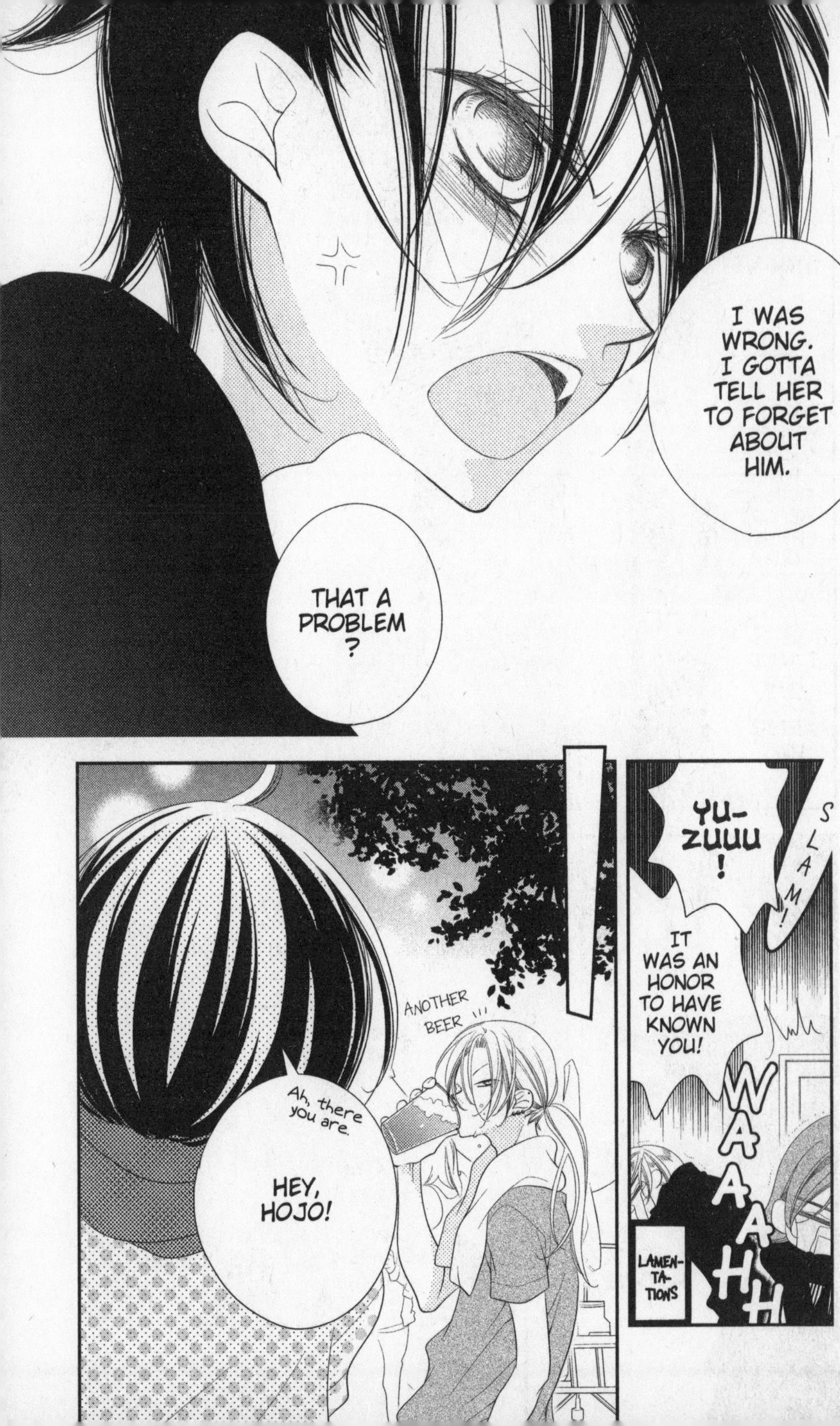
I WAS WRONG. I GOTTA TELL HER TO FORGET ABOUT HIM.
THAT A PROBLEM?
YU-ZUUU!
SLAM!
IT WAS AN HONOR TO HAVE KNOWN YOU!
WAAAAHH
LAMENTATIONS
!
ANOTHER BEER
Ah, there you are.
HEY, HOJO!

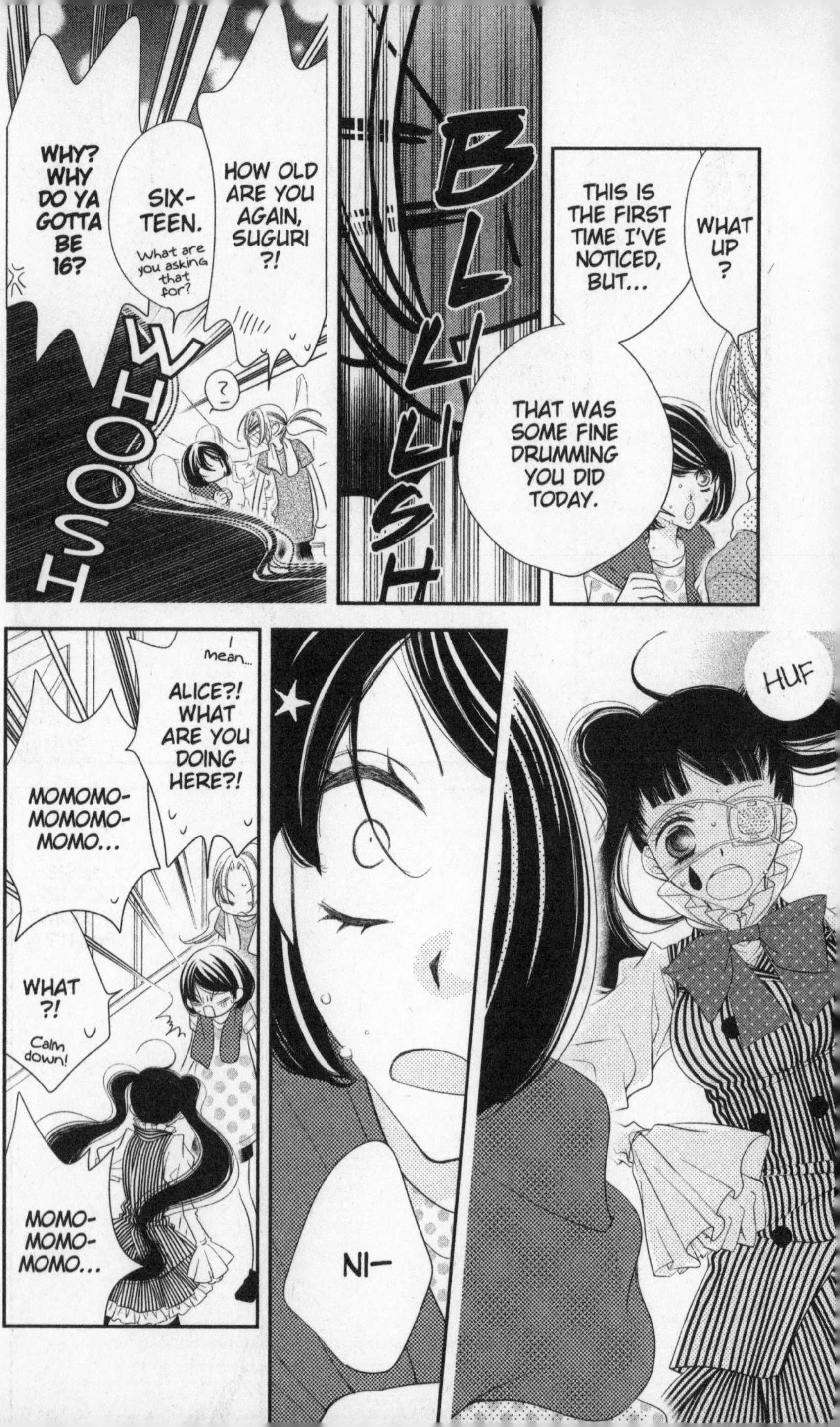
WHAT UP?
THIS IS THE FIRST TIME I'VE NOTICED, BUT...
THAT WAS SOME FINE DRUMMING YOU DID TODAY.
BLLUUSH
HOW OLD ARE YOU AGAIN, SUGURI?!
SIX-TEEN.
What are you asking that for?
WHY? WHY DO YA GOTTA BE 16?
?
WHOOOSH
HUF
NI—
ALICE?! WHAT ARE YOU DOING HERE?!
I mean...
MOMOMO-MOMOMO-MOMO...
WHAT?!
Calm down!
MOMO-MOMO-MOMO...

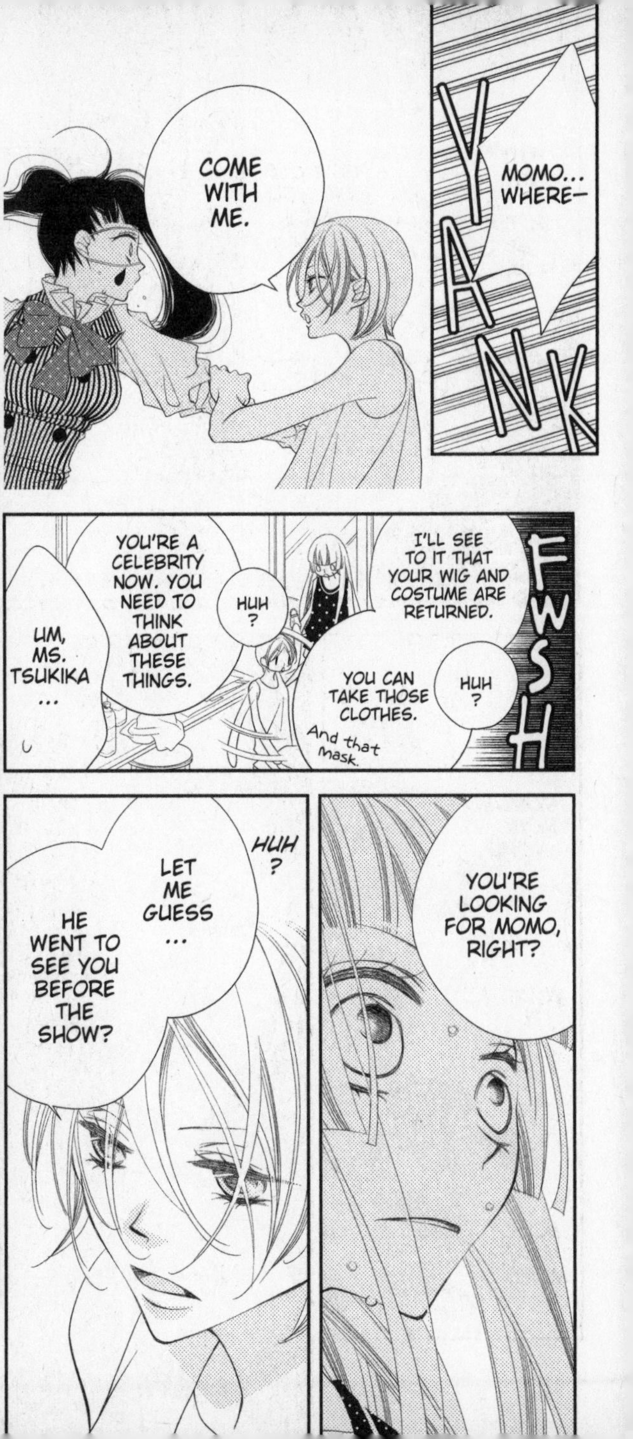
YANK
MOMO... WHERE—
COME WITH ME.
FWSH
I'LL SEE TO IT THAT YOUR WIG AND COSTUME ARE RETURNED.
HUH?
YOU CAN TAKE THOSE CLOTHES.
And that mask.
YOU'RE A CELEBRITY NOW. YOU NEED TO THINK ABOUT THESE THINGS.
HUH?
UM, MS. TSUKIKA...
YOU'RE LOOKING FOR MOMO, RIGHT?
HUH?
LET ME GUESS...
HE WENT TO SEE YOU BEFORE THE SHOW?

1

Greetings! This is Ryoko Fukuyama.

Thank you so much for reading Anonymous Noise volume 6! Kuro is on this volume's cover, which means that all six members of the main cast have now had their turn! I hope you're looking forward to seeing who will end up on the cover of volume 7 as much as I am—even I haven't decided yet!

YAY!!

I hope you enjoy this volume, brought to you by this easy-going frog!

AH, SUMMER.

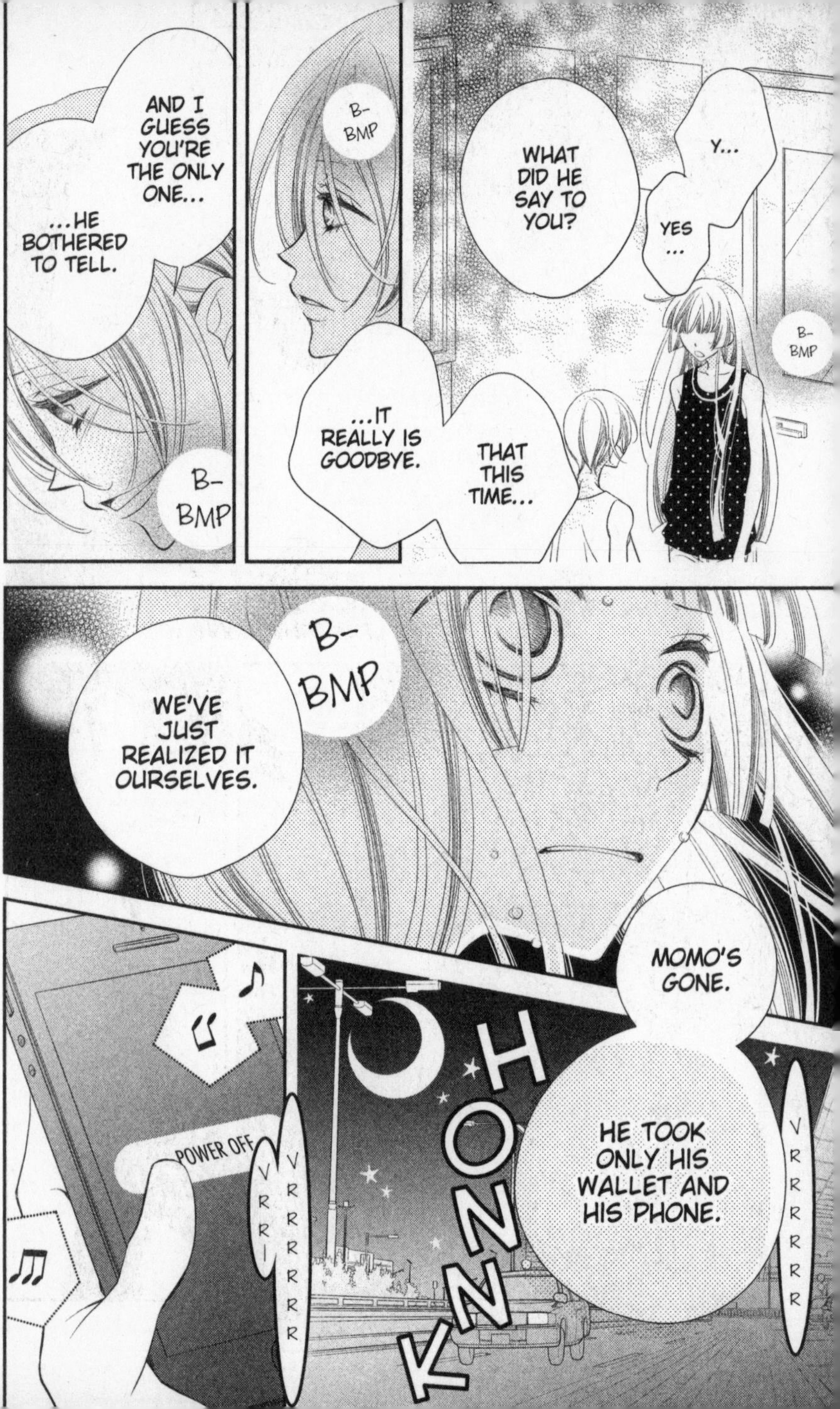
Y...
WHAT DID HE SAY TO YOU?
YES...
B-BMP
THAT THIS TIME...
...IT REALLY IS GOODBYE.
B-BMP
AND I GUESS YOU'RE THE ONLY ONE...
...HE BOTHERED TO TELL.
B-BMP
B-BMP
WE'VE JUST REALIZED IT OURSELVES.
MOMO'S GONE.
VRRRRRR
HE TOOK ONLY HIS WALLET AND HIS PHONE.
HONK
VRRRRRRR
VRRI
POWER OFF

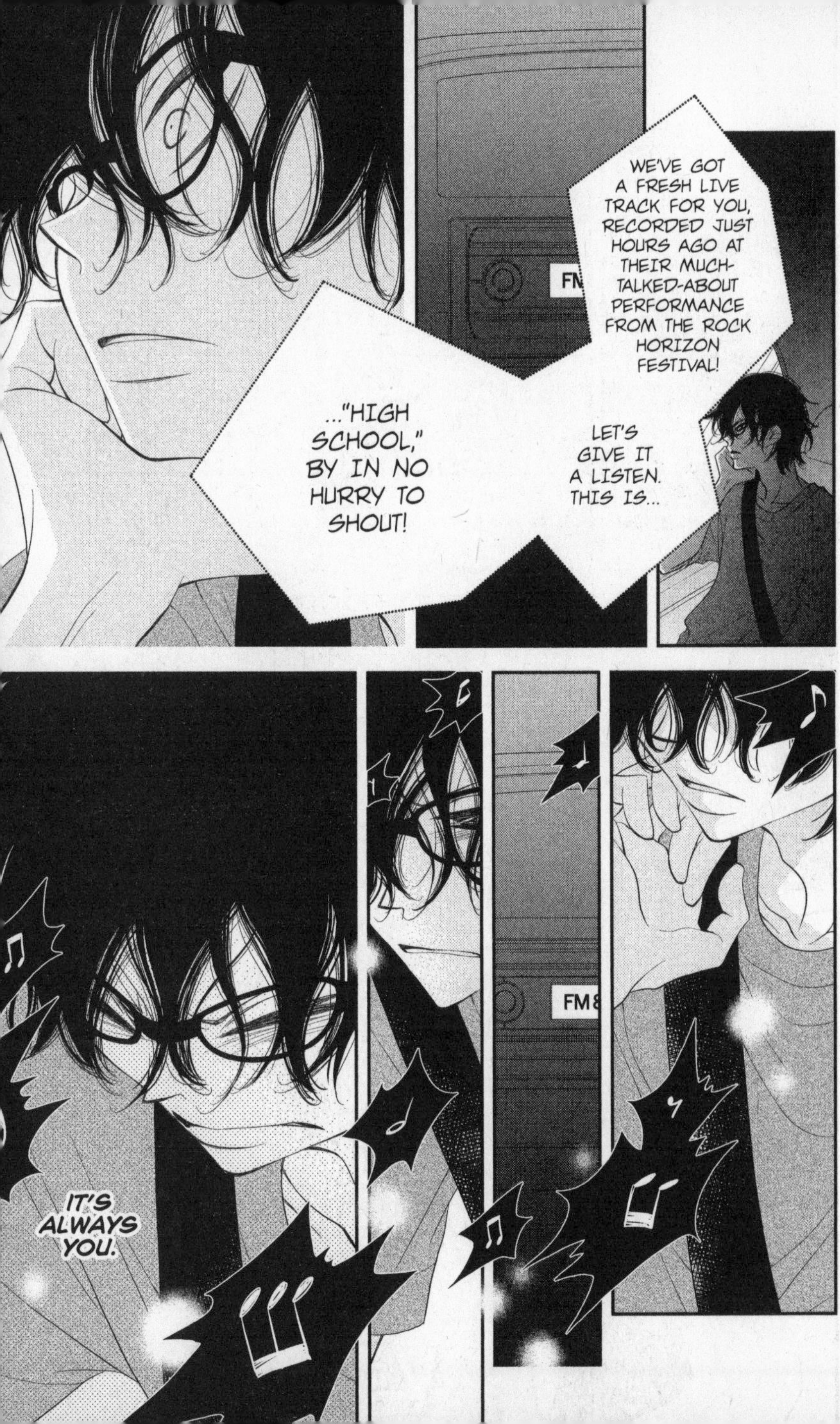
WE'VE GOT A FRESH LIVE TRACK FOR YOU, RECORDED JUST HOURS AGO AT THEIR MUCH-TALKED-ABOUT PERFORMANCE FROM THE ROCK HORIZON FESTIVAL!
LET'S GIVE IT A LISTEN. THIS IS...
..."HIGH SCHOOL," BY IN NO HURRY TO SHOUT!
FM
FM8
IT'S ALWAYS YOU.

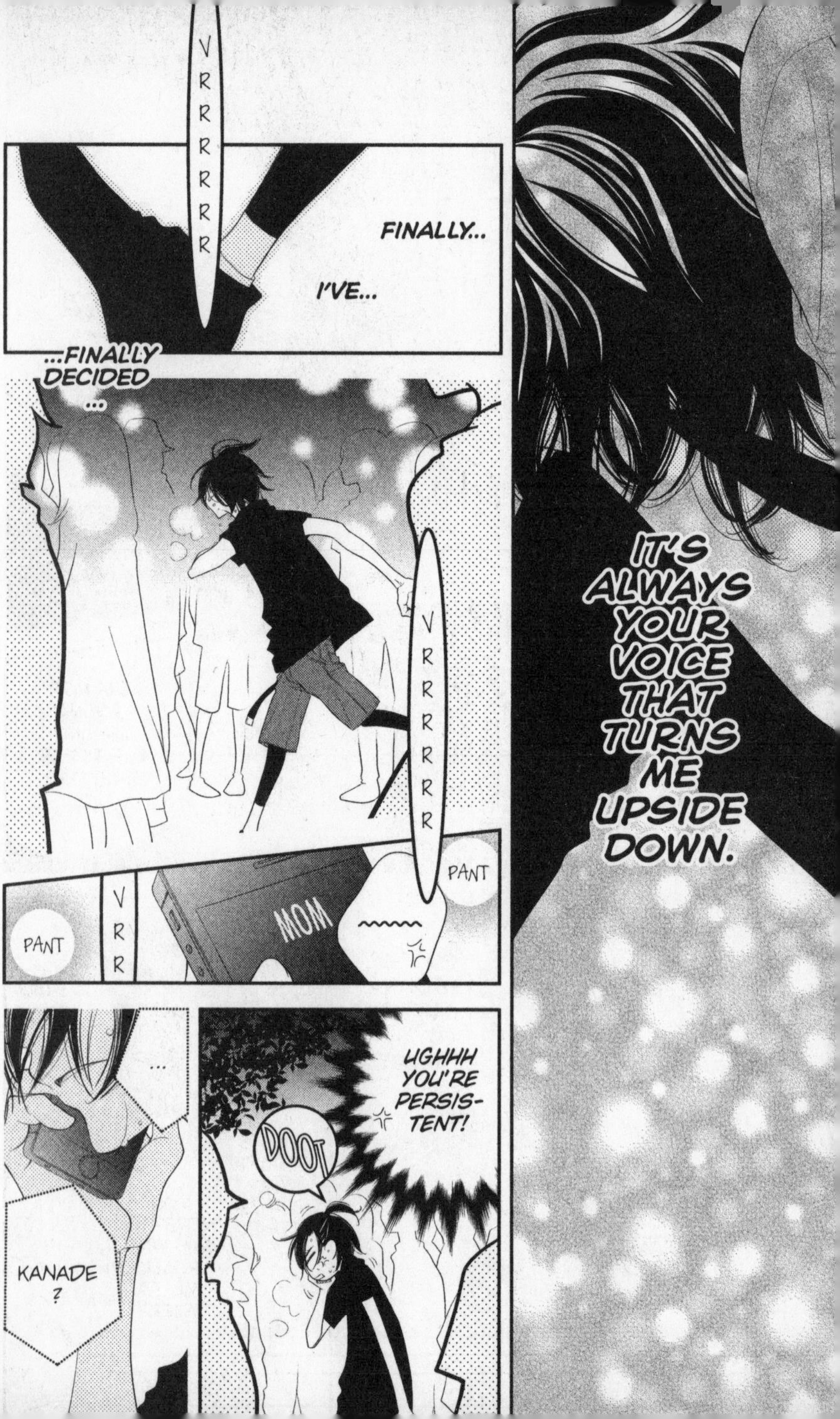
IT'S ALWAYS YOUR VOICE THAT TURNS ME UPSIDE DOWN.
VRRRRRR
FINALLY...
I'VE...
...FINALLY DECIDED...
VRRRRRRR
PANT
MOM
VRR
PANT
UGHHH YOU'RE PERSIS-TENT!
DOOT
...
KANADE?

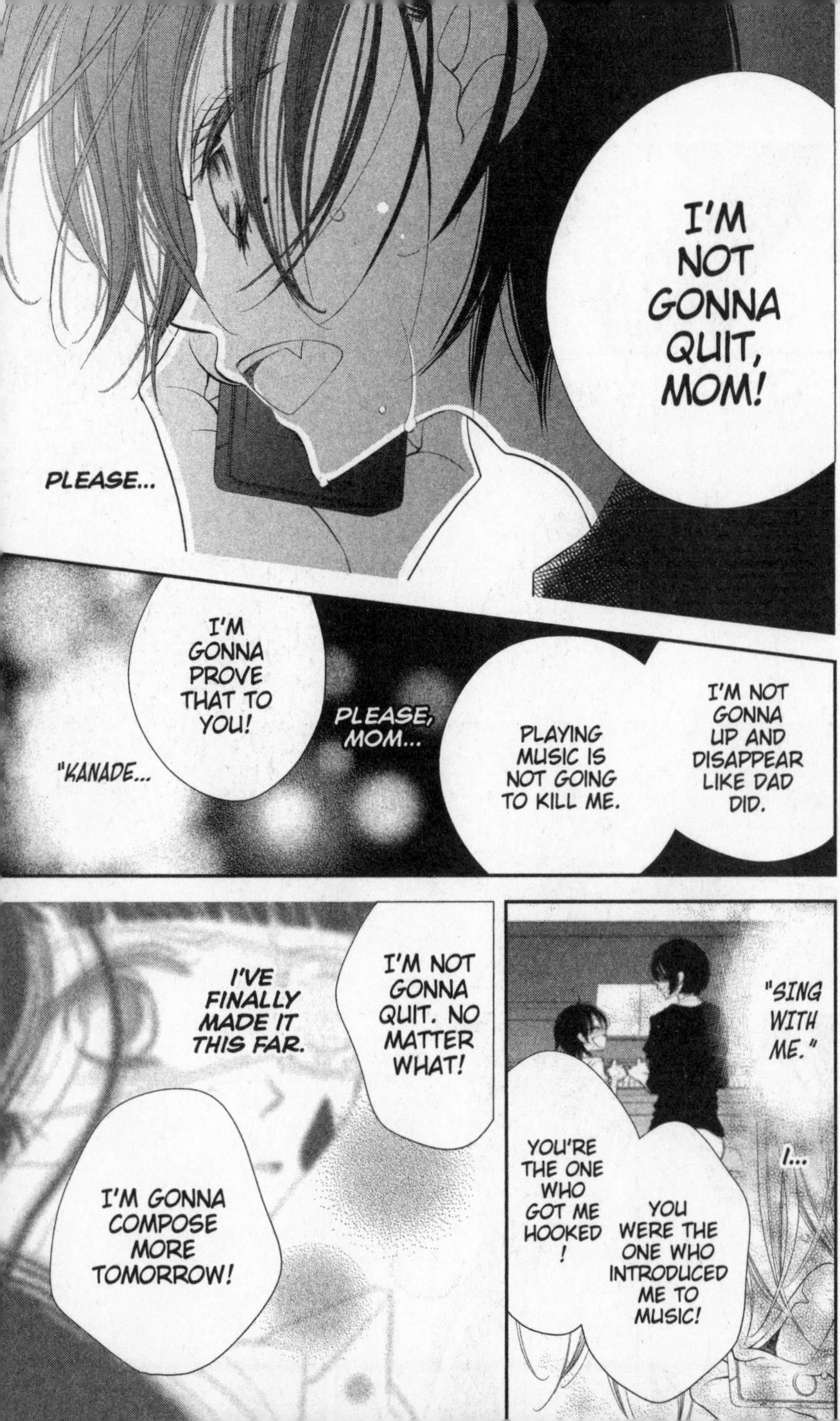
I'M NOT GONNA QUIT, MOM!
PLEASE...
I'M NOT GONNA UP AND DISAPPEAR LIKE DAD DID.
PLAYING MUSIC IS NOT GOING TO KILL ME.
PLEASE, MOM...
I'M GONNA PROVE THAT TO YOU!
"KANADE...
"SING WITH ME."
I...
YOU WERE THE ONE WHO INTRODUCED ME TO MUSIC!
YOU'RE THE ONE WHO GOT ME HOOKED!
I'M NOT GONNA QUIT. NO MATTER WHAT!
I'VE FINALLY MADE IT THIS FAR.
I'M GONNA COMPOSE MORE TOMORROW!

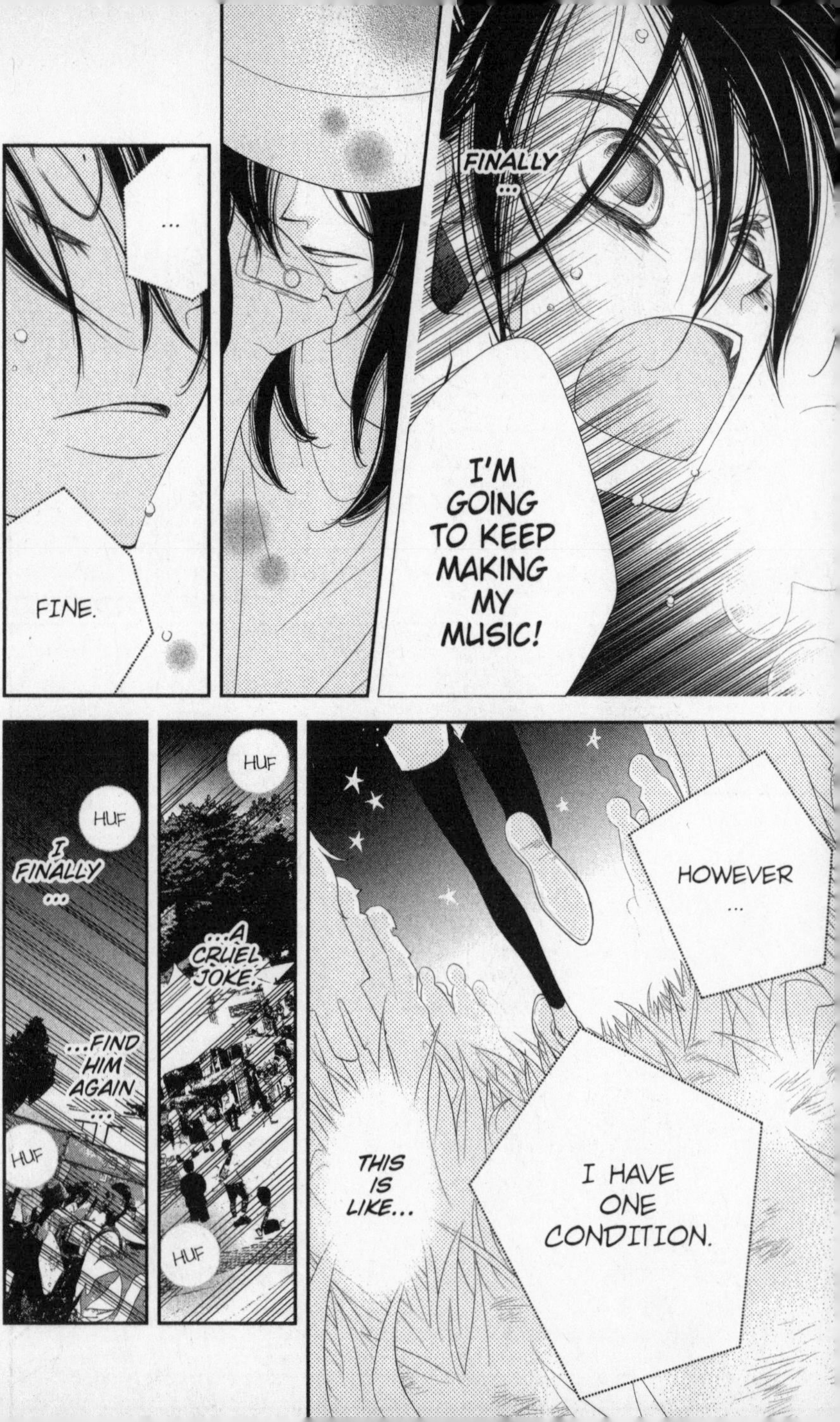
FINALLY ...
I'M GOING TO KEEP MAKING MY MUSIC!
...
FINE.
HOWEVER ...
I HAVE ONE CONDITION.
THIS IS LIKE...
HUF
...A CRUEL JOKE.
HUF
HUF
I FINALLY ...
...FIND HIM AGAIN ...
HUF

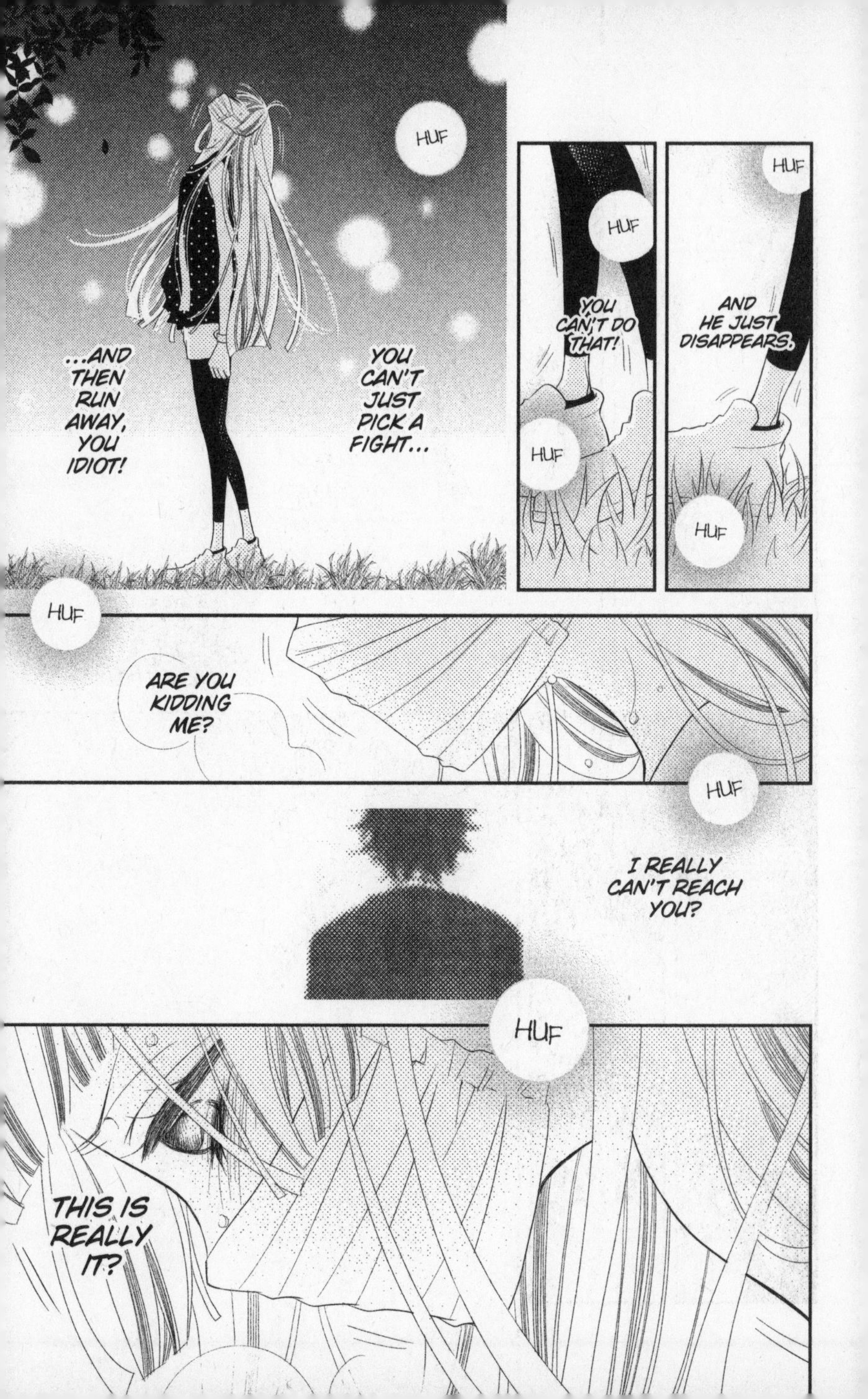
HUF
AND HE JUST DISAPPEARS.
HUF
HUF
YOU CAN'T DO THAT!
HUF
HUF
YOU CAN'T JUST PICK A FIGHT...
...AND THEN RUN AWAY, YOU IDIOT!
HUF
ARE YOU KIDDING ME?
HUF
I REALLY CAN'T REACH YOU?
HUF
THIS IS REALLY IT?

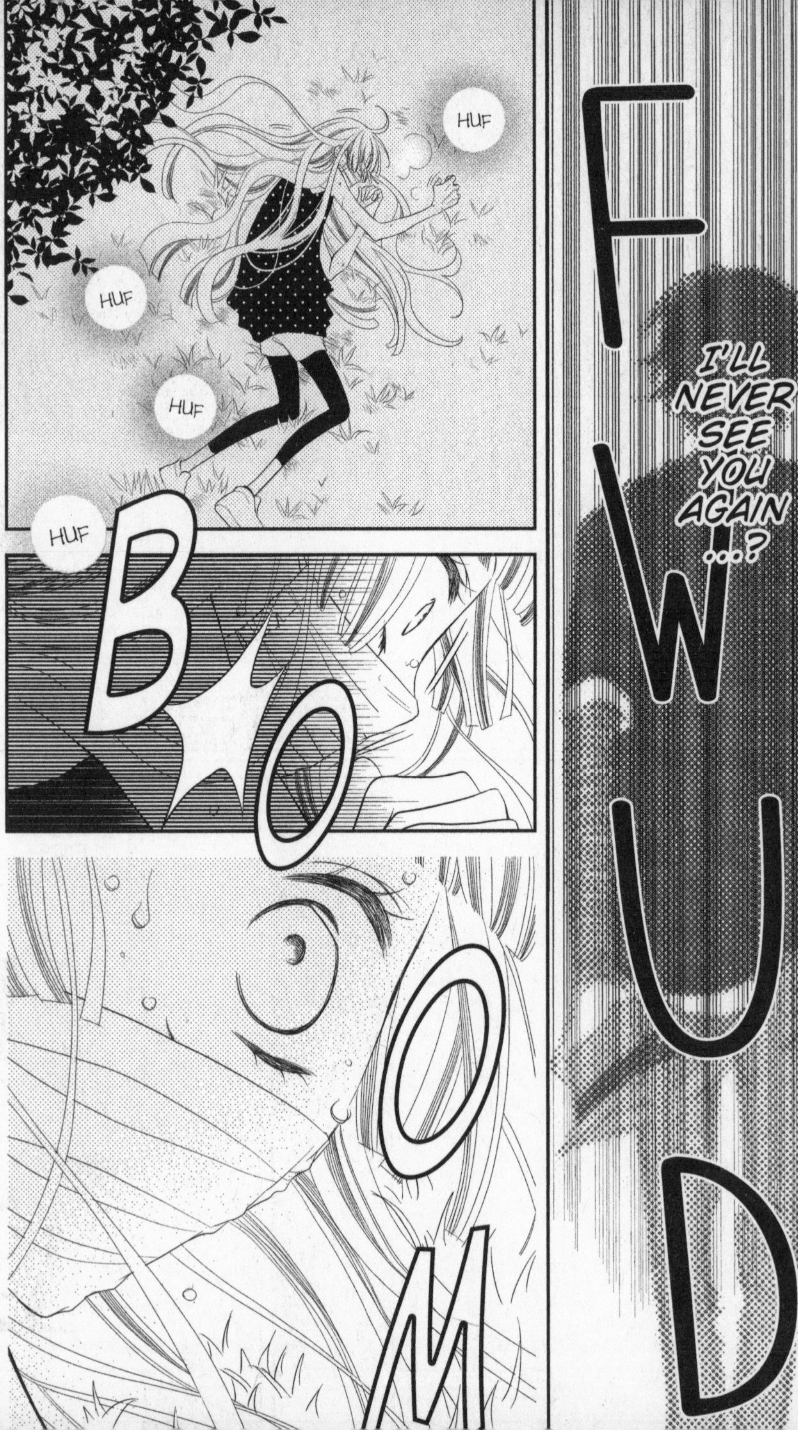
FWUD
I'LL NEVER SEE YOU AGAIN...?
HUF
HUF
HUF
HUF
BOOOM

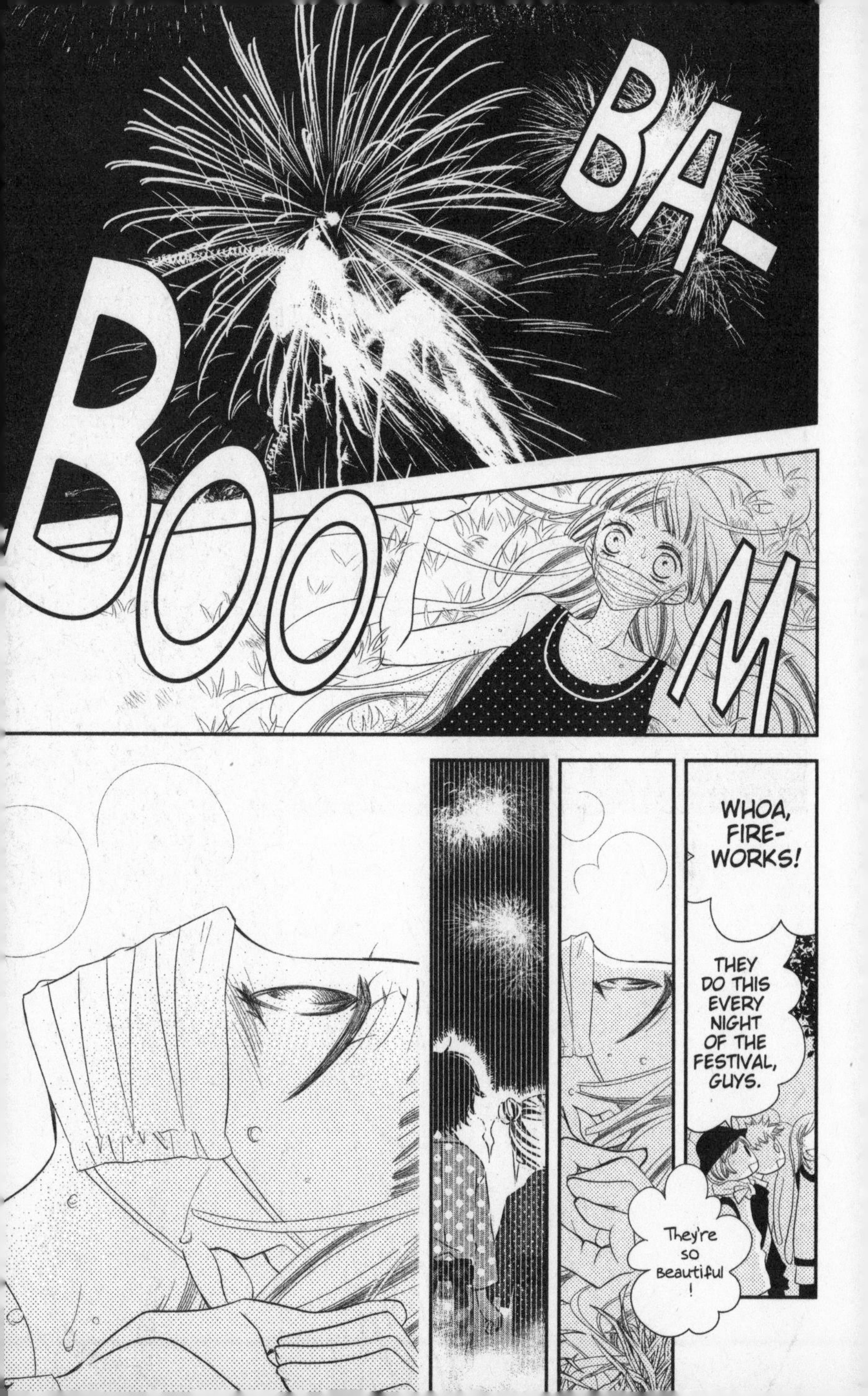
BA-BOOOM
WHOA, FIRE-WORKS!
THEY DO THIS EVERY NIGHT OF THE FESTIVAL, GUYS.
They're so beautiful!

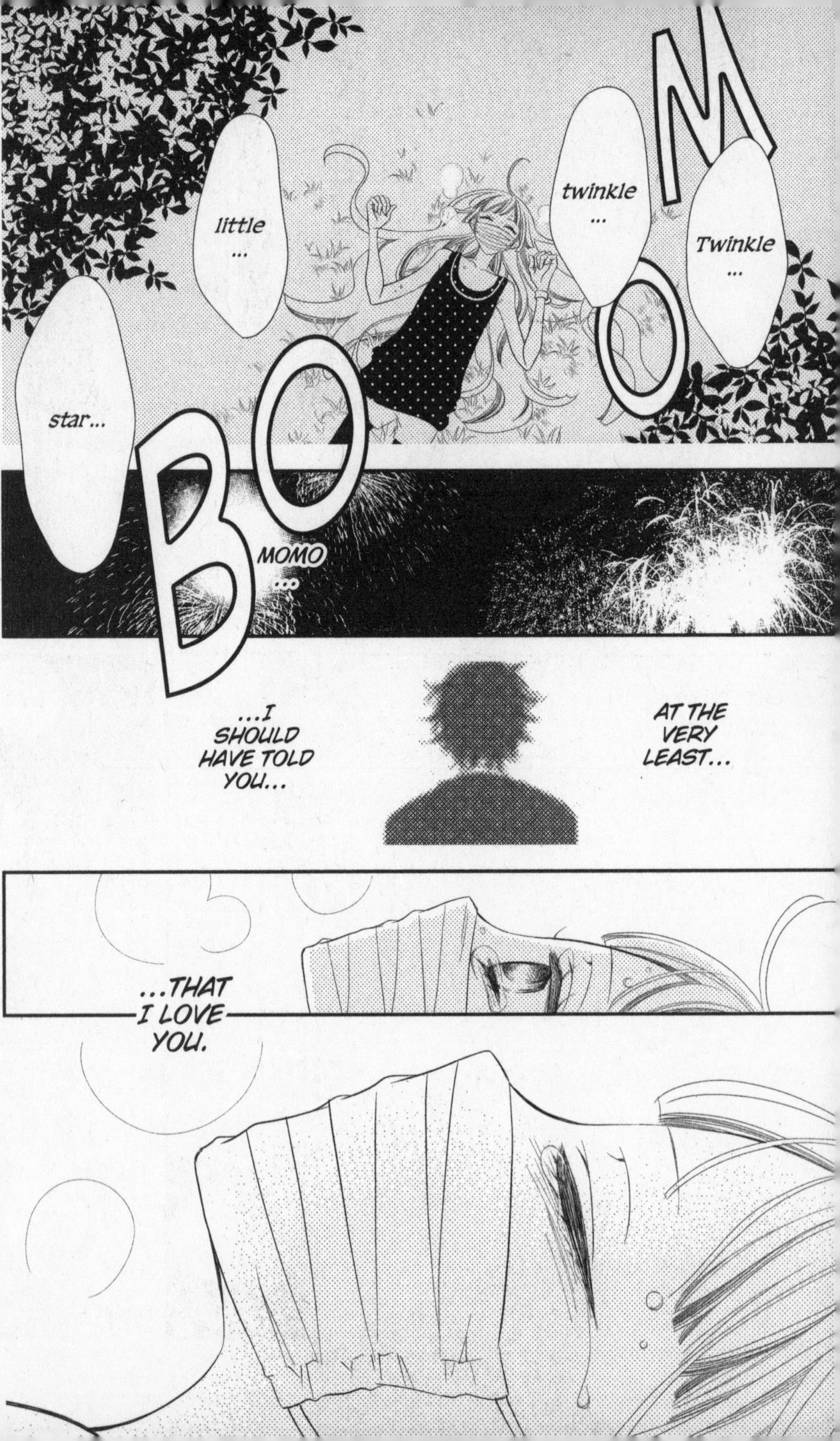
Twinkle...
twinkle...
little...
star...
BOOM
MOMO...
AT THE VERY LEAST...
...I SHOULD HAVE TOLD YOU...
...THAT I LOVE YOU.

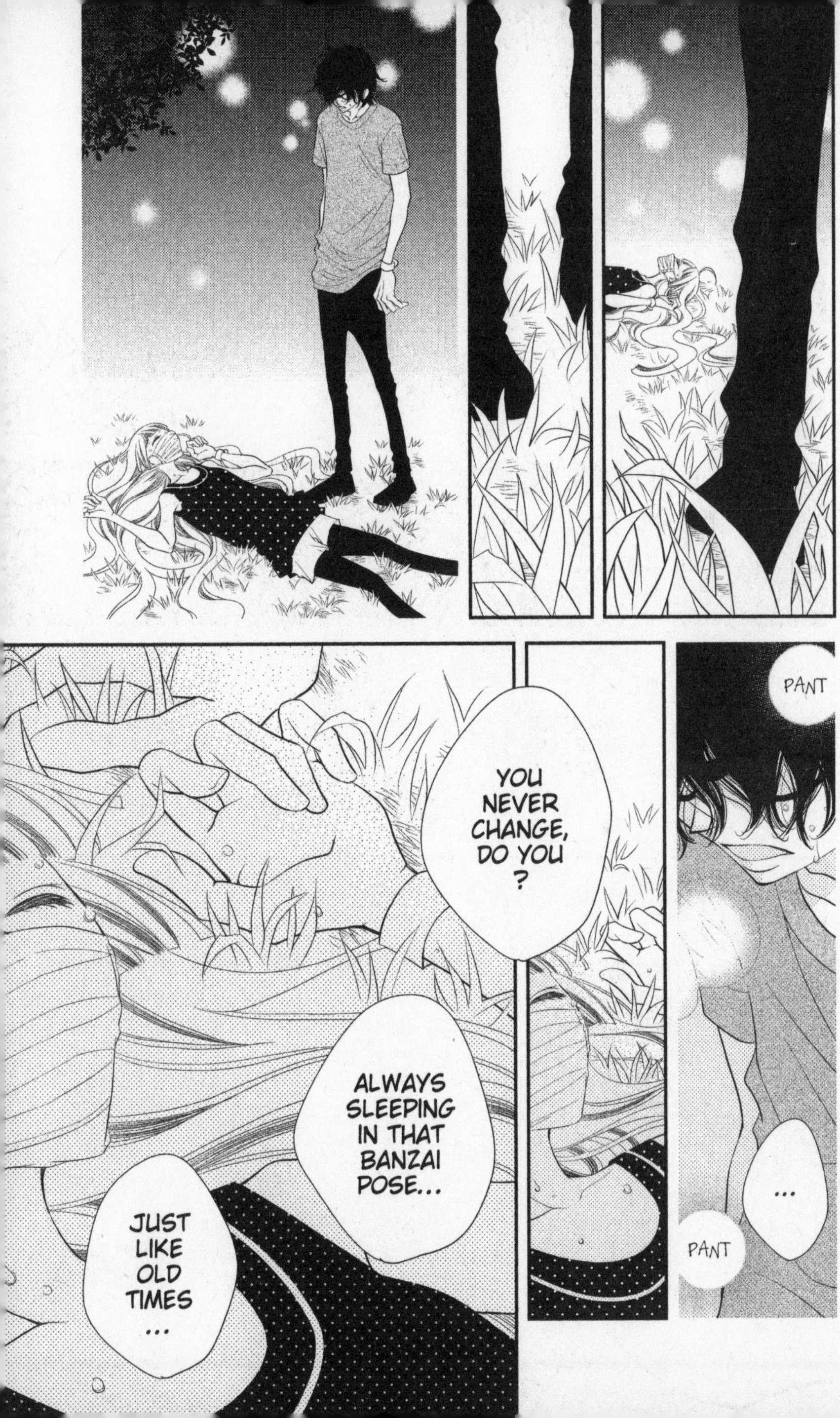
PANT
...
PANT
YOU NEVER CHANGE, DO YOU?
ALWAYS SLEEPING IN THAT BANZAI POSE...
JUST LIKE OLD TIMES...

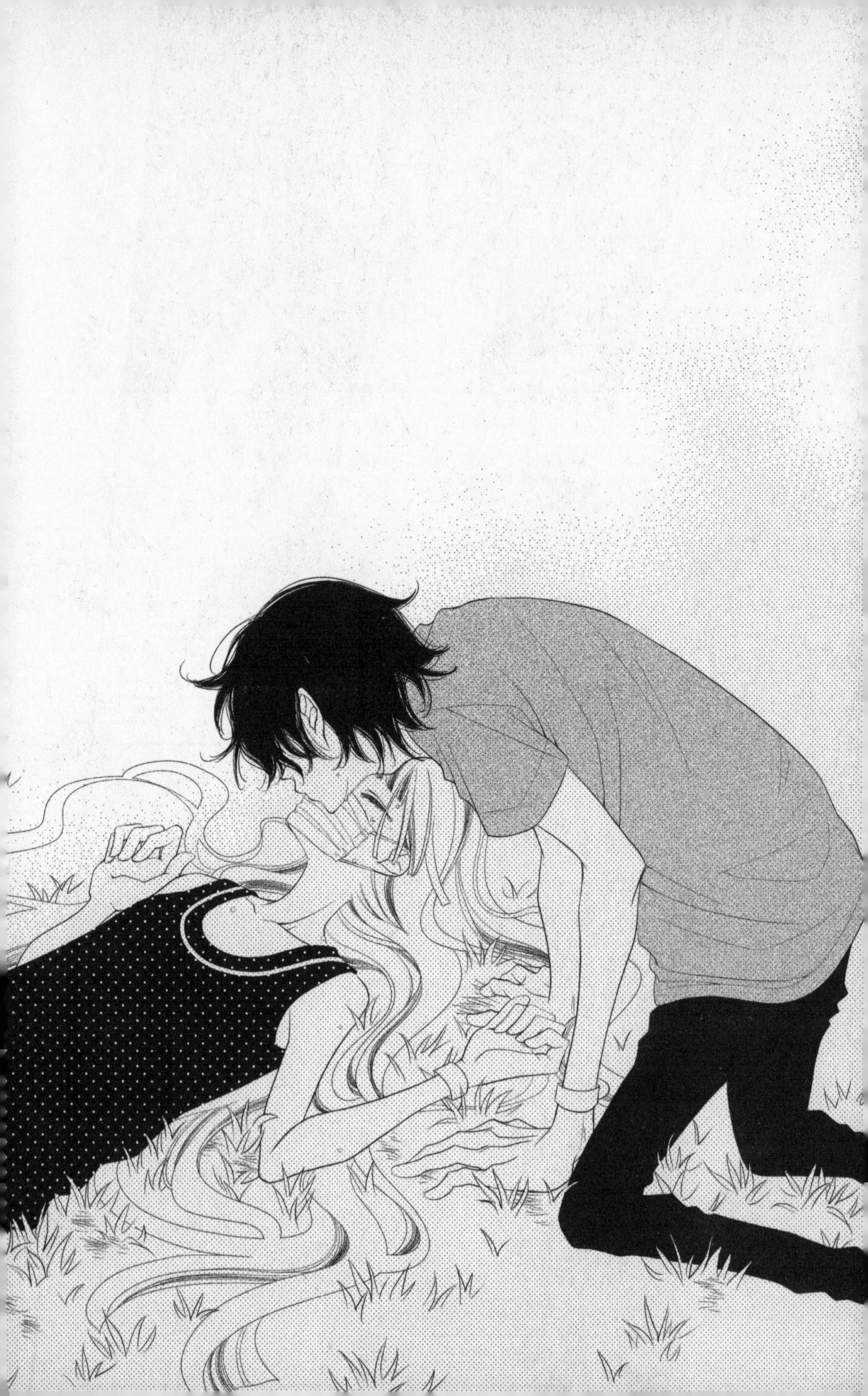

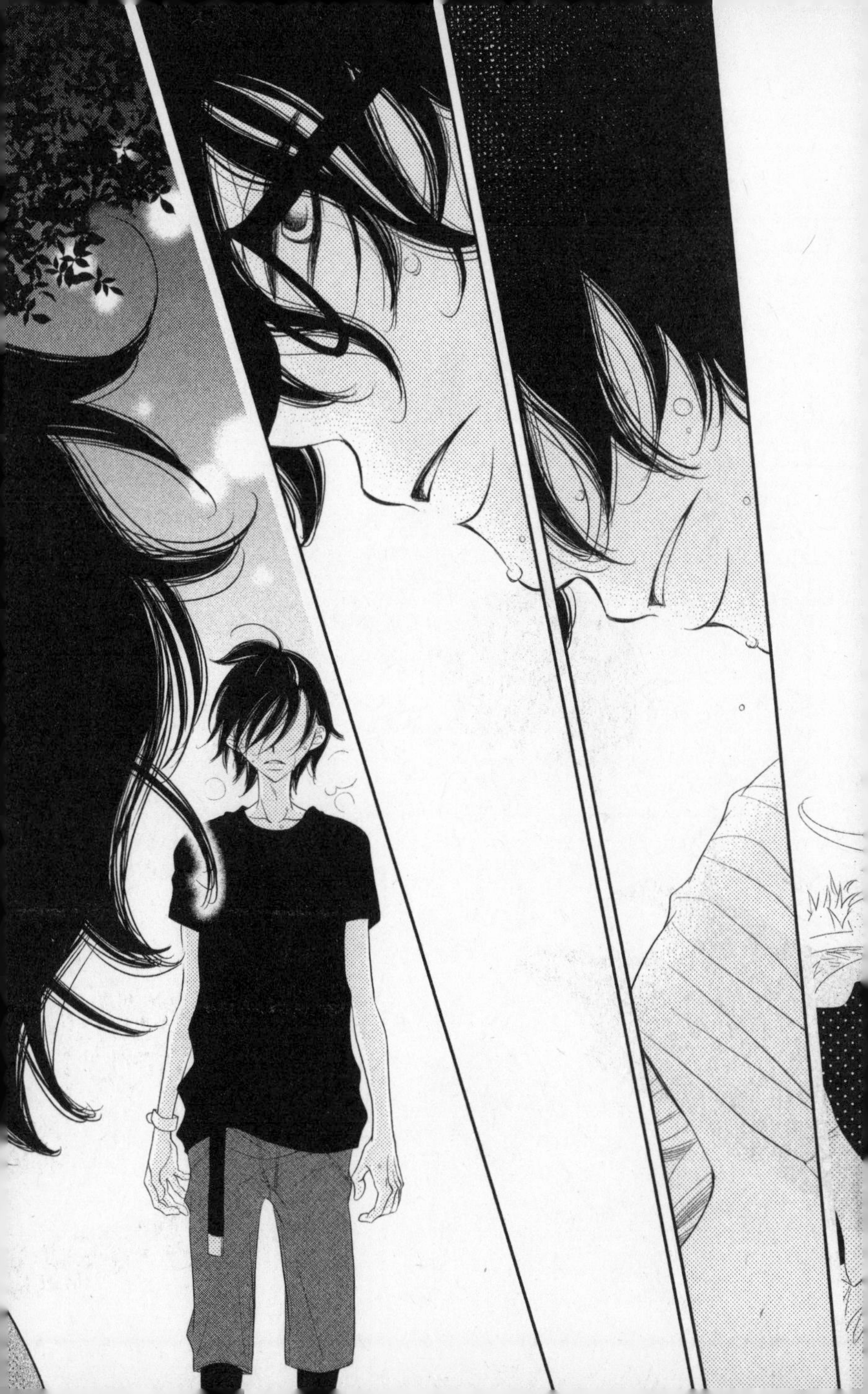

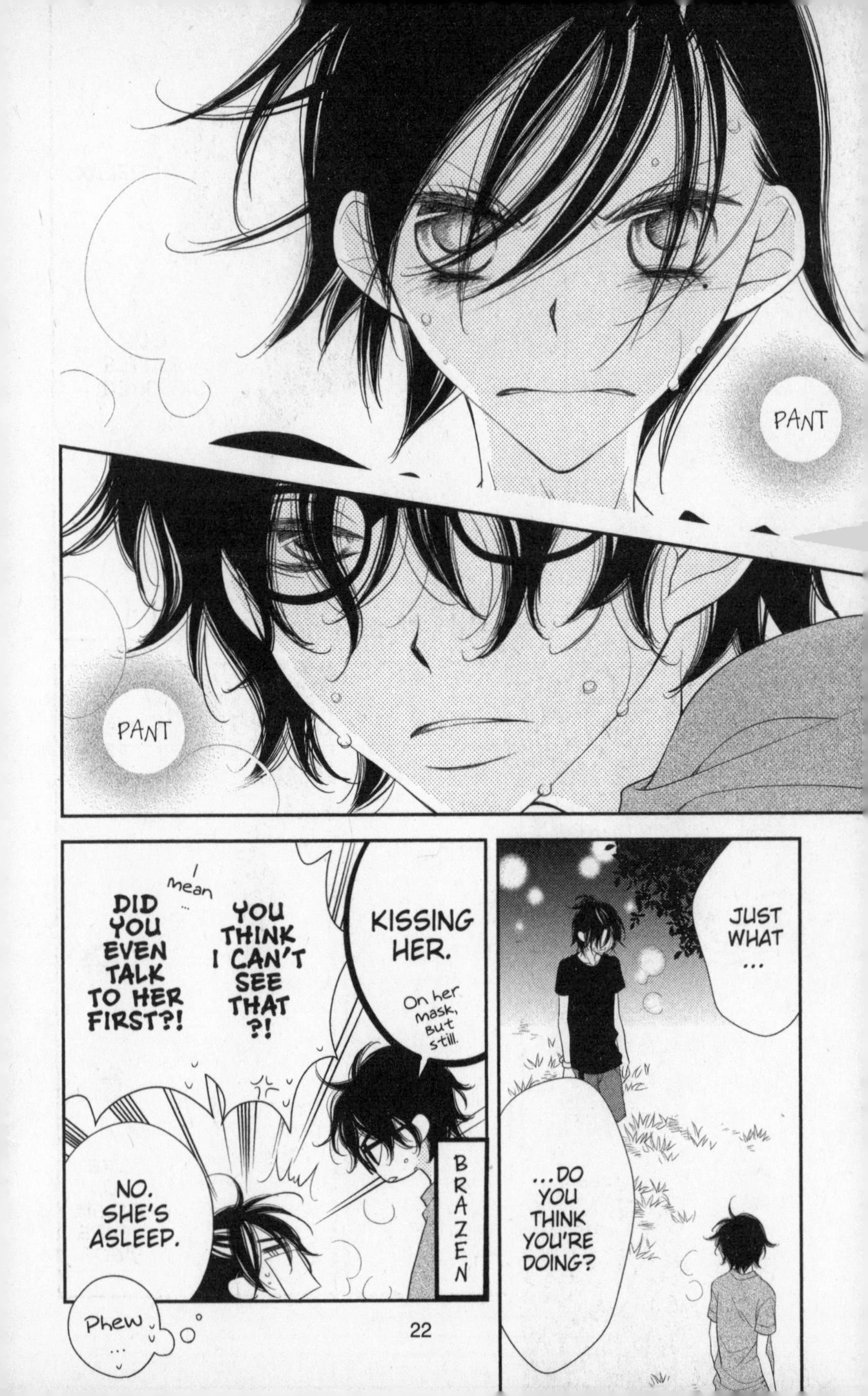
PANT
PANT
JUST WHAT ...
...DO YOU THINK YOU'RE DOING?
KISSING HER.
On her mask, But still.
YOU THINK I CAN'T SEE THAT?!
I mean ...
DID YOU EVEN TALK TO HER FIRST?!
BRAZEN
NO. SHE'S ASLEEP.
Phew ...

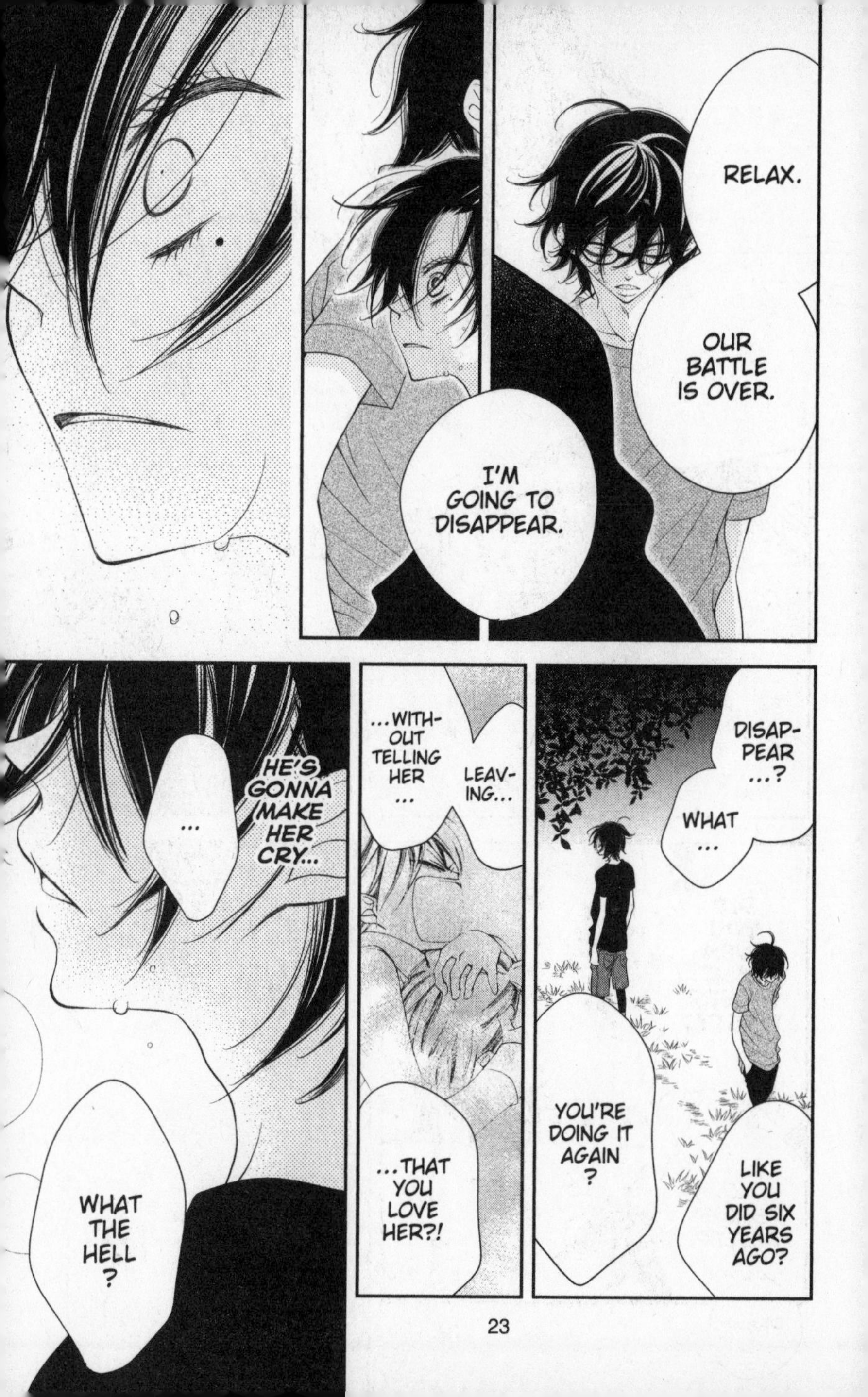
RELAX.
OUR BATTLE IS OVER.
I'M GOING TO DISAPPEAR.
DISAP-PEAR ...?
WHAT ...
YOU'RE DOING IT AGAIN ?
LIKE YOU DID SIX YEARS AGO?
LEAV-ING...
...WITH-OUT TELLING HER ...
...THAT YOU LOVE HER?!
...
HE'S GONNA MAKE HER CRY...
WHAT THE HELL ?

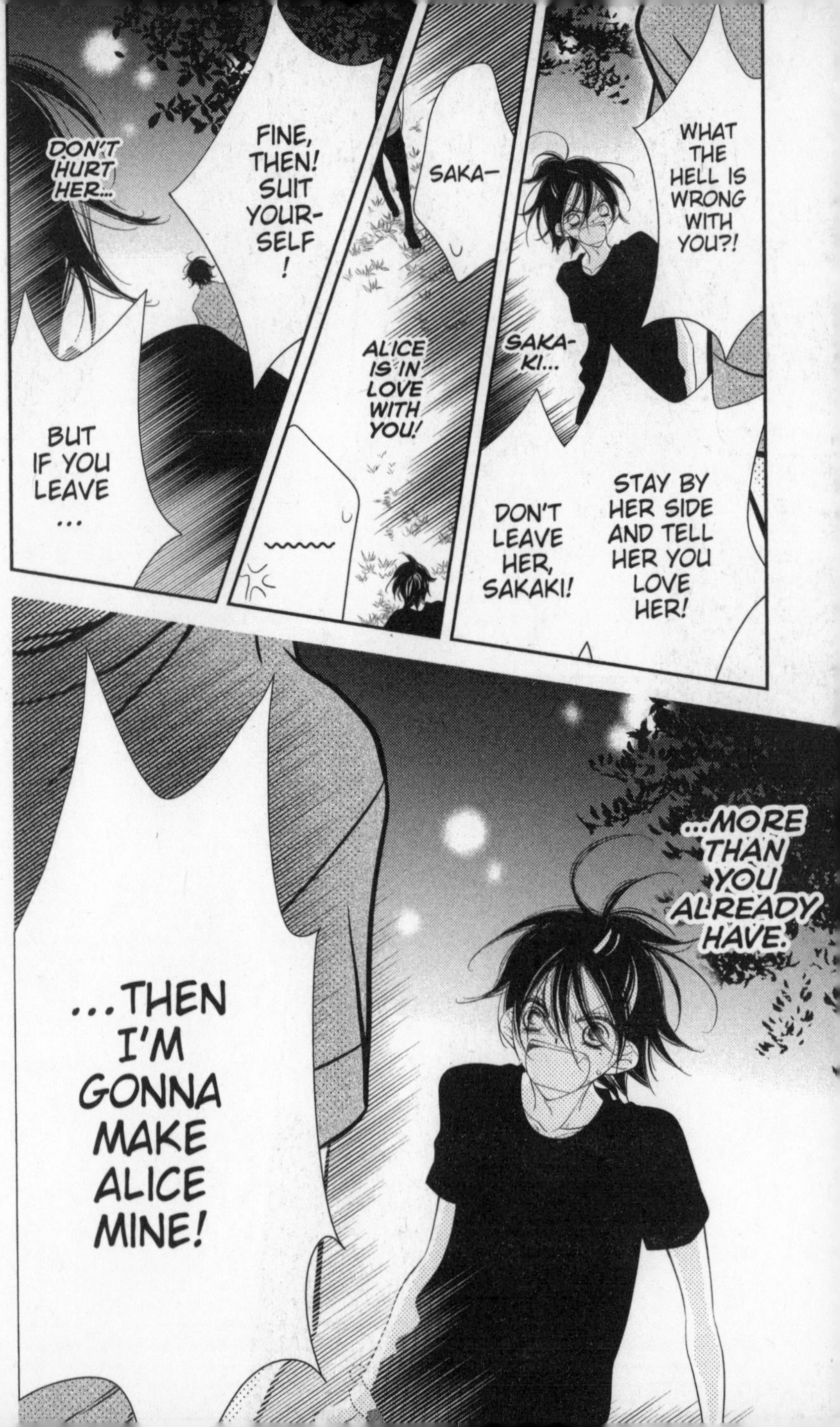
WHAT THE HELL IS WRONG WITH YOU?!
SAKA-KI...
STAY BY HER SIDE AND TELL HER YOU LOVE HER!
DON'T LEAVE HER, SAKAKI!
SAKA-
ALICE IS IN LOVE WITH YOU!
FINE, THEN! SUIT YOUR-SELF!
DON'T HURT HER...
BUT IF YOU LEAVE ...
...MORE THAN YOU ALREADY HAVE.
...THEN I'M GONNA MAKE ALICE MINE!

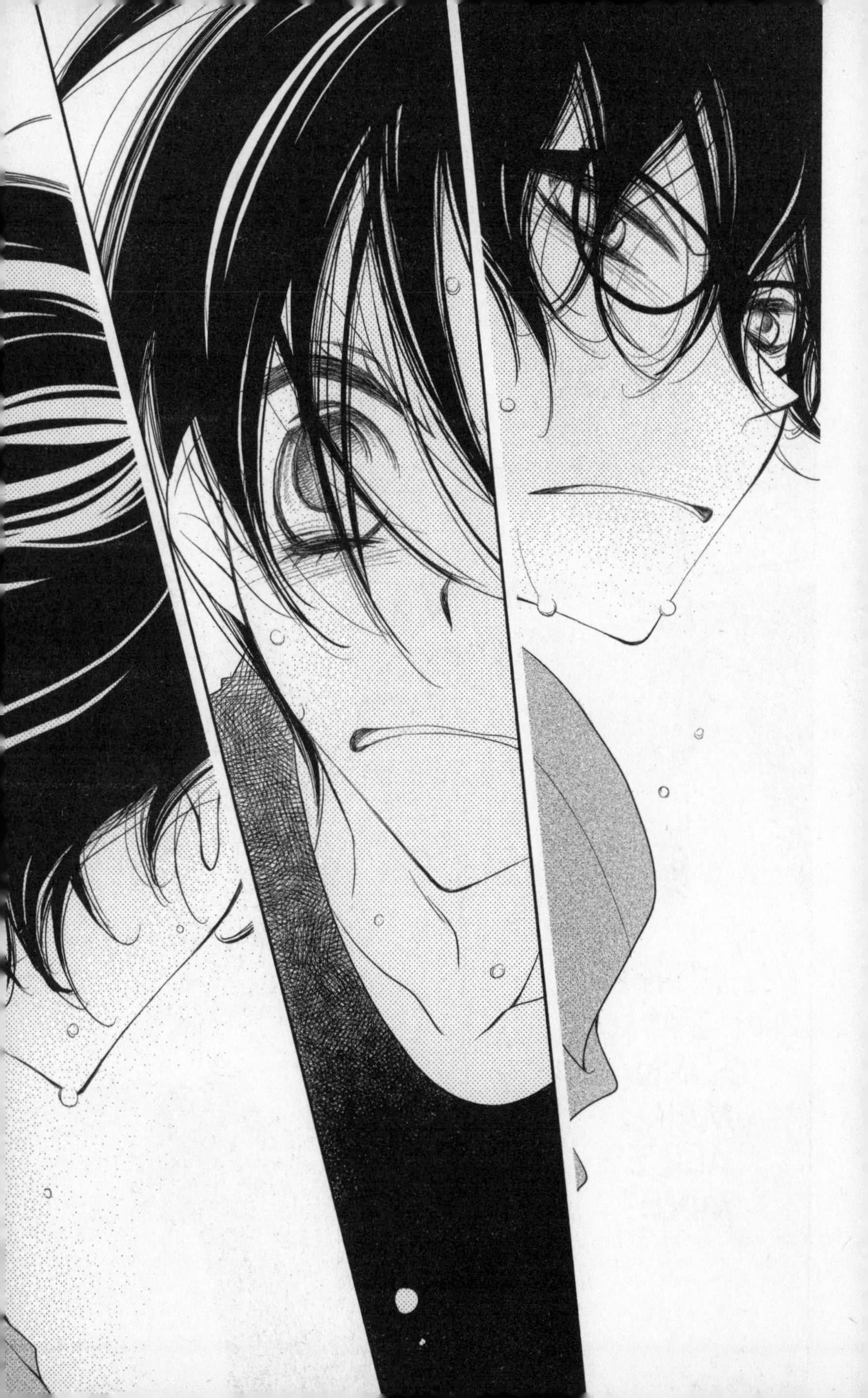

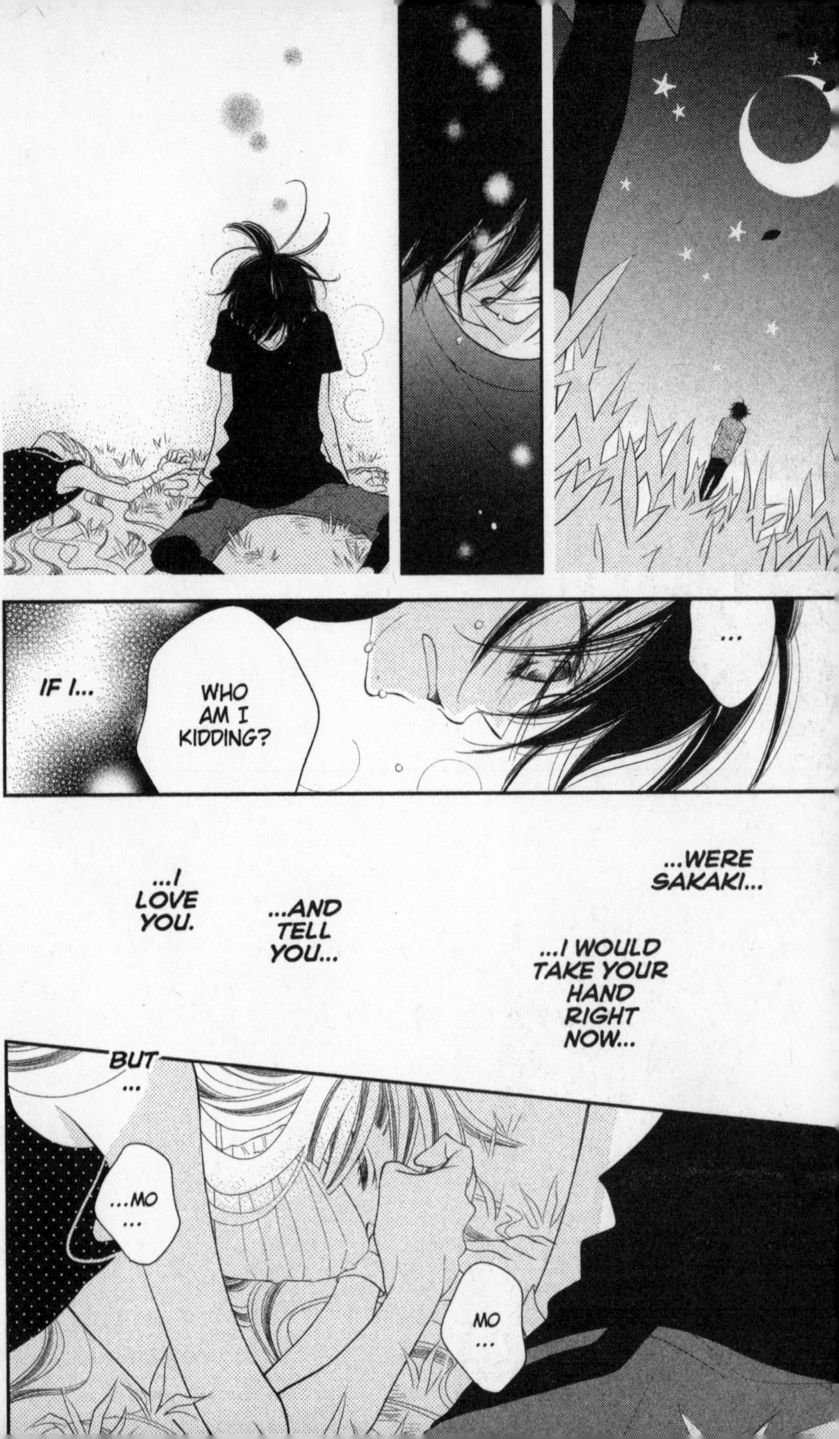

...
WHO AM I KIDDING?
IF I...
...WERE SAKAKI...
...I WOULD TAKE YOUR HAND RIGHT NOW...
...AND TELL YOU...
...I LOVE YOU.
BUT ...
MO ...
...MO ...

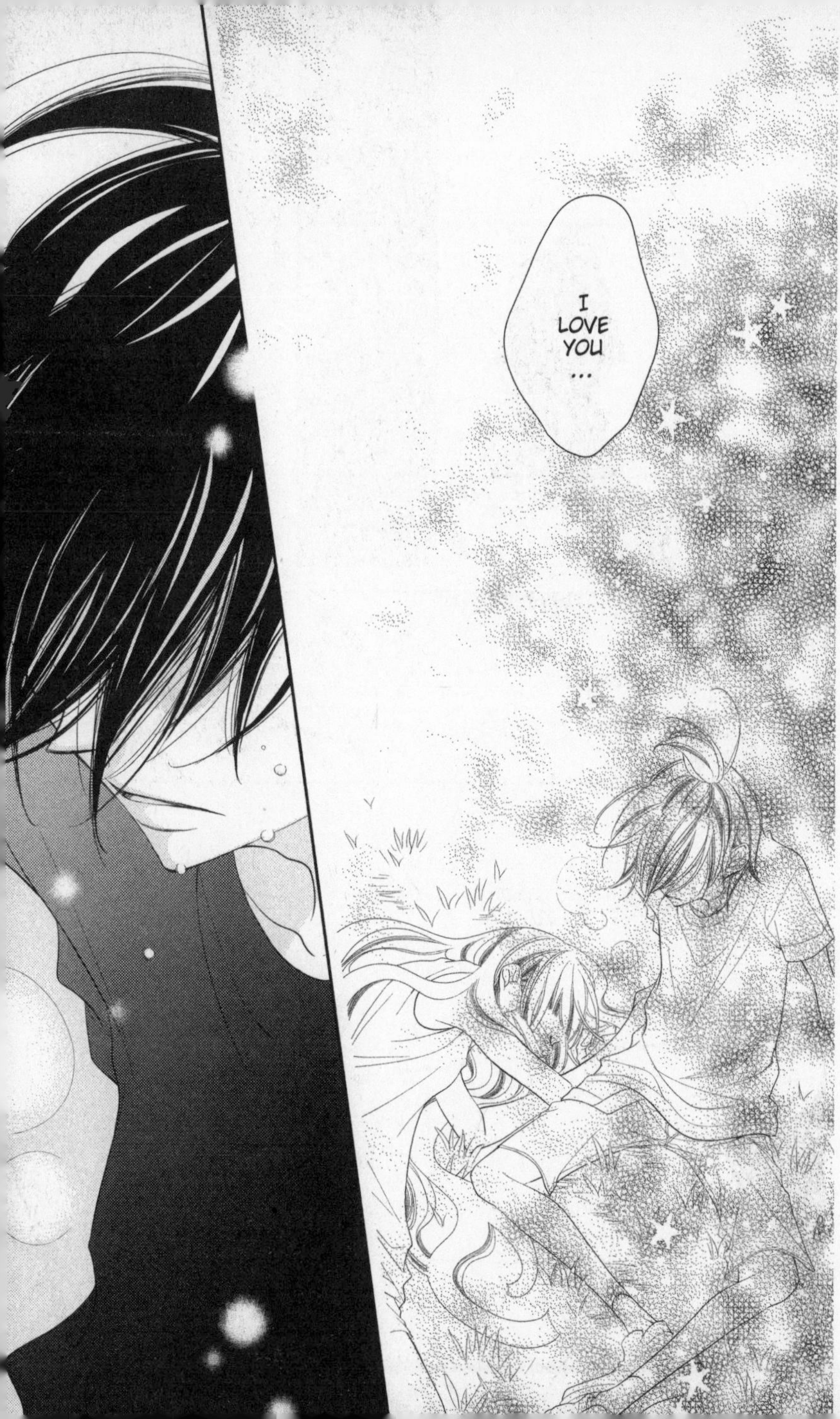
I LOVE YOU ...

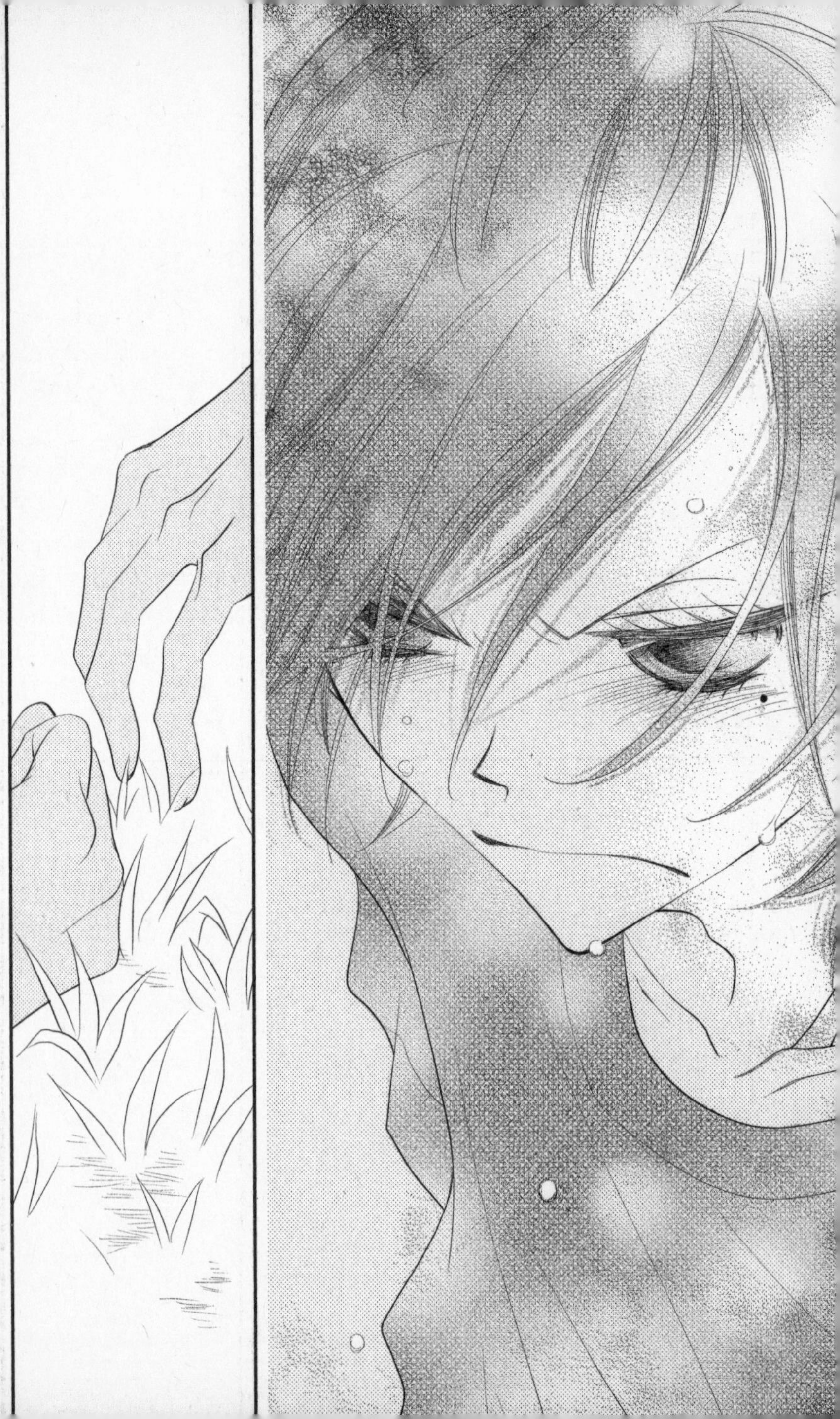

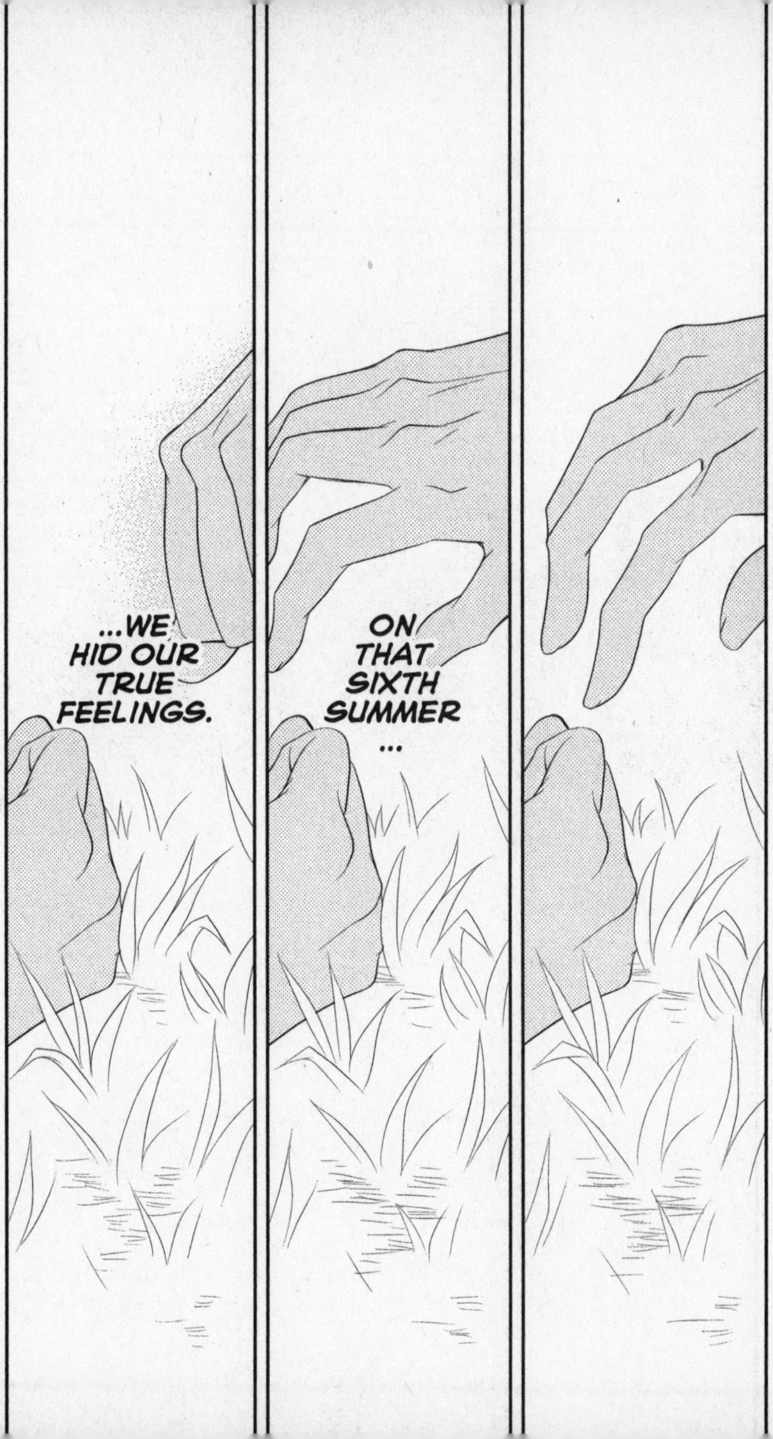
ON THAT SIXTH SUMMER ...
...WE HID OUR TRUE FEELINGS.

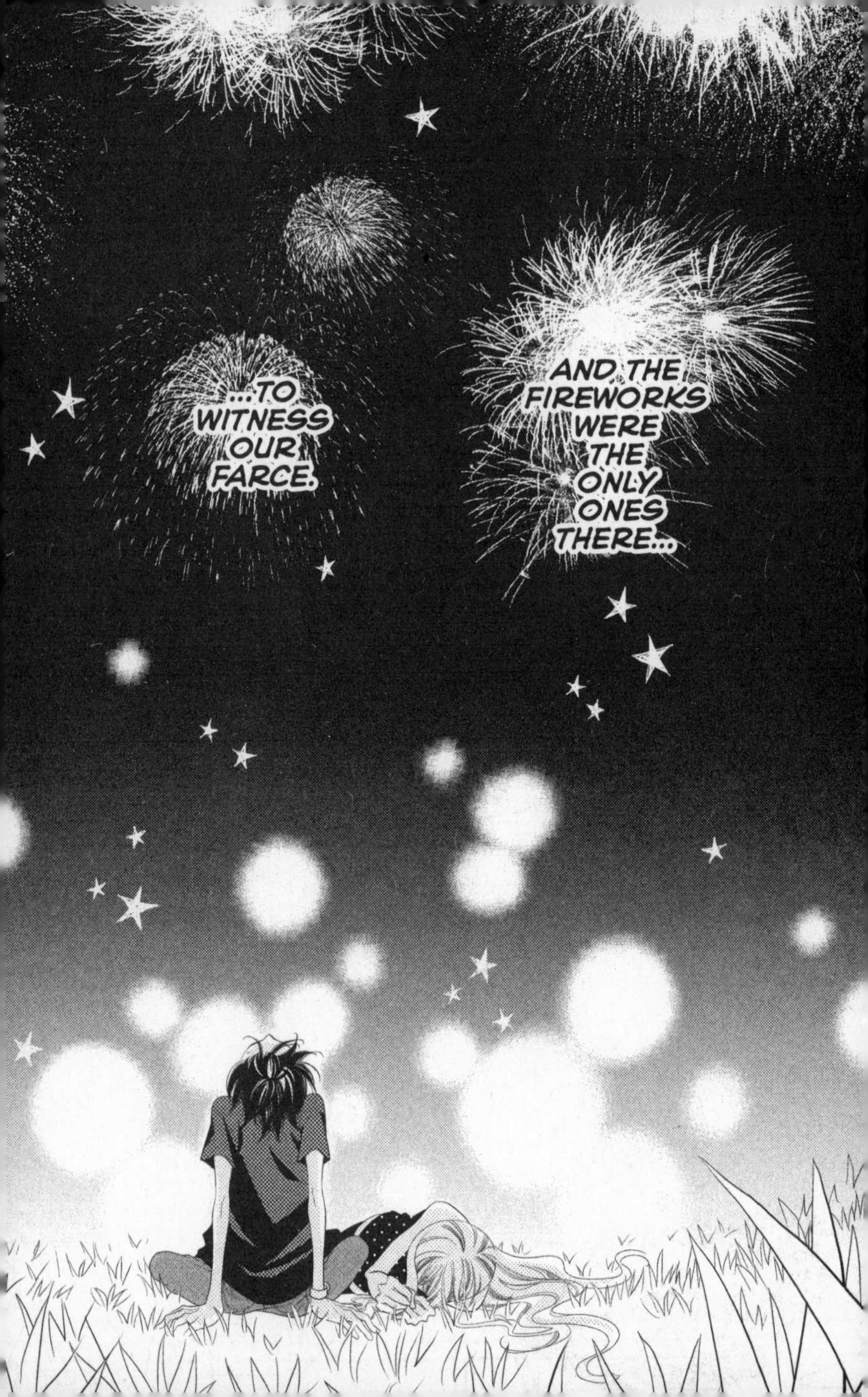
AND THE FIREWORKS WERE THE ONLY ONES THERE...
...TO WITNESS OUR FARCE.

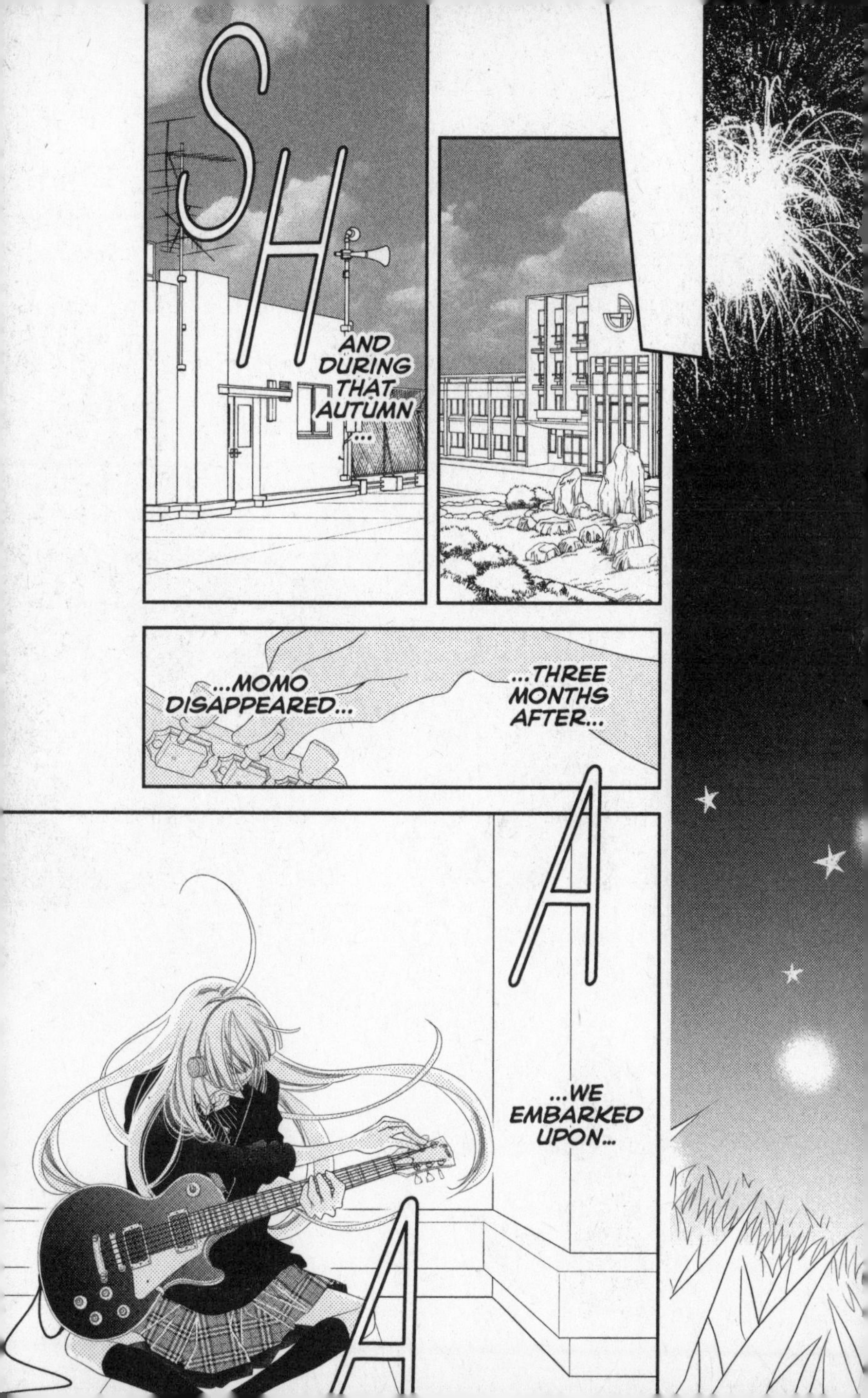
SH
AND DURING THAT AUTUMN...
...THREE MONTHS AFTER...
...MOMO DISAPPEARED...
A
...WE EMBARKED UPON...
A

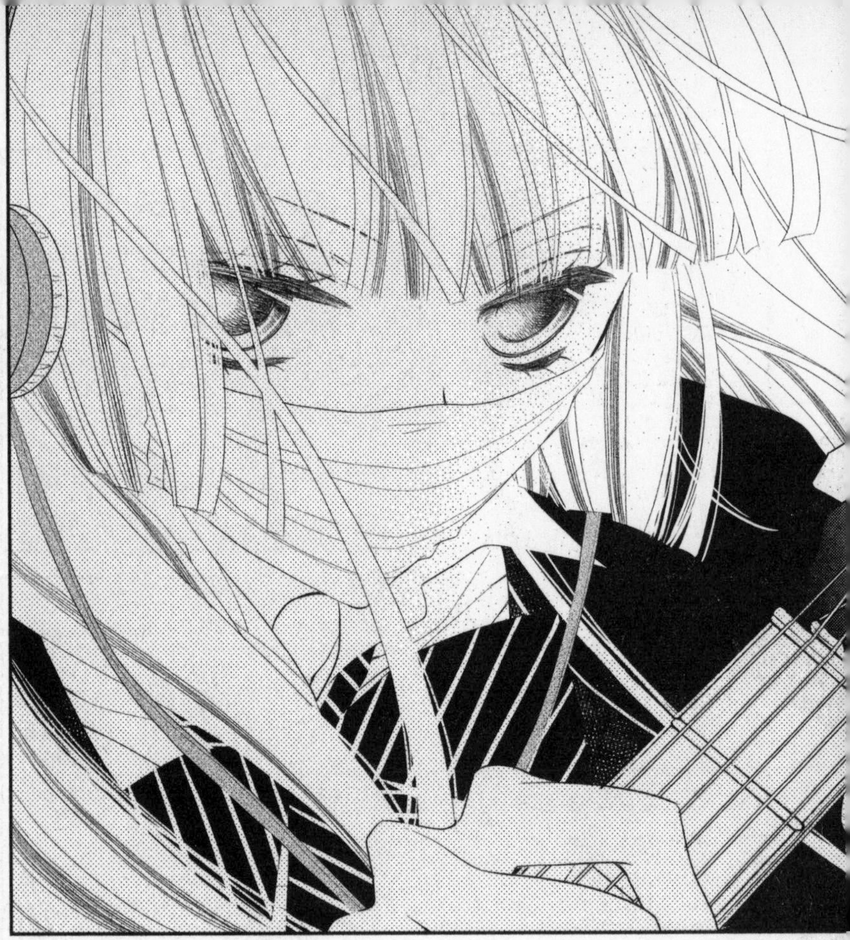

...OUR THIRD BEGINNING.

SONG 30

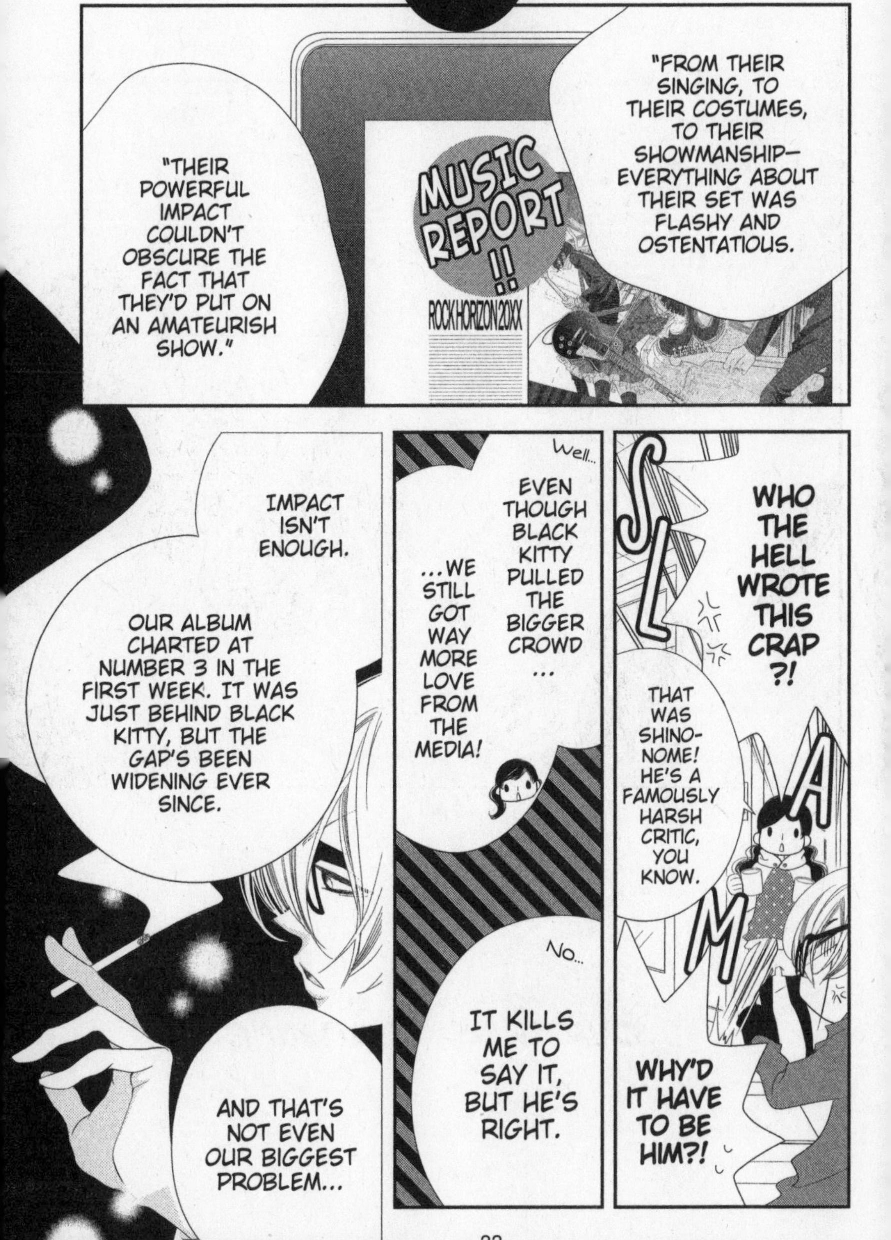
"FROM THEIR SINGING, TO THEIR COSTUMES, TO THEIR SHOWMANSHIP—EVERYTHING ABOUT THEIR SET WAS FLASHY AND OSTENTATIOUS.
MUSIC REPORT !!
ROCK HORIZON 20XX
"THEIR POWERFUL IMPACT COULDN'T OBSCURE THE FACT THAT THEY'D PUT ON AN AMATEURISH SHOW."
SLAM
WHO THE HELL WROTE THIS CRAP?!
THAT WAS SHINO-NOME! HE'S A FAMOUSLY HARSH CRITIC, YOU KNOW.
WHY'D IT HAVE TO BE HIM?!
Well...
EVEN THOUGH BLACK KITTY PULLED THE BIGGER CROWD...
...WE STILL GOT WAY MORE LOVE FROM THE MEDIA!
No...
IT KILLS ME TO SAY IT, BUT HE'S RIGHT.
IMPACT ISN'T ENOUGH.
OUR ALBUM CHARTED AT NUMBER 3 IN THE FIRST WEEK. IT WAS JUST BEHIND BLACK KITTY, BUT THE GAP'S BEEN WIDENING EVER SINCE.
AND THAT'S NOT EVEN OUR BIGGEST PROBLEM...

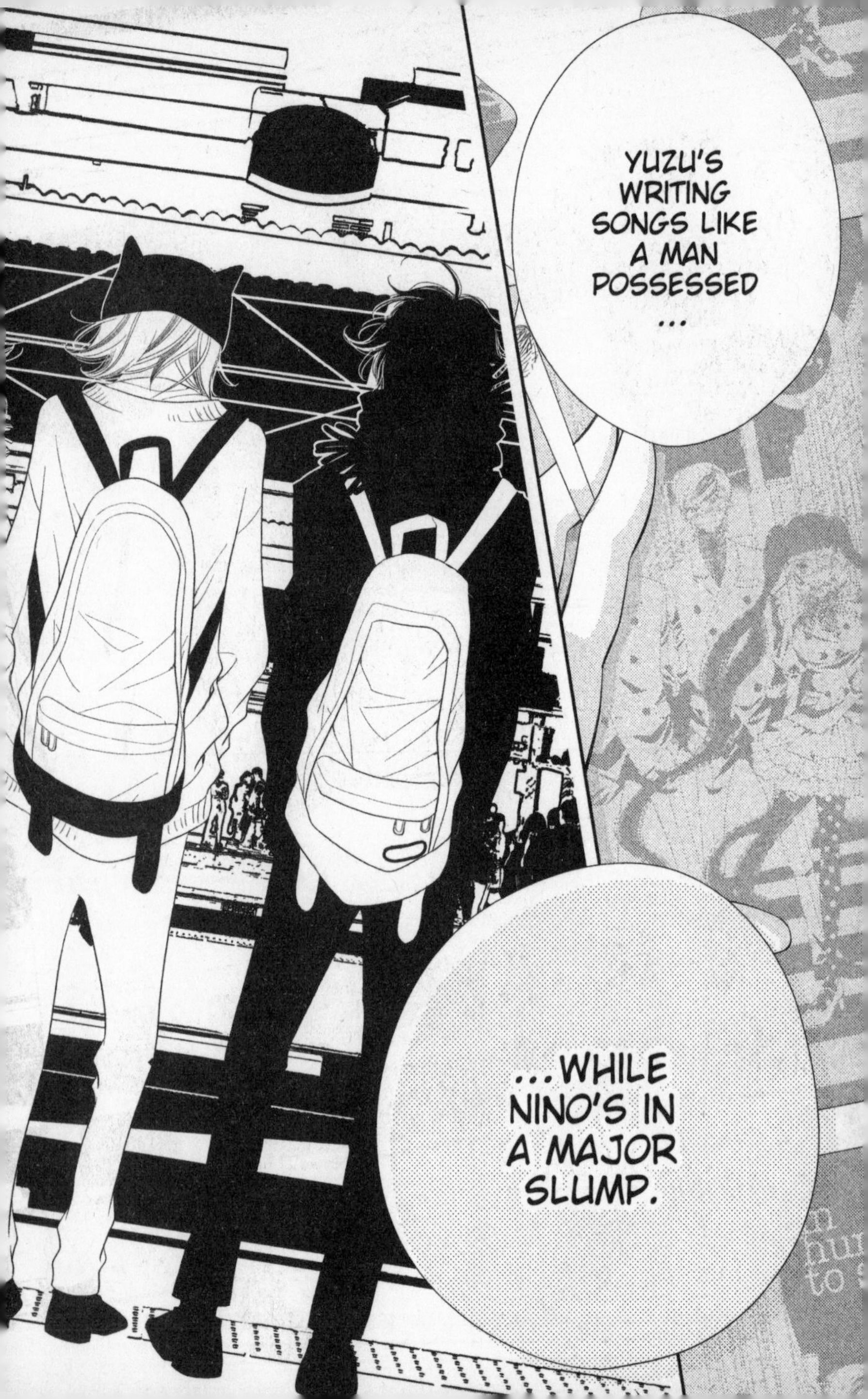
YUZU'S WRITING SONGS LIKE A MAN POSSESSED ...
...WHILE NINO'S IN A MAJOR SLUMP.

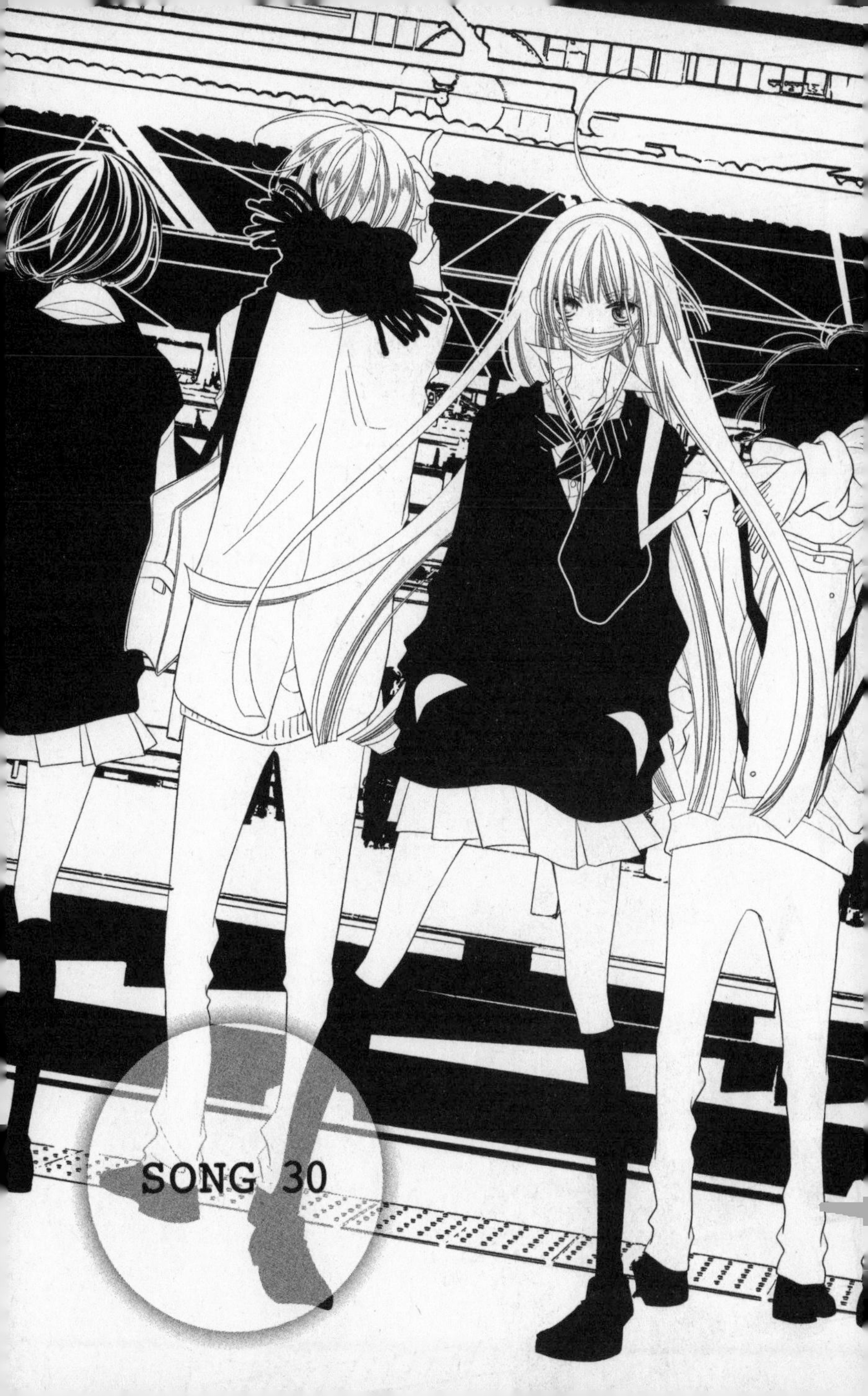
SONG 30

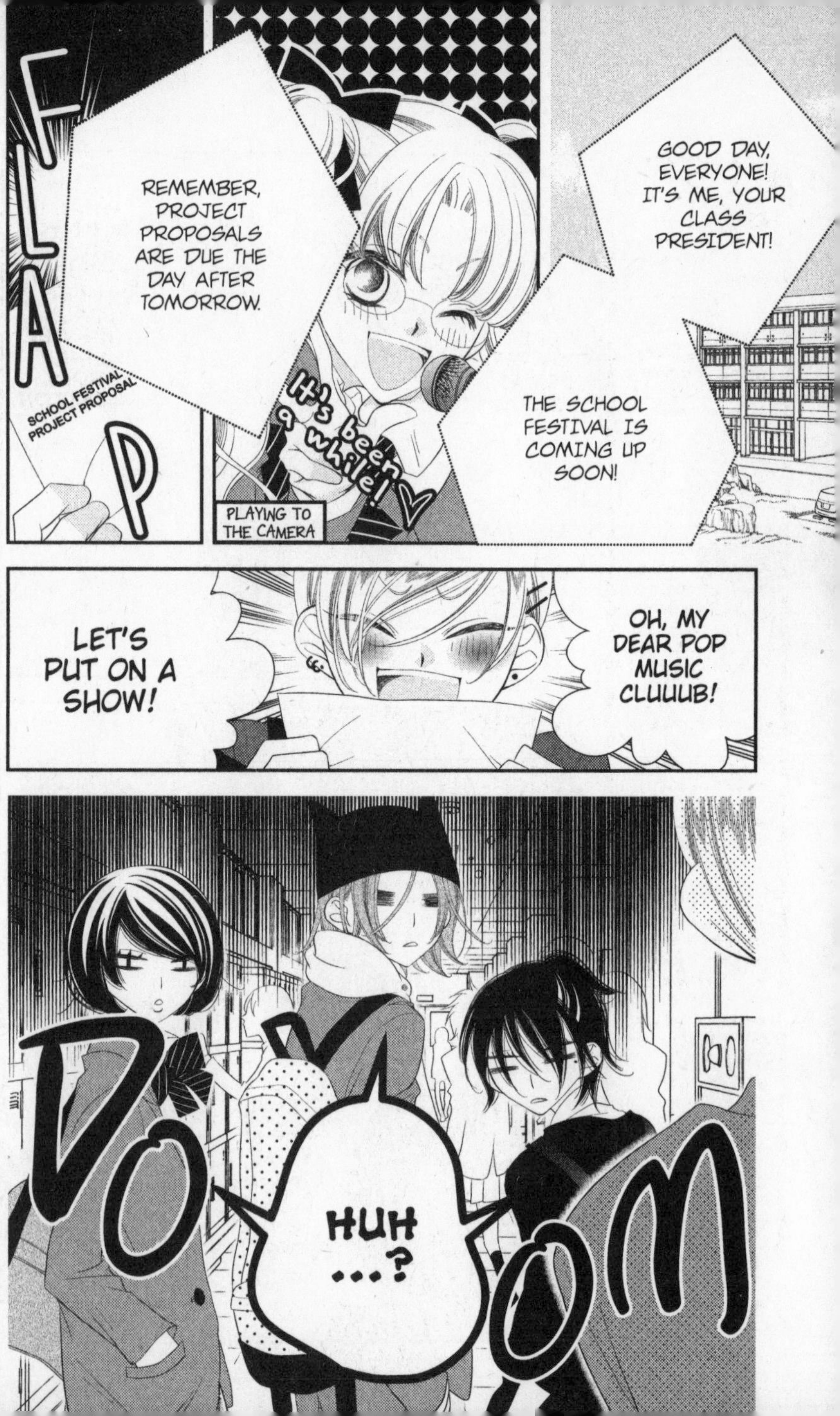
GOOD DAY, EVERYONE! IT'S ME, YOUR CLASS PRESIDENT!
THE SCHOOL FESTIVAL IS COMING UP SOON!
It's been a while! ♥
PLAYING TO THE CAMERA
REMEMBER, PROJECT PROPOSALS ARE DUE THE DAY AFTER TOMORROW.
FLAP
SCHOOL FESTIVAL PROJECT PROPOSAL
OH, MY DEAR POP MUSIC CLUUUB!
LET'S PUT ON A SHOW!
DOOM
HUH ...?

WHAT IS WITH YOU GUYS?! YOU'VE BEEN SLACK-ING OFF SINCE ROCK HORIZON!
I GOT SONGS TO WRITE. I'M OUT.
I HAVEN'T BEEN SLEEPING WELL SINCE I MOVED BACK HOME. I'M OUT.
I'M TAKING A BREAK FROM PER-FORMING. I'M OUT.
WE'RE IN A RUT HERE! A RUT!
WOULDN'T IT BE FUN TO GET NINO IN? WE COULD DO DUAL VOCALS!
YEAH, NO. I'M THE ONLY VOCALIST WE NEED.
NO! THE WAY SHE IS RIGHT NOW, THIS COULD BE THE PERFECT—
NOT GONNA HAPPEN, HARUYOSHI.

2

I've always loved seeing live music, but I've been on a real concert kick lately, so I've been going to shows every month. This month, I went to three of them! Since I started working on Anonymous Noise, I've been lucky enough to receive lots of invitations to shows, and it's been a real thrill to experience all sorts of different music scenes that I've never experienced before.

Despite playing piano and having been in a band before, I've always suffered from stage fright. So to all the artists doing battle onstage live like that—

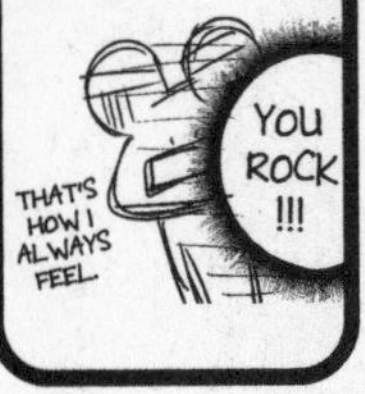

YOU ROCK!!!
THAT'S HOW I ALWAYS FEEL.

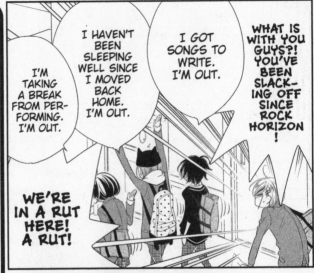

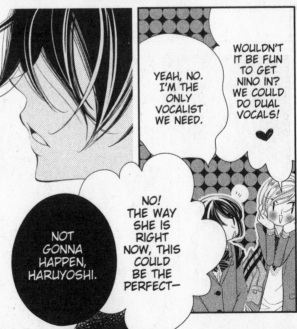

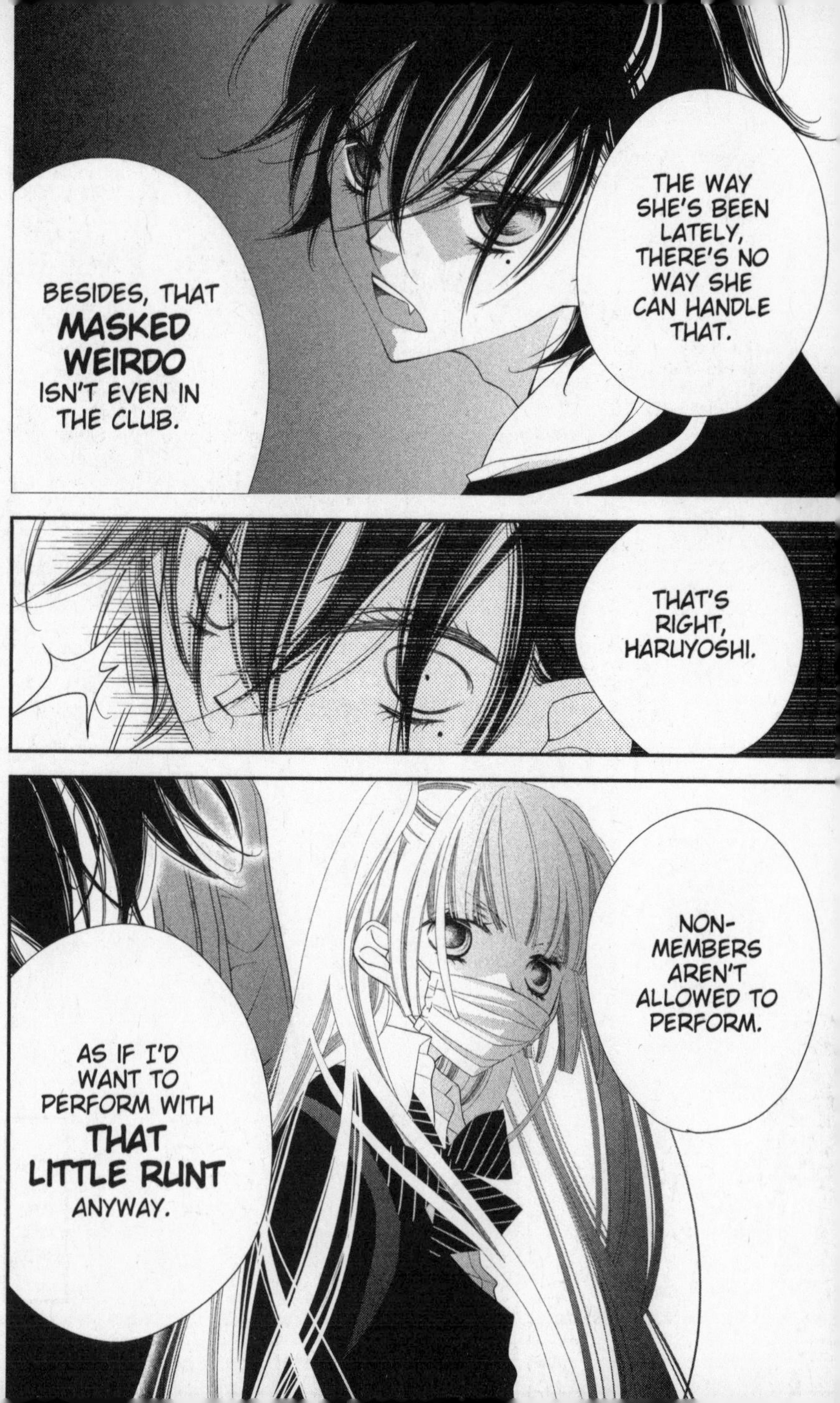
THE WAY SHE'S BEEN LATELY, THERE'S NO WAY SHE CAN HANDLE THAT.
BESIDES, THAT **MASKED WEIRDO** ISN'T EVEN IN THE CLUB.
THAT'S RIGHT, HARUYOSHI.
NON-MEMBERS AREN'T ALLOWED TO PERFORM.
AS IF I'D WANT TO PERFORM WITH **THAT LITTLE RUNT** ANYWAY.

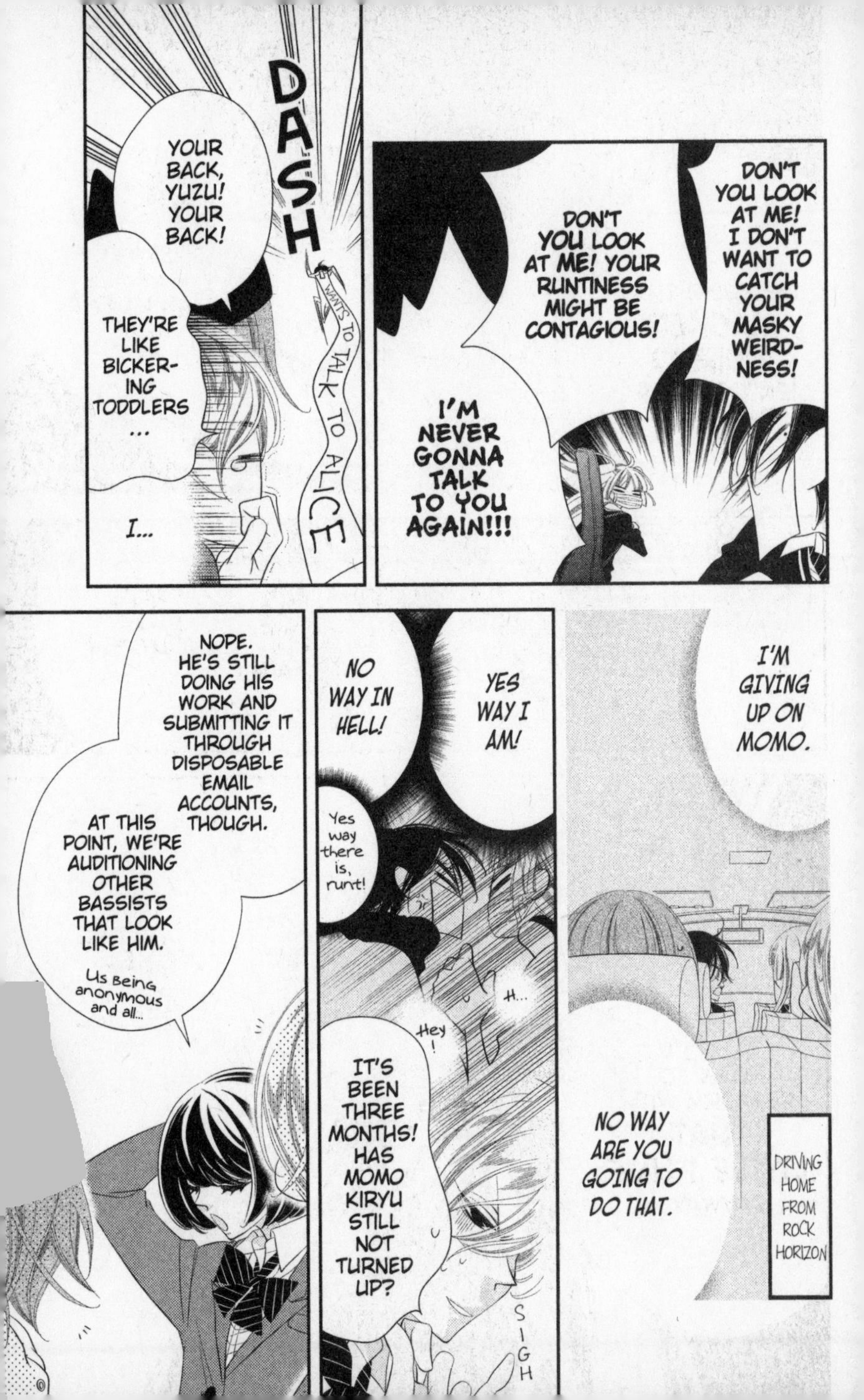
DON'T YOU LOOK AT ME! I DON'T WANT TO CATCH YOUR MASKY WEIRDNESS!
DON'T YOU LOOK AT ME! YOUR RUNTINESS MIGHT BE CONTAGIOUS!
I'M NEVER GONNA TALK TO YOU AGAIN!!!
DASH
YOUR BACK, YUZU! YOUR BACK!
WANTS TO TALK TO ALICE
THEY'RE LIKE BICKERING TODDLERS ...
I...
DRIVING HOME FROM ROCK HORIZON
I'M GIVING UP ON MOMO.
NO WAY ARE YOU GOING TO DO THAT.
YES WAY I AM!
NO WAY IN HELL!
Yes way there is, runt!
H...
Hey!
IT'S BEEN THREE MONTHS! HAS MOMO KIRYU STILL NOT TURNED UP?
SIGH
NOPE. HE'S STILL DOING HIS WORK AND SUBMITTING IT THROUGH DISPOSABLE EMAIL ACCOUNTS, THOUGH.
AT THIS POINT, WE'RE AUDITIONING OTHER BASSISTS THAT LOOK LIKE HIM.
Us being anonymous and all...

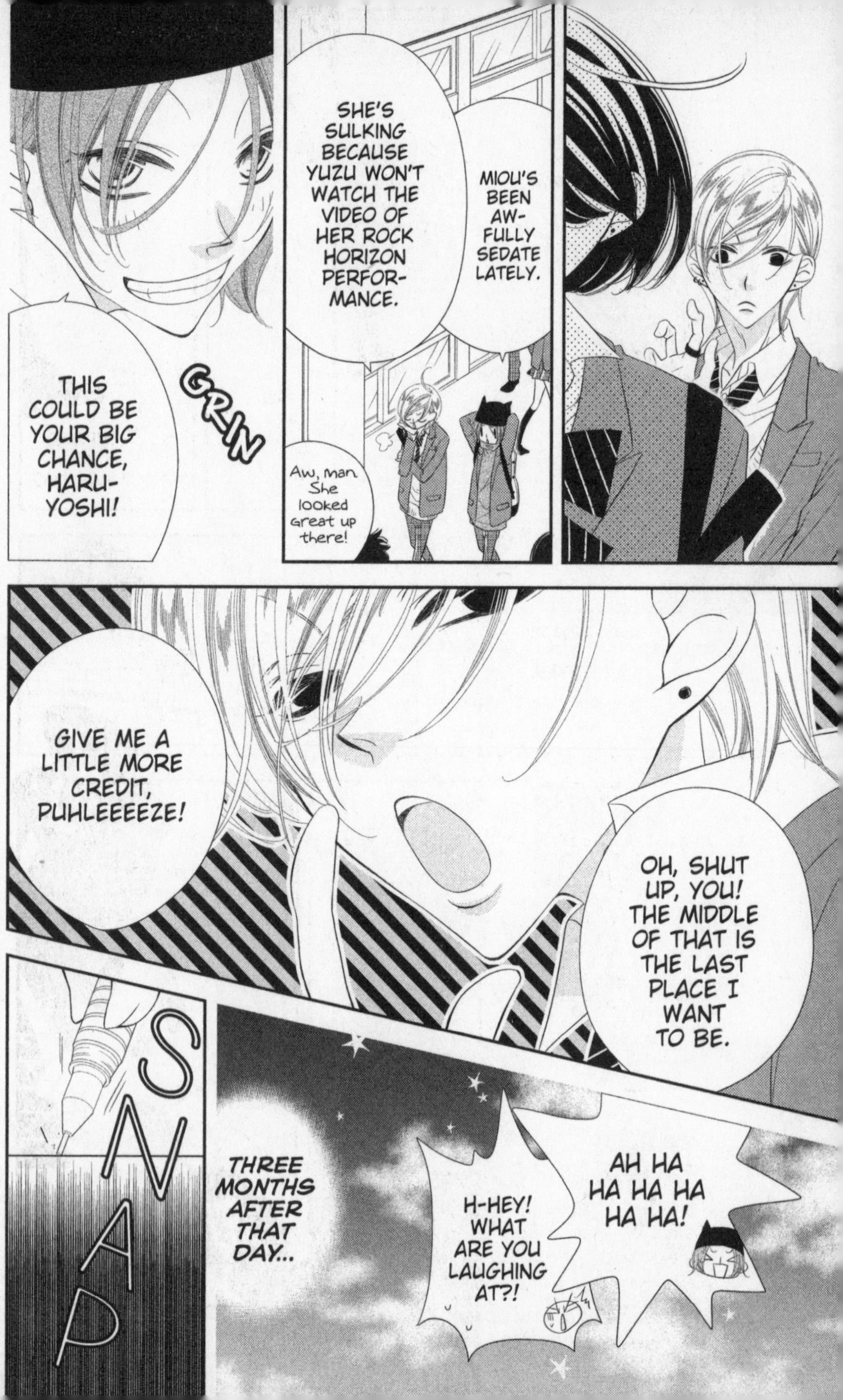
MIOU'S BEEN AW-FULLY SEDATE LATELY.
SHE'S SULKING BECAUSE YUZU WON'T WATCH THE VIDEO OF HER ROCK HORIZON PERFOR-MANCE.
Aw, man She looked great up there!
GRIN
THIS COULD BE YOUR BIG CHANCE, HARU-YOSHI!
GIVE ME A LITTLE MORE CREDIT, PUHLEEEEZE!
OH, SHUT UP, YOU! THE MIDDLE OF THAT IS THE LAST PLACE I WANT TO BE.
AH HA HA HA HA HA HA!
H-HEY! WHAT ARE YOU LAUGHING AT?!
THREE MONTHS AFTER THAT DAY...
SNAP

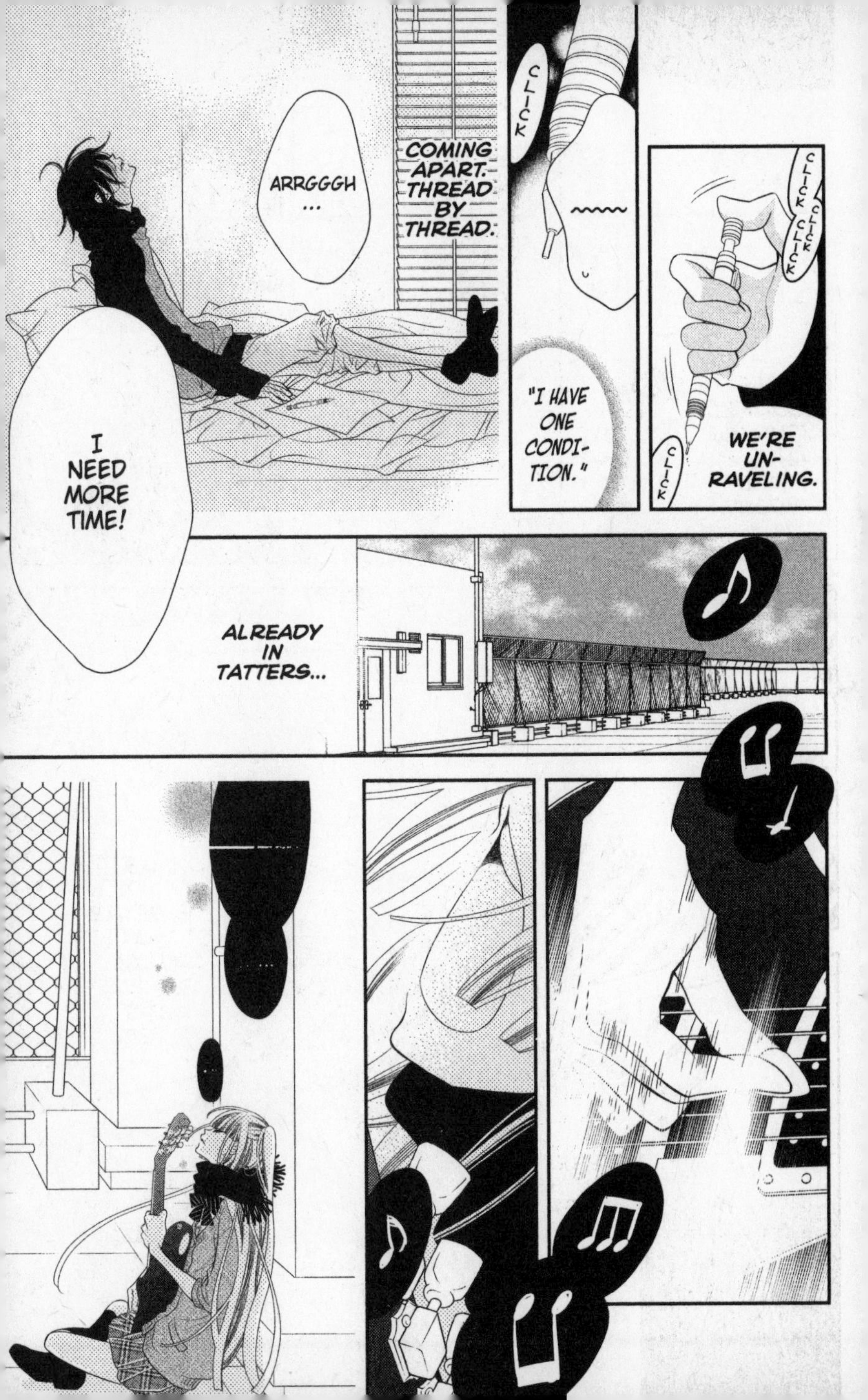
CLICK CLICK CLICK CLICK
WE'RE UN-RAVELING.
CLICK
CLICK
~~~~
"I HAVE ONE CONDI-TION."
COMING APART. THREAD BY THREAD.
ARRGGGH ...
I NEED MORE TIME!
ALREADY IN TATTERS...
~~~~

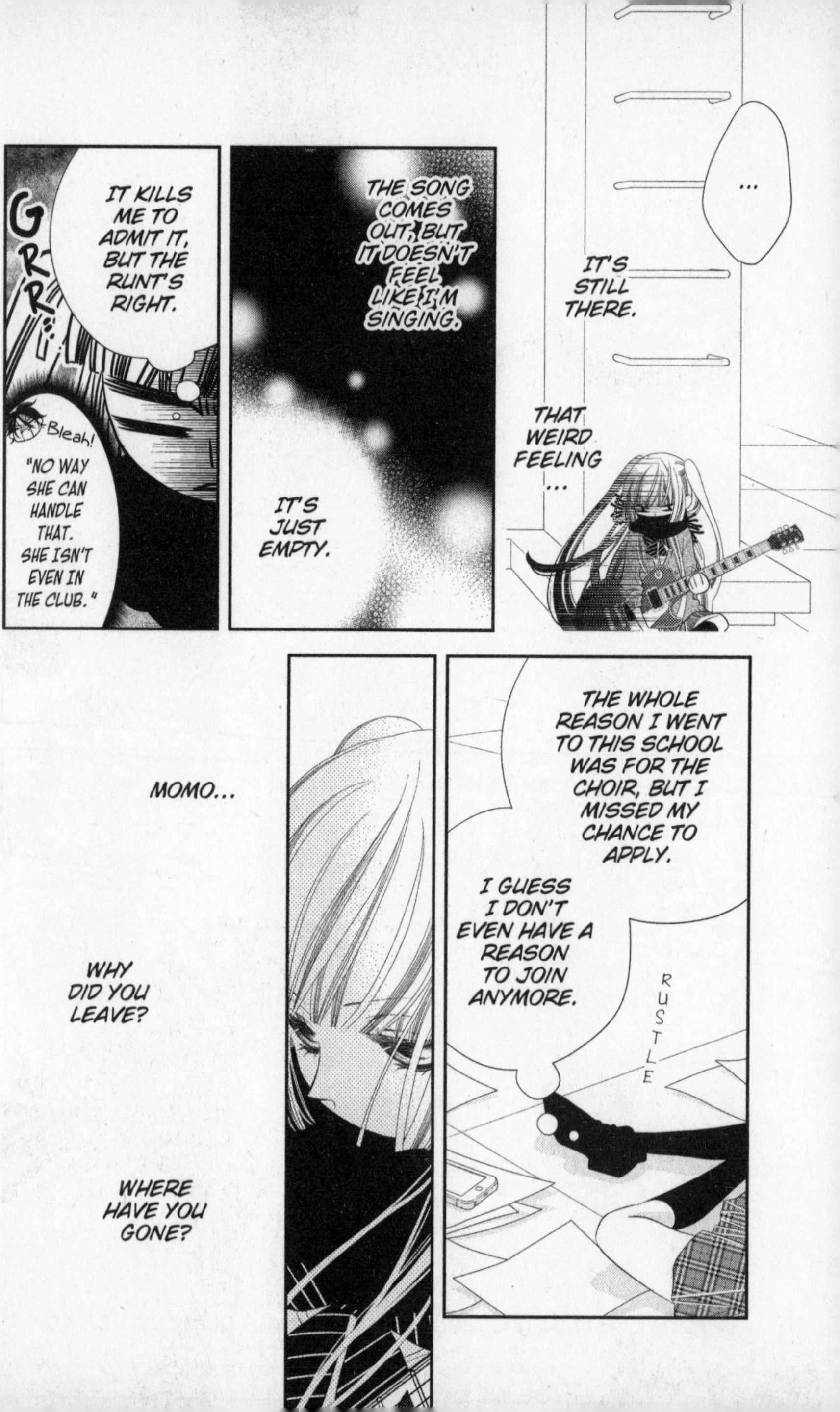
...
IT'S STILL THERE.
THAT WEIRD FEELING...
THE SONG COMES OUT, BUT IT DOESN'T FEEL LIKE I'M SINGING.
IT'S JUST EMPTY.
IT KILLS ME TO ADMIT IT, BUT THE RUNT'S RIGHT.
GRR
Bleah!
"NO WAY SHE CAN HANDLE THAT. SHE ISN'T EVEN IN THE CLUB."
THE WHOLE REASON I WENT TO THIS SCHOOL WAS FOR THE CHOIR, BUT I MISSED MY CHANCE TO APPLY.
I GUESS I DON'T EVEN HAVE A REASON TO JOIN ANYMORE.
RUSTLE
MOMO...
WHY DID YOU LEAVE?
WHERE HAVE YOU GONE?

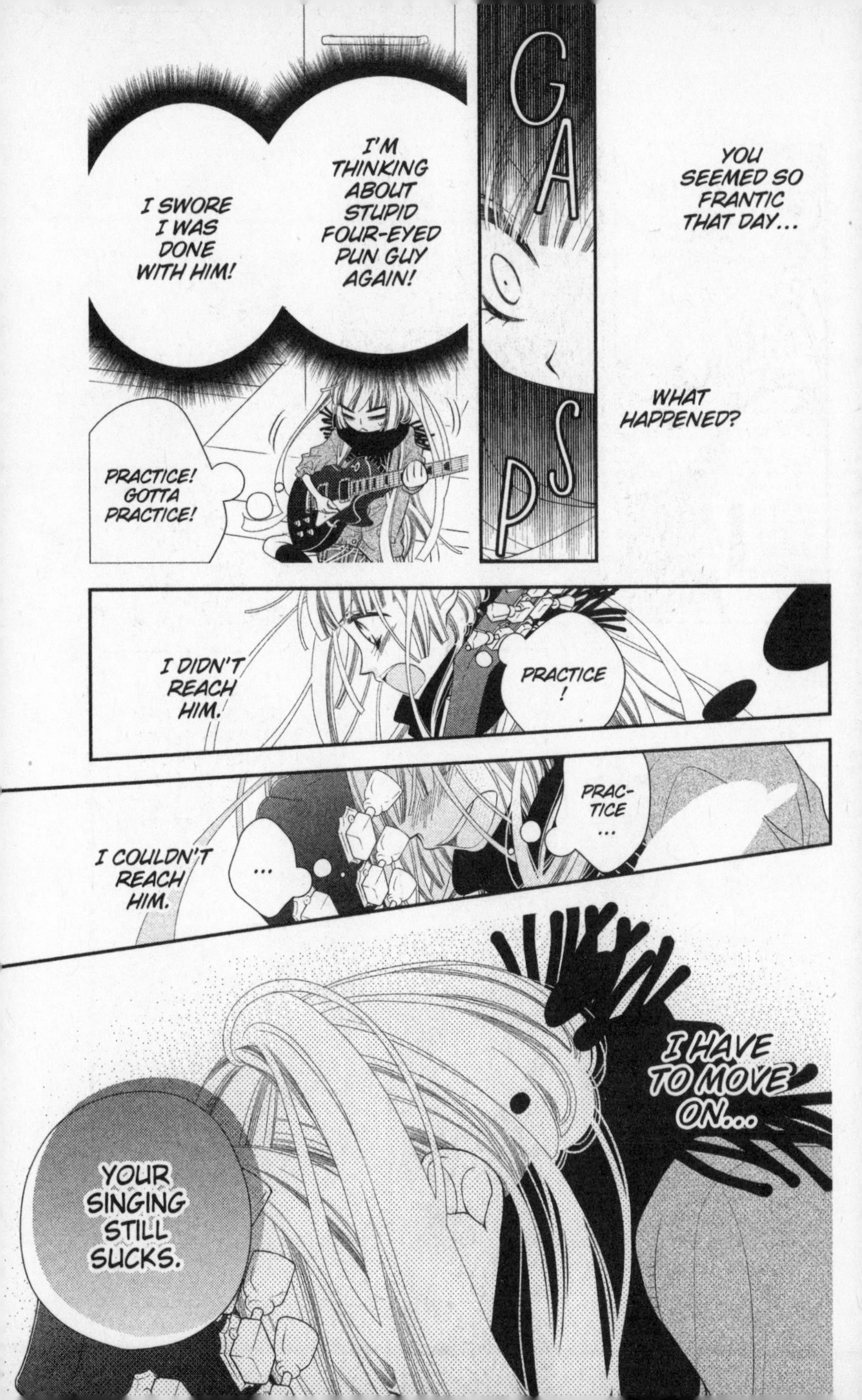
YOU SEEMED SO FRANTIC THAT DAY...
WHAT HAPPENED?
GASP
I'M THINKING ABOUT STUPID FOUR-EYED PUN GUY AGAIN!
I SWORE I WAS DONE WITH HIM!
PRACTICE! GOTTA PRACTICE!
PRACTICE!
I DIDN'T REACH HIM.
PRAC-TICE...
...
I COULDN'T REACH HIM.
I HAVE TO MOVE ON...
YOUR SINGING STILL SUCKS.

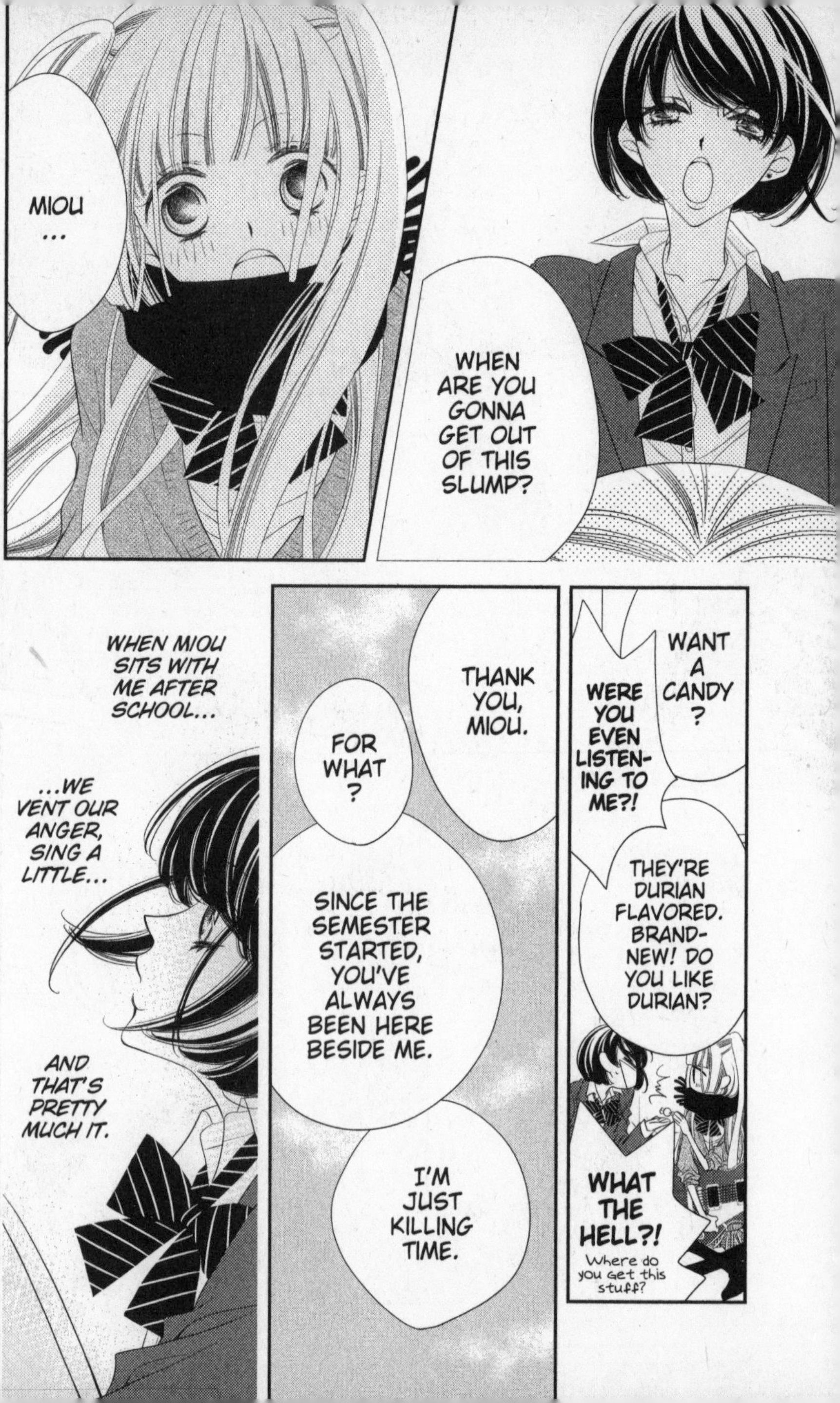
WHEN ARE YOU GONNA GET OUT OF THIS SLUMP?
MIOU ...
WANT A CANDY?
WERE YOU EVEN LISTENING TO ME?!
THEY'RE DURIAN FLAVORED. BRAND-NEW! DO YOU LIKE DURIAN?
WHAT THE HELL?!
Where do you get this stuff?
THANK YOU, MIOU.
FOR WHAT?
SINCE THE SEMESTER STARTED, YOU'VE ALWAYS BEEN HERE BESIDE ME.
I'M JUST KILLING TIME.
WHEN MIOU SITS WITH ME AFTER SCHOOL...
...WE VENT OUR ANGER, SING A LITTLE...
AND THAT'S PRETTY MUCH IT.

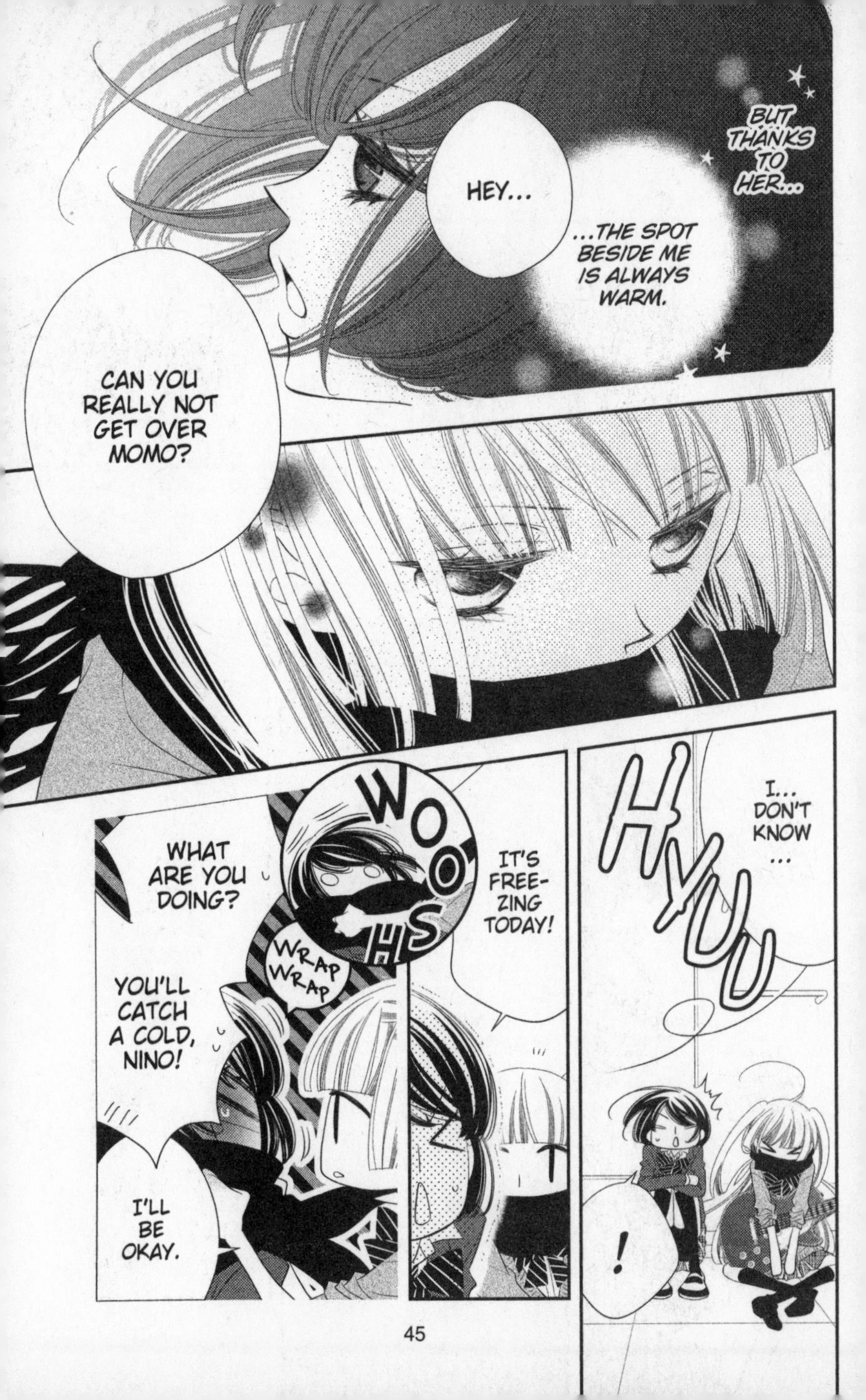
BUT THANKS TO HER...
...THE SPOT BESIDE ME IS ALWAYS WARM.
HEY...
CAN YOU REALLY NOT GET OVER MOMO?
I... DON'T KNOW ...
HYUU
!
IT'S FREEZING TODAY!
WHOOSH
WRAP WRAP
WHAT ARE YOU DOING?
YOU'LL CATCH A COLD, NINO!
I'LL BE OKAY.

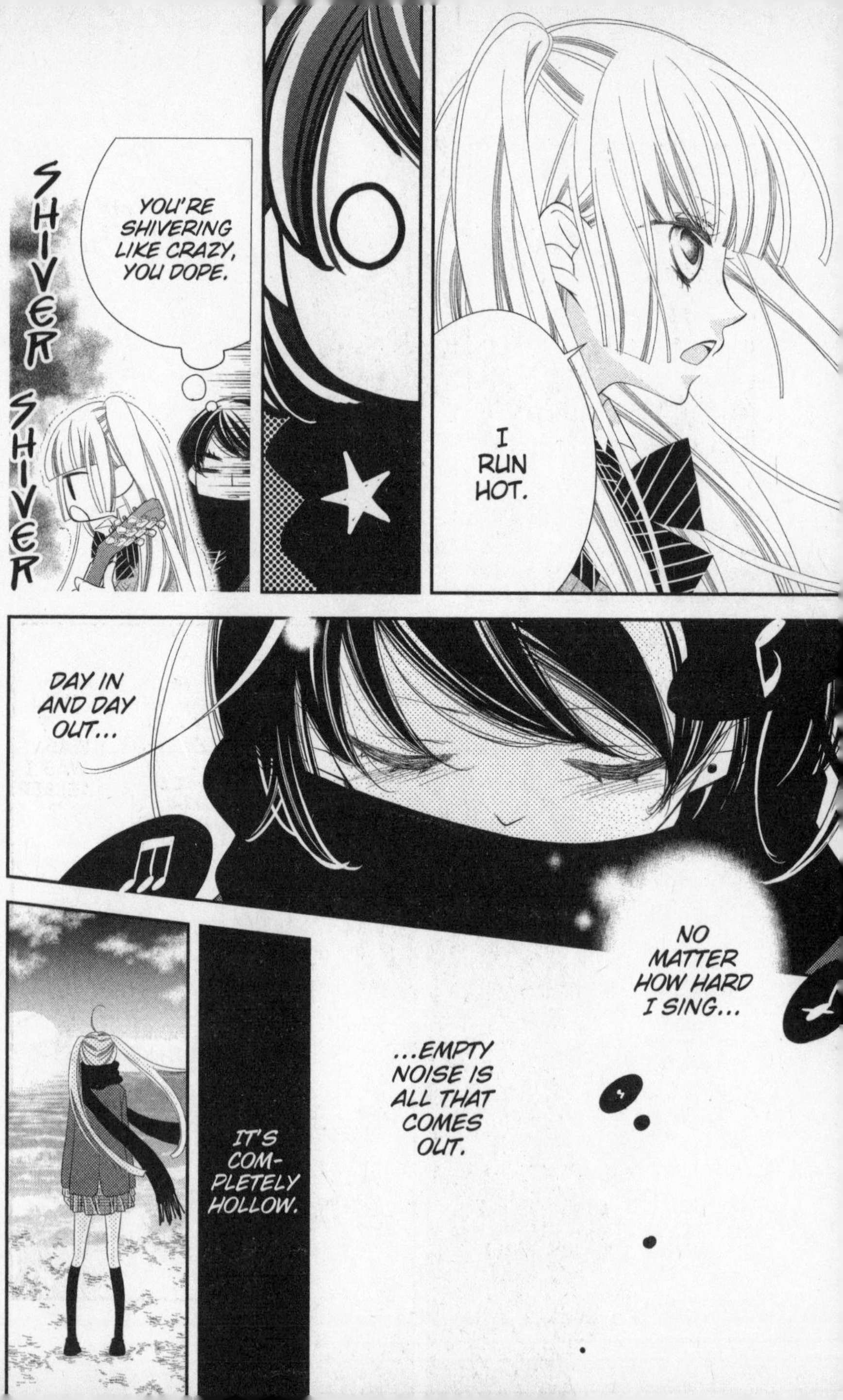
I RUN HOT.
YOU'RE SHIVERING LIKE CRAZY, YOU DOPE.
SHIVER SHIVER
DAY IN AND DAY OUT...
NO MATTER HOW HARD I SING...
...EMPTY NOISE IS ALL THAT COMES OUT.
IT'S COM-PLETELY HOLLOW.

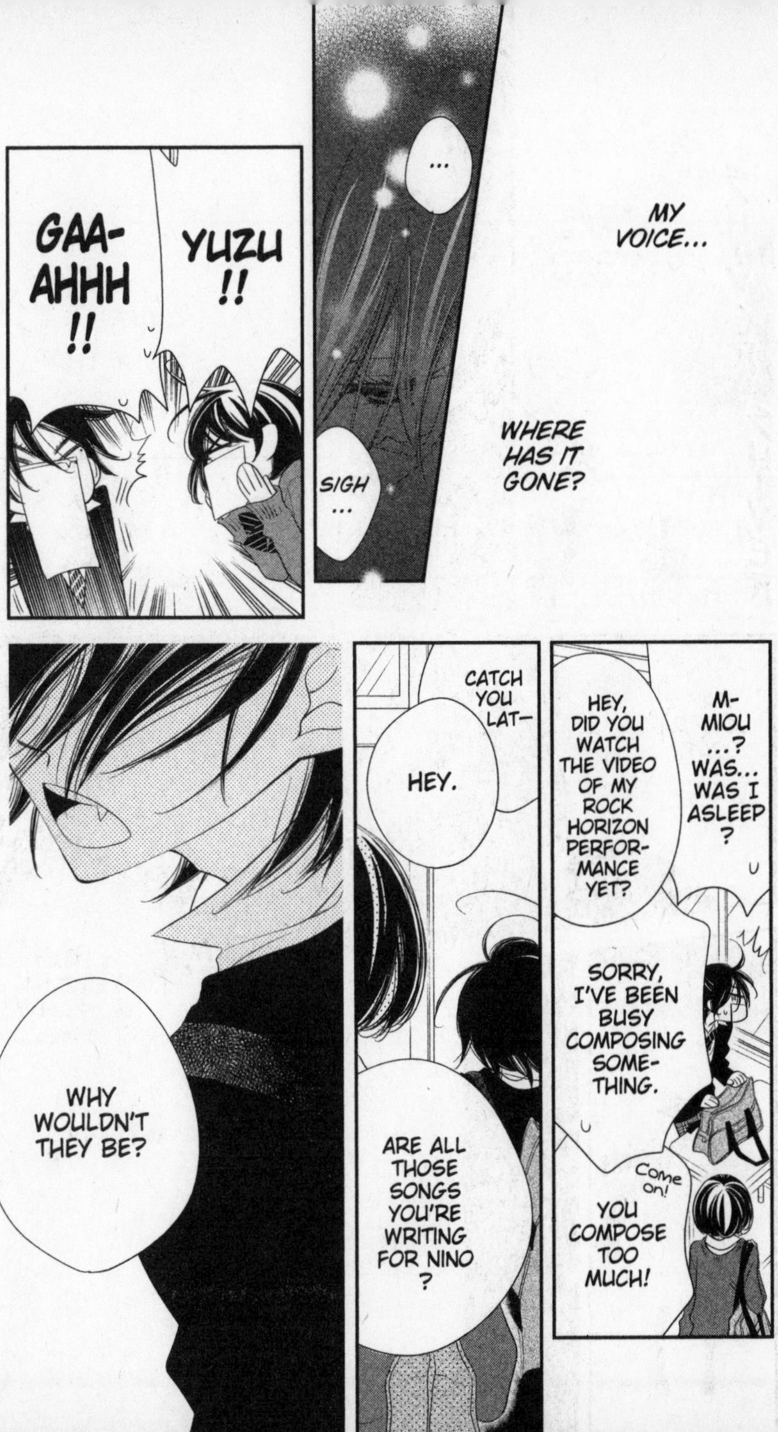
MY VOICE...
WHERE HAS IT GONE?
...
SIGH...
YUZU!!
GAA-AHHH!!
M-MIOU...? WAS... WAS I ASLEEP?
HEY, DID YOU WATCH THE VIDEO OF MY ROCK HORIZON PERFORMANCE YET?
SORRY, I'VE BEEN BUSY COMPOSING SOMETHING.
Come on!
YOU COMPOSE TOO MUCH!
CATCH YOU LAT—
HEY.
ARE ALL THOSE SONGS YOU'RE WRITING FOR NINO?
WHY WOULDN'T THEY BE?

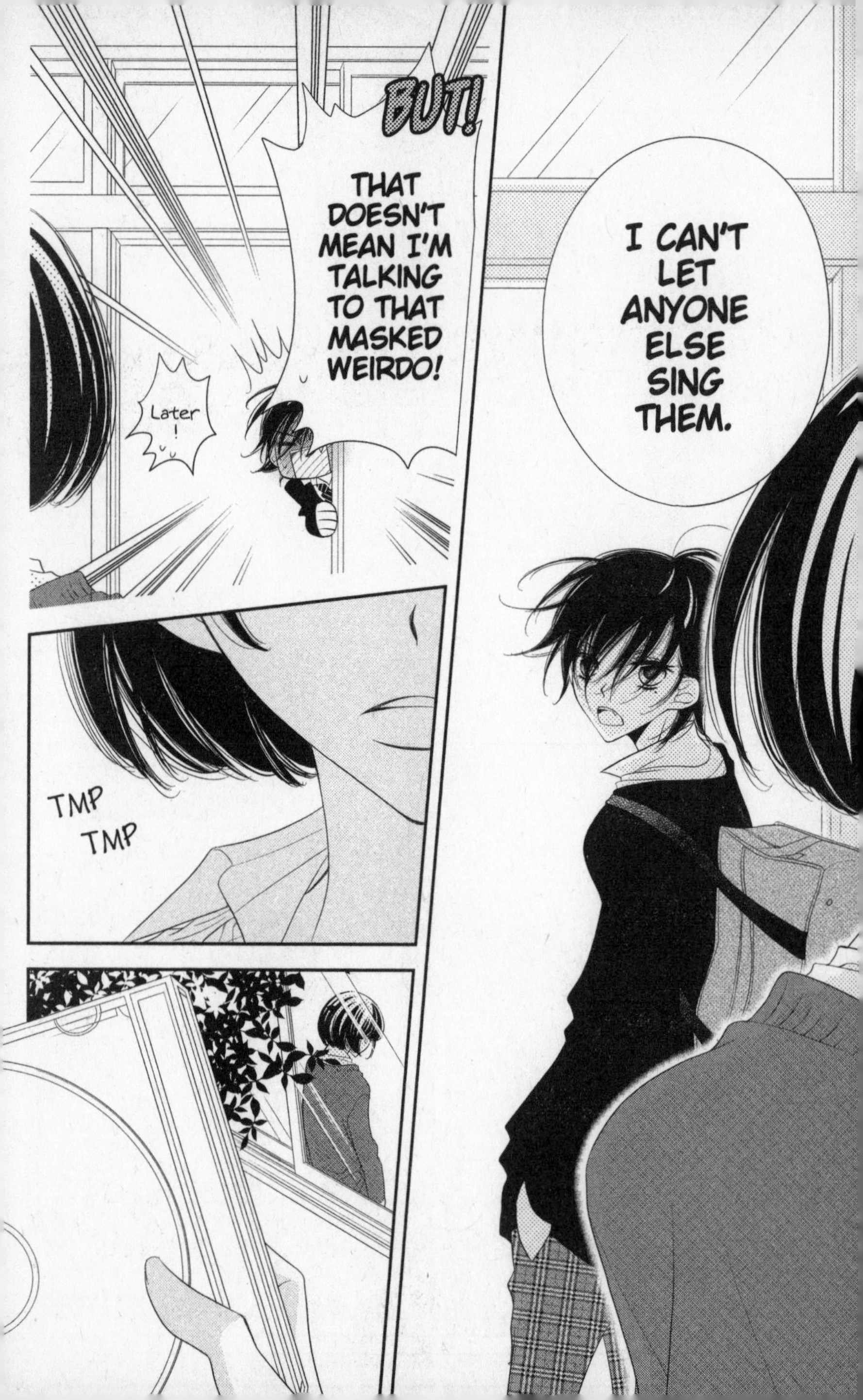
I CAN'T LET ANYONE ELSE SING THEM.
BUT!
THAT DOESN'T MEAN I'M TALKING TO THAT MASKED WEIRDO!
Later!
TMP TMP

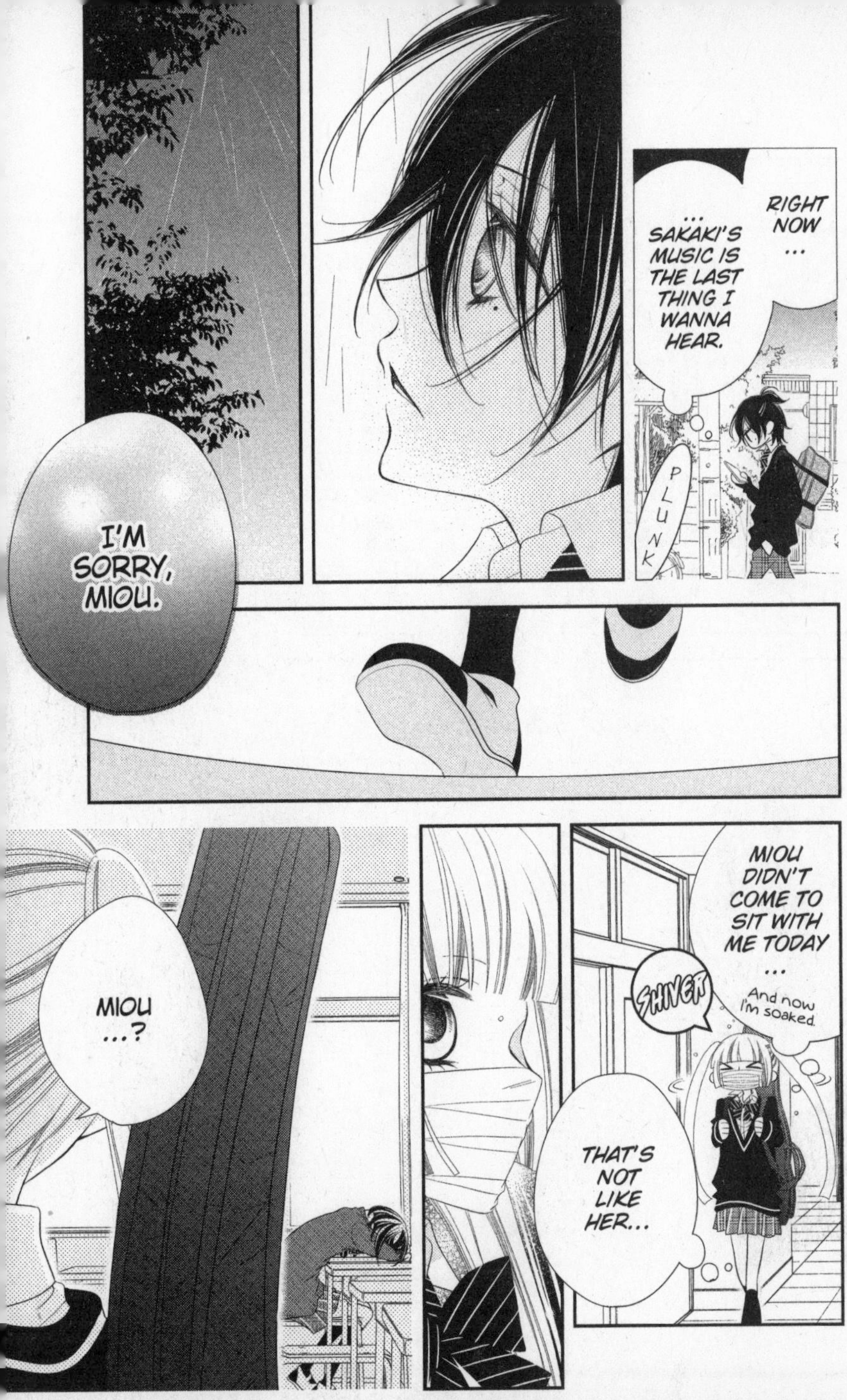
RIGHT NOW ...
... SAKAKI'S MUSIC IS THE LAST THING I WANNA HEAR.
PLUNK
I'M SORRY, MIOU.
MIOU DIDN'T COME TO SIT WITH ME TODAY ...
And now I'm soaked.
SHIVER
THAT'S NOT LIKE HER...
MIOU ...?

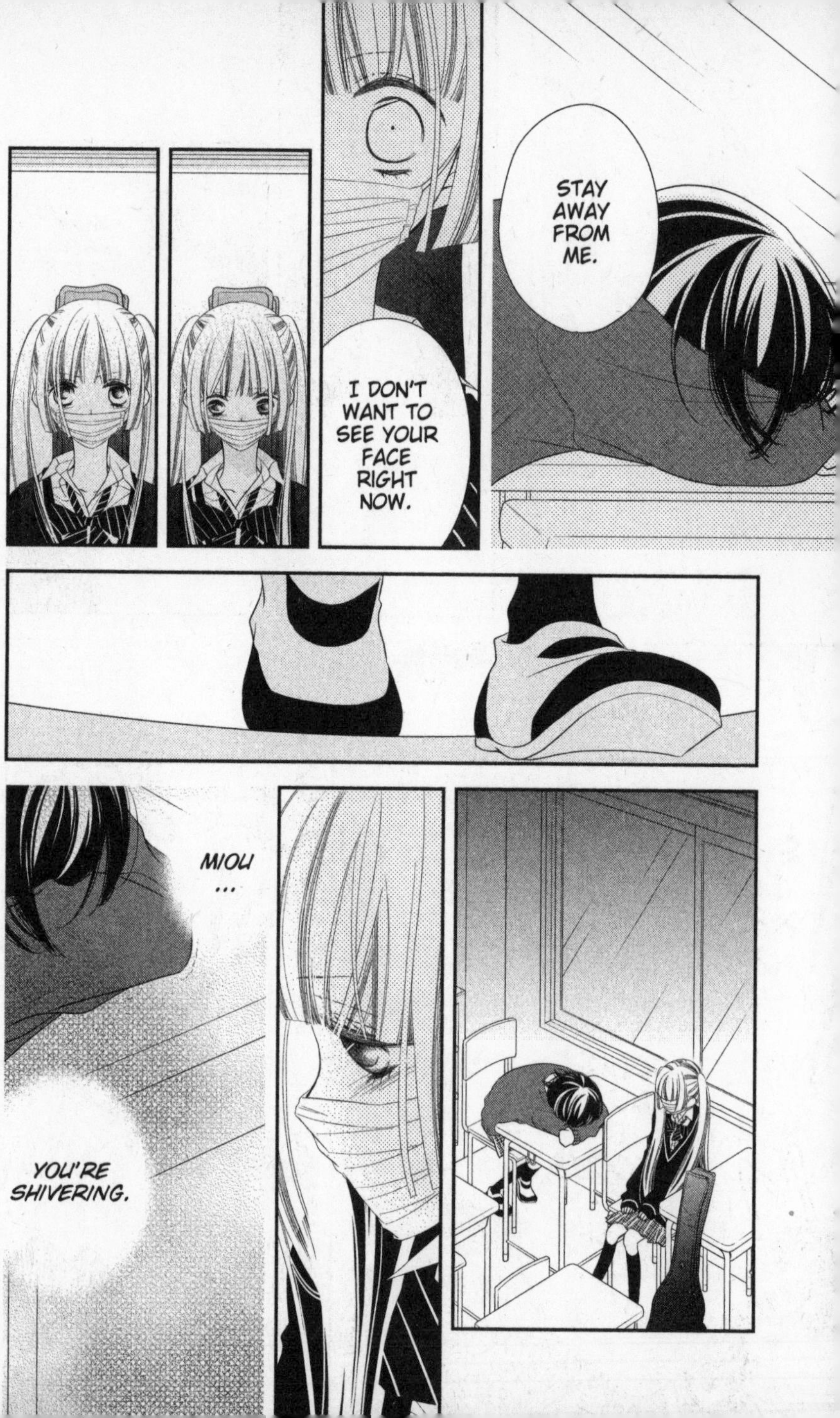
STAY AWAY FROM ME.
I DON'T WANT TO SEE YOUR FACE RIGHT NOW.
MIOU ...
YOU'RE SHIVERING.

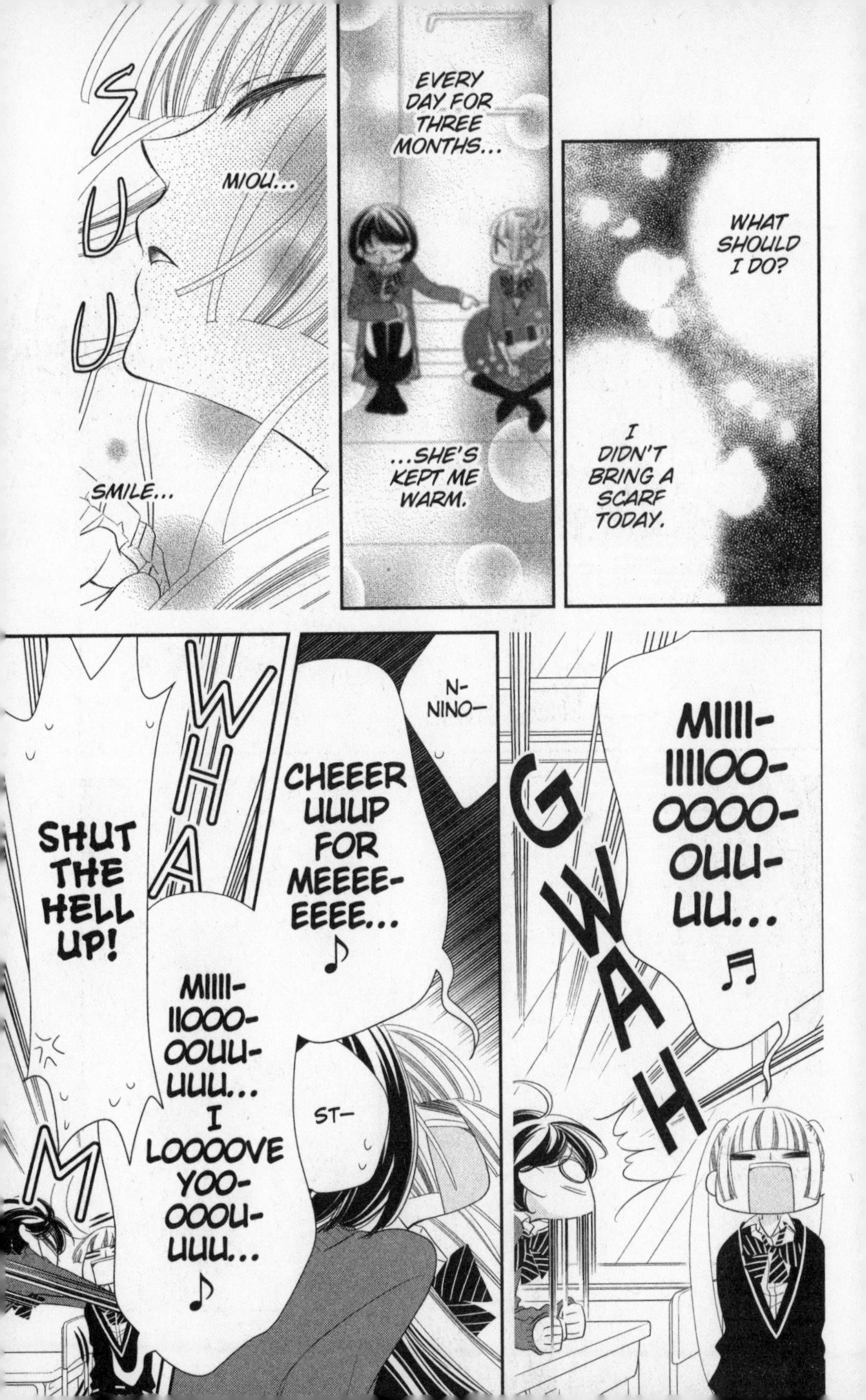
WHAT SHOULD I DO?
I DIDN'T BRING A SCARF TODAY.
EVERY DAY FOR THREE MONTHS...
...SHE'S KEPT ME WARM.
SUUU
MIOU...
SMILE...
MIIII-IIIIOO-OOOO-OUUU-UU... ♬
GWAH
N-NINO—
CHEEER UUUP FOR MEEEE-EEEE... ♪
WHA
SHUT THE HELL UP!
ST—
MIIII-IIOOO-OOUU-UUU... I LOOOOVE YOO-OOOU-UUU... ♪
M

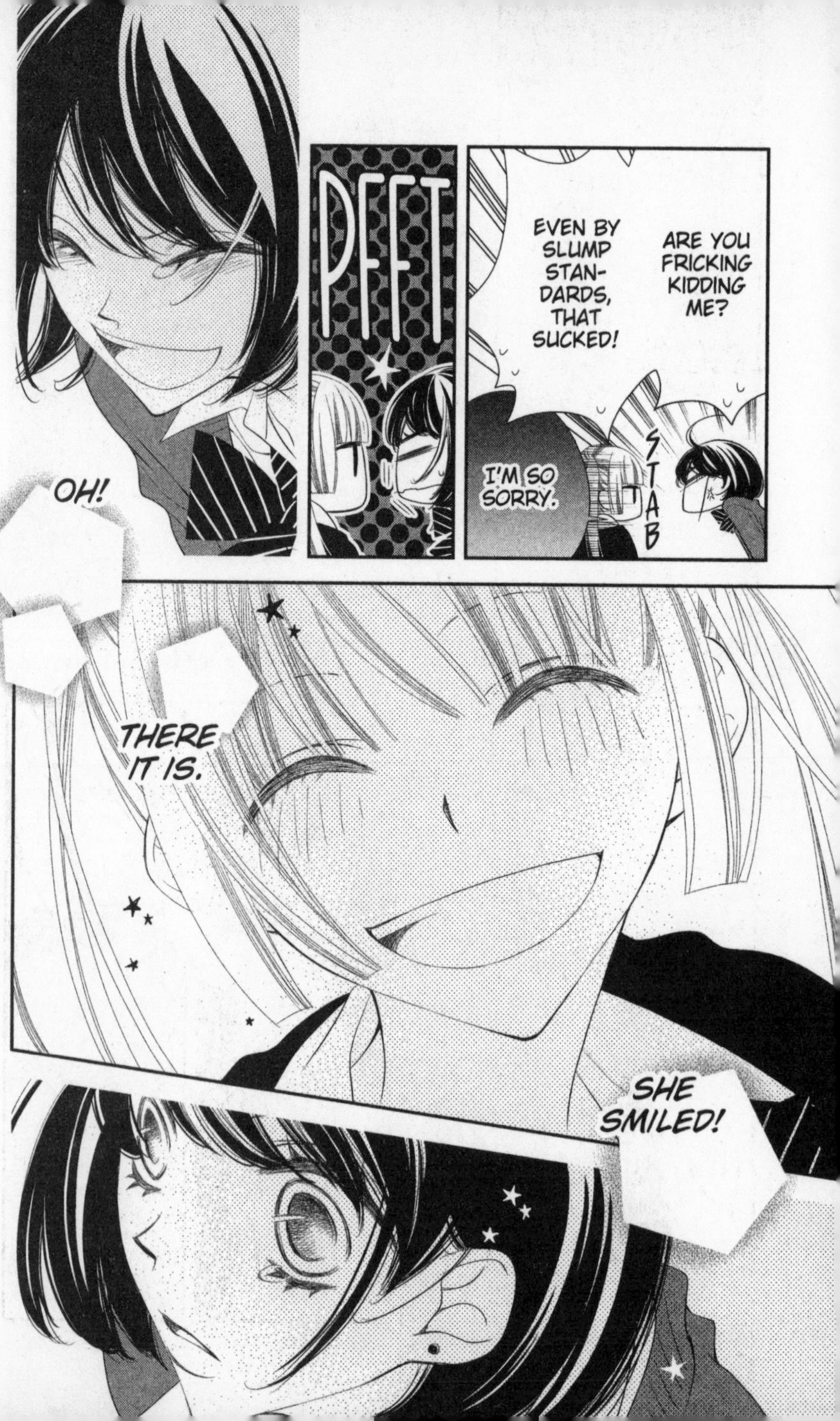
ARE YOU FRICKING KIDDING ME?
EVEN BY SLUMP STAN-DARDS, THAT SUCKED!
STAB
I'M SO SORRY.
PFFT
OH!
THERE IT IS.
SHE SMILED!

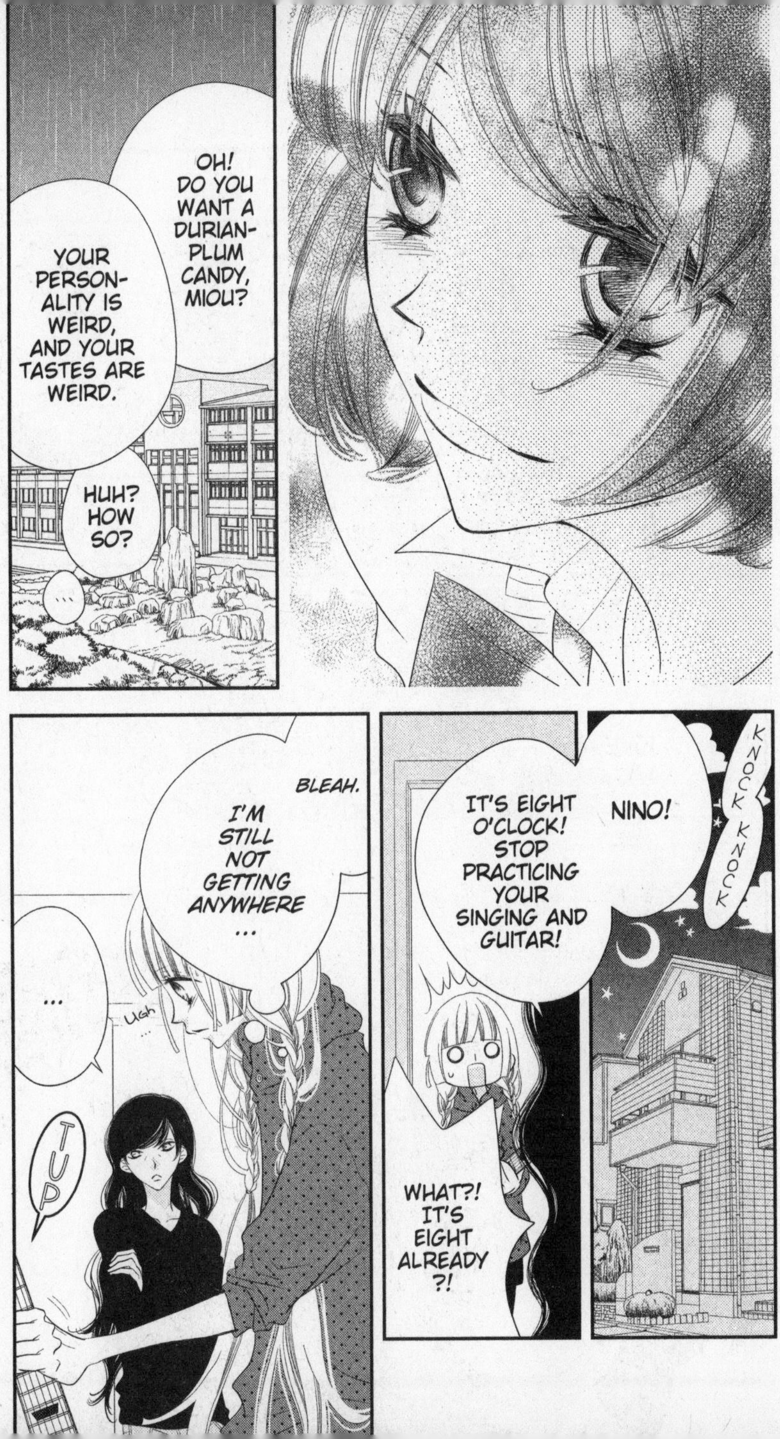
OH! DO YOU WANT A DURIAN-PLUM CANDY, MIOU?
YOUR PERSONALITY IS WEIRD, AND YOUR TASTES ARE WEIRD.
HUH? HOW SO?
...
KNOCK KNOCK
NINO!
IT'S EIGHT O'CLOCK! STOP PRACTICING YOUR SINGING AND GUITAR!
WHAT?! IT'S EIGHT ALREADY?!
BLEAH.
I'M STILL NOT GETTING ANYWHERE...
Ugh...
...
TUP

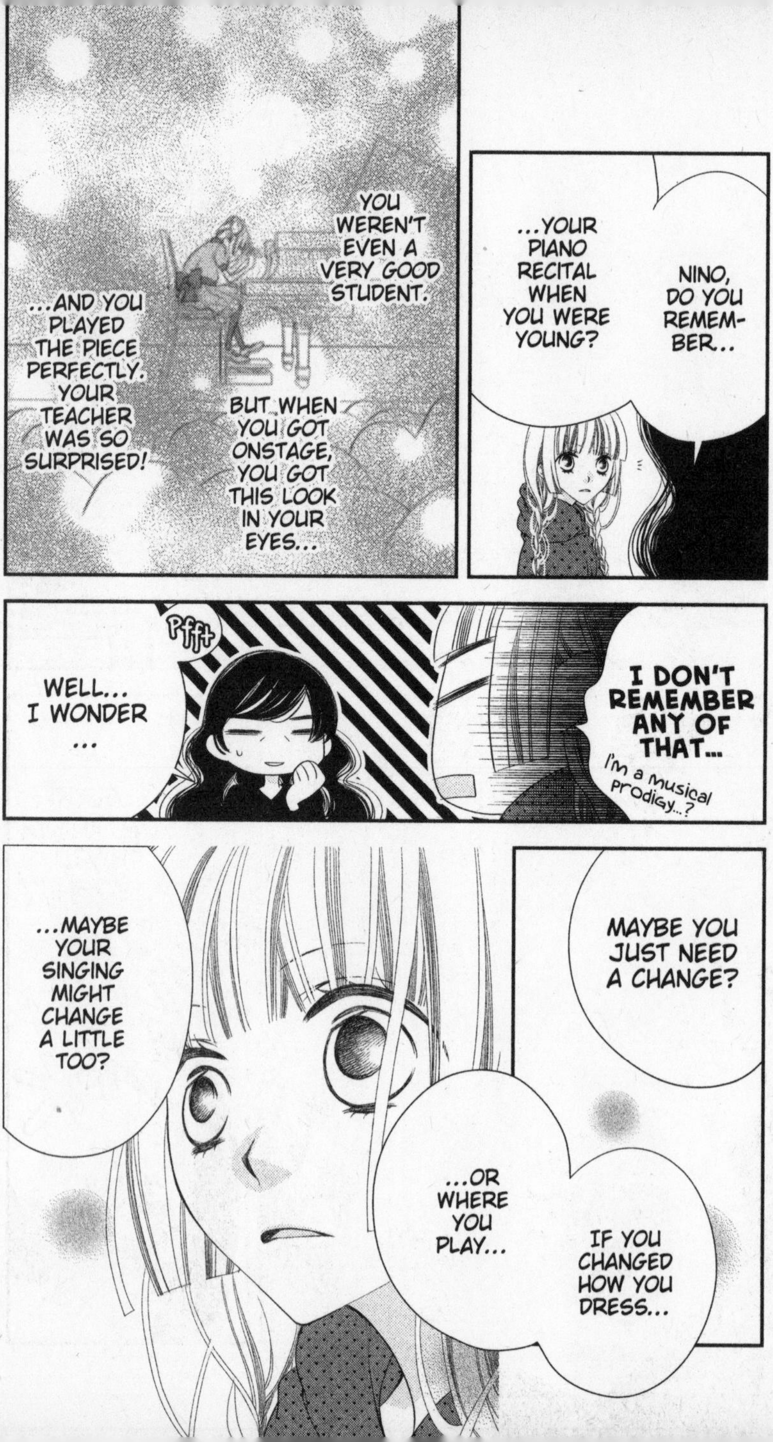
NINO, DO YOU REMEMBER...
...YOUR PIANO RECITAL WHEN YOU WERE YOUNG?
YOU WEREN'T EVEN A VERY GOOD STUDENT.
BUT WHEN YOU GOT ONSTAGE, YOU GOT THIS LOOK IN YOUR EYES...
...AND YOU PLAYED THE PIECE PERFECTLY. YOUR TEACHER WAS SO SURPRISED!
I DON'T REMEMBER ANY OF THAT...
I'm a musical prodigy...?
Pfft
WELL... I WONDER ...
MAYBE YOU JUST NEED A CHANGE?
IF YOU CHANGED HOW YOU DRESS...
...OR WHERE YOU PLAY...
...MAYBE YOUR SINGING MIGHT CHANGE A LITTLE TOO?

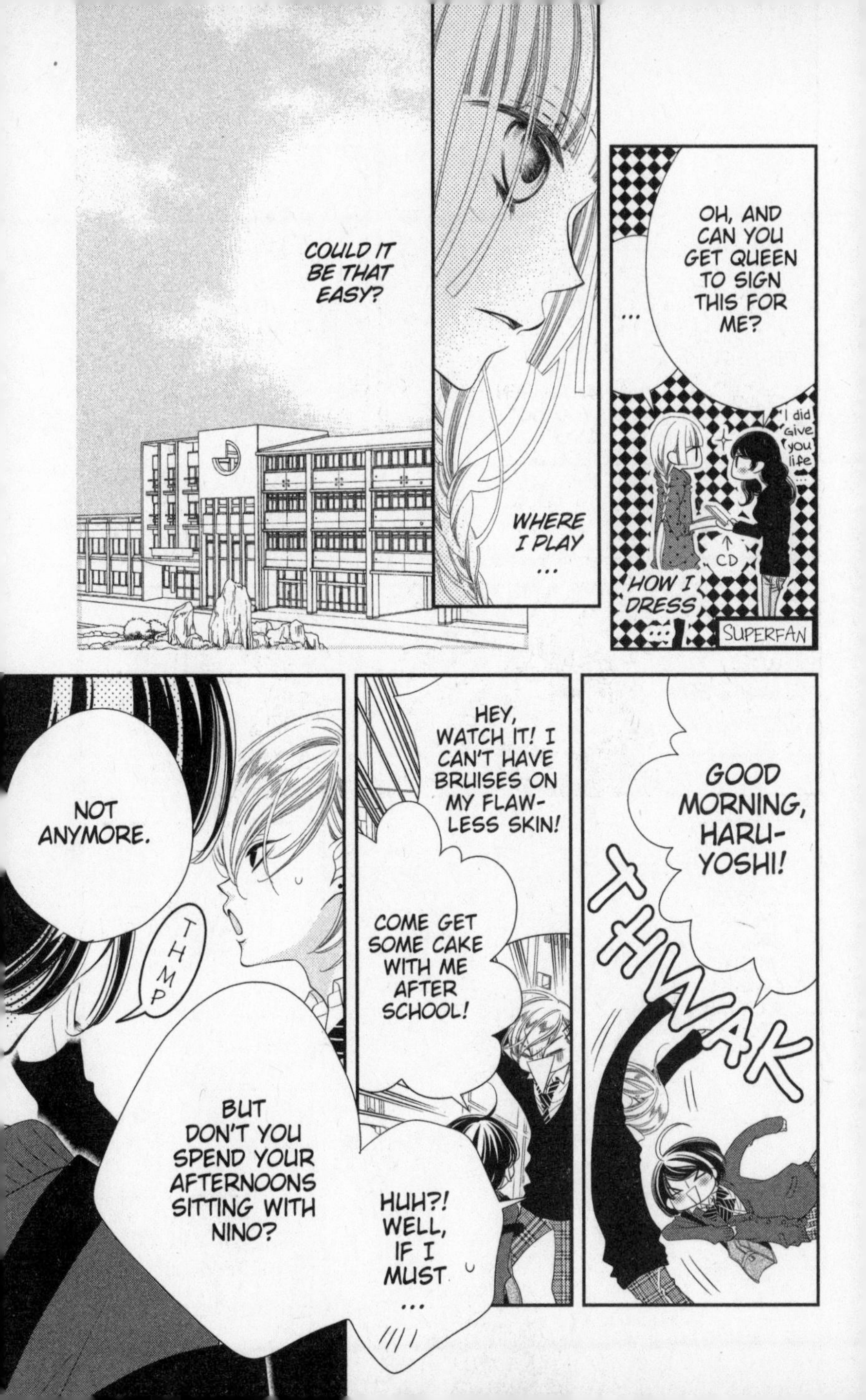
OH, AND CAN YOU GET QUEEN TO SIGN THIS FOR ME?
...
I did Give you life ...
CD
HOW I DRESS ...
SUPERFAN
WHERE I PLAY ...
COULD IT BE THAT EASY?
GOOD MORNING, HARU-YOSHI!
THWAK
HEY, WATCH IT! I CAN'T HAVE BRUISES ON MY FLAW-LESS SKIN!
COME GET SOME CAKE WITH ME AFTER SCHOOL!
HUH?! WELL, IF I MUST ...
BUT DON'T YOU SPEND YOUR AFTERNOONS SITTING WITH NINO?
THMP
NOT ANYMORE.

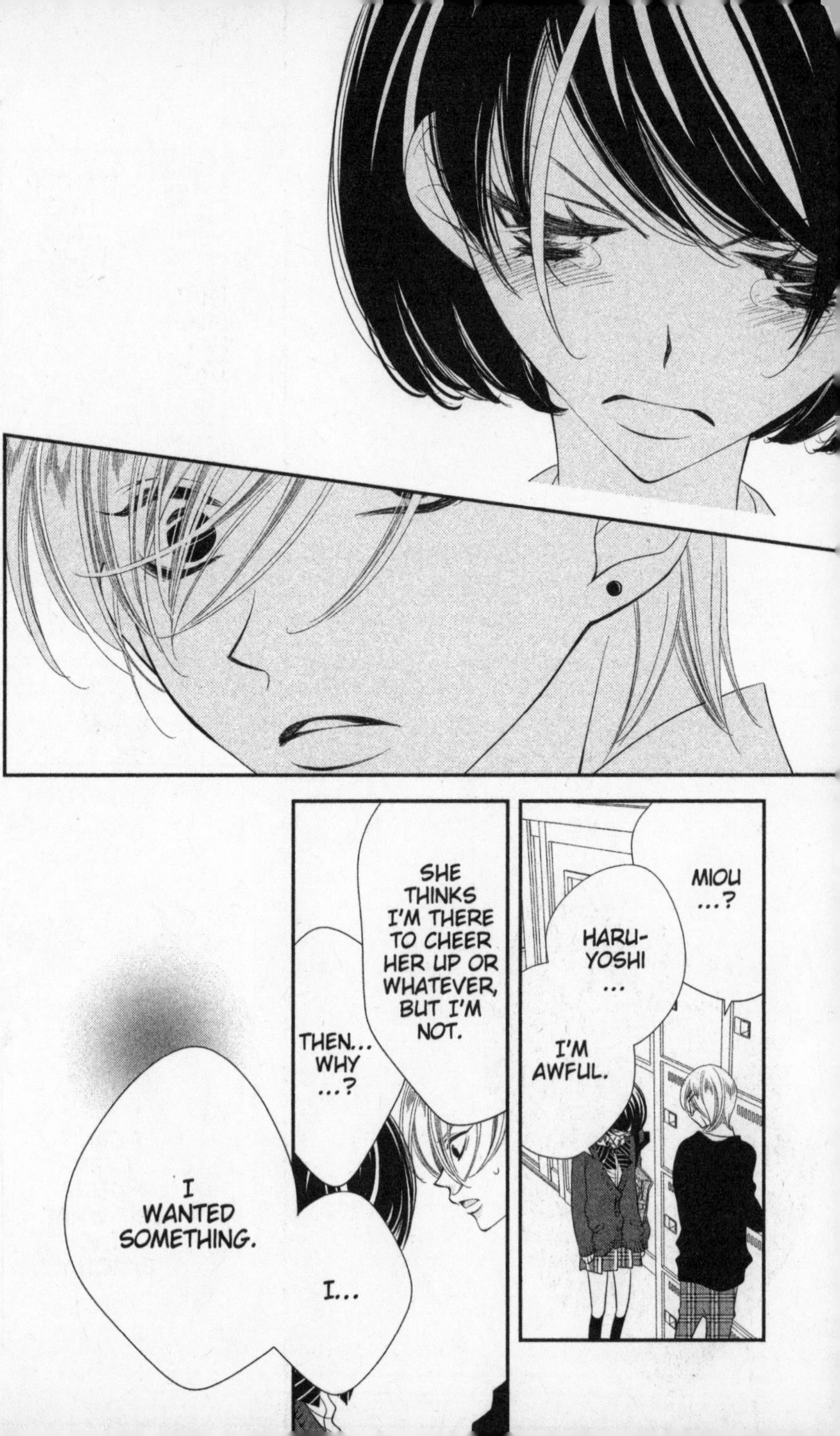
MIOU ...?
HARU-YOSHI ...
I'M AWFUL.
SHE THINKS I'M THERE TO CHEER HER UP OR WHATEVER, BUT I'M NOT.
THEN... WHY ...?
I...
I WANTED SOMETHING.

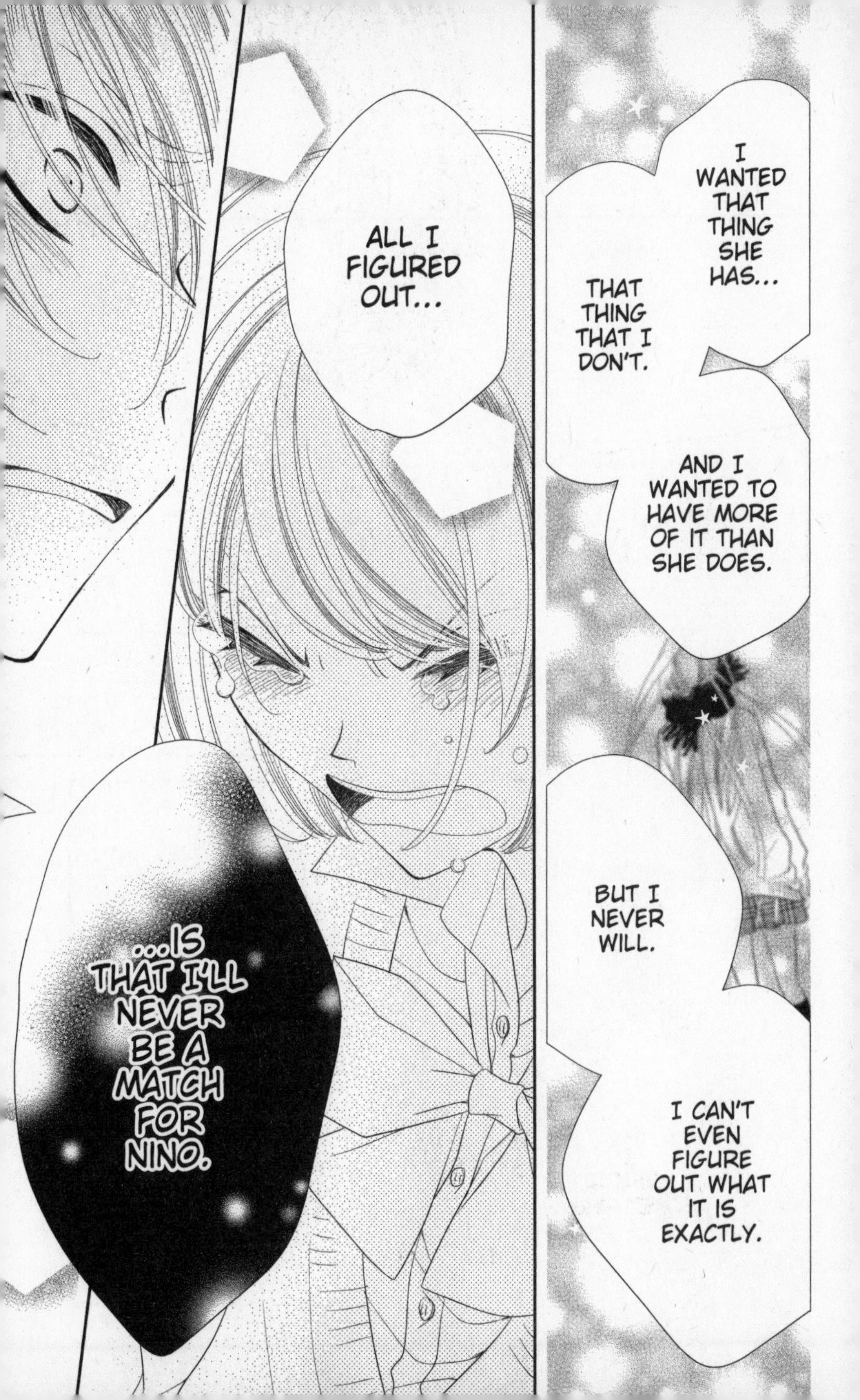
I WANTED THAT THING SHE HAS...
THAT THING THAT I DON'T.
AND I WANTED TO HAVE MORE OF IT THAN SHE DOES.
BUT I NEVER WILL.
I CAN'T EVEN FIGURE OUT WHAT IT IS EXACTLY.
ALL I FIGURED OUT...
...IS THAT I'LL NEVER BE A MATCH FOR NINO.

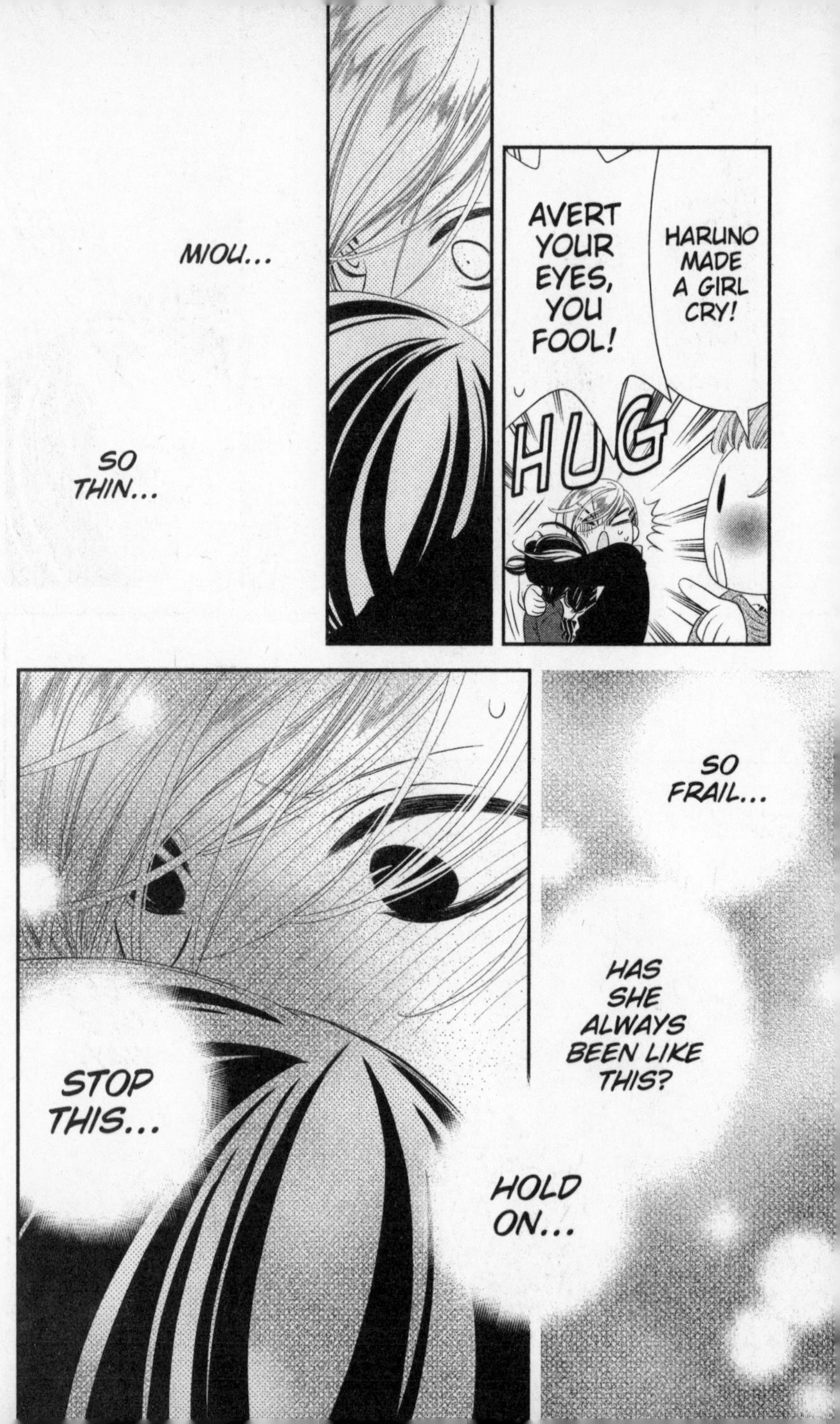
HARUNO MADE A GIRL CRY!
AVERT YOUR EYES, YOU FOOL!
HUG
MIOU...
SO THIN...
SO FRAIL...
HAS SHE ALWAYS BEEN LIKE THIS?
HOLD ON...
STOP THIS...

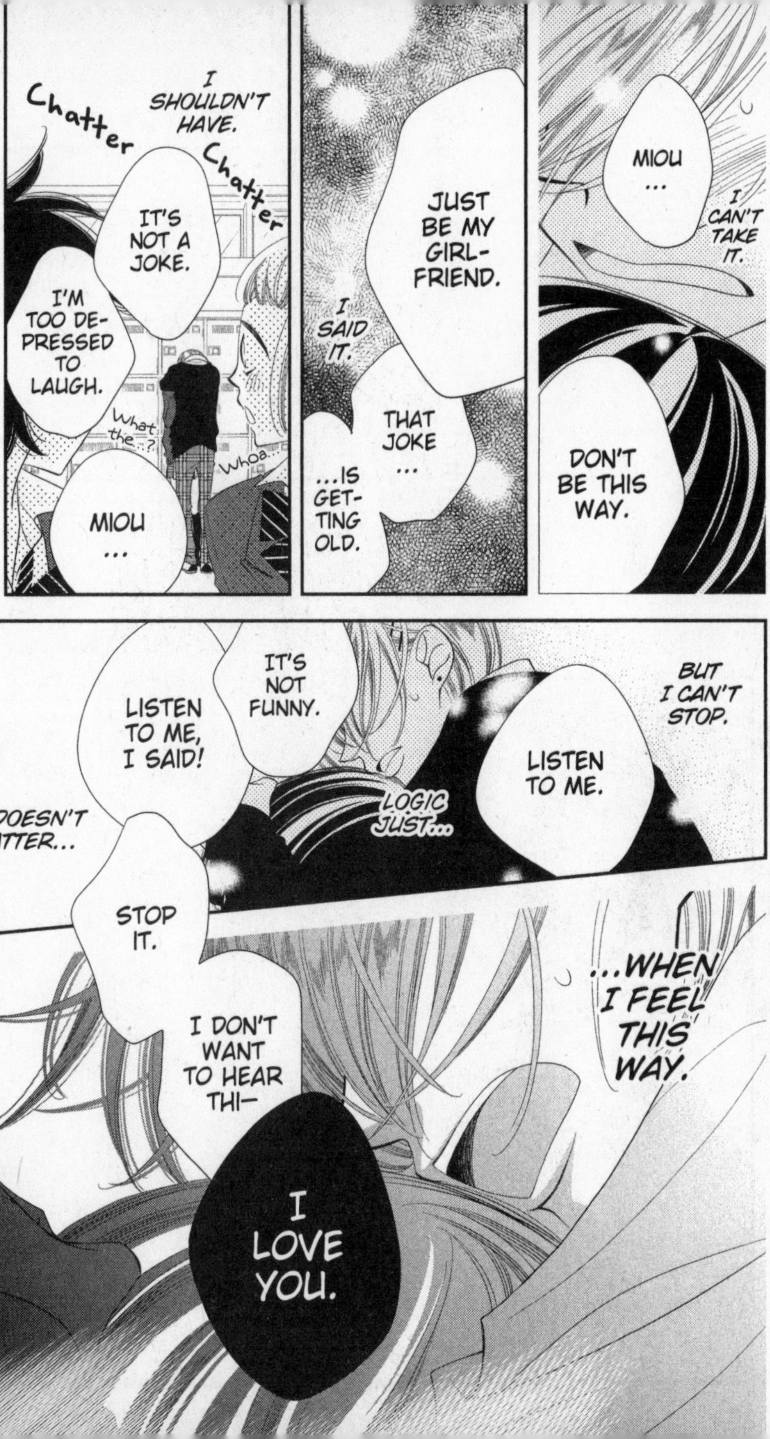
MIOU...
I CAN'T TAKE IT.
DON'T BE THIS WAY.
JUST BE MY GIRLFRIEND.
I SAID IT.
THAT JOKE...
...IS GETTING OLD.
I SHOULDN'T HAVE.
Chatter
Chatter
IT'S NOT A JOKE.
I'M TOO DEPRESSED TO LAUGH.
What the...?
Whoa...
MIOU...
BUT I CAN'T STOP.
LISTEN TO ME.
LOGIC JUST...
IT'S NOT FUNNY.
LISTEN TO ME, I SAID!
...DOESN'T MATTER...
...WHEN I FEEL THIS WAY.
STOP IT.
I DON'T WANT TO HEAR THI—
I LOVE YOU.

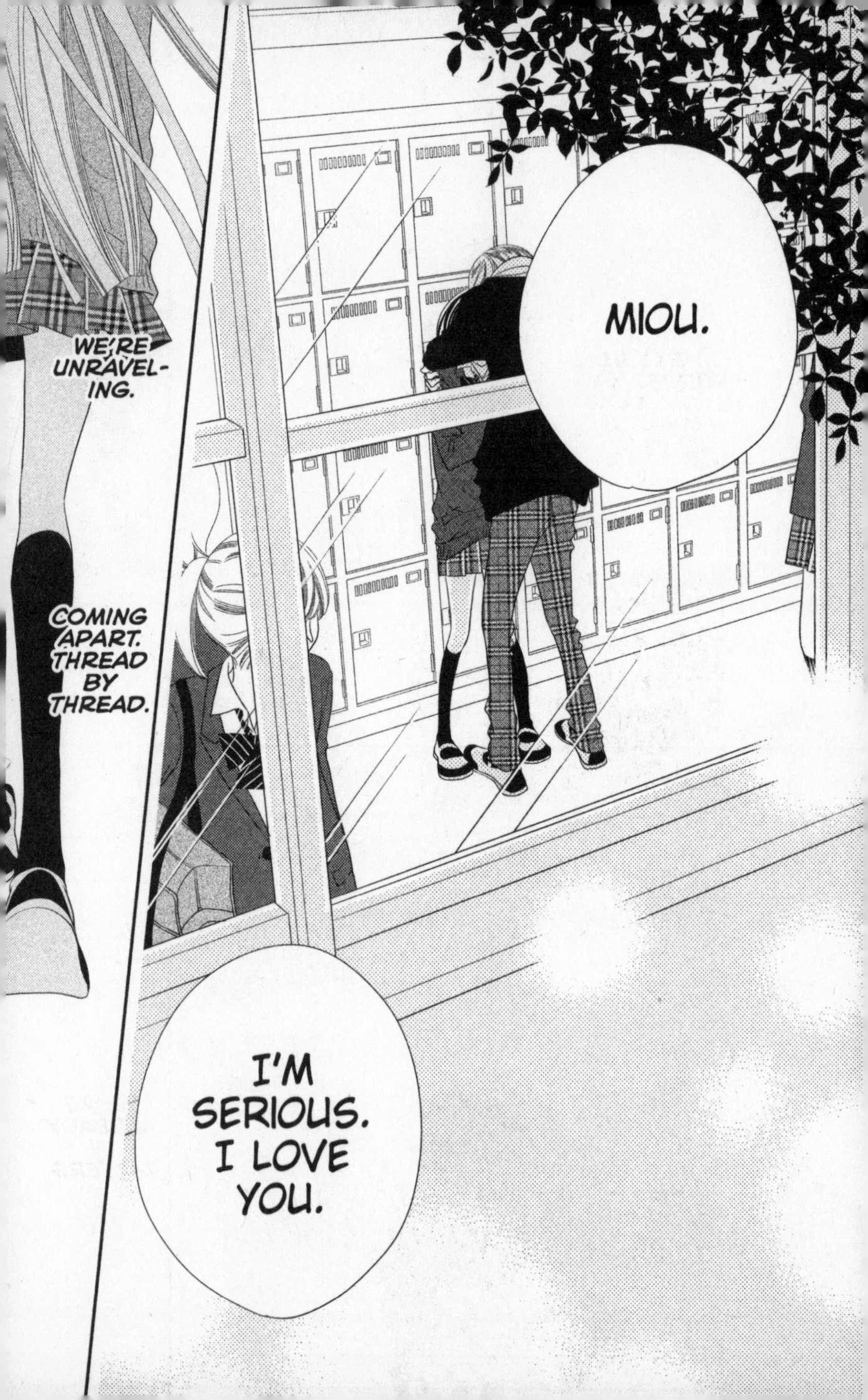
MIOU.
I'M SERIOUS. I LOVE YOU.
WE'RE UNRAVELING.
COMING APART. THREAD BY THREAD.

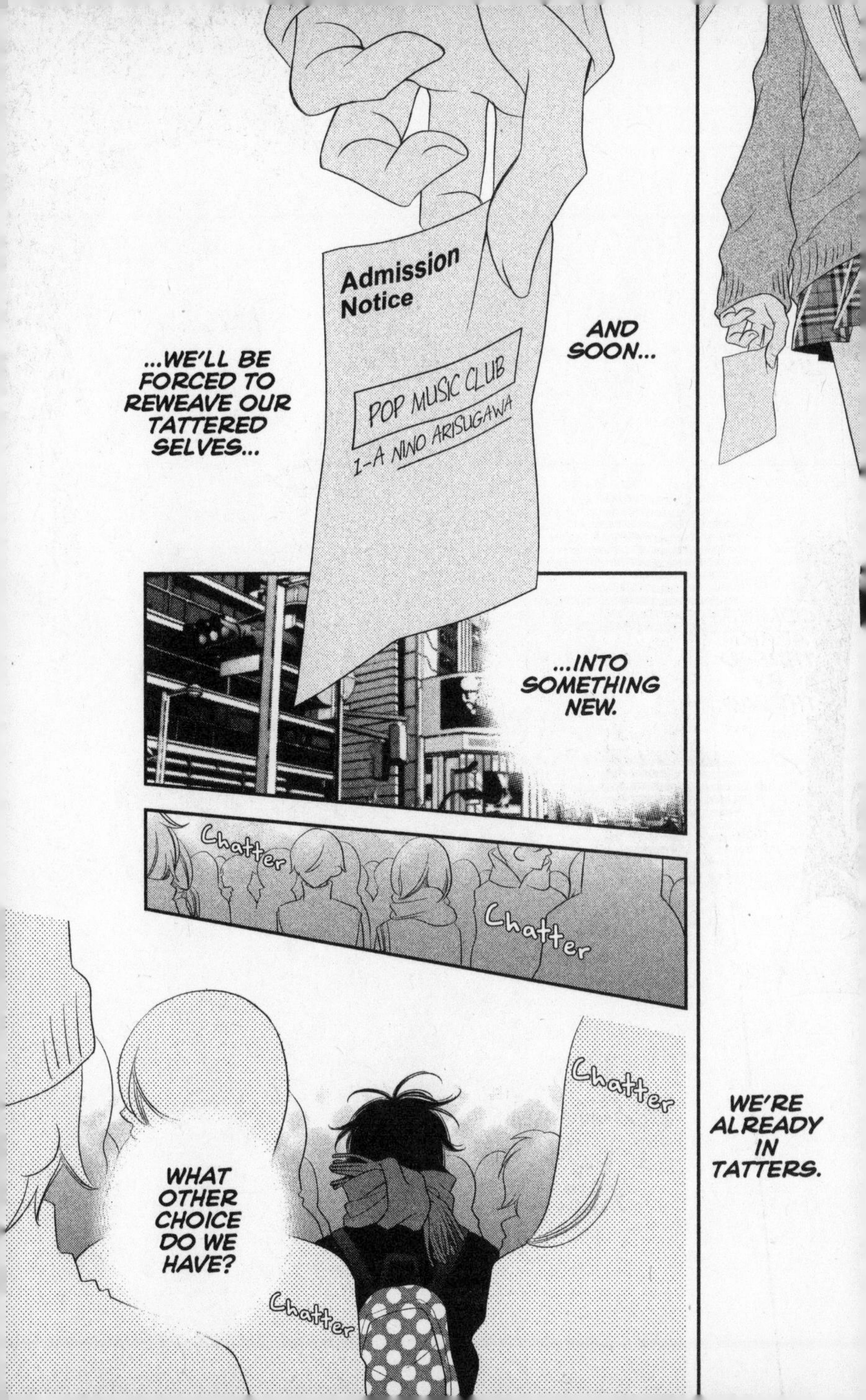
WE'RE ALREADY IN TATTERS.
Admission Notice
POP MUSIC CLUB
1-A NINO ARISUGAWA
AND SOON...
...WE'LL BE FORCED TO REWEAVE OUR TATTERED SELVES...
...INTO SOMETHING NEW.
Chatter
Chatter
Chatter
WHAT OTHER CHOICE DO WE HAVE?
Chatter

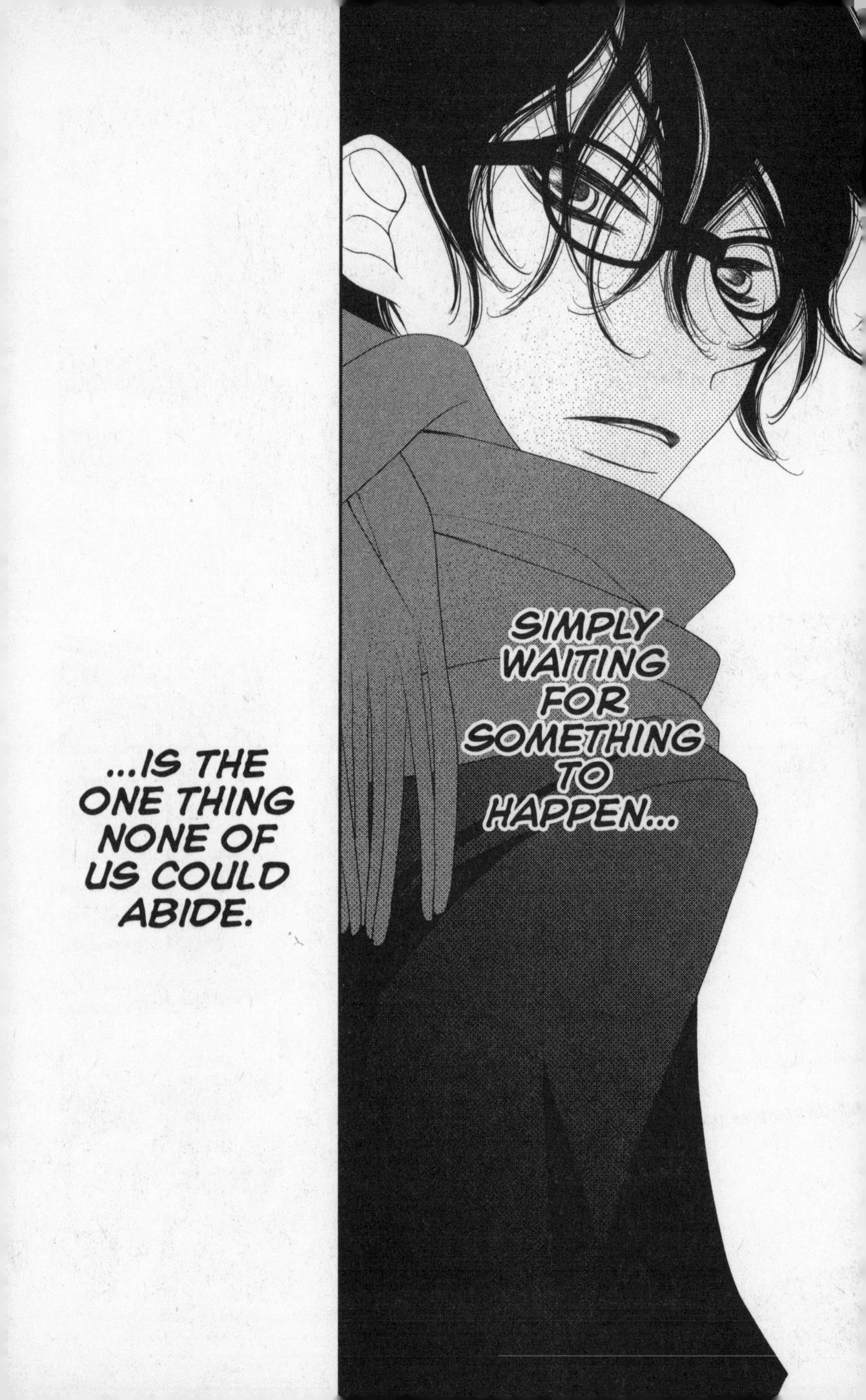
SIMPLY WAITING FOR SOMETHING TO HAPPEN...
...IS THE ONE THING NONE OF US COULD ABIDE.

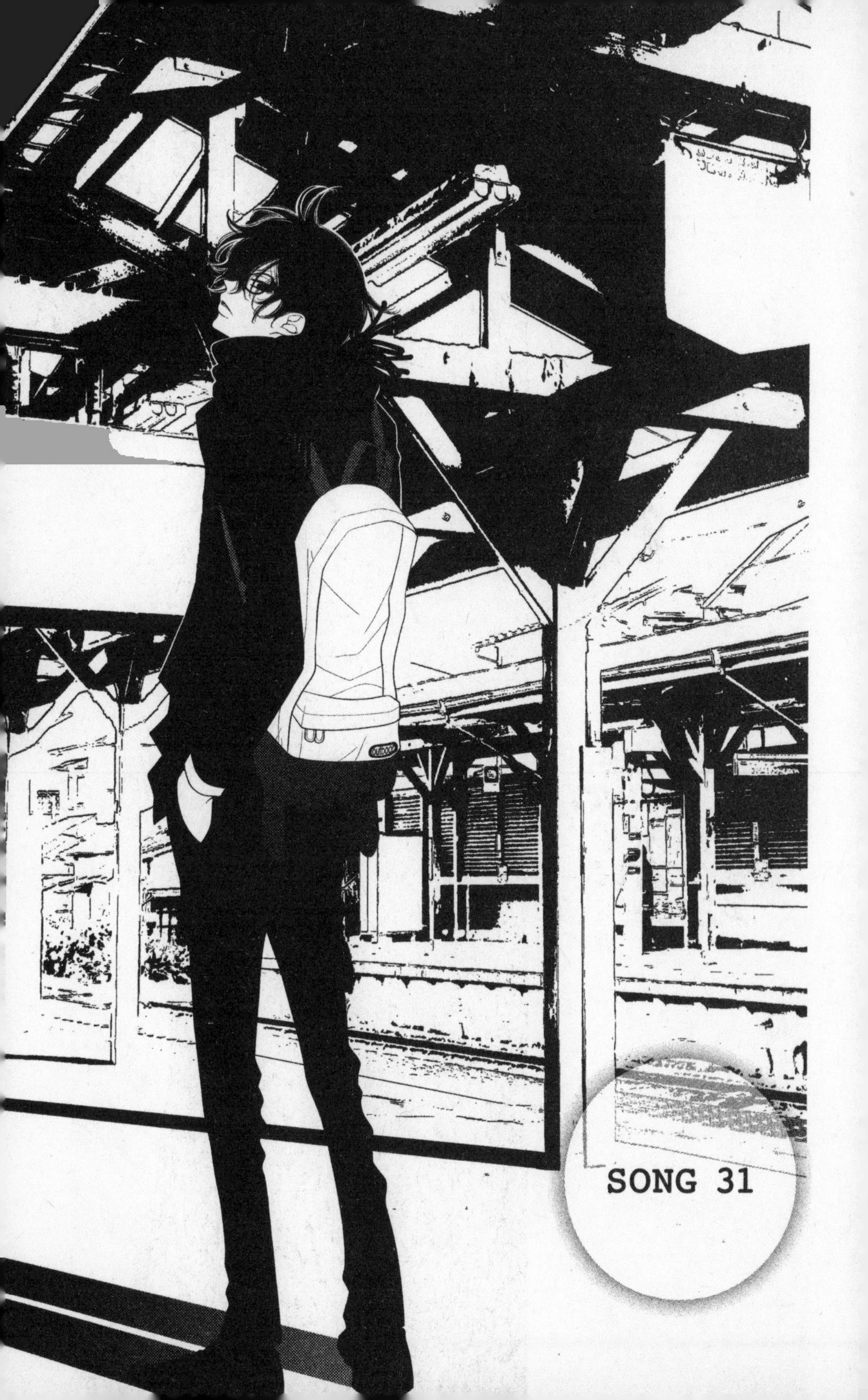
SONG 31

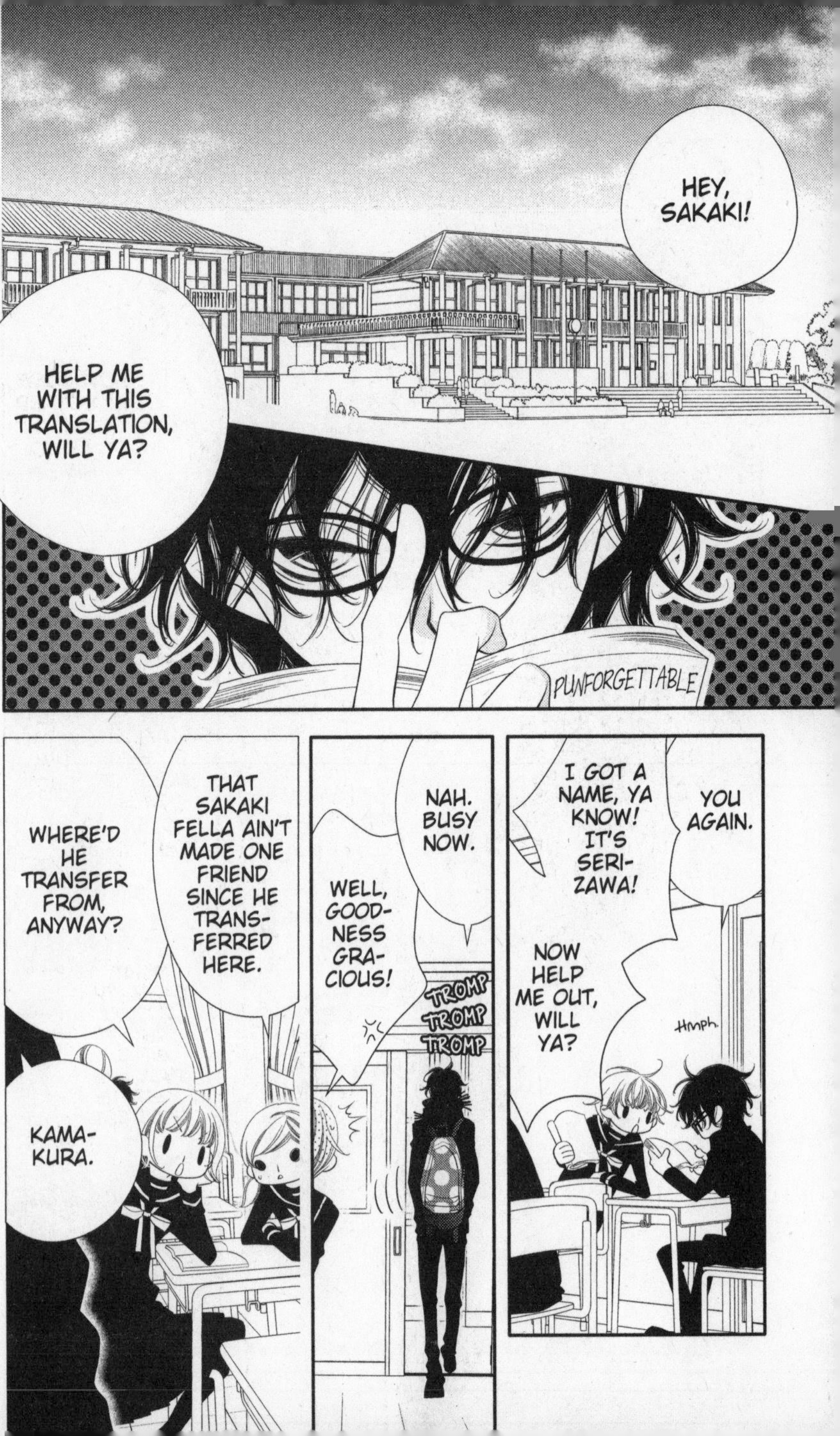
HEY, SAKAKI!
HELP ME WITH THIS TRANSLATION, WILL YA?
PUNFORGETTABLE
YOU AGAIN.
I GOT A NAME, YA KNOW! IT'S SERI-ZAWA!
NOW HELP ME OUT, WILL YA?
Hmph.
NAH. BUSY NOW.
WELL, GOODNESS GRACIOUS!
TROMP TROMP TROMP
THAT SAKAKI FELLA AIN'T MADE ONE FRIEND SINCE HE TRANS-FERRED HERE.
WHERE'D HE TRANSFER FROM, ANYWAY?
KAMA-KURA.

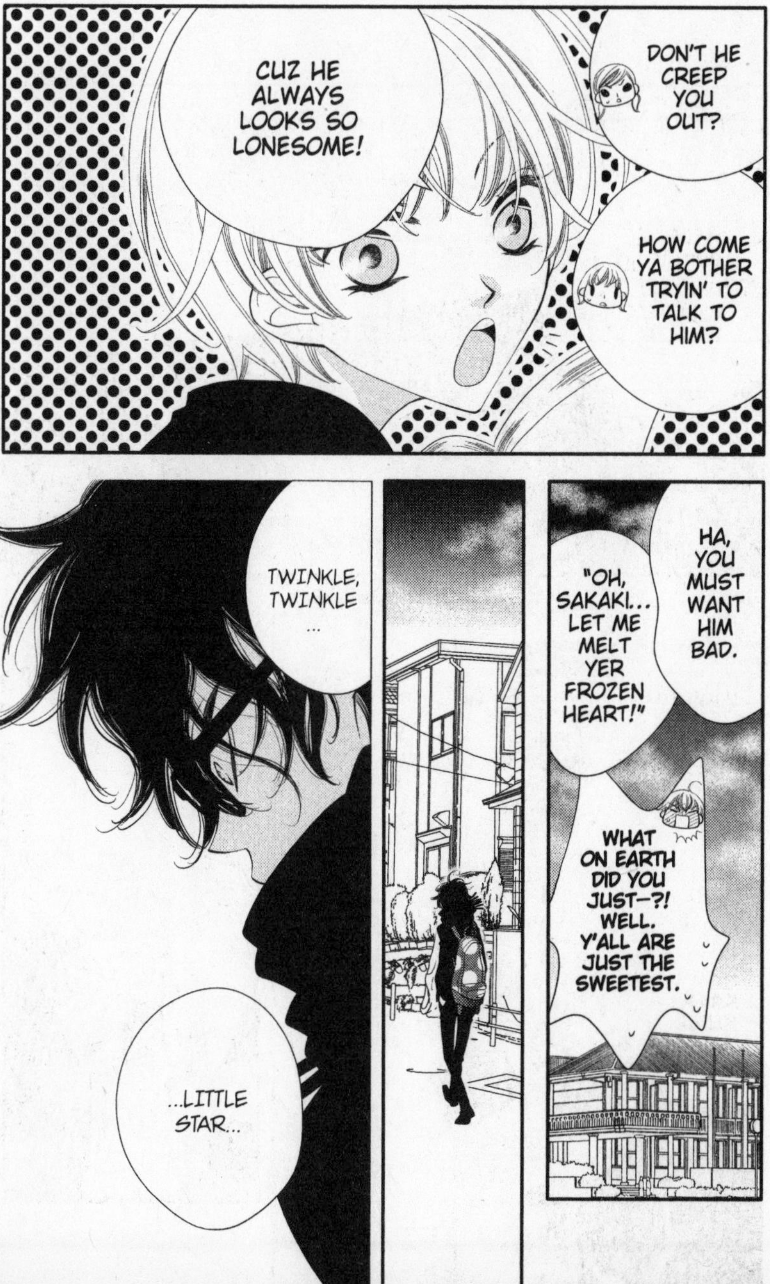
DON'T HE CREEP YOU OUT?
HOW COME YA BOTHER TRYIN' TO TALK TO HIM?
CUZ HE ALWAYS LOOKS SO LONESOME!
HA, YOU MUST WANT HIM BAD.
"OH, SAKAKI... LET ME MELT YER FROZEN HEART!"
WHAT ON EARTH DID YOU JUST—?! WELL. Y'ALL ARE JUST THE SWEETEST.
TWINKLE, TWINKLE...
...LITTLE STAR...

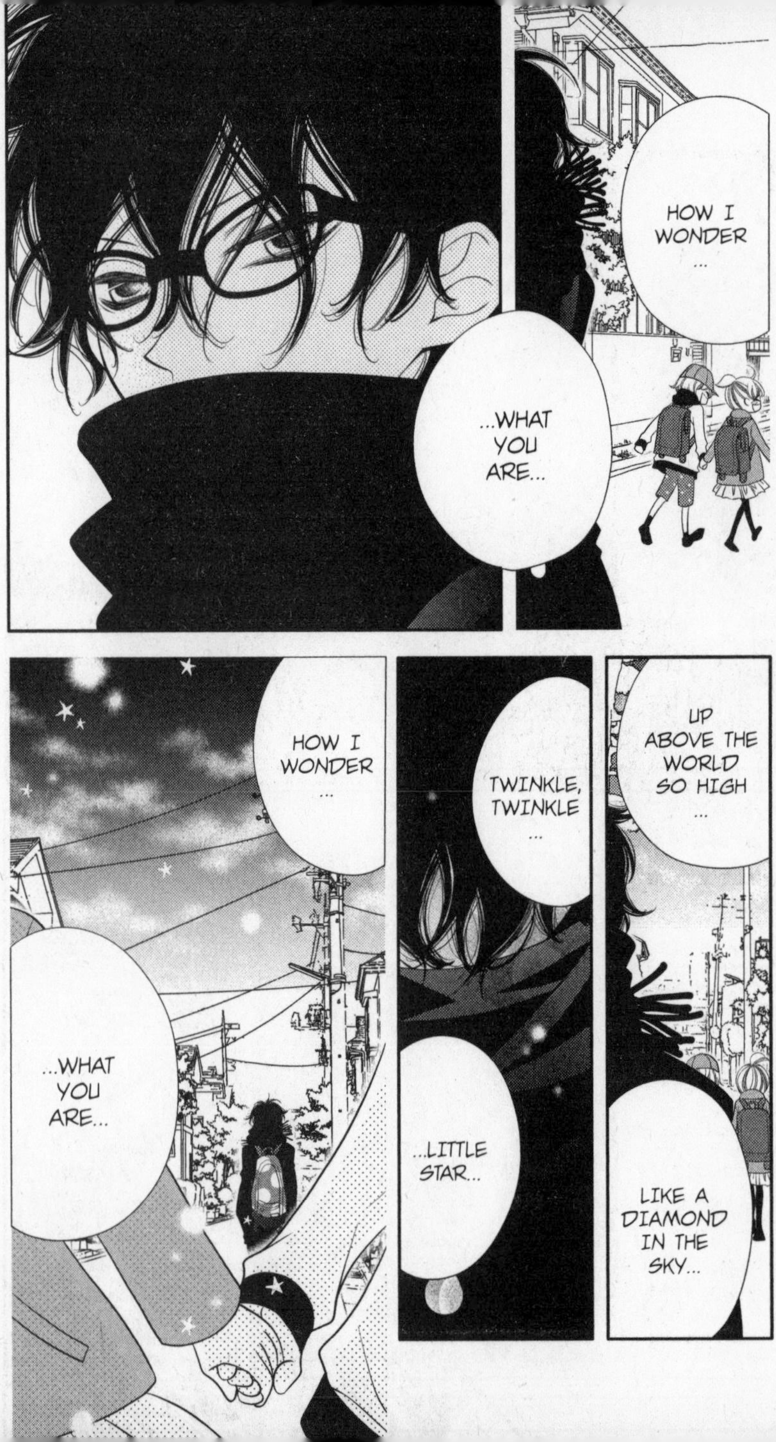
HOW I WONDER ...
...WHAT YOU ARE...
UP ABOVE THE WORLD SO HIGH ...
LIKE A DIAMOND IN THE SKY...
TWINKLE, TWINKLE ...
...LITTLE STAR...
HOW I WONDER ...
...WHAT YOU ARE...

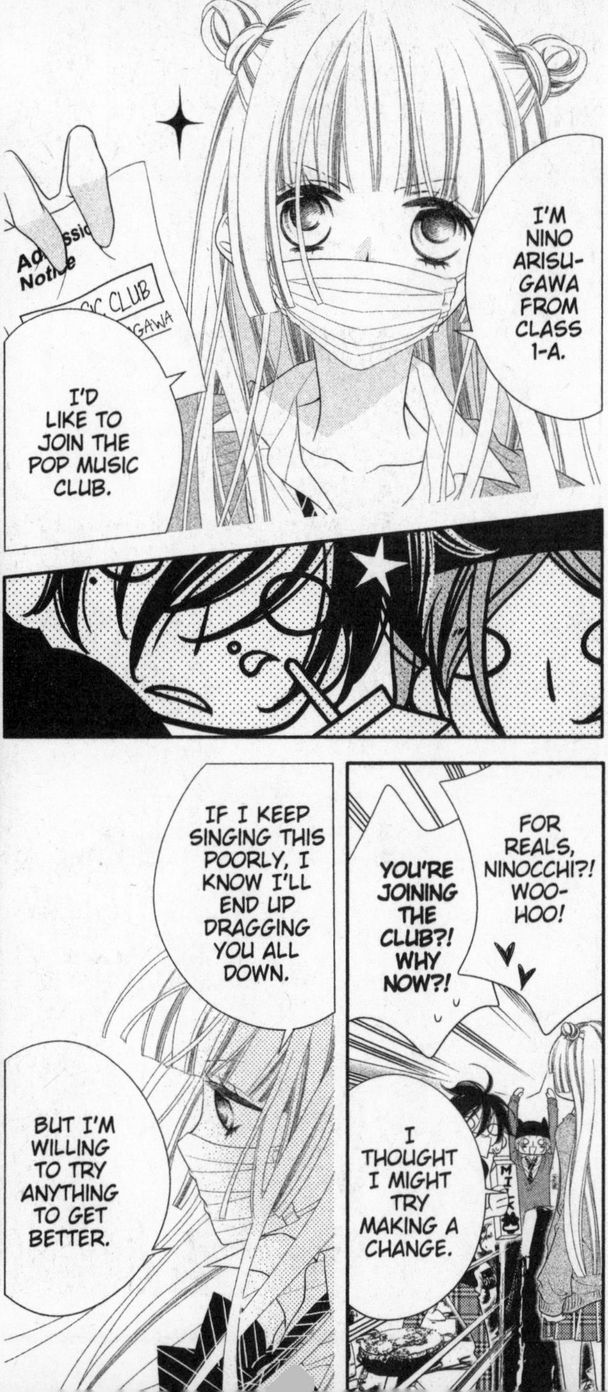
I'M NINO ARISUGAWA FROM CLASS 1-A.
I'D LIKE TO JOIN THE POP MUSIC CLUB.
FOR REALS, NINOCCHI?! WOO-HOO!
YOU'RE JOINING THE CLUB?! WHY NOW?!
I THOUGHT I MIGHT TRY MAKING A CHANGE.
IF I KEEP SINGING THIS POORLY, I KNOW I'LL END UP DRAGGING YOU ALL DOWN.
BUT I'M WILLING TO TRY ANYTHING TO GET BETTER.

3

I've become addicted to playing Ingress on my phone.

In a nutshell, it's a game where a blue team and a green team compete to control as much of Earth as possible. I was having so much fun with it that I suggested my editor play it, and...

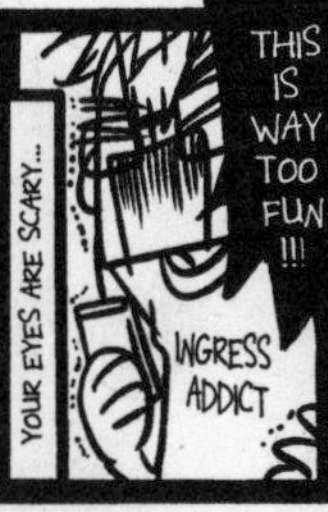
THIS IS WAY TOO FUN!!!
YOUR EYES ARE SCARY...
INGRESS ADDICT

It doesn't look like we'll be giving it up anytime soon—my editor and I were even fighting to control Hibiya Park (he's on the enemy team) when we went to see CreepHyp there the other day.

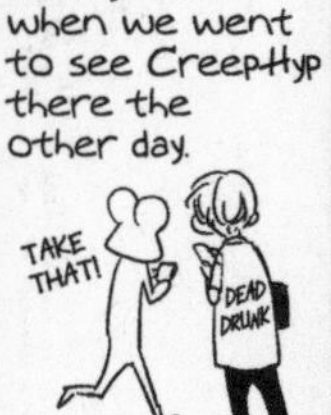
TAKE THAT!
DEAD DRUNK

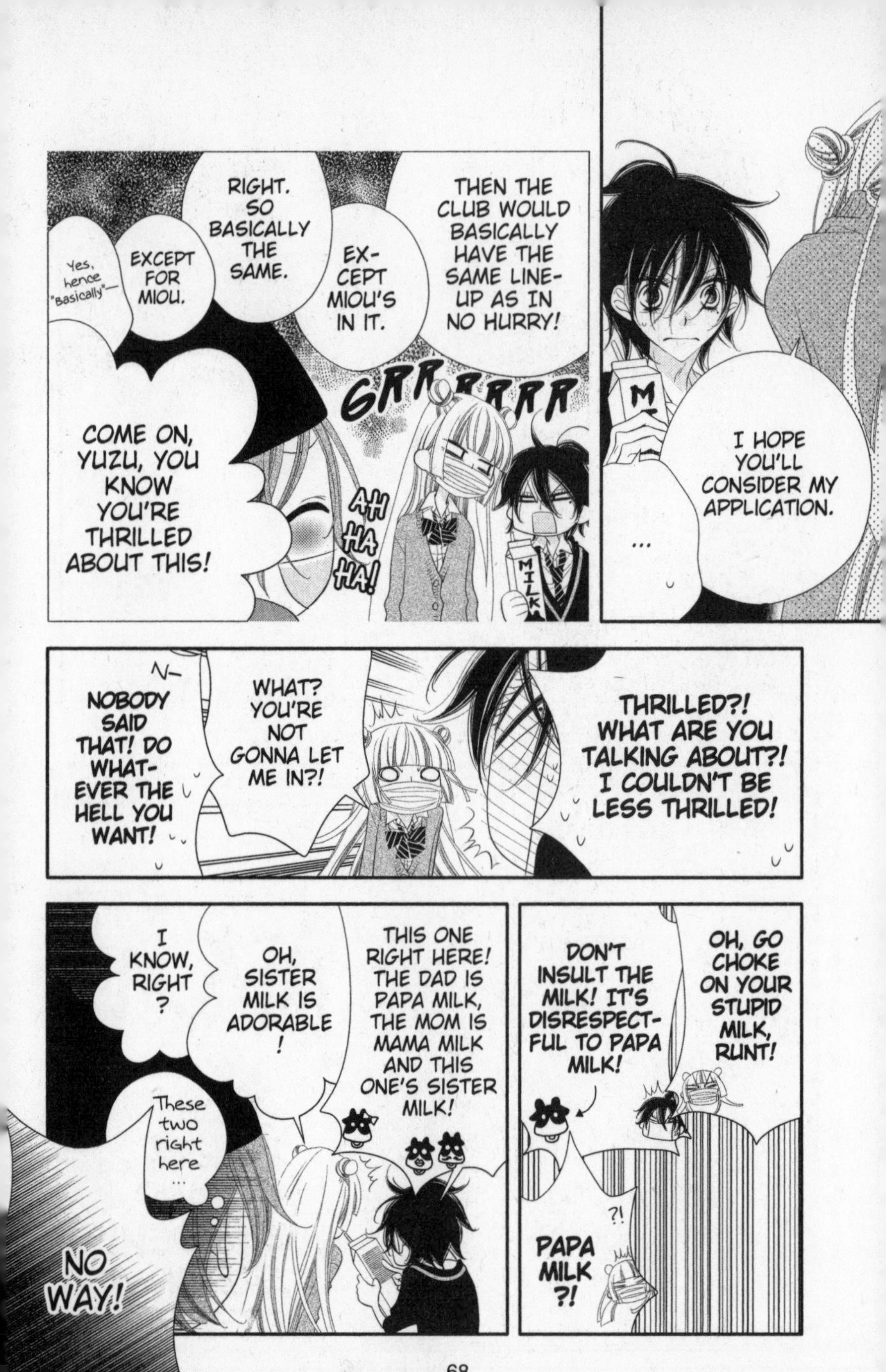
I HOPE YOU'LL CONSIDER MY APPLICATION.
...
THEN THE CLUB WOULD BASICALLY HAVE THE SAME LINE-UP AS IN NO HURRY!
EX-CEPT MIOU'S IN IT.
RIGHT. SO BASICALLY THE SAME.
EXCEPT FOR MIOU.
Yes, hence "basically"—
GRRRRRRR
COME ON, YUZU, YOU KNOW YOU'RE THRILLED ABOUT THIS!
AH HA HA!
MILK
THRILLED?! WHAT ARE YOU TALKING ABOUT?! I COULDN'T BE LESS THRILLED!
WHAT? YOU'RE NOT GONNA LET ME IN?!
N— NOBODY SAID THAT! DO WHAT-EVER THE HELL YOU WANT!
OH, GO CHOKE ON YOUR STUPID MILK, RUNT!
DON'T INSULT THE MILK! IT'S DISRESPECT-FUL TO PAPA MILK!
?!
PAPA MILK ?!
THIS ONE RIGHT HERE! THE DAD IS PAPA MILK, THE MOM IS MAMA MILK AND THIS ONE'S SISTER MILK!
OH, SISTER MILK IS ADORABLE!
I KNOW, RIGHT?
These two right here ...
NO WAY!

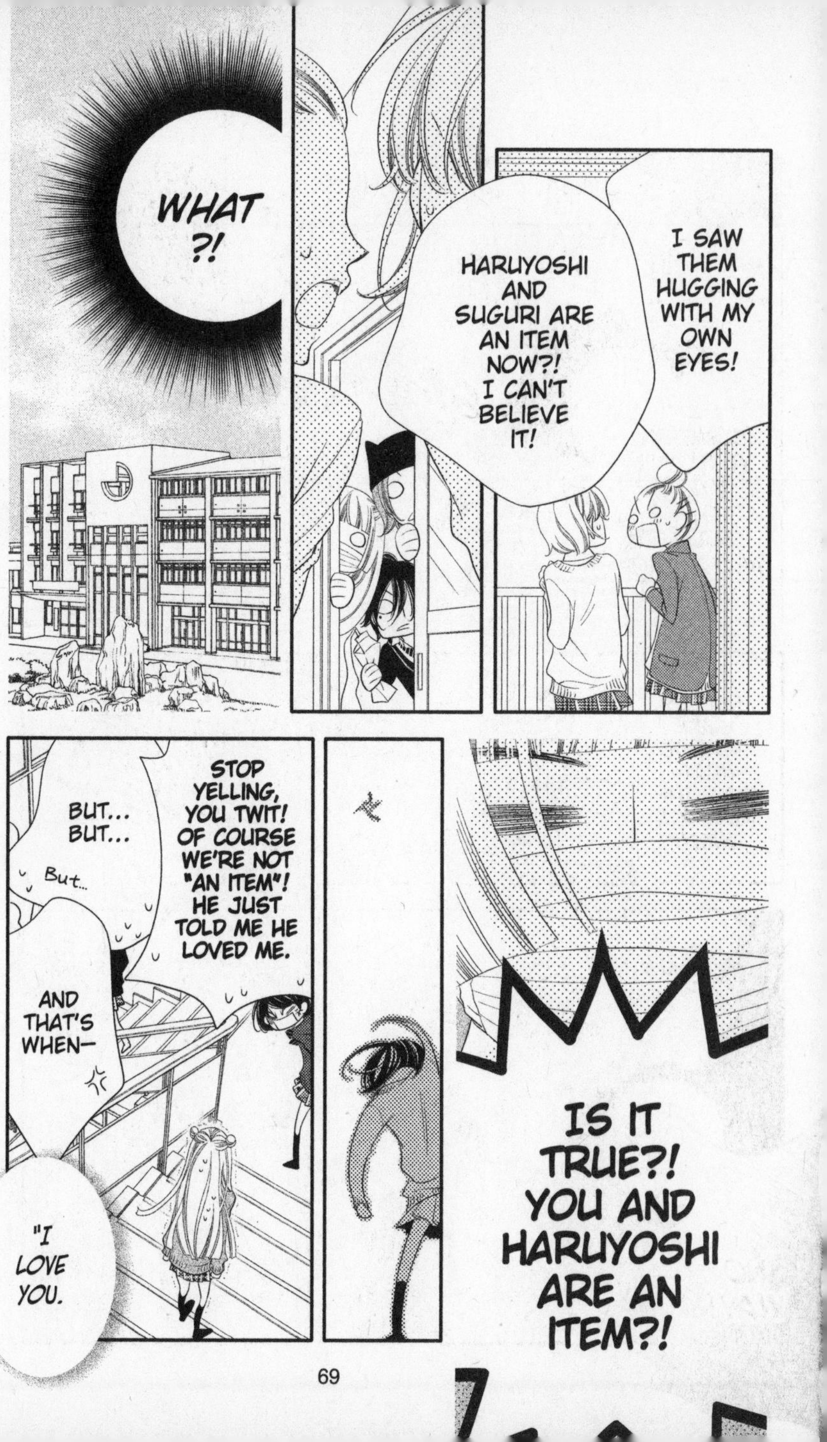
I SAW THEM HUGGING WITH MY OWN EYES!
HARUYOSHI AND SUGURI ARE AN ITEM NOW?! I CAN'T BELIEVE IT!
WHAT ?!
IS IT TRUE?! YOU AND HARUYOSHI ARE AN ITEM?!
STOP YELLING, YOU TWIT! OF COURSE WE'RE NOT "AN ITEM"! HE JUST TOLD ME HE LOVED ME.
BUT... BUT...
But...
AND THAT'S WHEN—
"I LOVE YOU.

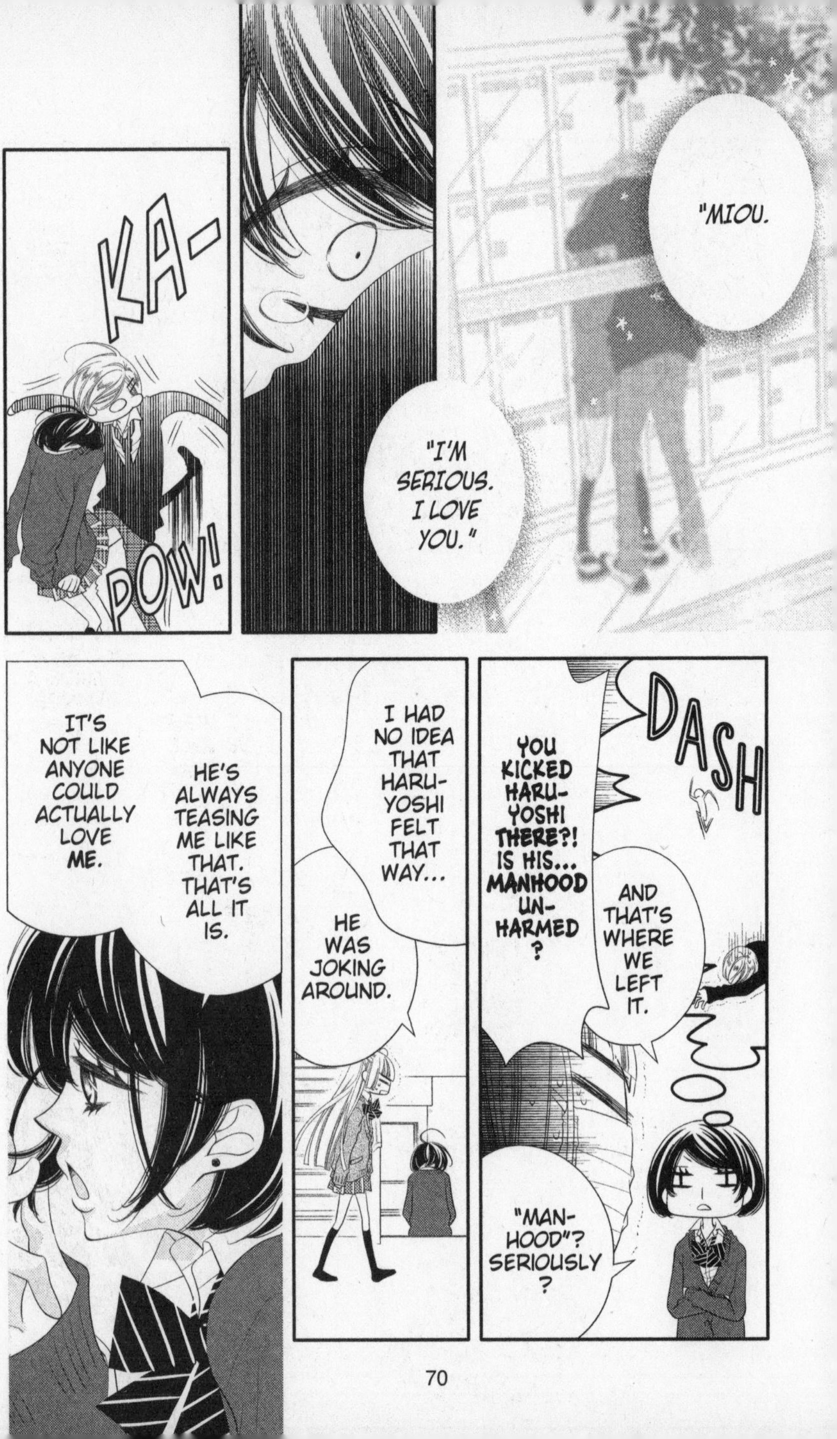
"MIOU.
"I'M SERIOUS. I LOVE YOU."
KA-POW!
DASH
YOU KICKED HARUYOSHI THERE?! IS HIS... MANHOOD UNHARMED?
AND THAT'S WHERE WE LEFT IT.
"MANHOOD"? SERIOUSLY?
I HAD NO IDEA THAT HARUYOSHI FELT THAT WAY...
HE WAS JOKING AROUND.
HE'S ALWAYS TEASING ME LIKE THAT. THAT'S ALL IT IS.
IT'S NOT LIKE ANYONE COULD ACTUALLY LOVE ME.

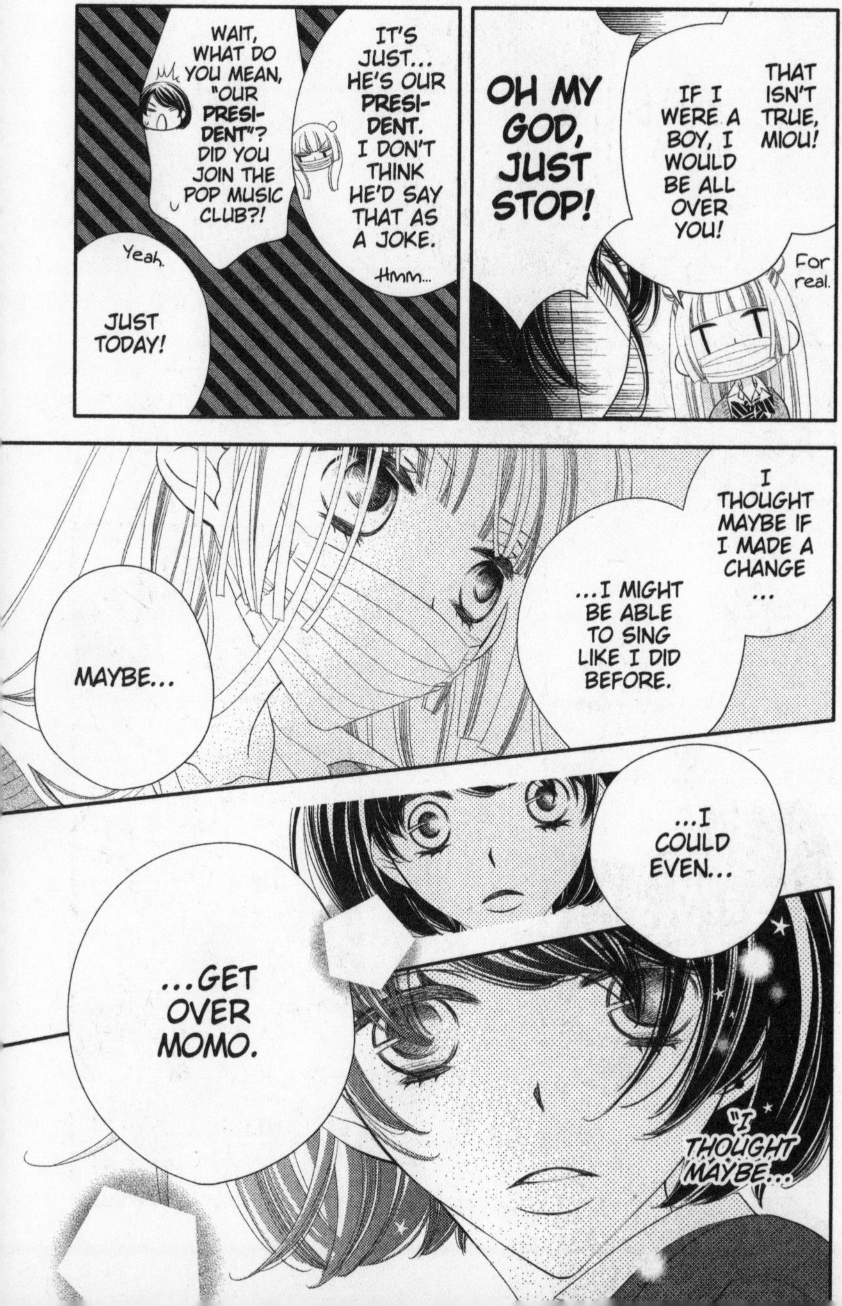
THAT ISN'T TRUE, MIOU!
IF I WERE A BOY, I WOULD BE ALL OVER YOU!
For real.
OH MY GOD, JUST STOP!
IT'S JUST... HE'S OUR PRESIDENT. I DON'T THINK HE'D SAY THAT AS A JOKE.
Hmm...
WAIT, WHAT DO YOU MEAN, "OUR PRESIDENT"? DID YOU JOIN THE POP MUSIC CLUB?!
Yeah.
JUST TODAY!
I THOUGHT MAYBE IF I MADE A CHANGE...
...I MIGHT BE ABLE TO SING LIKE I DID BEFORE.
MAYBE...
...I COULD EVEN...
...GET OVER MOMO.
"I THOUGHT MAYBE..."

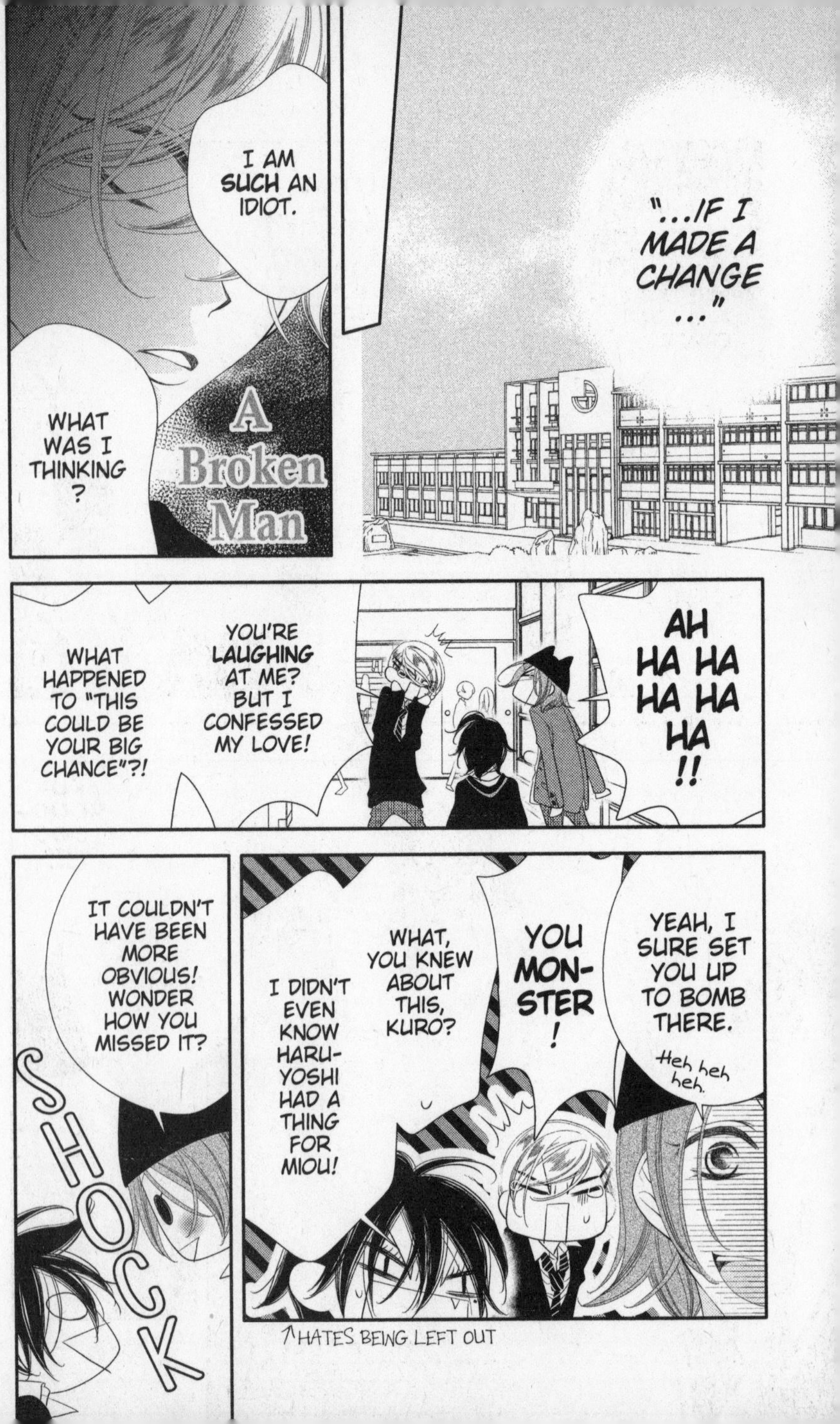
"...IF I MADE A CHANGE ..."
I AM SUCH AN IDIOT.
WHAT WAS I THINKING?
A Broken Man
AH HA HA HA HA HA!!
YOU'RE LAUGHING AT ME? BUT I CONFESSED MY LOVE!
WHAT HAPPENED TO "THIS COULD BE YOUR BIG CHANCE"?!
YEAH, I SURE SET YOU UP TO BOMB THERE.
Heh heh heh.
YOU MON-STER!
WHAT, YOU KNEW ABOUT THIS, KURO?
I DIDN'T EVEN KNOW HARU-YOSHI HAD A THING FOR MIOU!
↑HATES BEING LEFT OUT
IT COULDN'T HAVE BEEN MORE OBVIOUS! WONDER HOW YOU MISSED IT?
SHOCK

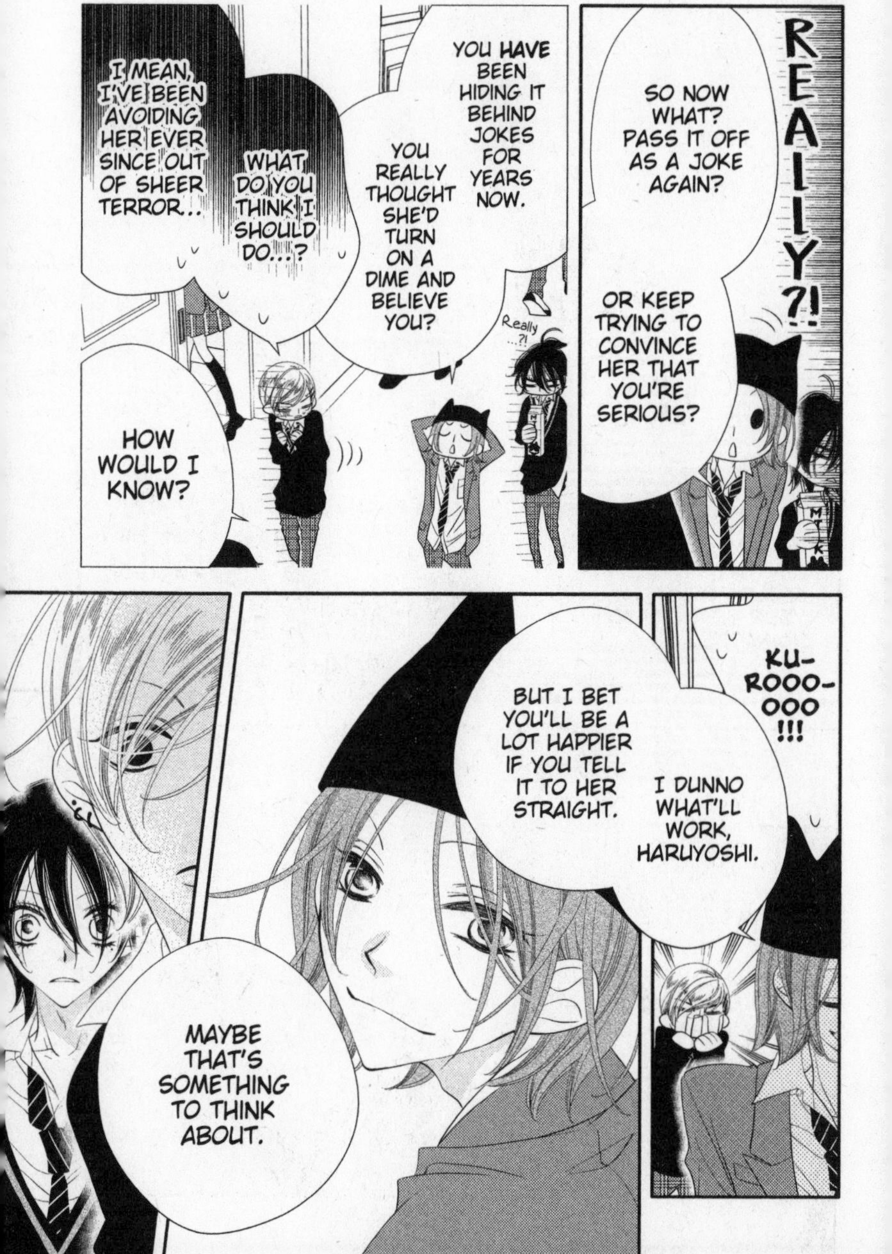
REALLY?!
SO NOW WHAT? PASS IT OFF AS A JOKE AGAIN?
OR KEEP TRYING TO CONVINCE HER THAT YOU'RE SERIOUS?
YOU HAVE BEEN HIDING IT BEHIND JOKES FOR YEARS NOW.
YOU REALLY THOUGHT SHE'D TURN ON A DIME AND BELIEVE YOU?
Really ...?!
WHAT DO YOU THINK I SHOULD DO...?
I MEAN, I'VE BEEN AVOIDING HER EVER SINCE OUT OF SHEER TERROR...
HOW WOULD I KNOW?
KU-ROOO-OOO!!!
I DUNNO WHAT'LL WORK, HARUYOSHI.
BUT I BET YOU'LL BE A LOT HAPPIER IF YOU TELL IT TO HER STRAIGHT.
MAYBE THAT'S SOMETHING TO THINK ABOUT.

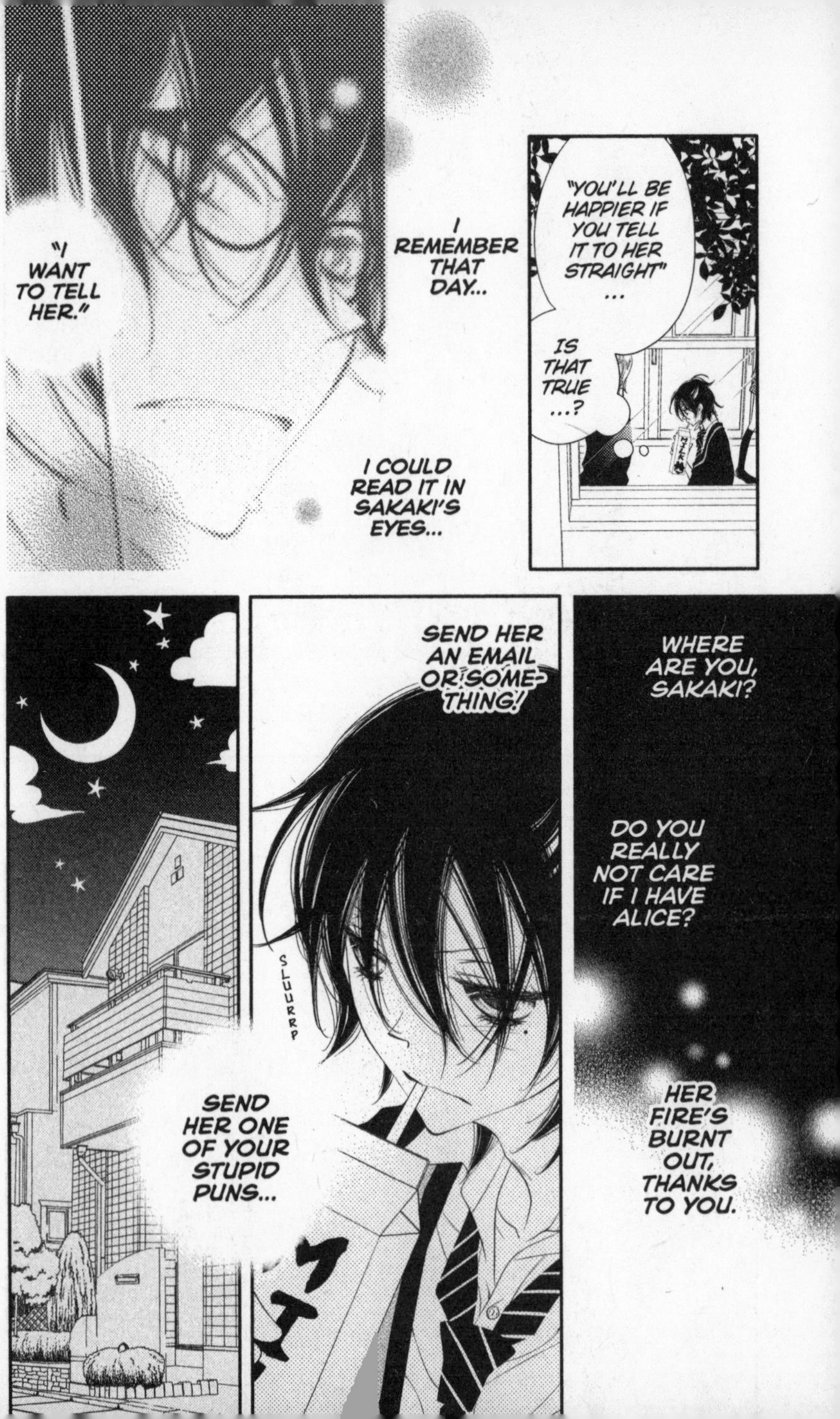
"YOU'LL BE HAPPIER IF YOU TELL IT TO HER STRAIGHT" ...
IS THAT TRUE ...?
I REMEMBER THAT DAY...
I COULD READ IT IN SAKAKI'S EYES...
"I WANT TO TELL HER."
WHERE ARE YOU, SAKAKI?
DO YOU REALLY NOT CARE IF I HAVE ALICE?
HER FIRE'S BURNT OUT, THANKS TO YOU.
SEND HER AN EMAIL OR SOME-THING!
SLUURRP
SEND HER ONE OF YOUR STUPID PUNS...

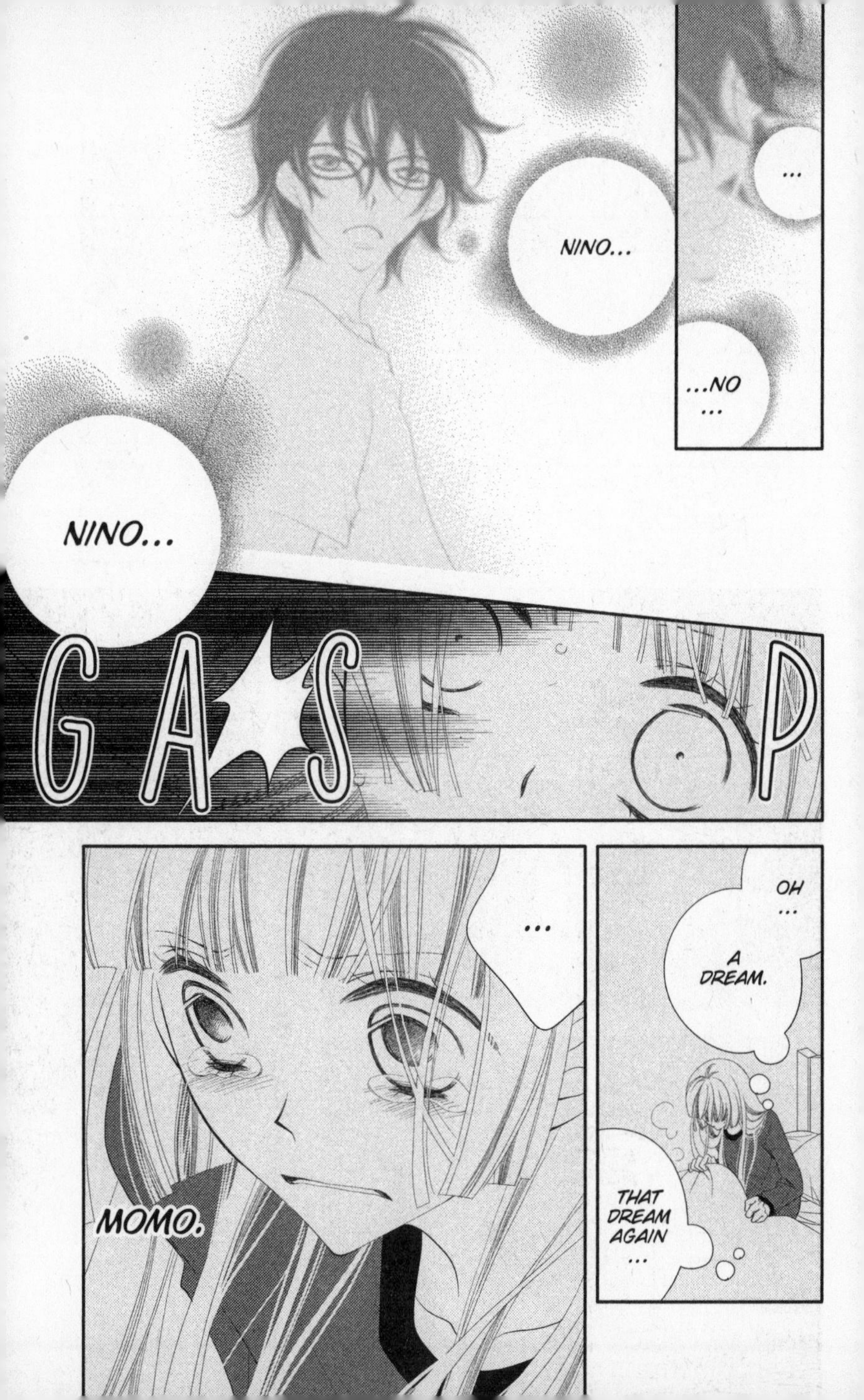
...
...NO ...
NINO...
NINO...
GASP
OH ...
A DREAM.
THAT DREAM AGAIN ...
...
MOMO.

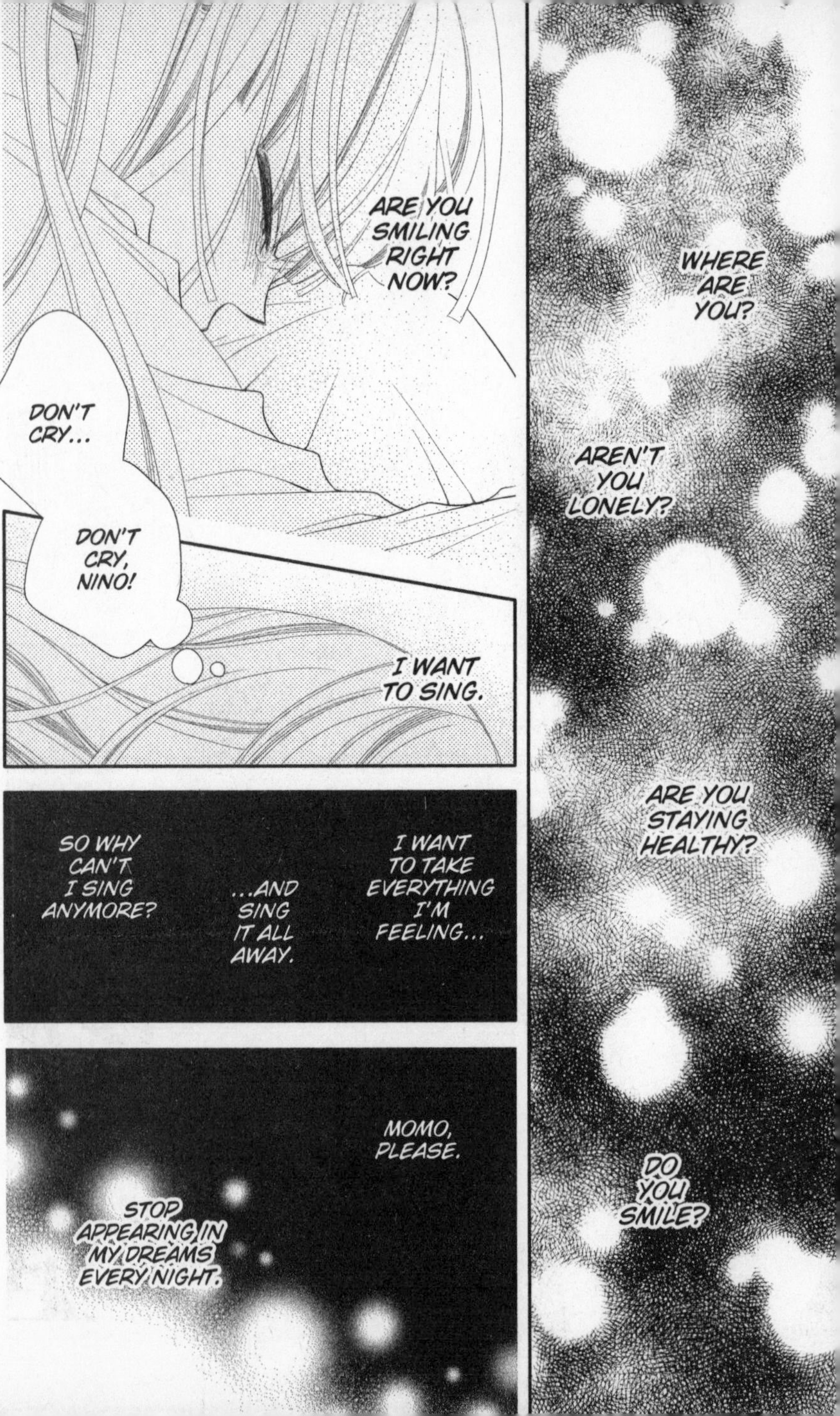
WHERE ARE YOU?
AREN'T YOU LONELY?
ARE YOU STAYING HEALTHY?
DO YOU SMILE?
ARE YOU SMILING RIGHT NOW?
DON'T CRY...
DON'T CRY, NINO!
I WANT TO SING.
I WANT TO TAKE EVERYTHING I'M FEELING...
...AND SING IT ALL AWAY.
SO WHY CAN'T I SING ANYMORE?
MOMO, PLEASE.
STOP APPEARING IN MY DREAMS EVERY NIGHT.

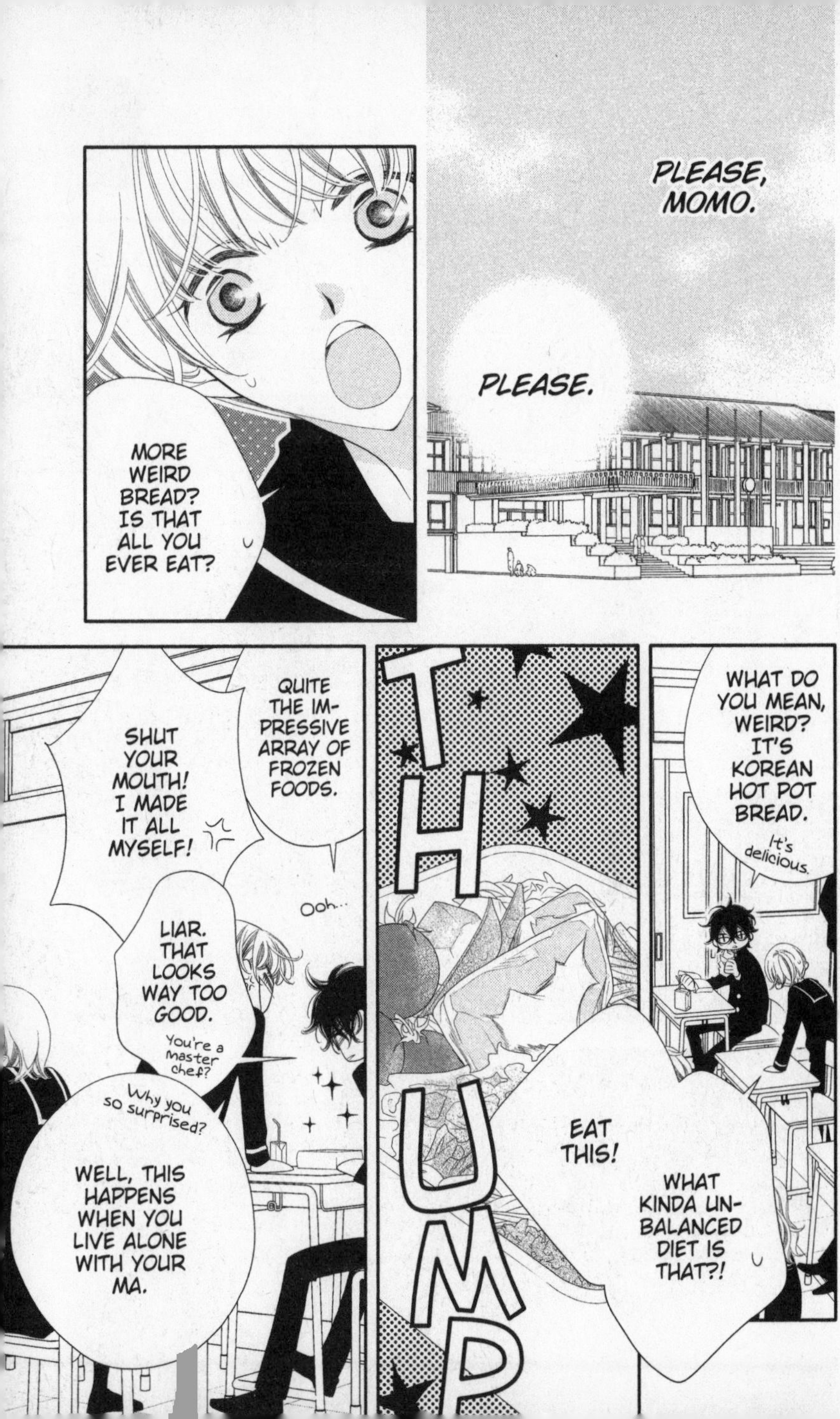
PLEASE, MOMO.
PLEASE.
MORE WEIRD BREAD? IS THAT ALL YOU EVER EAT?
WHAT DO YOU MEAN, WEIRD? IT'S KOREAN HOT POT BREAD.
It's delicious.
WHAT KINDA UN-BALANCED DIET IS THAT?!
THUMP
EAT THIS!
QUITE THE IM-PRESSIVE ARRAY OF FROZEN FOODS.
SHUT YOUR MOUTH! I MADE IT ALL MYSELF!
Ooh...
LIAR. THAT LOOKS WAY TOO GOOD.
You're a master chef?
Why you so surprised?
WELL, THIS HAPPENS WHEN YOU LIVE ALONE WITH YOUR MA.

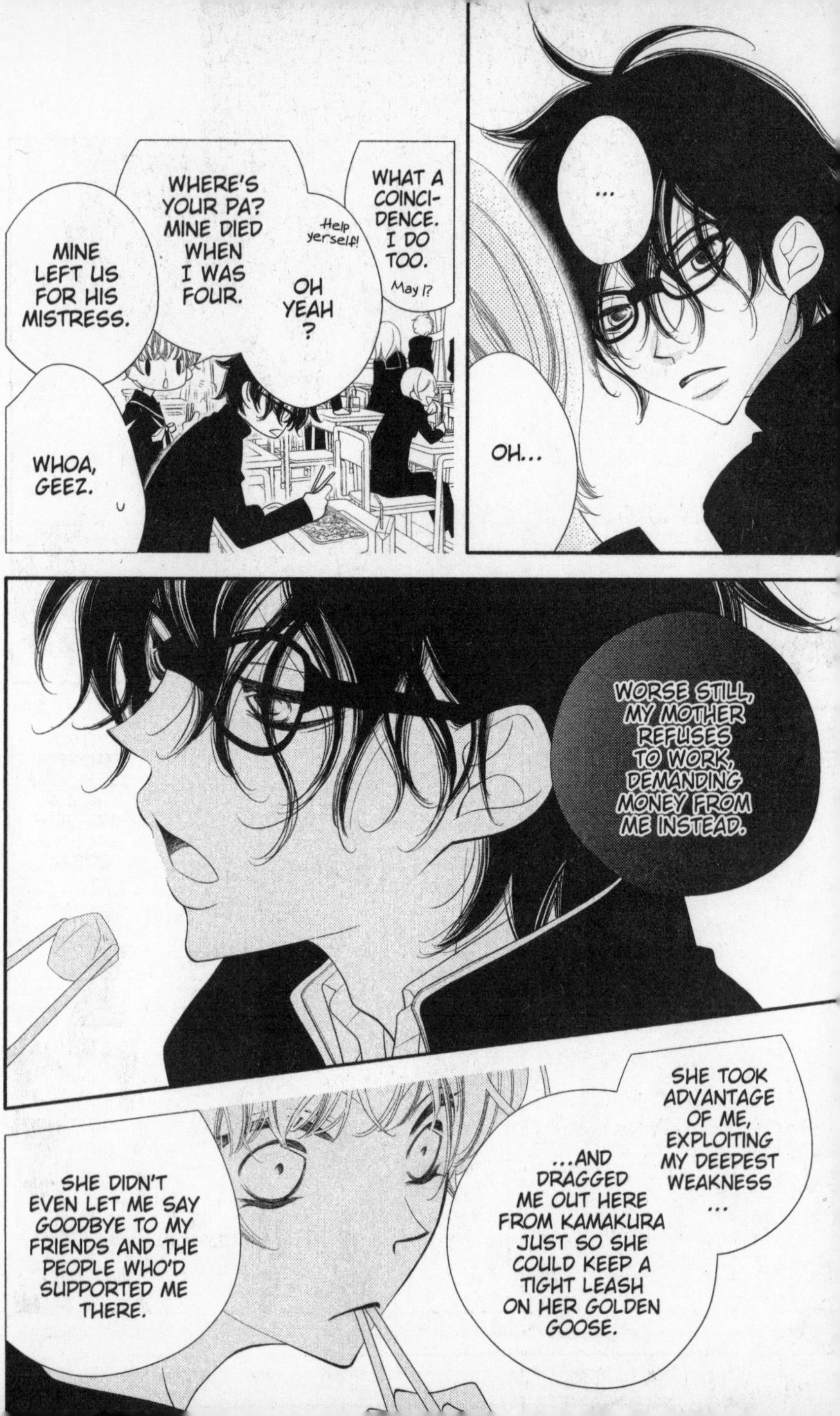
...
OH...
WHAT A COINCIDENCE. I DO TOO.
May I?
Help yerself!
OH YEAH?
WHERE'S YOUR PA? MINE DIED WHEN I WAS FOUR.
MINE LEFT US FOR HIS MISTRESS.
WHOA, GEEZ.
WORSE STILL, MY MOTHER REFUSES TO WORK, DEMANDING MONEY FROM ME INSTEAD.
SHE TOOK ADVANTAGE OF ME, EXPLOITING MY DEEPEST WEAKNESS...
...AND DRAGGED ME OUT HERE FROM KAMAKURA JUST SO SHE COULD KEEP A TIGHT LEASH ON HER GOLDEN GOOSE.
SHE DIDN'T EVEN LET ME SAY GOODBYE TO MY FRIENDS AND THE PEOPLE WHO'D SUPPORTED ME THERE.

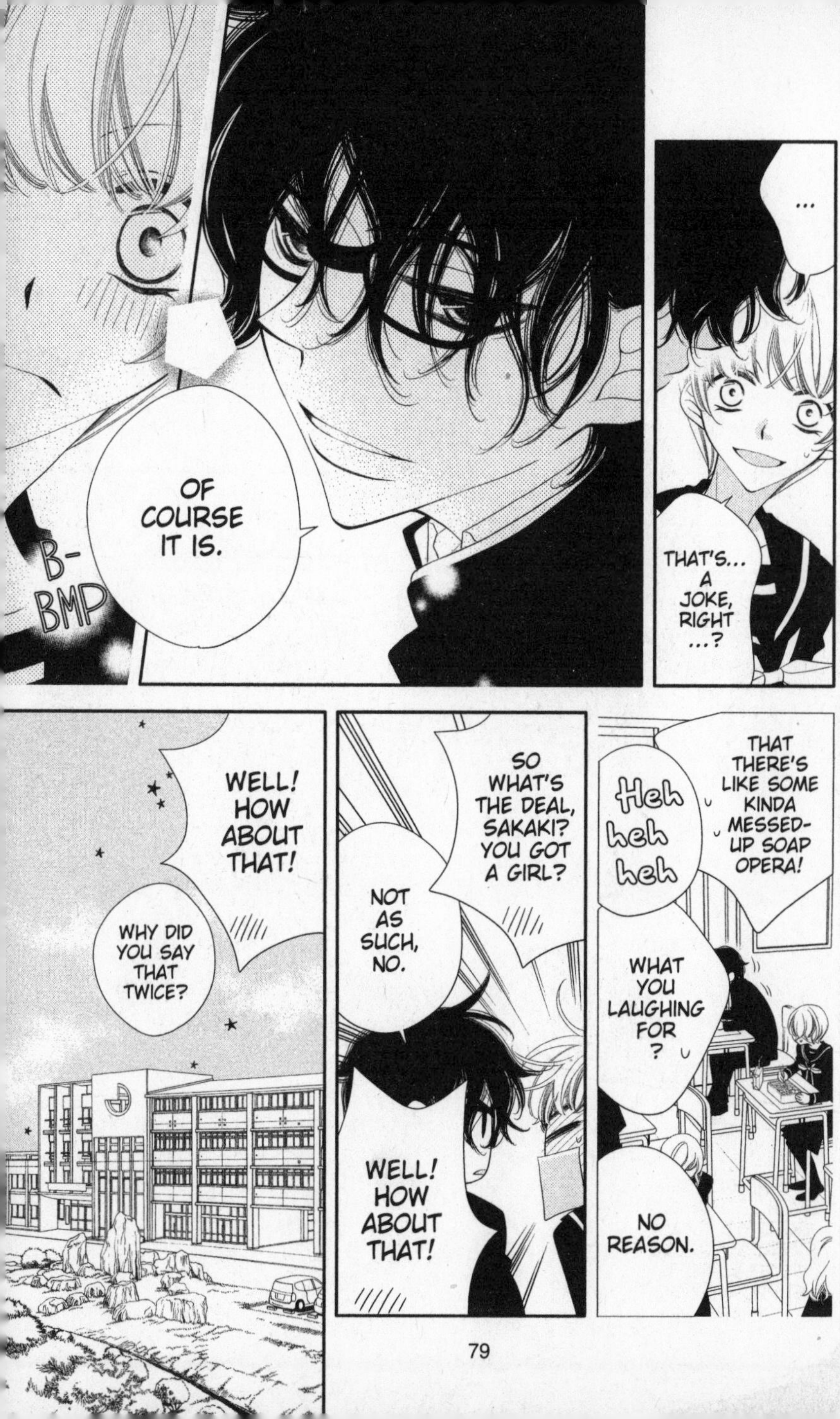
...
THAT'S... A JOKE, RIGHT ...?
OF COURSE IT IS.
B-BMP
THAT THERE'S LIKE SOME KINDA MESSED-UP SOAP OPERA!
Heh heh heh
WHAT YOU LAUGHING FOR?
NO REASON.
SO WHAT'S THE DEAL, SAKAKI? YOU GOT A GIRL?
NOT AS SUCH, NO.
WELL! HOW ABOUT THAT!
WELL! HOW ABOUT THAT!
WHY DID YOU SAY THAT TWICE?

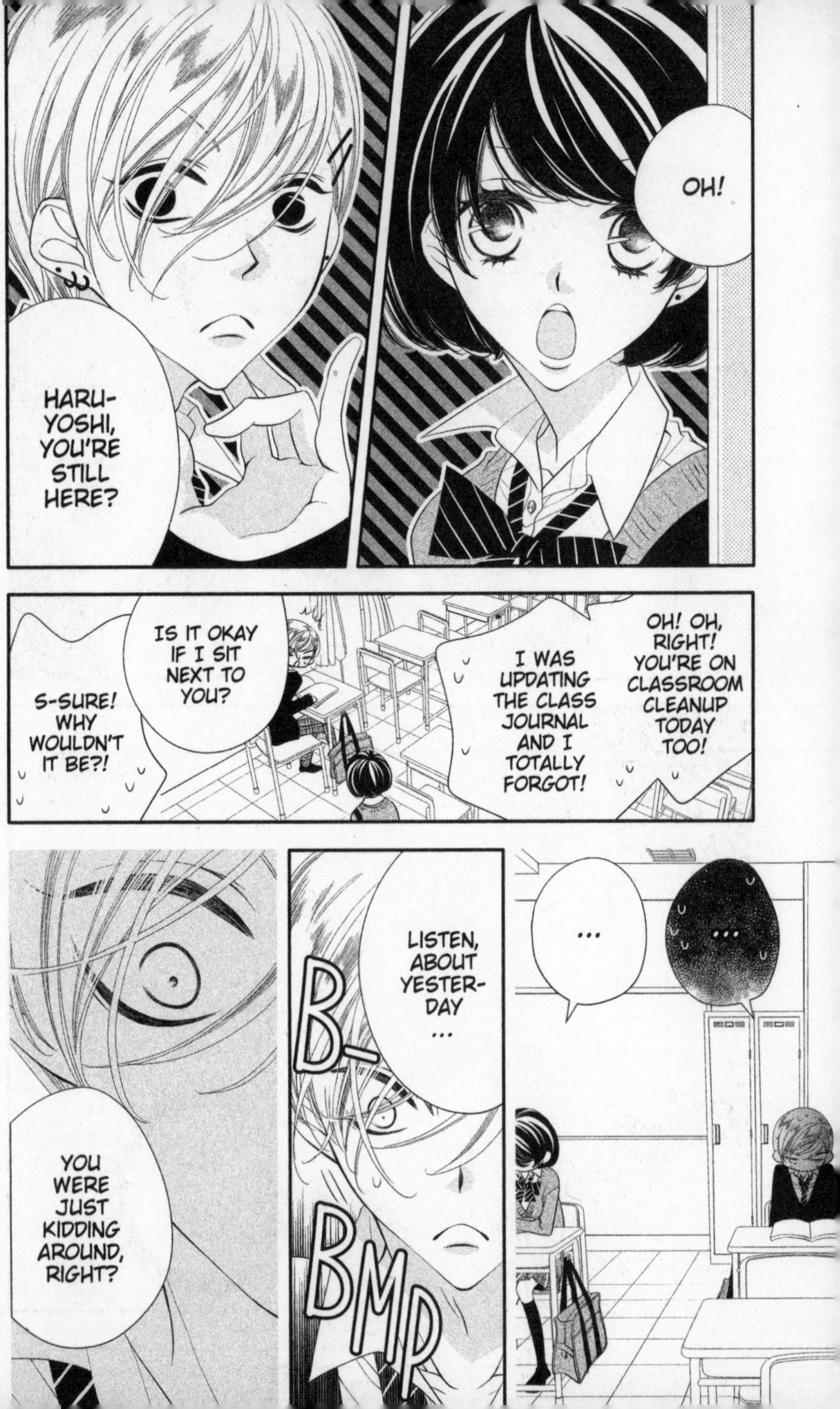
OH!
HARU-YOSHI, YOU'RE STILL HERE?
OH! OH, RIGHT! YOU'RE ON CLASSROOM CLEANUP TODAY TOO!
I WAS UPDATING THE CLASS JOURNAL AND I TOTALLY FORGOT!
IS IT OKAY IF I SIT NEXT TO YOU?
S-SURE! WHY WOULDN'T IT BE?!
...
...
LISTEN, ABOUT YESTER-DAY ...
B-BMP
YOU WERE JUST KIDDING AROUND, RIGHT?

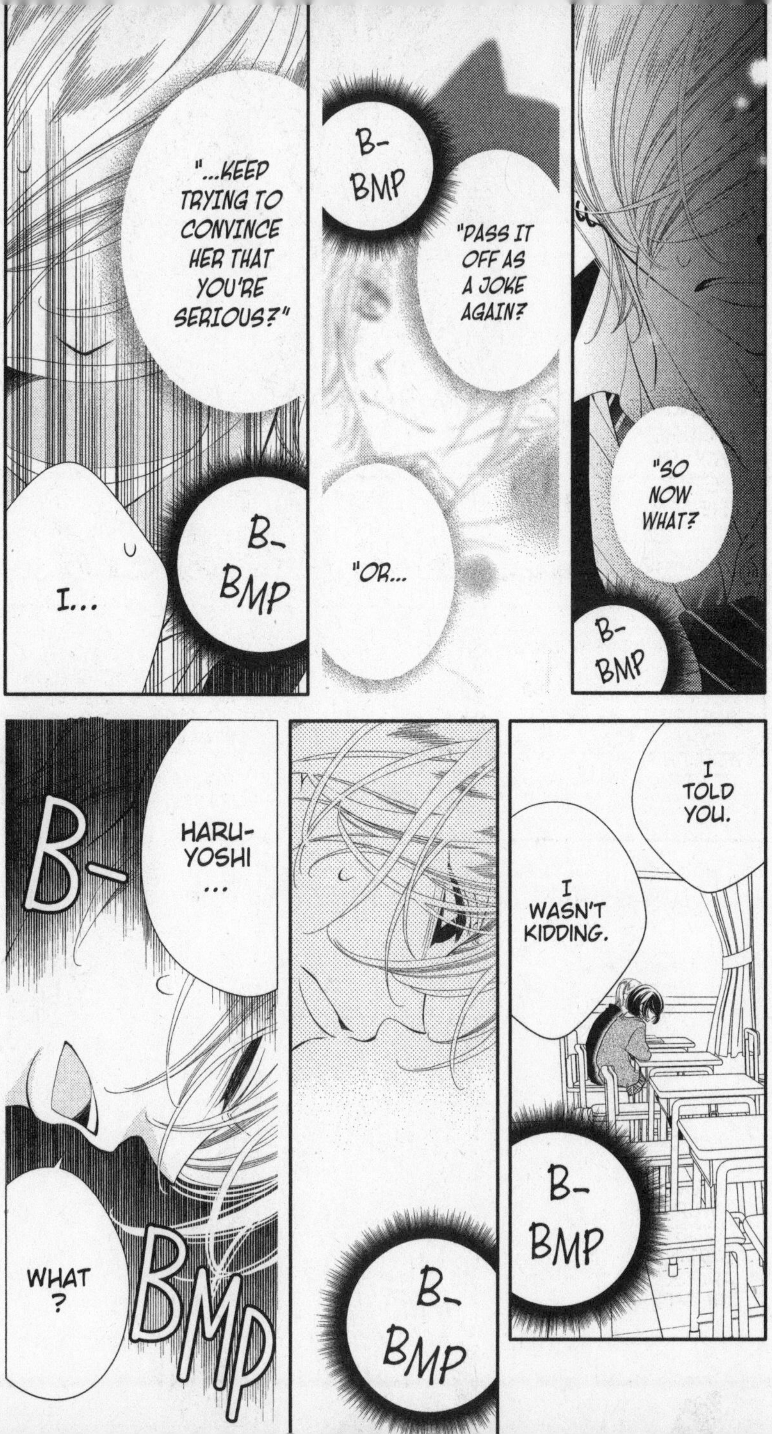
"SO NOW WHAT?
B-BMP
B-BMP
"PASS IT OFF AS A JOKE AGAIN?
"OR...
"...KEEP TRYING TO CONVINCE HER THAT YOU'RE SERIOUS?"
B-BMP
I...
I TOLD YOU.
I WASN'T KIDDING.
B-BMP
B-BMP
HARU-YOSHI...
B-BMP
WHAT?

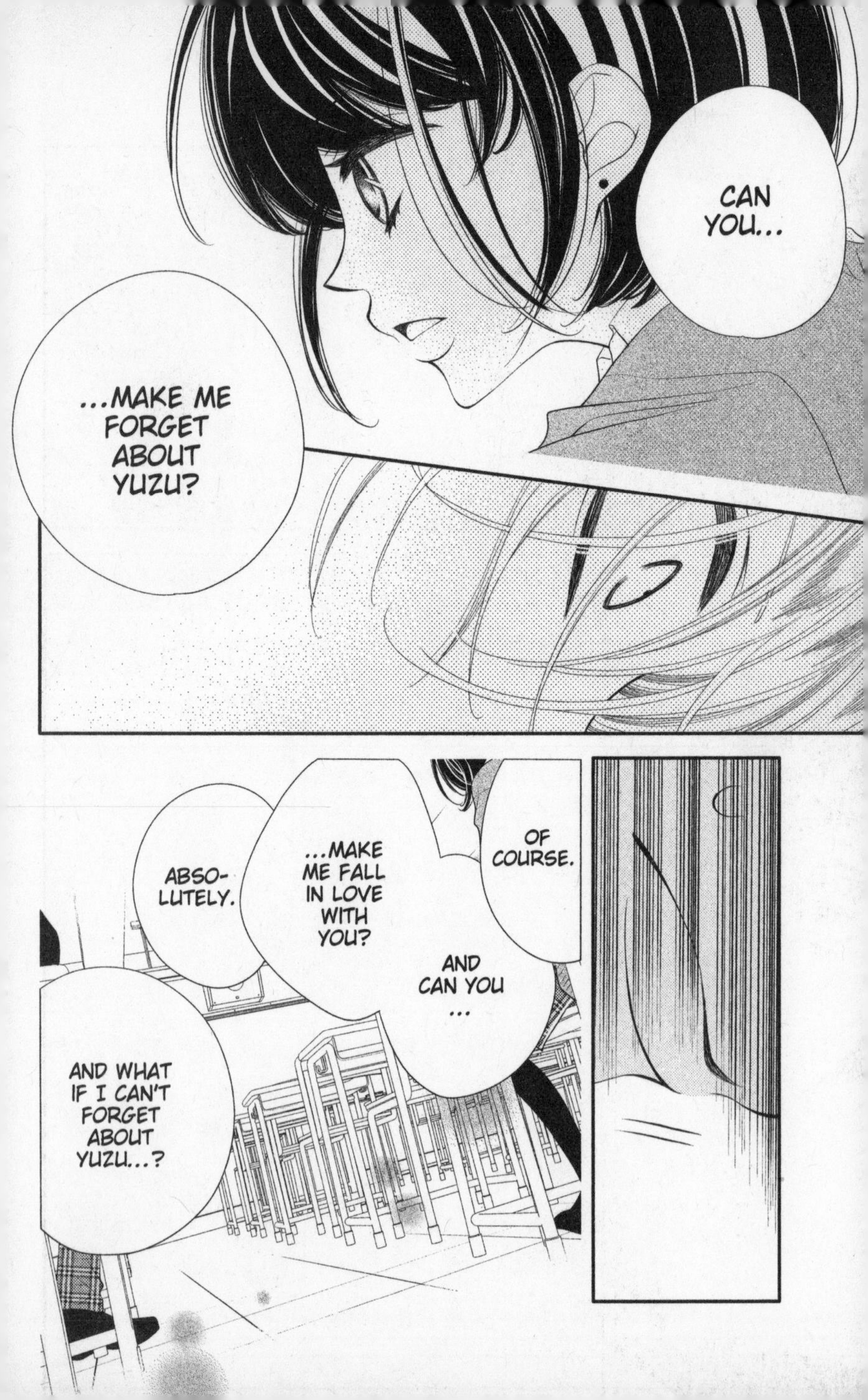
CAN YOU...
...MAKE ME FORGET ABOUT YUZU?
OF COURSE.
AND CAN YOU ...
...MAKE ME FALL IN LOVE WITH YOU?
ABSO-LUTELY.
AND WHAT IF I CAN'T FORGET ABOUT YUZU...?

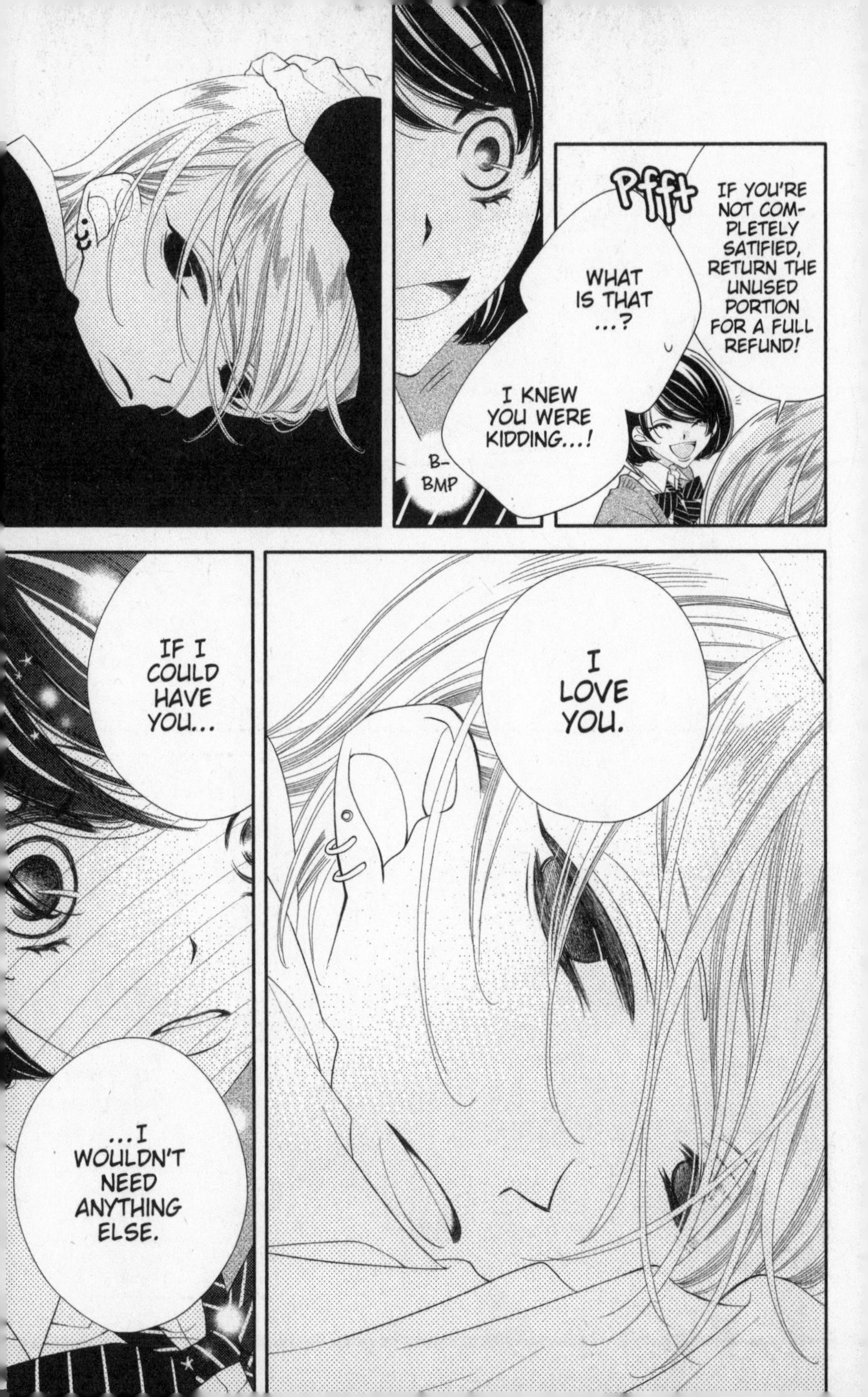
Pfft
IF YOU'RE NOT COMPLETELY SATIFIED, RETURN THE UNUSED PORTION FOR A FULL REFUND!
WHAT IS THAT ...?
I KNEW YOU WERE KIDDING...!
B-BMP
I LOVE YOU.
IF I COULD HAVE YOU...
...I WOULDN'T NEED ANYTHING ELSE.

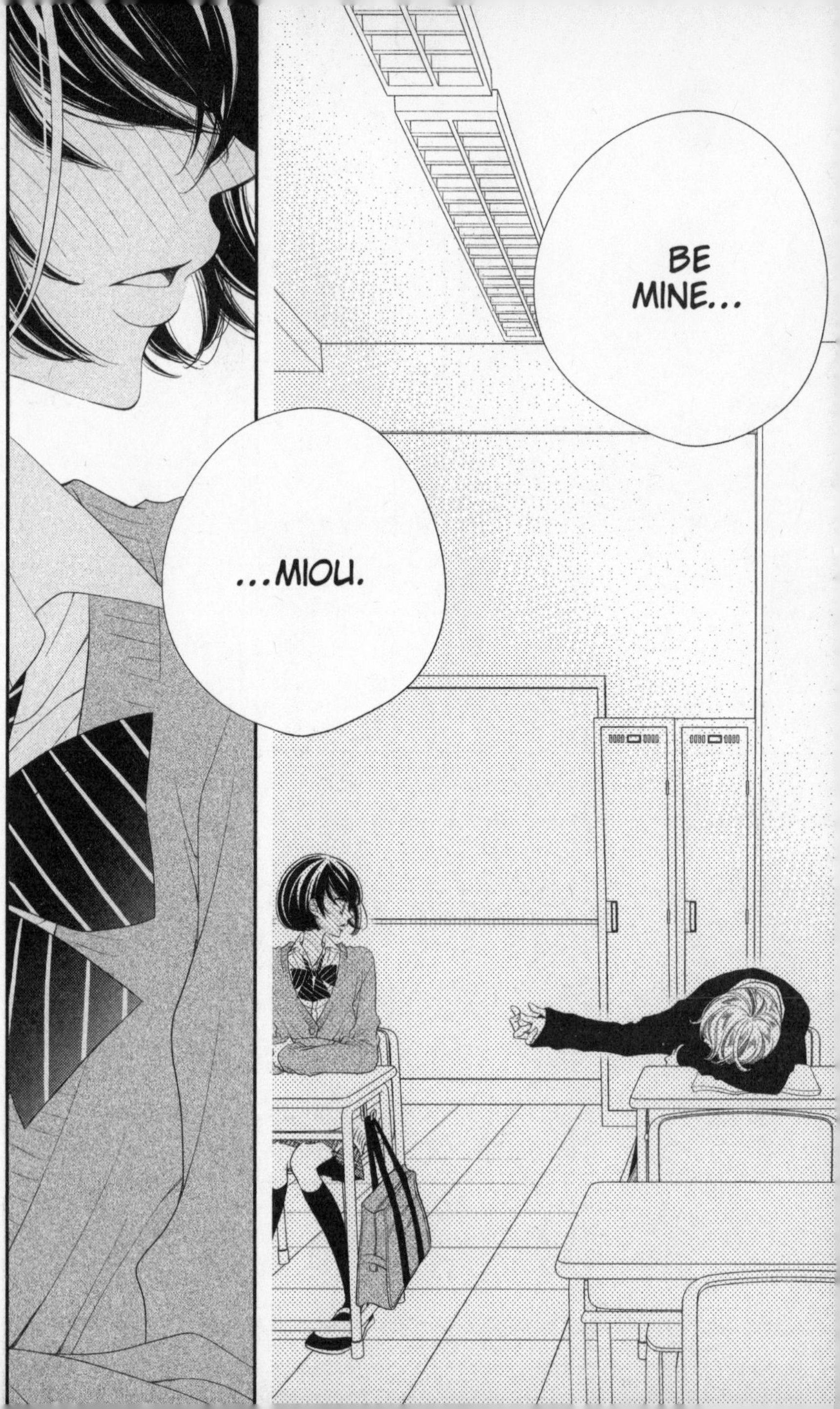
BE MINE...
...MIOU.

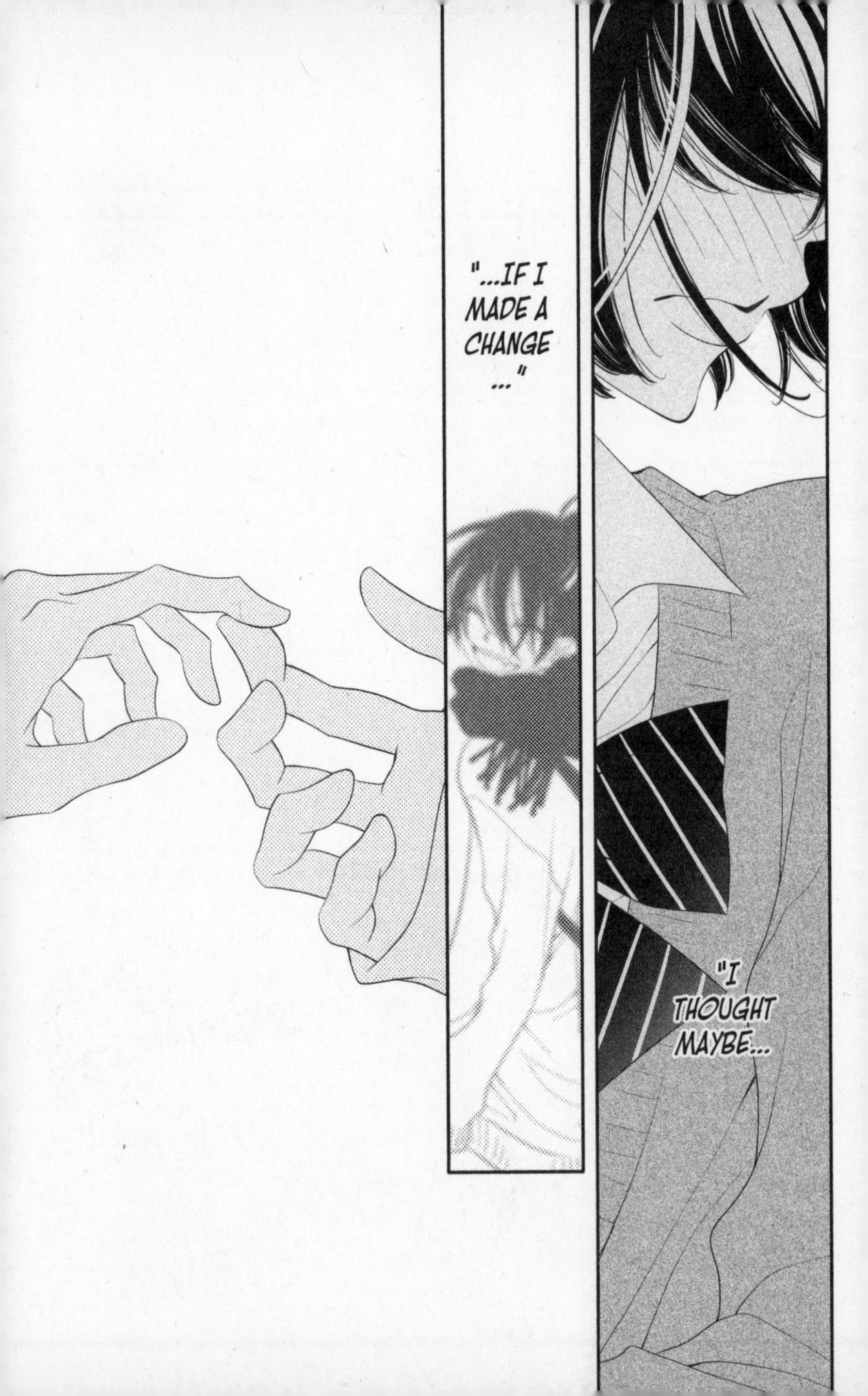
"...IF I MADE A CHANGE ..."
"I THOUGHT MAYBE...

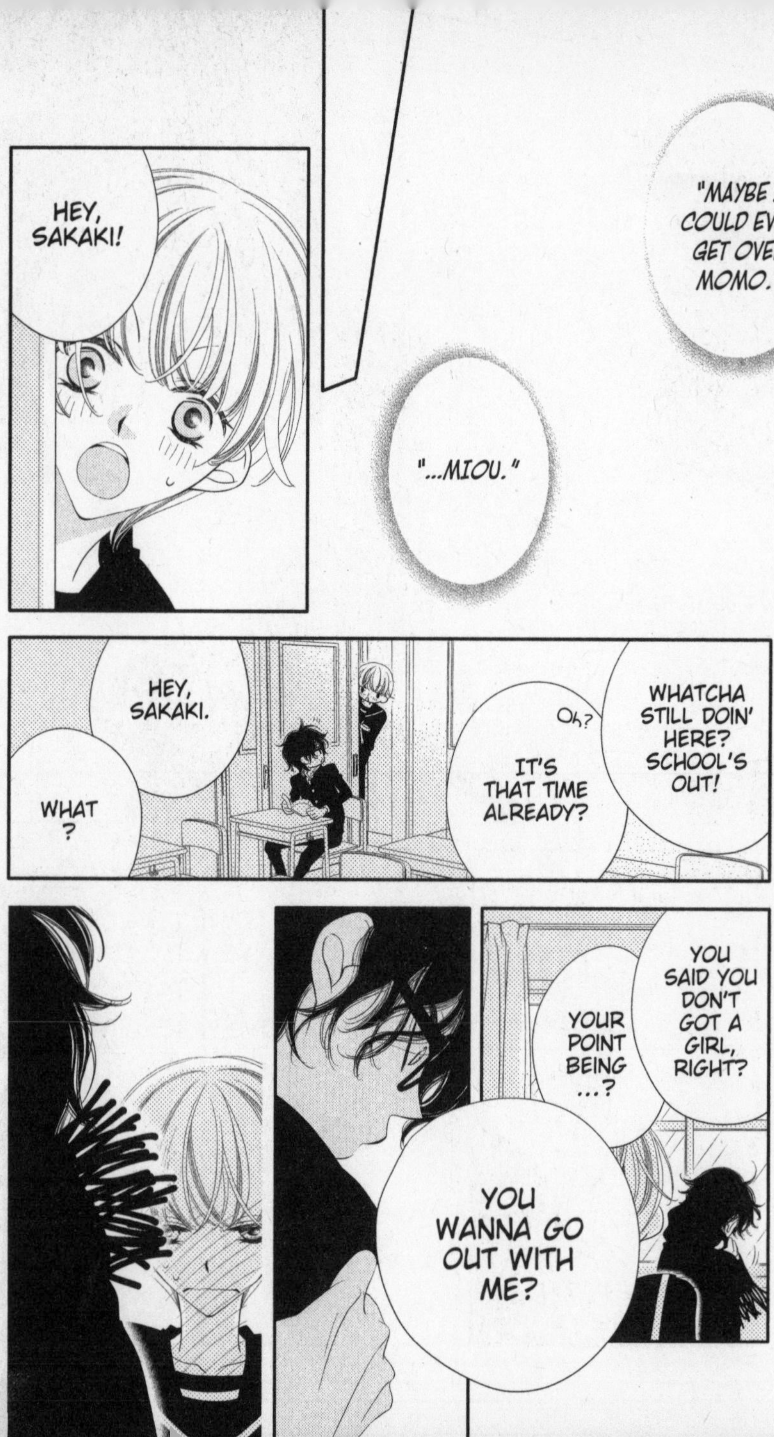
"MAYBE I COULD EVEN GET OVER MOMO."
"...MIOU."
HEY, SAKAKI!
WHATCHA STILL DOIN' HERE? SCHOOL'S OUT!
Oh?
IT'S THAT TIME ALREADY?
HEY, SAKAKI.
WHAT?
YOU SAID YOU DON'T GOT A GIRL, RIGHT?
YOUR POINT BEING ...?
YOU WANNA GO OUT WITH ME?

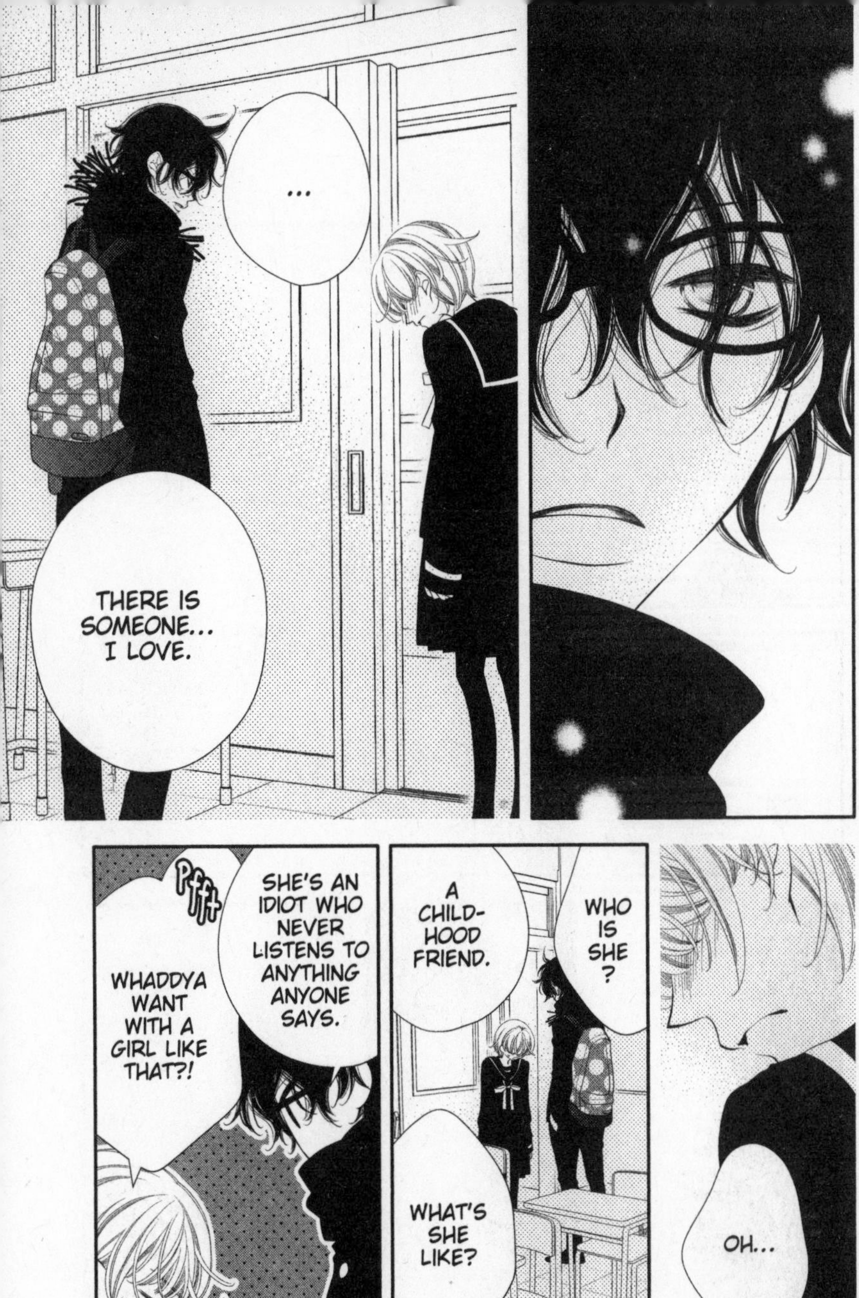
...
THERE IS SOMEONE... I LOVE.
OH...
WHO IS SHE?
A CHILDHOOD FRIEND.
WHAT'S SHE LIKE?
SHE'S AN IDIOT WHO NEVER LISTENS TO ANYTHING ANYONE SAYS.
Pfft
WHADDYA WANT WITH A GIRL LIKE THAT?!

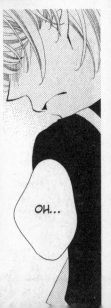

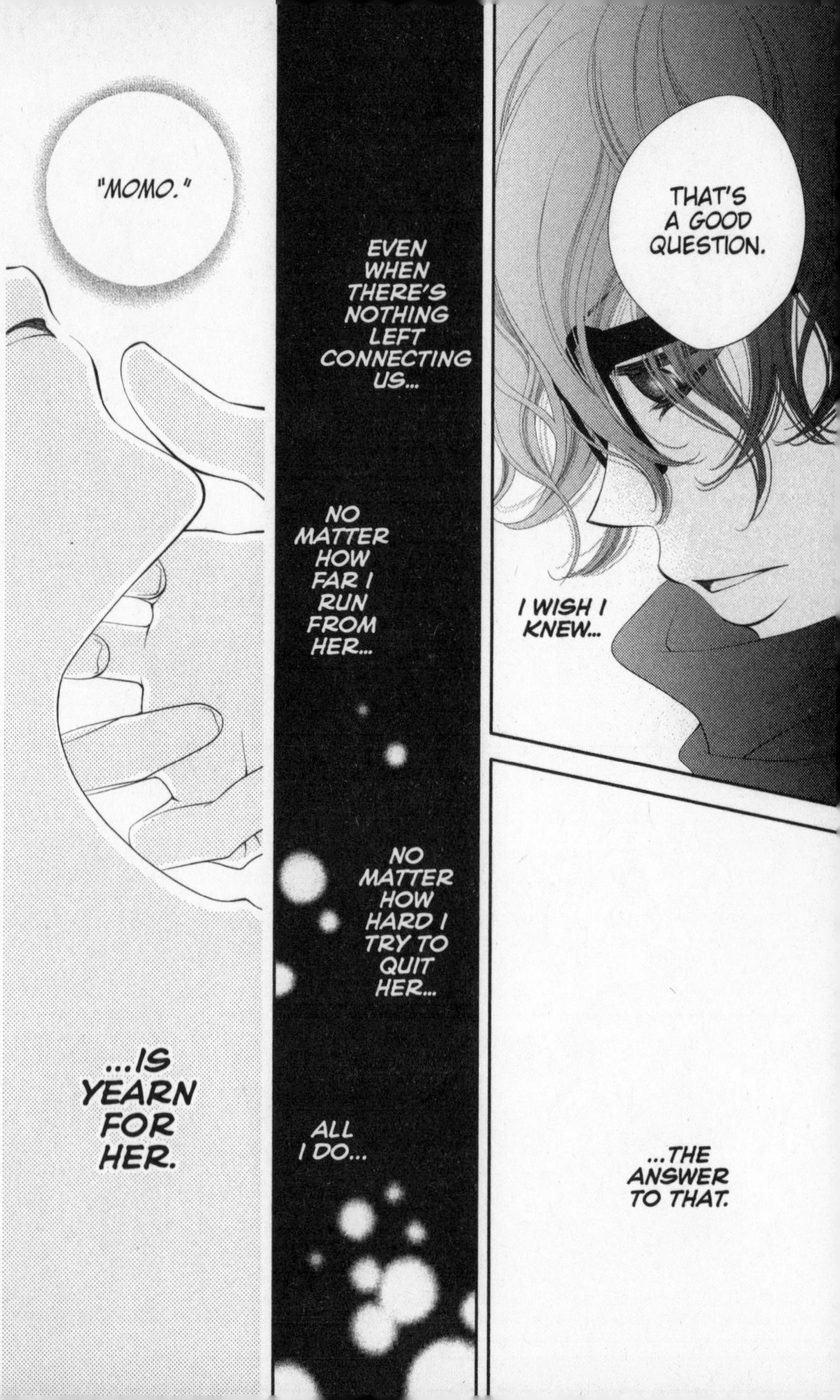
THAT'S A GOOD QUESTION.
I WISH I KNEW...
...THE ANSWER TO THAT.
EVEN WHEN THERE'S NOTHING LEFT CONNECTING US...
NO MATTER HOW FAR I RUN FROM HER...
NO MATTER HOW HARD I TRY TO QUIT HER...
ALL I DO...
"MOMO."
...IS YEARN FOR HER.

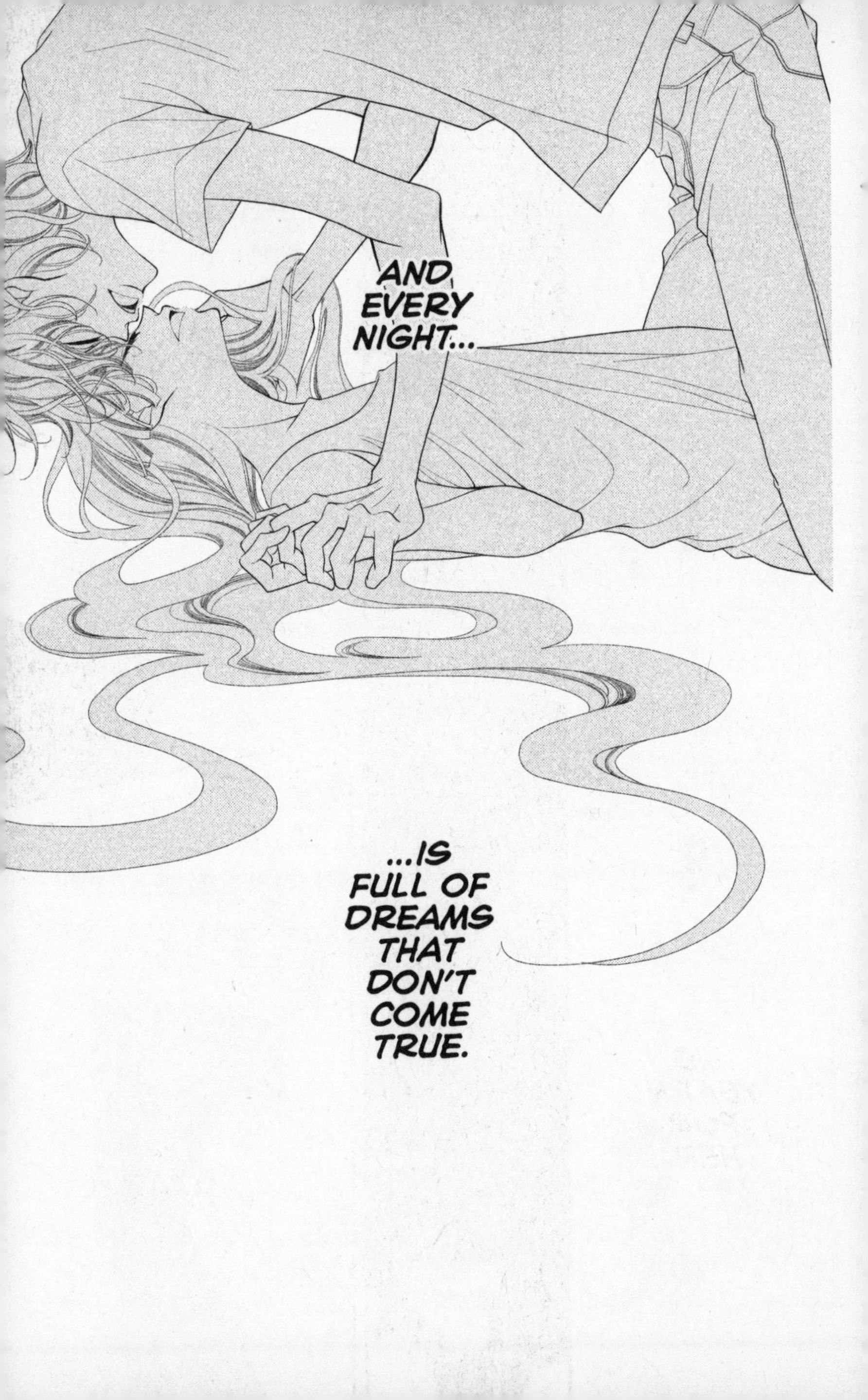
AND EVERY NIGHT...
...IS FULL OF DREAMS THAT DON'T COME TRUE.

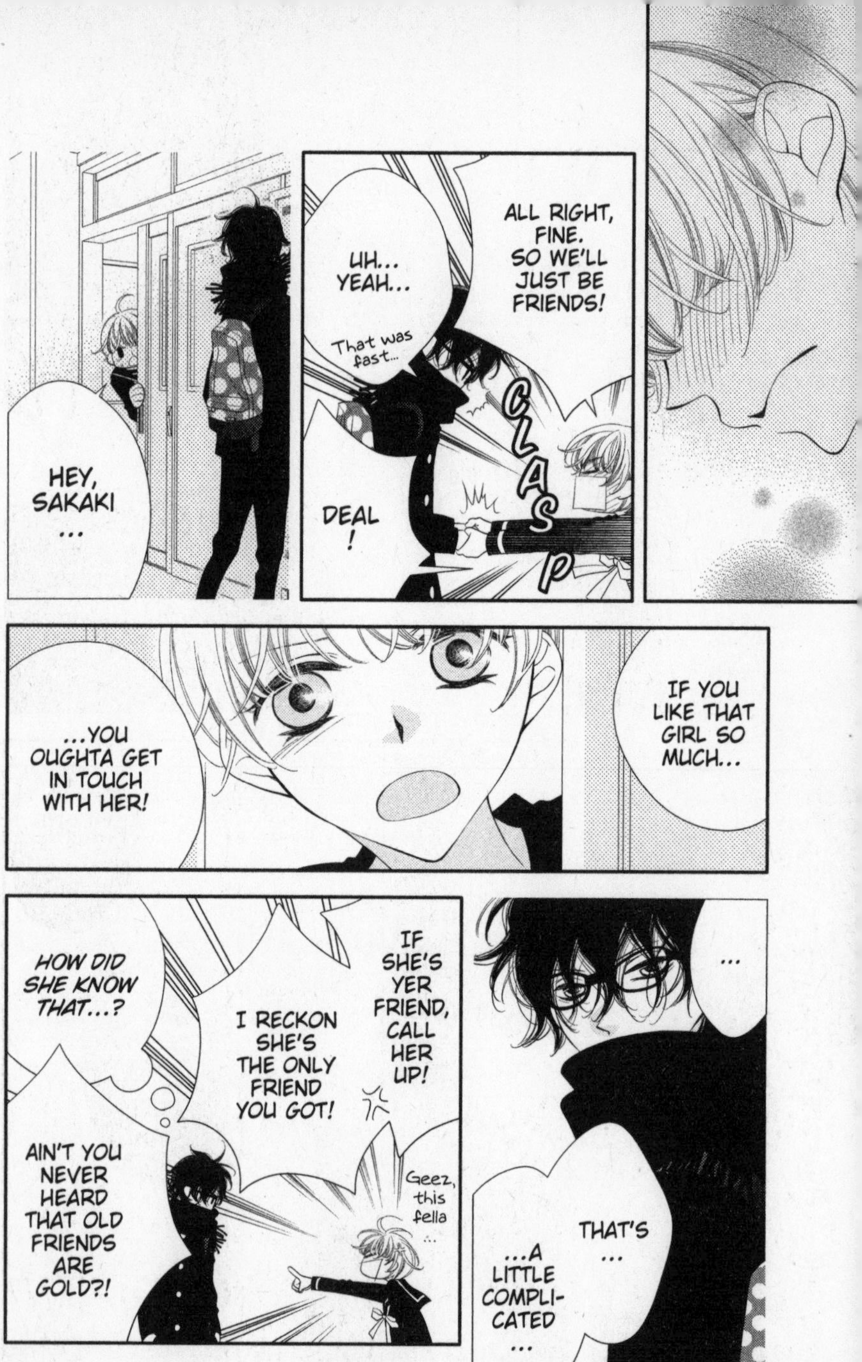
ALL RIGHT, FINE. SO WE'LL JUST BE FRIENDS!
UH... YEAH...
That was fast...
CLASP
DEAL!
HEY, SAKAKI ...
IF YOU LIKE THAT GIRL SO MUCH...
...YOU OUGHTA GET IN TOUCH WITH HER!
...
THAT'S ...
...A LITTLE COMPLI-CATED ...
IF SHE'S YER FRIEND, CALL HER UP!
I RECKON SHE'S THE ONLY FRIEND YOU GOT!
HOW DID SHE KNOW THAT...?
Geez, this fella ...
AIN'T YOU NEVER HEARD THAT OLD FRIENDS ARE GOLD?!

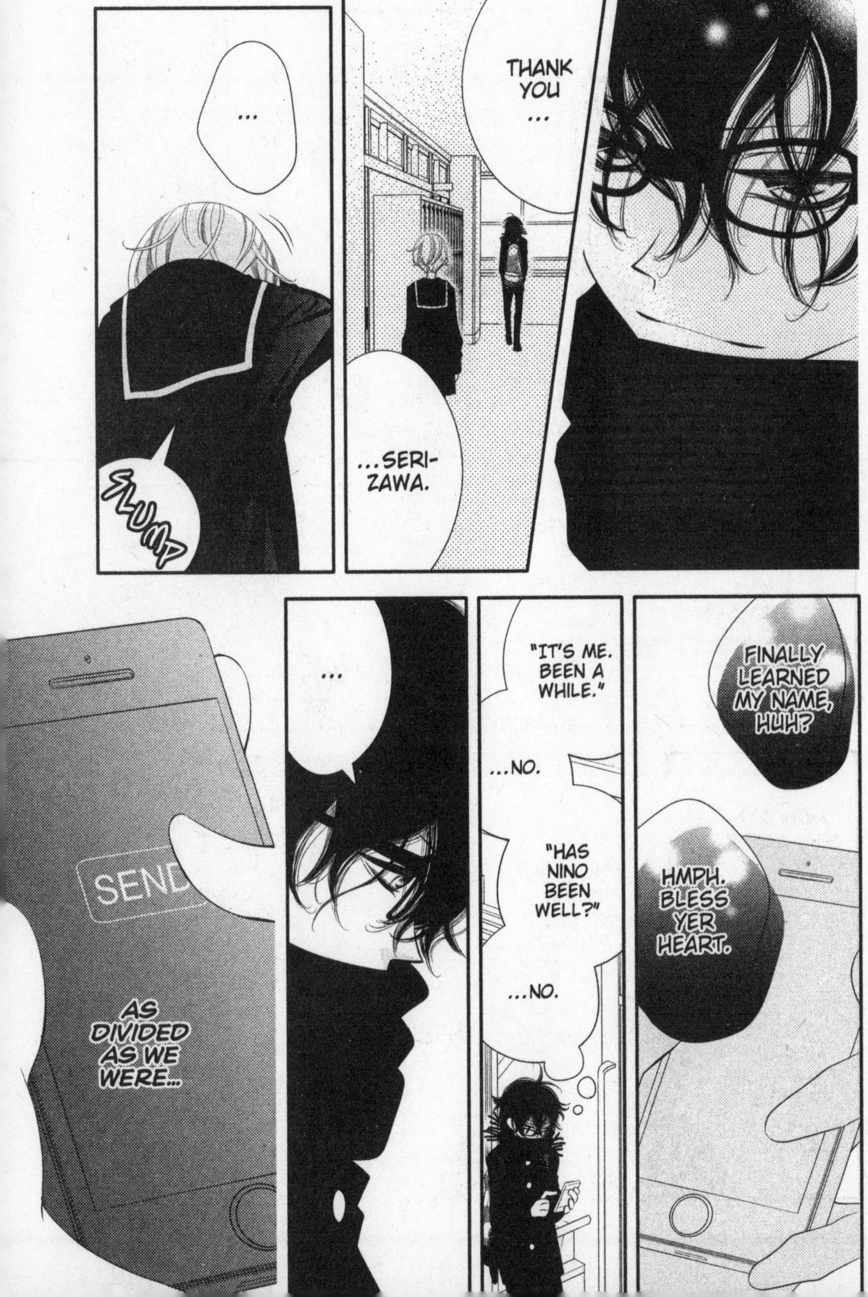
THANK YOU ...
...SERI-ZAWA.
...
SLUMP
FINALLY LEARNED MY NAME, HUH?
HMPH. BLESS YER HEART.
"IT'S ME. BEEN A WHILE."
...NO.
"HAS NINO BEEN WELL?"
...NO.
...
SEND
AS DIVIDED AS WE WERE...

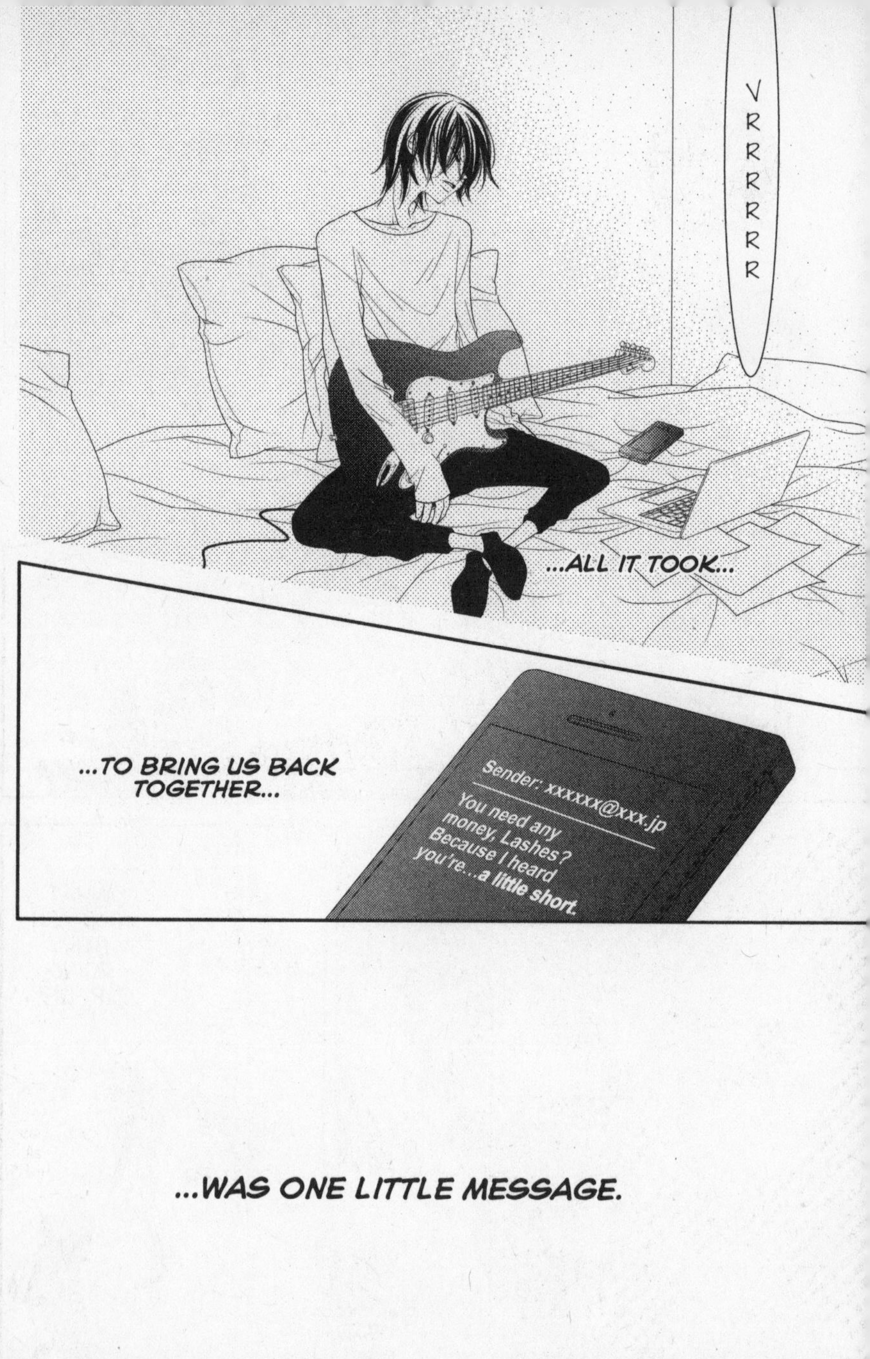
VRRRRRR
...ALL IT TOOK...
Sender: xxxxxx@xxx.jp
You need any money, Lashes? Because I heard you're...a little short.
...TO BRING US BACK TOGETHER...
...WAS ONE LITTLE MESSAGE.

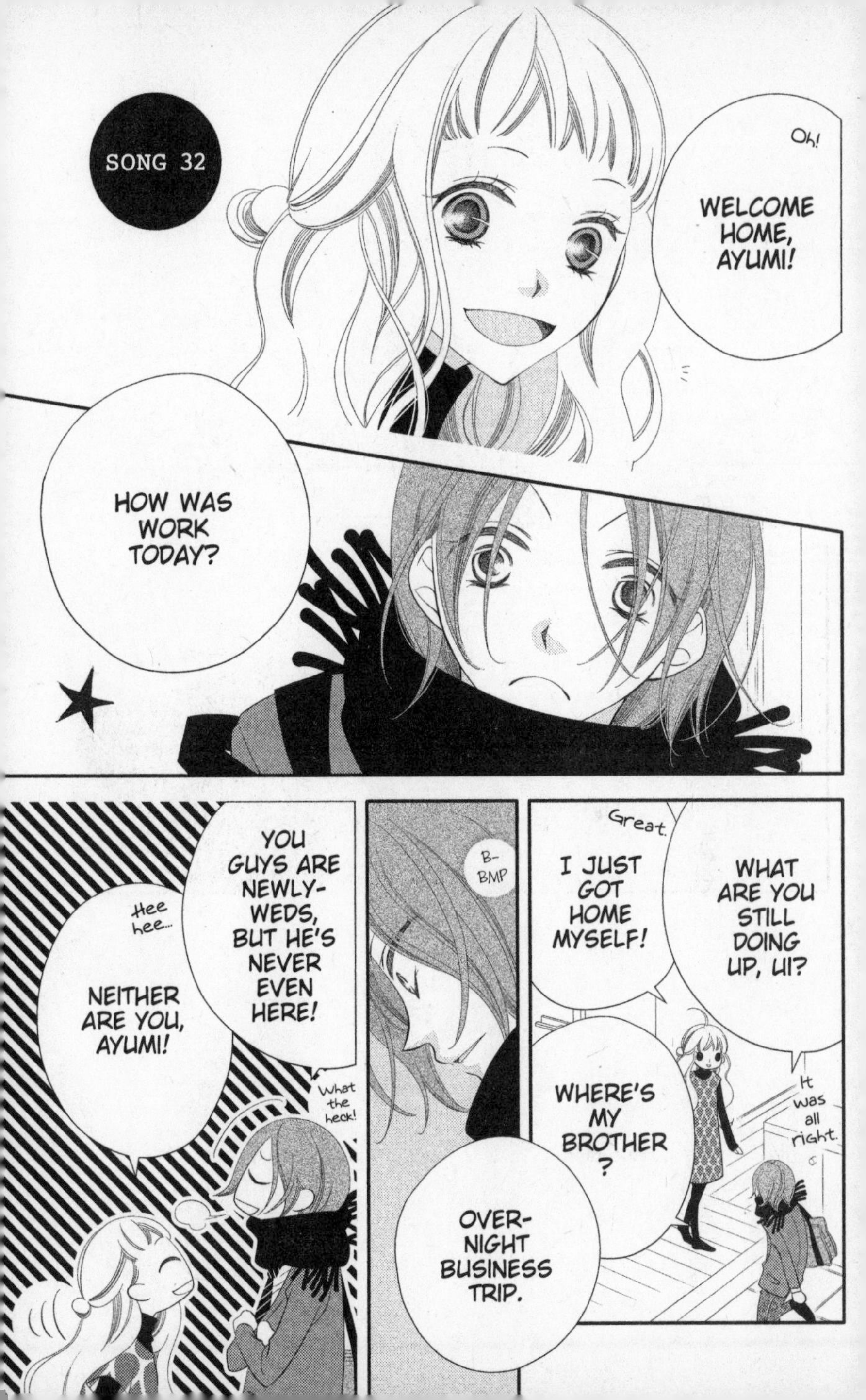
SONG 32
Oh!
WELCOME HOME, AYUMI!
HOW WAS WORK TODAY?
It was all right.
Great.
WHAT ARE YOU STILL DOING UP, UI?
I JUST GOT HOME MYSELF!
WHERE'S MY BROTHER?
OVER-NIGHT BUSINESS TRIP.
B-BMP
YOU GUYS ARE NEWLY-WEDS, BUT HE'S NEVER EVEN HERE!
Hee hee...
NEITHER ARE YOU, AYUMI!
What the heck!

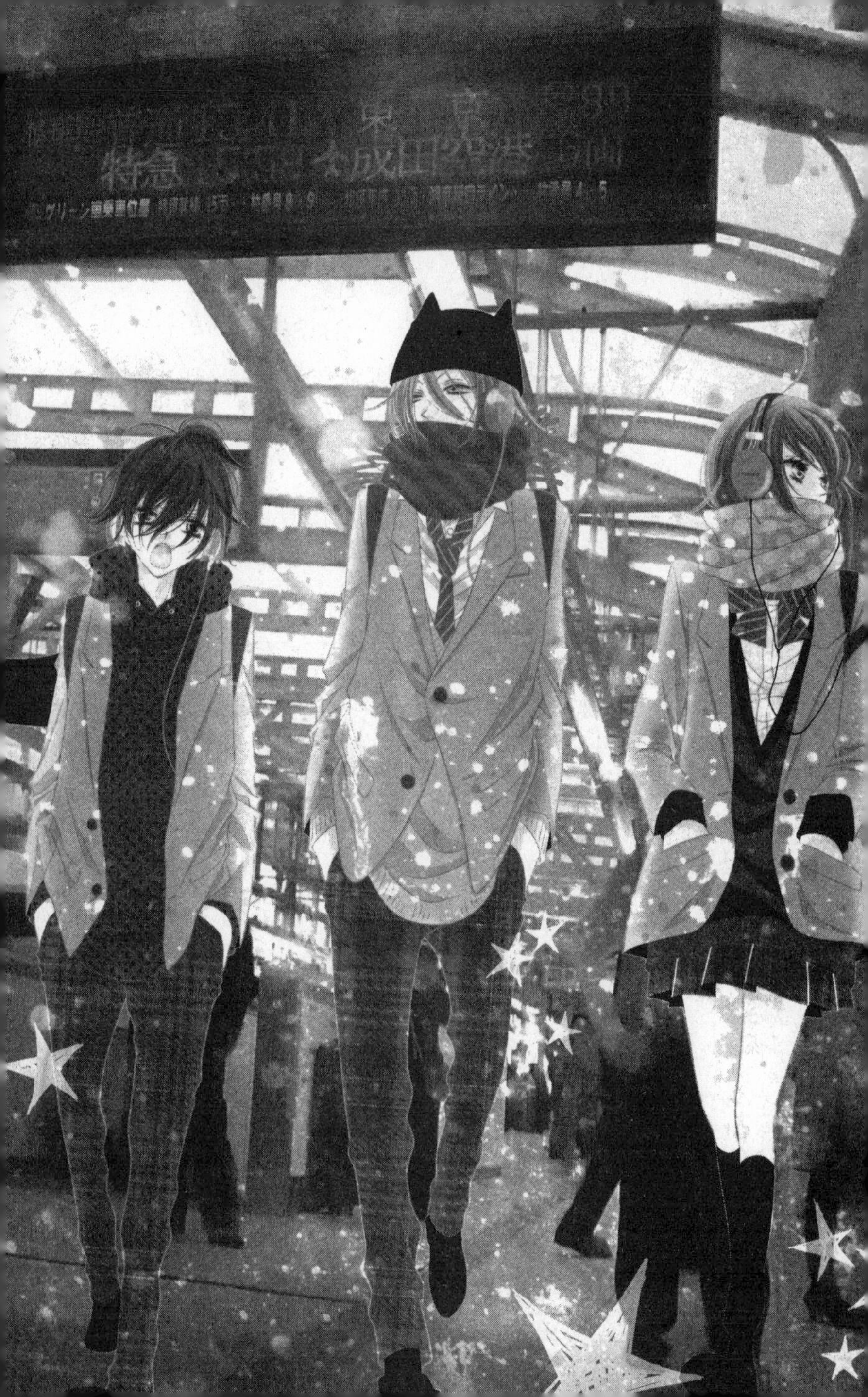
特急
成田空港

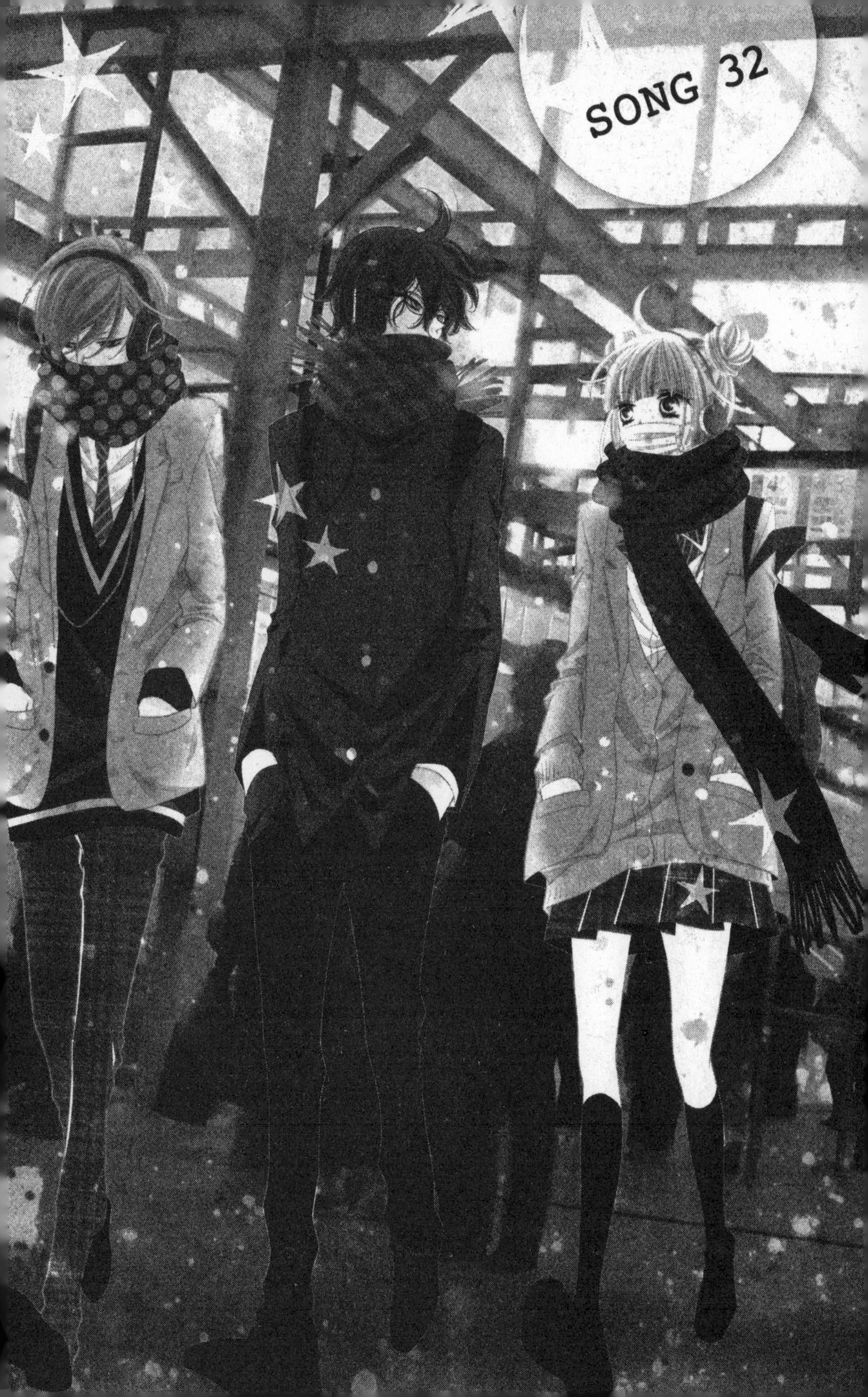
SONG 32

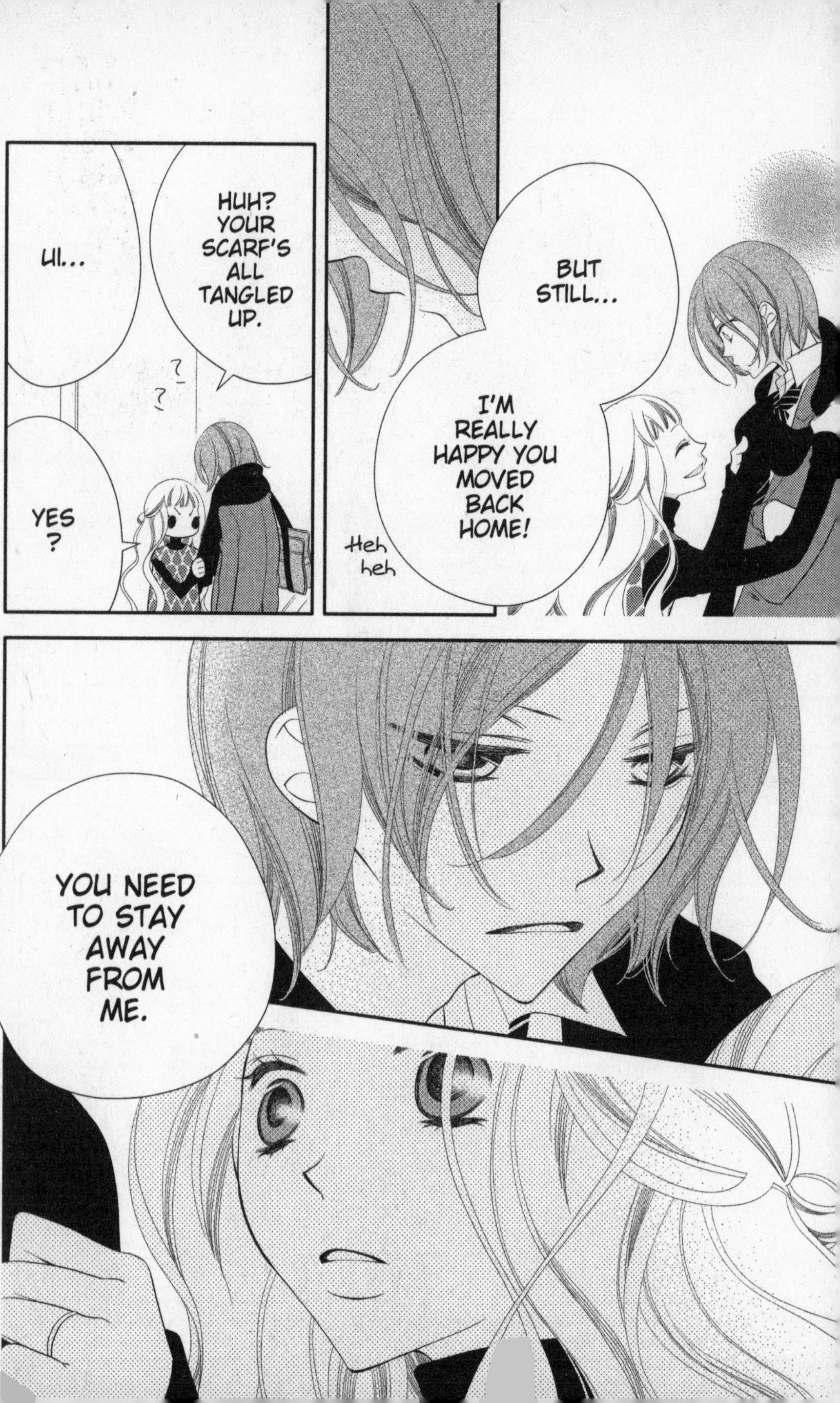
BUT STILL...
I'M REALLY HAPPY YOU MOVED BACK HOME!
Heh heh
HUH? YOUR SCARF'S ALL TANGLED UP.
UI...
? ?
YES?
YOU NEED TO STAY AWAY FROM ME.

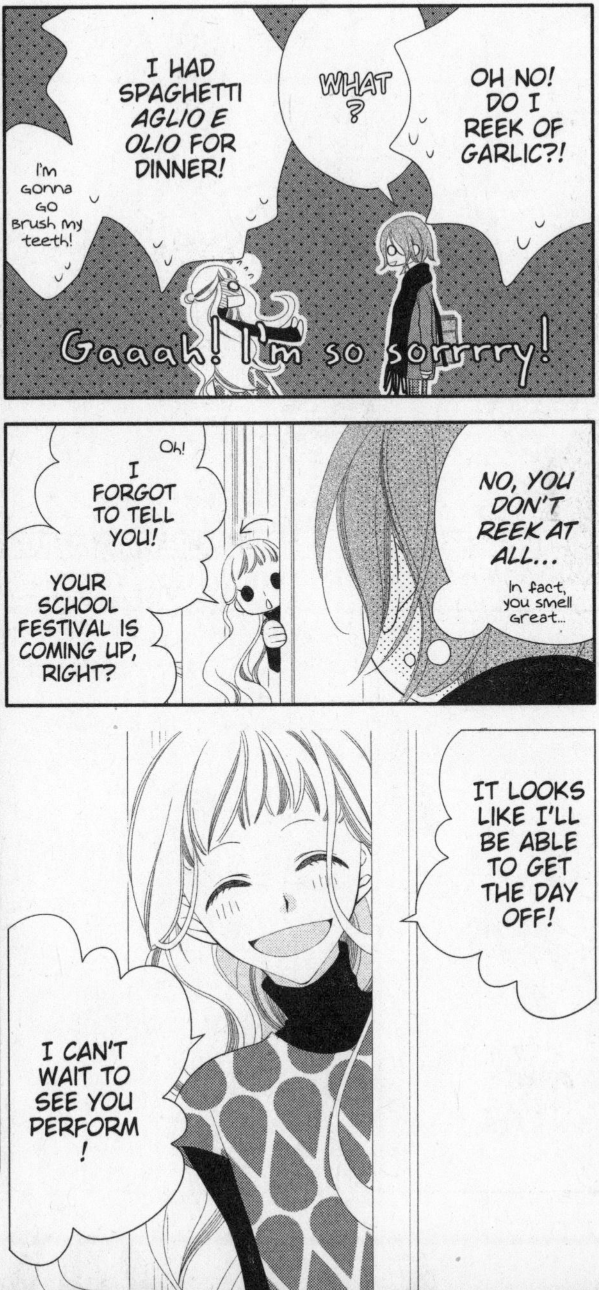
OH NO! DO I REEK OF GARLIC?!
WHAT?
I HAD SPAGHETTI AGLIO E OLIO FOR DINNER!
I'm gonna go brush my teeth!
Gaaah! I'm so sorrrry!
NO, YOU DON'T REEK AT ALL...
In fact, you smell great...
Oh!
I FORGOT TO TELL YOU!
YOUR SCHOOL FESTIVAL IS COMING UP, RIGHT?
IT LOOKS LIKE I'LL BE ABLE TO GET THE DAY OFF!
I CAN'T WAIT TO SEE YOU PERFORM!

4

Volume 5 came out way back in January in Japan, so it's been half a year since I last talked to my graphic novel readers! How have you been?!

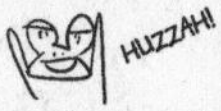
HUZZAH!

I think that's the longest gap yet, so this feels really weird. In the interim, I've gone full digital with my drawing. (Strictly speaking, it started at the end of volume 5.) This was true of my analog stuff as well, but there's a lot to it!

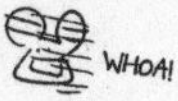
WHOA!

Lately I've felt like the art is finally getting close to where I want it to be, but I'm still firmly in the trial-and-error stage.

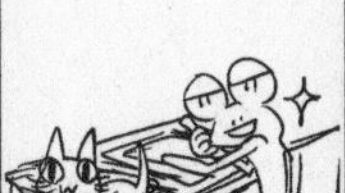

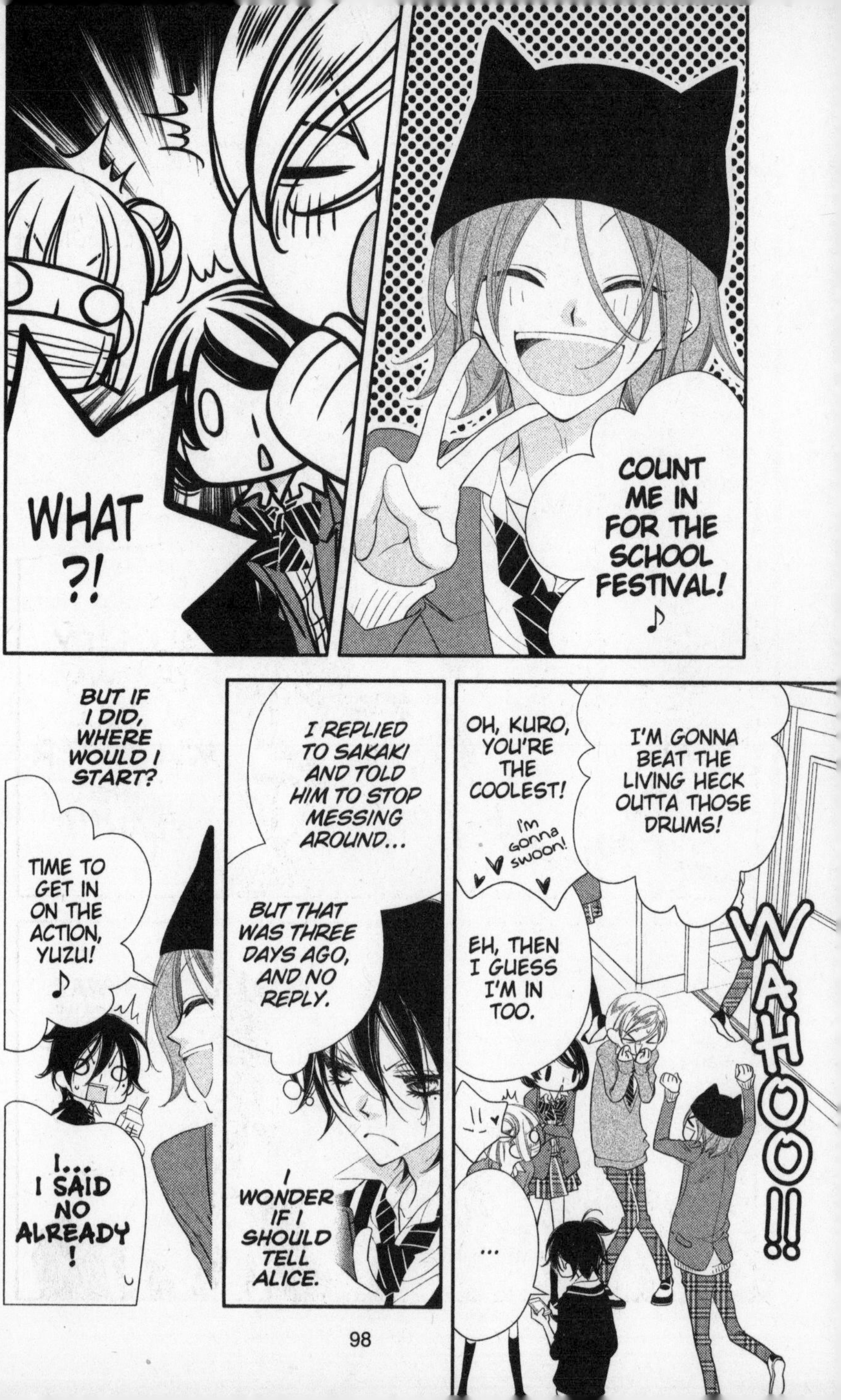
COUNT ME IN FOR THE SCHOOL FESTIVAL! ♪
WHAT?!
I'M GONNA BEAT THE LIVING HECK OUTTA THOSE DRUMS!
WAHOO!!
OH, KURO, YOU'RE THE COOLEST!
I'm gonna swoon!
EH, THEN I GUESS I'M IN TOO.
...
I REPLIED TO SAKAKI AND TOLD HIM TO STOP MESSING AROUND...
BUT THAT WAS THREE DAYS AGO, AND NO REPLY.
I WONDER IF I SHOULD TELL ALICE.
BUT IF I DID, WHERE WOULD I START?
TIME TO GET IN ON THE ACTION, YUZU! ♪
I... I SAID NO ALREADY!

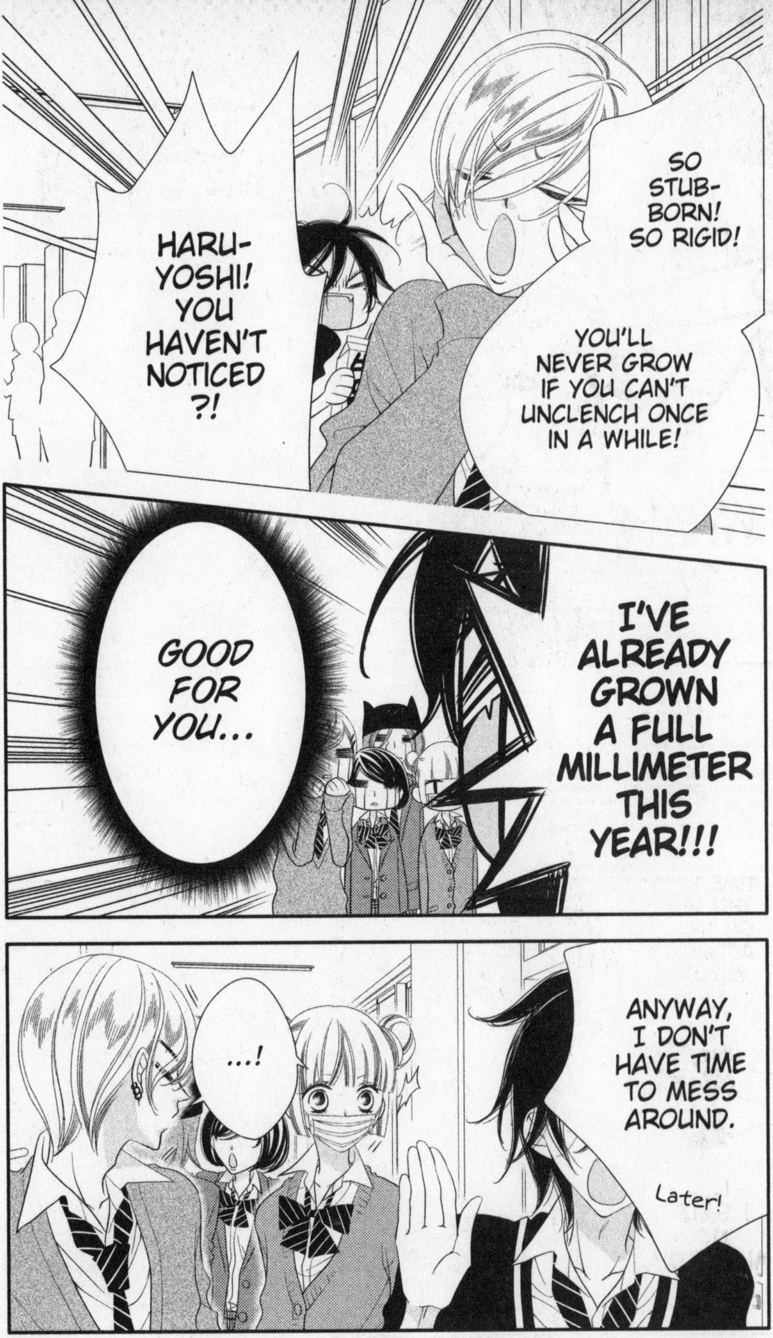
SO STUB-BORN! SO RIGID!
YOU'LL NEVER GROW IF YOU CAN'T UNCLENCH ONCE IN A WHILE!
HARU-YOSHI! YOU HAVEN'T NOTICED?!
I'VE ALREADY GROWN A FULL MILLIMETER THIS YEAR!!!
GOOD FOR YOU...
ANYWAY, I DON'T HAVE TIME TO MESS AROUND.
Later!
...!

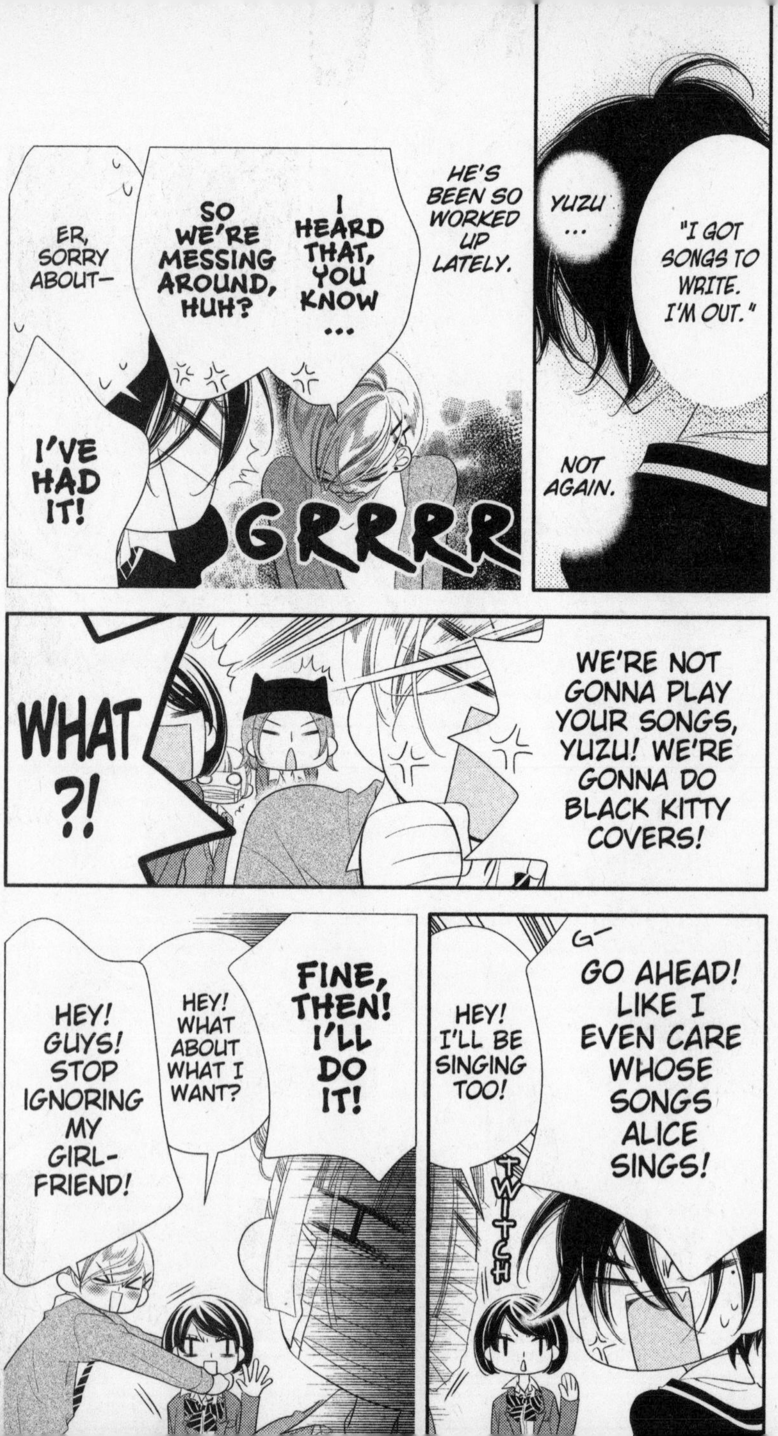
"I GOT SONGS TO WRITE. I'M OUT."
YUZU ...
NOT AGAIN.
HE'S BEEN SO WORKED UP LATELY.
I HEARD THAT, YOU KNOW ...
SO WE'RE MESSING AROUND, HUH?
ER, SORRY ABOUT—
I'VE HAD IT!
GRRRR
WE'RE NOT GONNA PLAY YOUR SONGS, YUZU! WE'RE GONNA DO BLACK KITTY COVERS!
WHAT ?!
G—
GO AHEAD! LIKE I EVEN CARE WHOSE SONGS ALICE SINGS!
HEY! I'LL BE SINGING TOO!
TWITCH
FINE, THEN! I'LL DO IT!
HEY! WHAT ABOUT WHAT I WANT?
HEY! GUYS! STOP IGNORING MY GIRL-FRIEND!

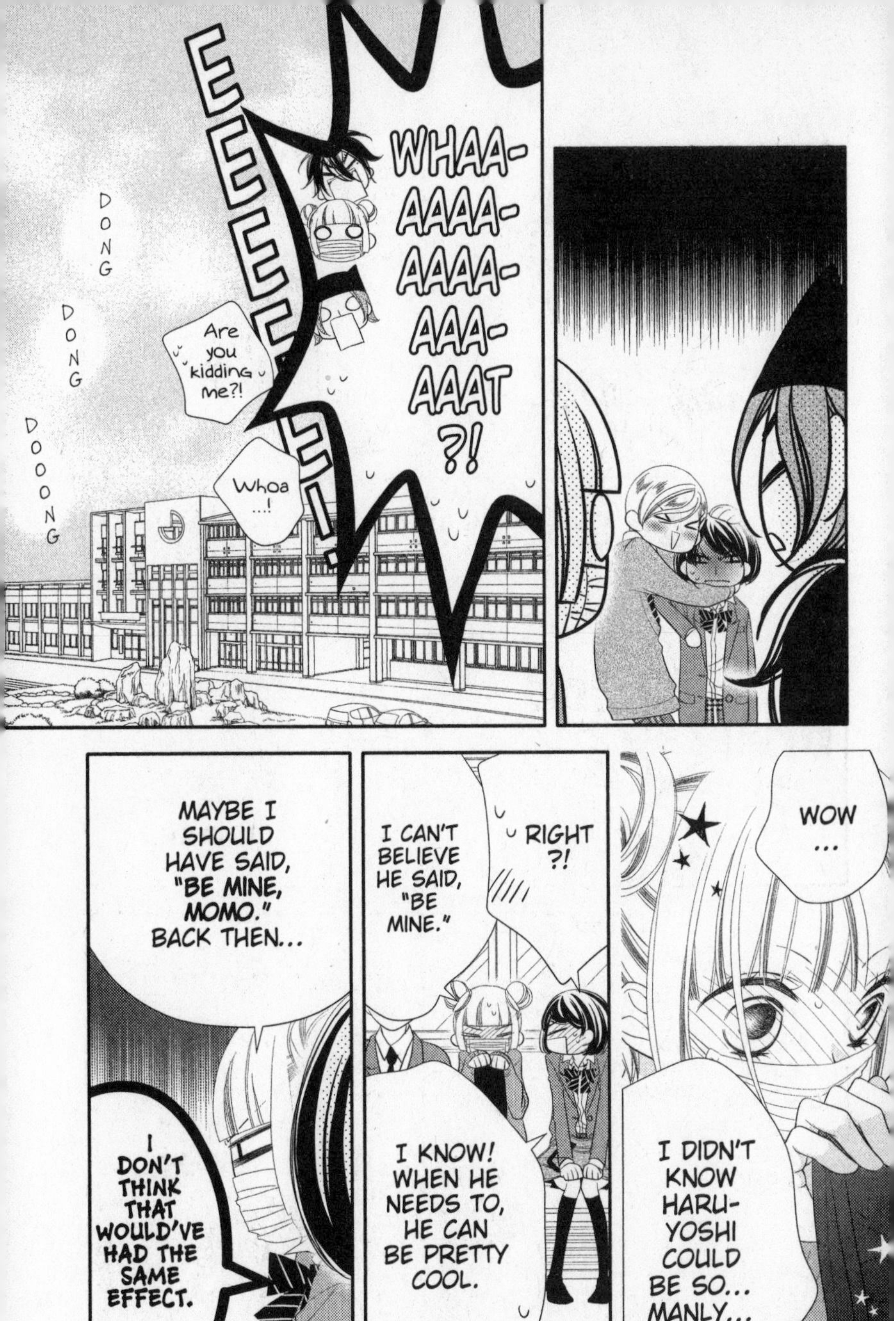
WHAA-AAAA-AAAA-AAA-AAAT?!
Are you kidding me?!
Whoa...!
DONG
DONG
DOOOONG
WOW...
I DIDN'T KNOW HARUYOSHI COULD BE SO... MANLY...
RIGHT?!
I CAN'T BELIEVE HE SAID, "BE MINE."
I KNOW! WHEN HE NEEDS TO, HE CAN BE PRETTY COOL.
MAYBE I SHOULD HAVE SAID, "BE MINE, MOMO." BACK THEN...
I DON'T THINK THAT WOULD'VE HAD THE SAME EFFECT.

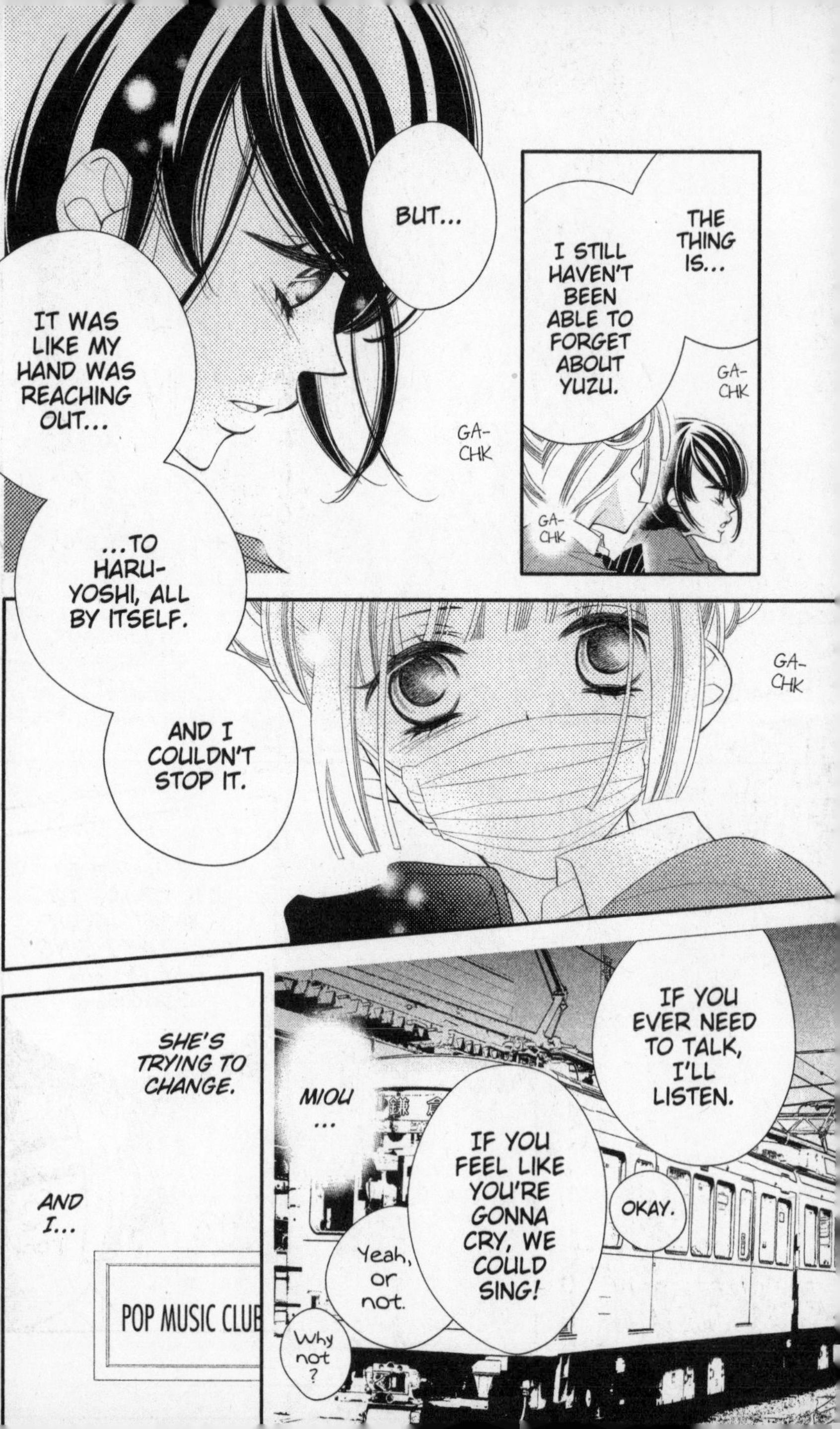
THE THING IS...
I STILL HAVEN'T BEEN ABLE TO FORGET ABOUT YUZU.
GA-CHK
GA-CHK
BUT...
IT WAS LIKE MY HAND WAS REACHING OUT...
GA-CHK
...TO HARU-YOSHI, ALL BY ITSELF.
GA-CHK
AND I COULDN'T STOP IT.
IF YOU EVER NEED TO TALK, I'LL LISTEN.
IF YOU FEEL LIKE YOU'RE GONNA CRY, WE COULD SING!
OKAY.
Yeah, or not.
Why not?
MIOU...
SHE'S TRYING TO CHANGE.
AND I...
POP MUSIC CLUB

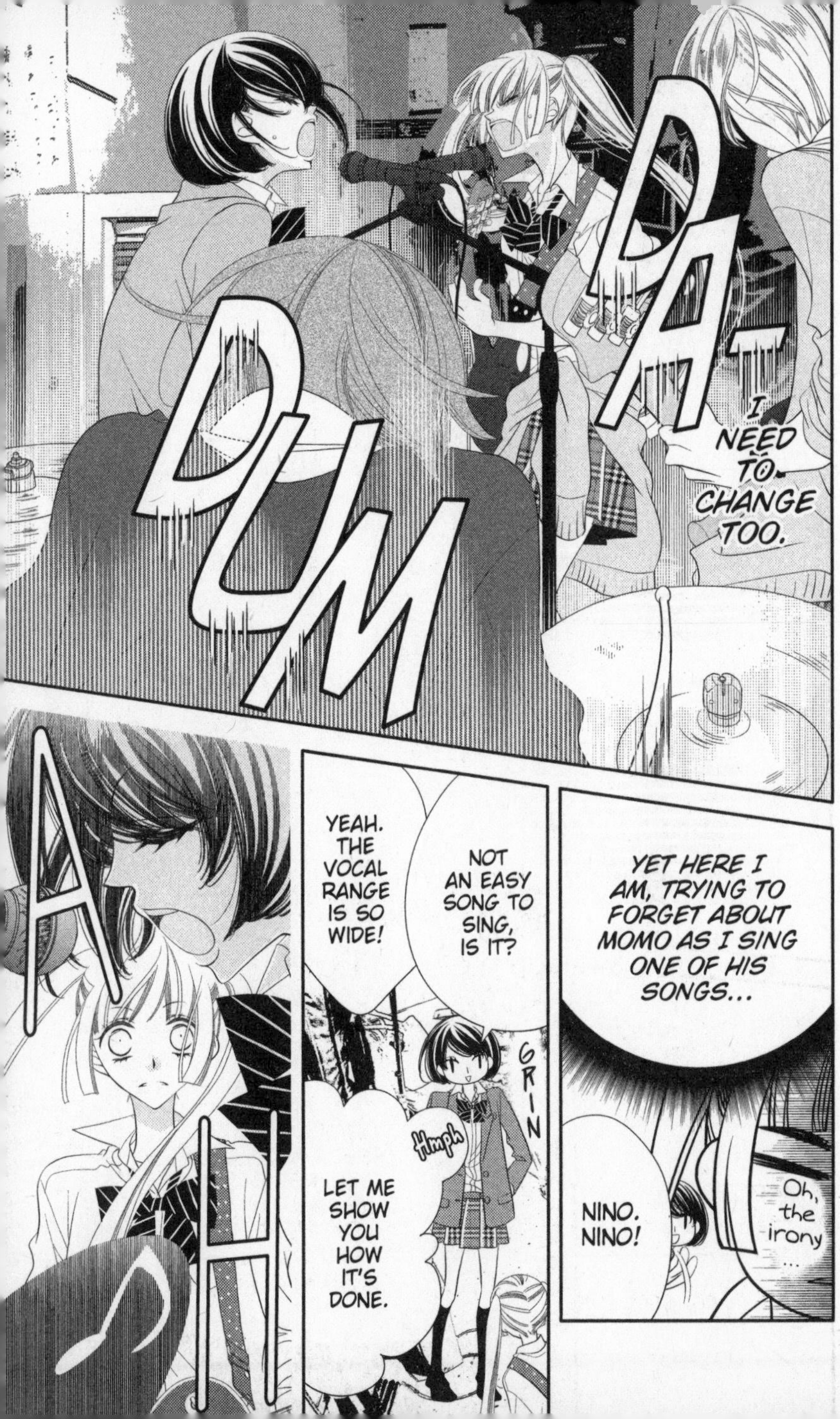
DA-
I NEED TO CHANGE TOO.
DUM
YET HERE I AM, TRYING TO FORGET ABOUT MOMO AS I SING ONE OF HIS SONGS...
Oh, the irony...
NINO. NINO!
NOT AN EASY SONG TO SING, IS IT?
YEAH. THE VOCAL RANGE IS SO WIDE!
GRIN
Hmph
LET ME SHOW YOU HOW IT'S DONE.
AH

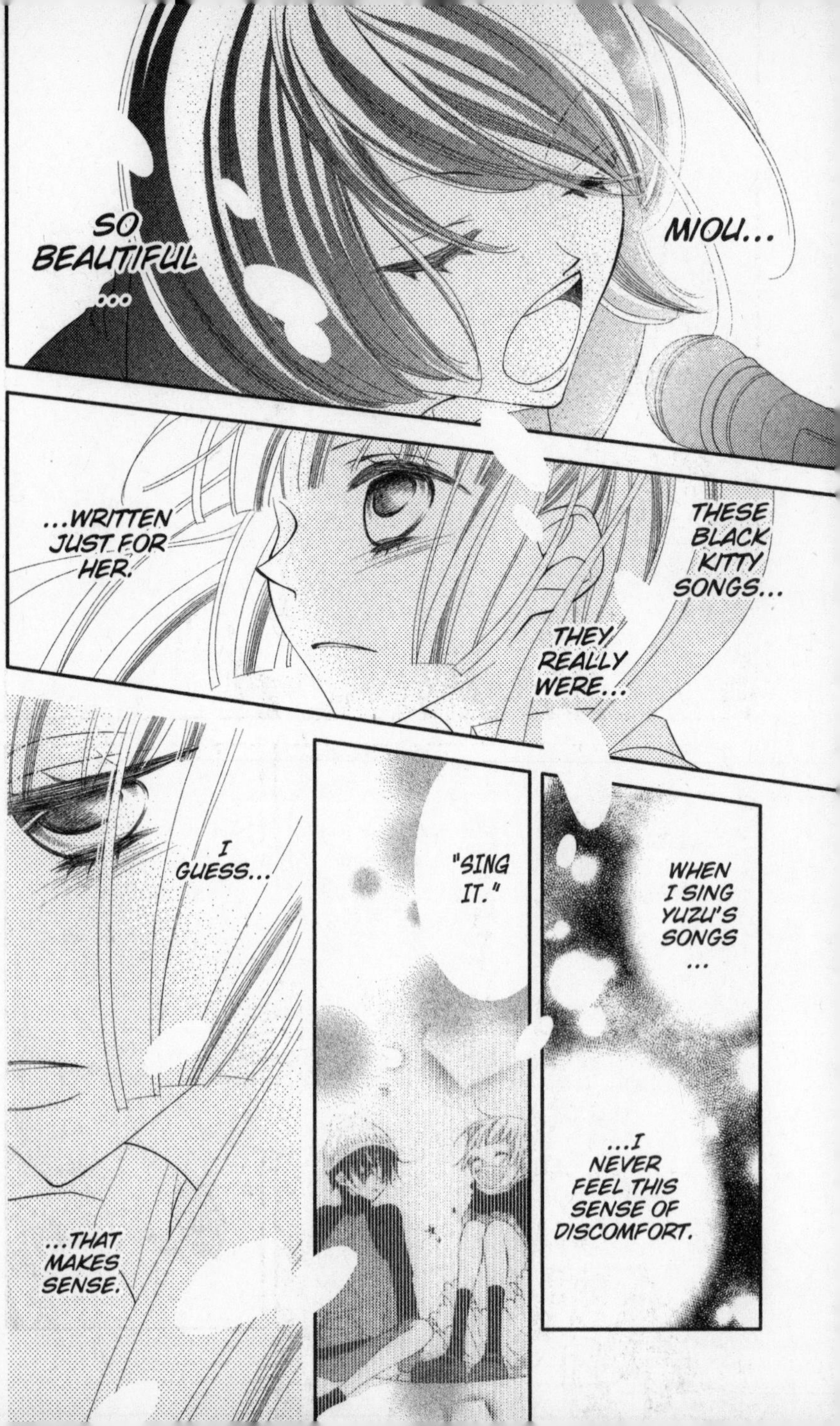
MIOU...
SO BEAUTIFUL ...
THESE BLACK KITTY SONGS...
THEY REALLY WERE...
...WRITTEN JUST FOR HER.
WHEN I SING YUZU'S SONGS ...
...I NEVER FEEL THIS SENSE OF DISCOMFORT.
"SING IT."
I GUESS...
...THAT MAKES SENSE.

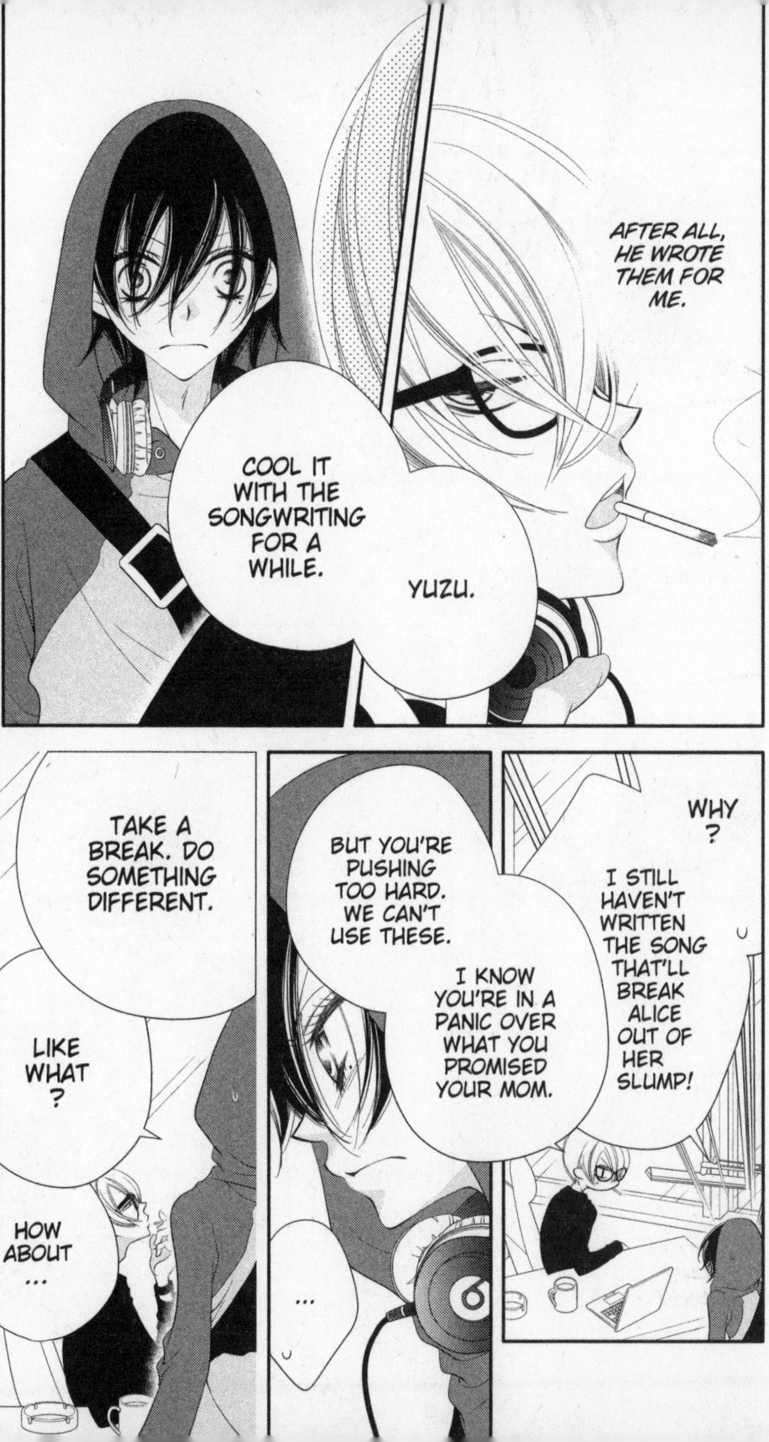
AFTER ALL, HE WROTE THEM FOR ME.
YUZU.
COOL IT WITH THE SONGWRITING FOR A WHILE.
WHY?
I STILL HAVEN'T WRITTEN THE SONG THAT'LL BREAK ALICE OUT OF HER SLUMP!
I KNOW YOU'RE IN A PANIC OVER WHAT YOU PROMISED YOUR MOM.
BUT YOU'RE PUSHING TOO HARD. WE CAN'T USE THESE.
...
TAKE A BREAK. DO SOMETHING DIFFERENT.
LIKE WHAT?
HOW ABOUT ...

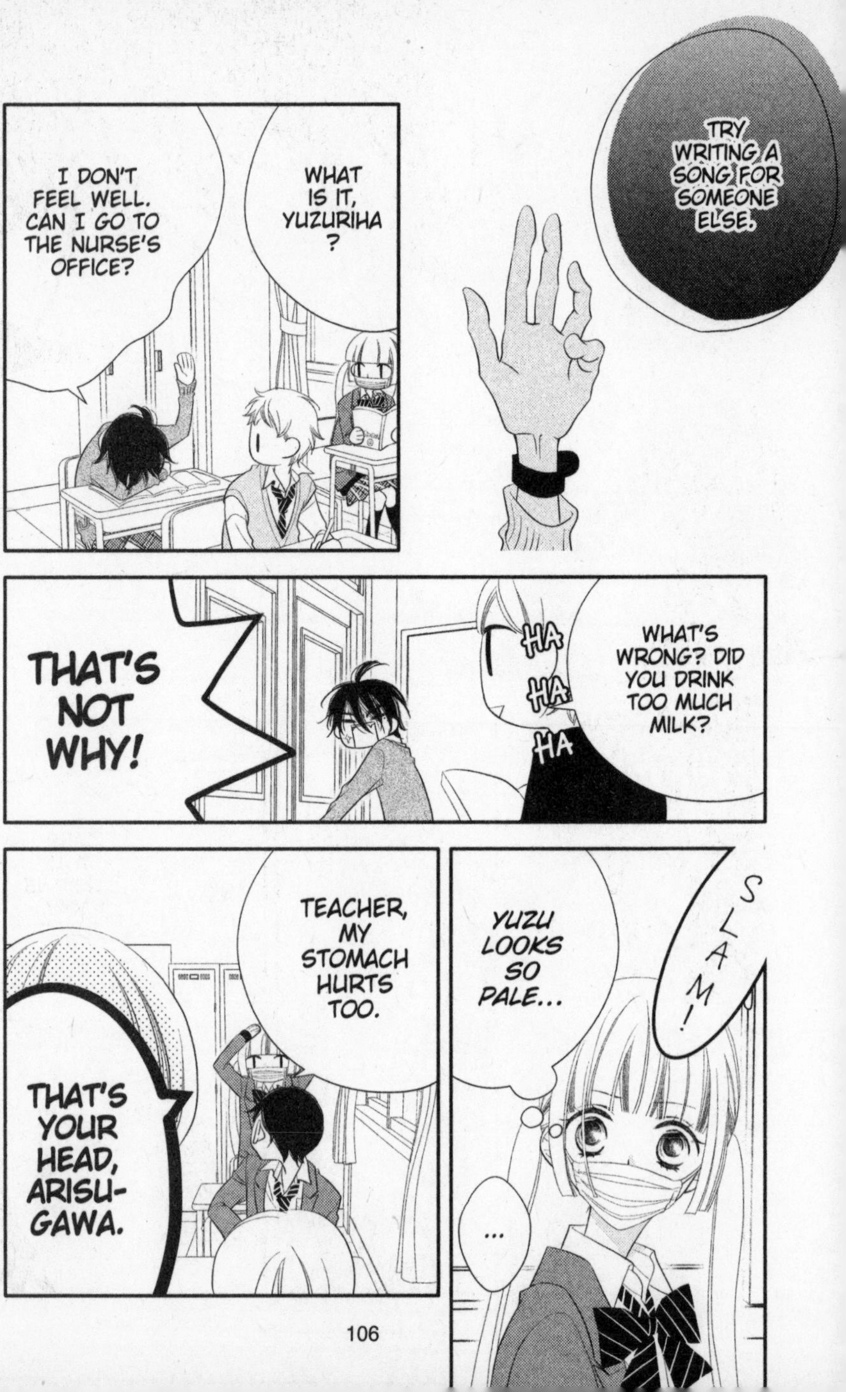
TRY WRITING A SONG FOR SOMEONE ELSE.
WHAT IS IT, YUZURIHA?
I DON'T FEEL WELL. CAN I GO TO THE NURSE'S OFFICE?
WHAT'S WRONG? DID YOU DRINK TOO MUCH MILK?
HA HA HA
THAT'S NOT WHY!
SLAM!
YUZU LOOKS SO PALE...
...
TEACHER, MY STOMACH HURTS TOO.
THAT'S YOUR HEAD, ARISUGAWA.

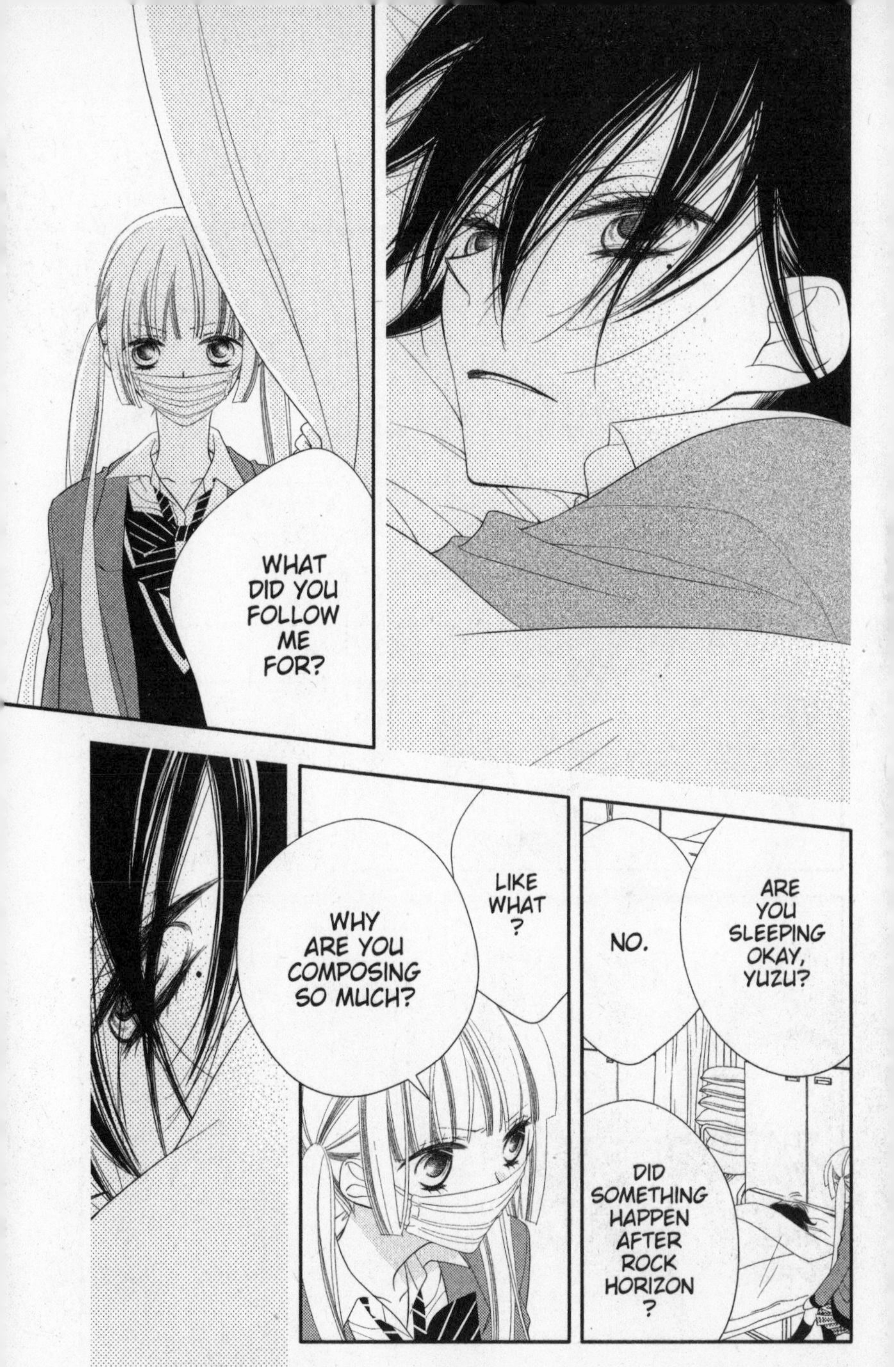
WHAT DID YOU FOLLOW ME FOR?
ARE YOU SLEEPING OKAY, YUZU?
NO.
DID SOMETHING HAPPEN AFTER ROCK HORIZON?
LIKE WHAT?
WHY ARE YOU COMPOSING SO MUCH?

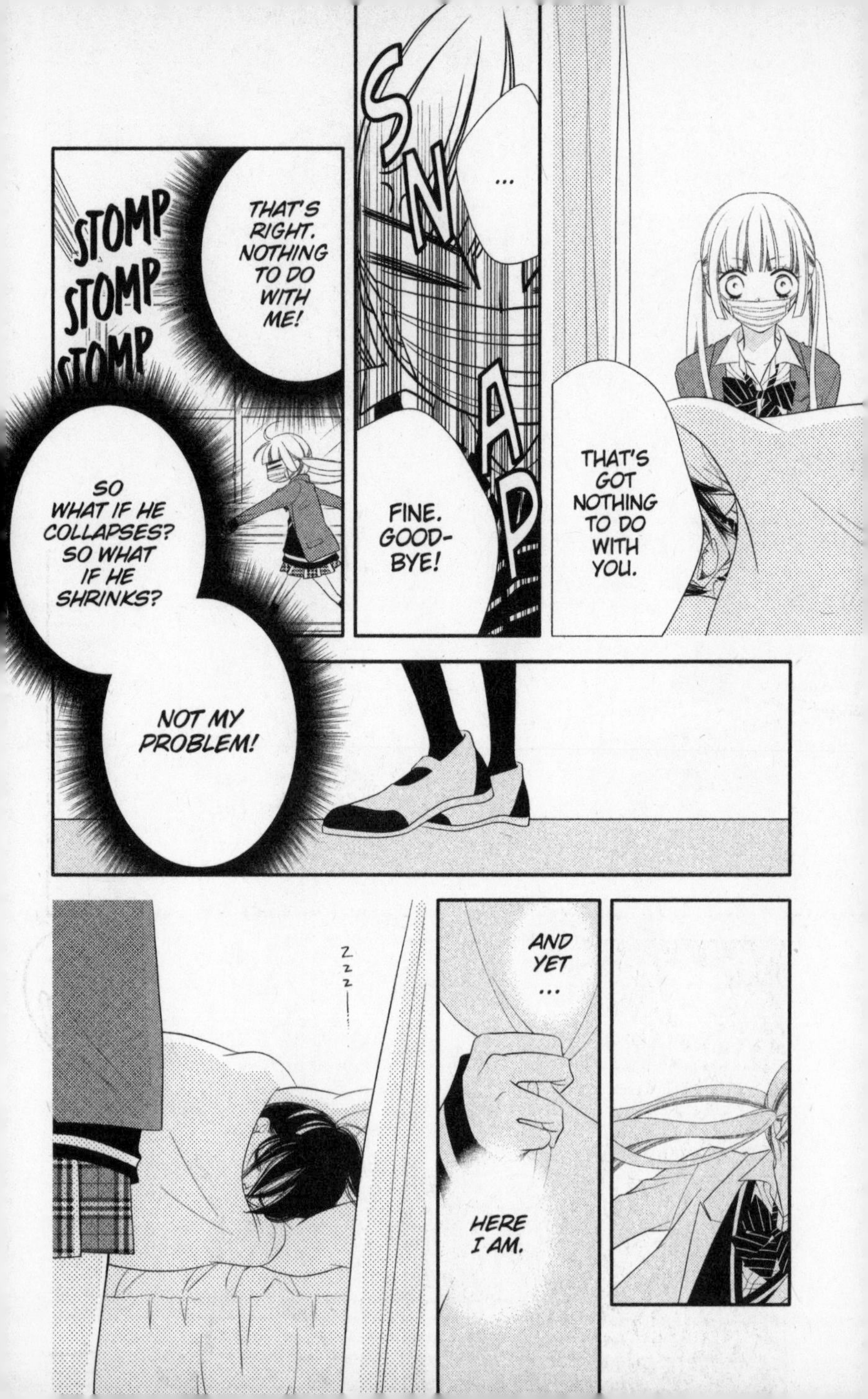
THAT'S GOT NOTHING TO DO WITH YOU.
...
SNAP
FINE. GOOD-BYE!
STOMP STOMP STOMP
THAT'S RIGHT. NOTHING TO DO WITH ME!
SO WHAT IF HE COLLAPSES? SO WHAT IF HE SHRINKS?
NOT MY PROBLEM!
AND YET ...
HERE I AM.
ZZZ

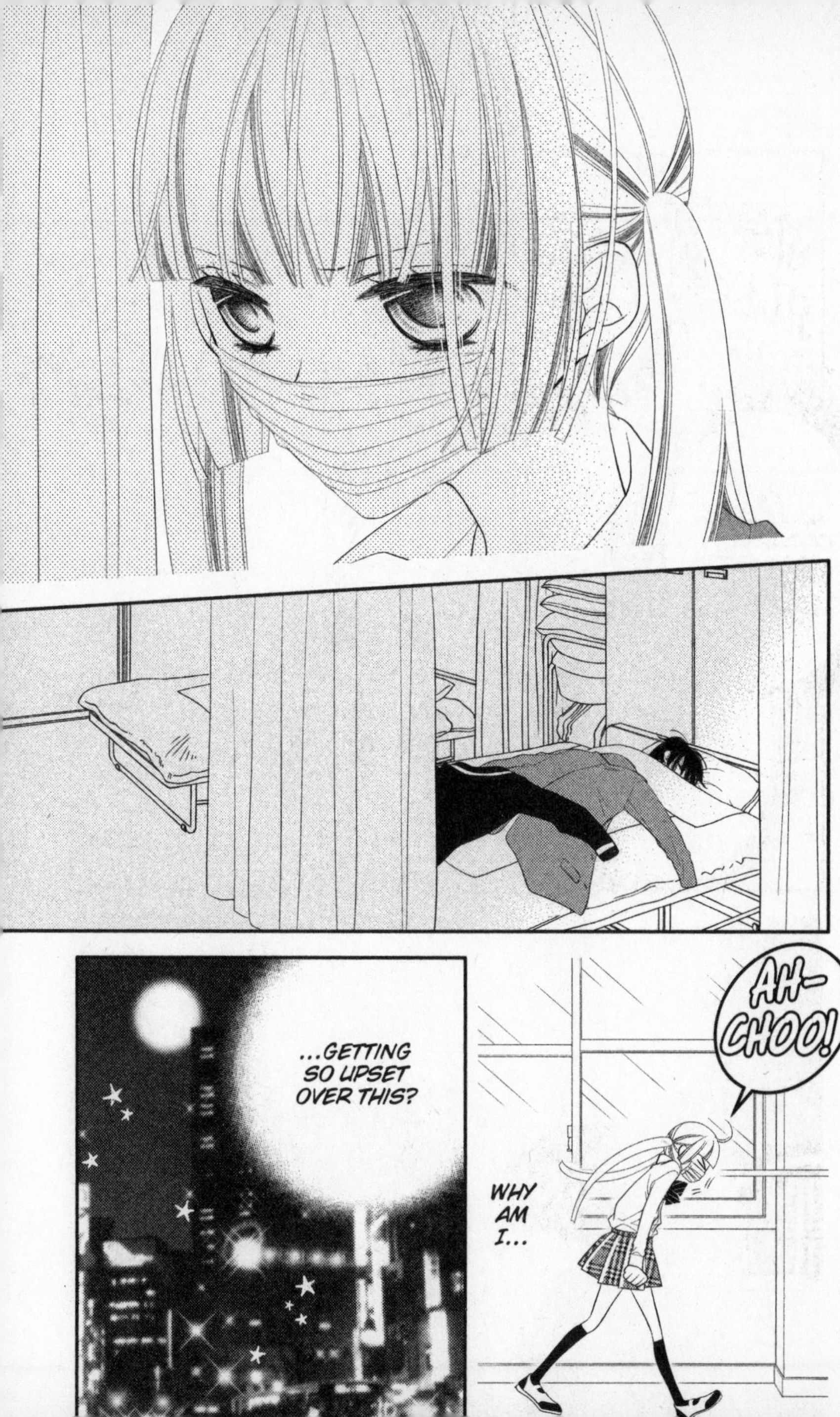
AH-CHOO!
WHY AM I...
...GETTING SO UPSET OVER THIS?

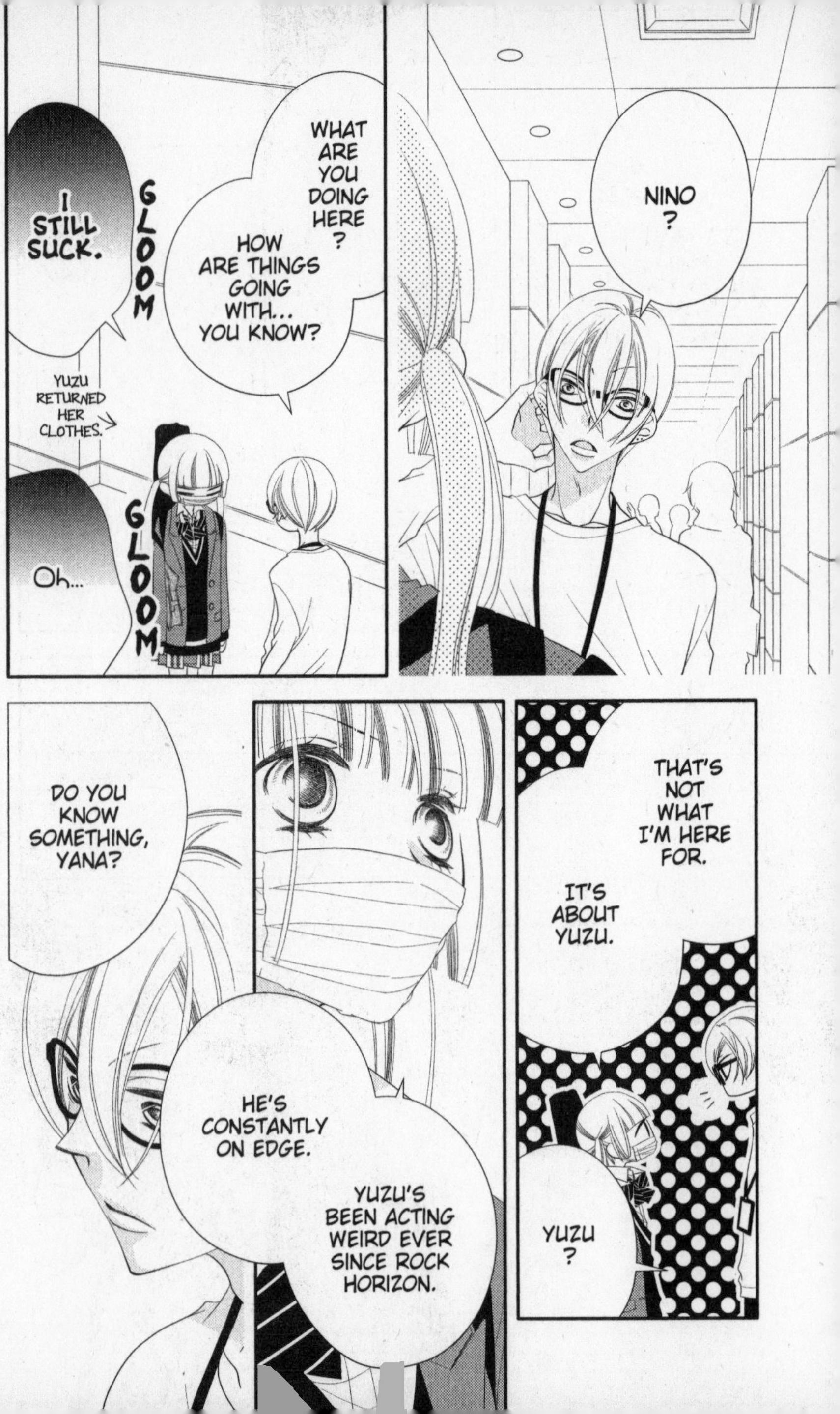
NINO?
WHAT ARE YOU DOING HERE?
HOW ARE THINGS GOING WITH... YOU KNOW?
GLOOM
I STILL SUCK.
GLOOM
YUZU RETURNED HER CLOTHES.
Oh...
THAT'S NOT WHAT I'M HERE FOR.
IT'S ABOUT YUZU.
YUZU?
YUZU'S BEEN ACTING WEIRD EVER SINCE ROCK HORIZON.
HE'S CONSTANTLY ON EDGE.
DO YOU KNOW SOMETHING, YANA?

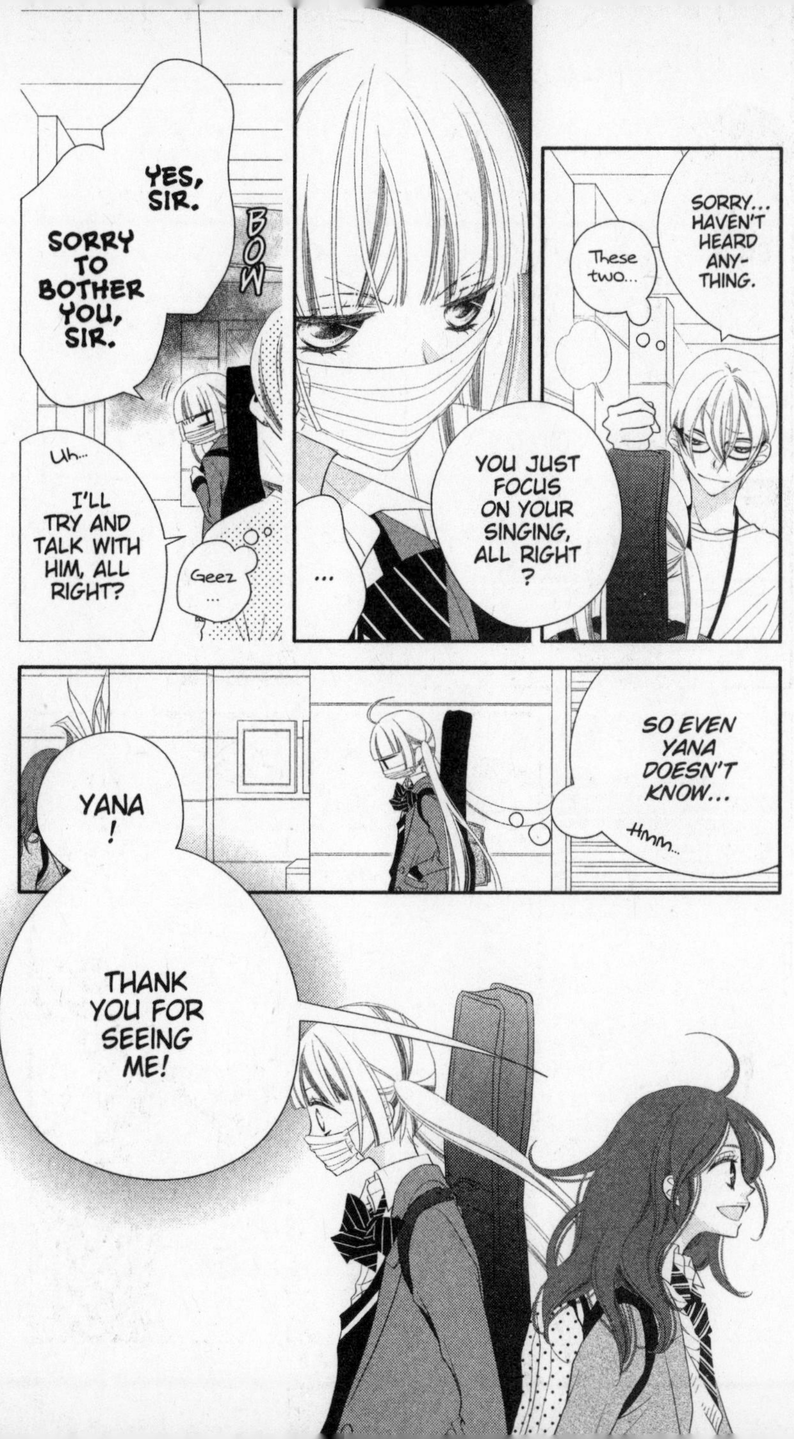
SORRY... HAVEN'T HEARD ANYTHING.
These two...
YOU JUST FOCUS ON YOUR SINGING, ALL RIGHT?
...
YES, SIR.
SORRY TO BOTHER YOU, SIR.
BOW
Uh...
I'LL TRY AND TALK WITH HIM, ALL RIGHT?
Geez...
SO EVEN YANA DOESN'T KNOW...
Hmm...
YANA!
THANK YOU FOR SEEING ME!

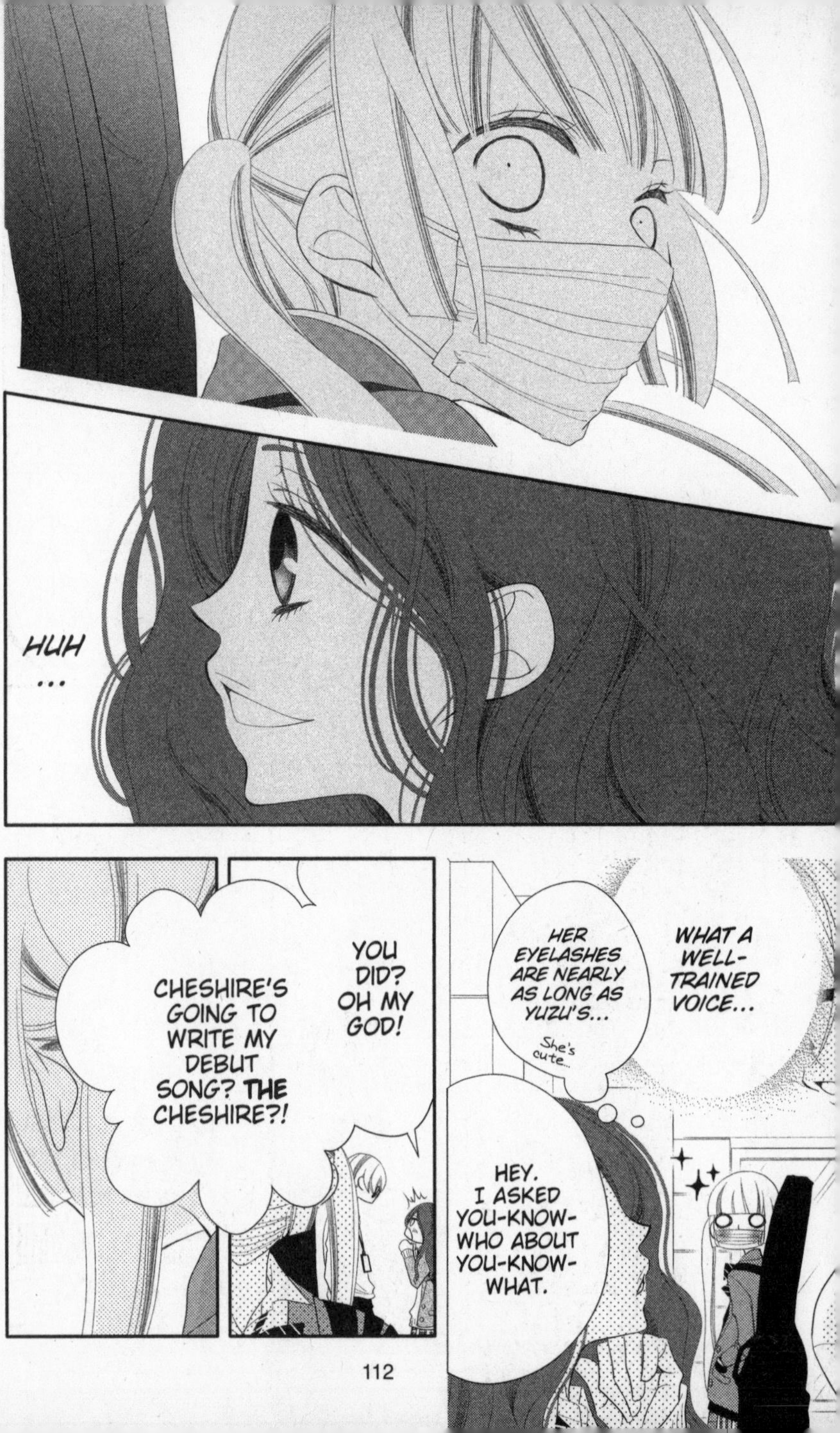
HUH ...
WHAT A WELL-TRAINED VOICE...
HER EYELASHES ARE NEARLY AS LONG AS YUZU'S...
She's cute...
HEY. I ASKED YOU-KNOW-WHO ABOUT YOU-KNOW-WHAT.
YOU DID? OH MY GOD!
CHESHIRE'S GOING TO WRITE MY DEBUT SONG? **THE** CHESHIRE?!

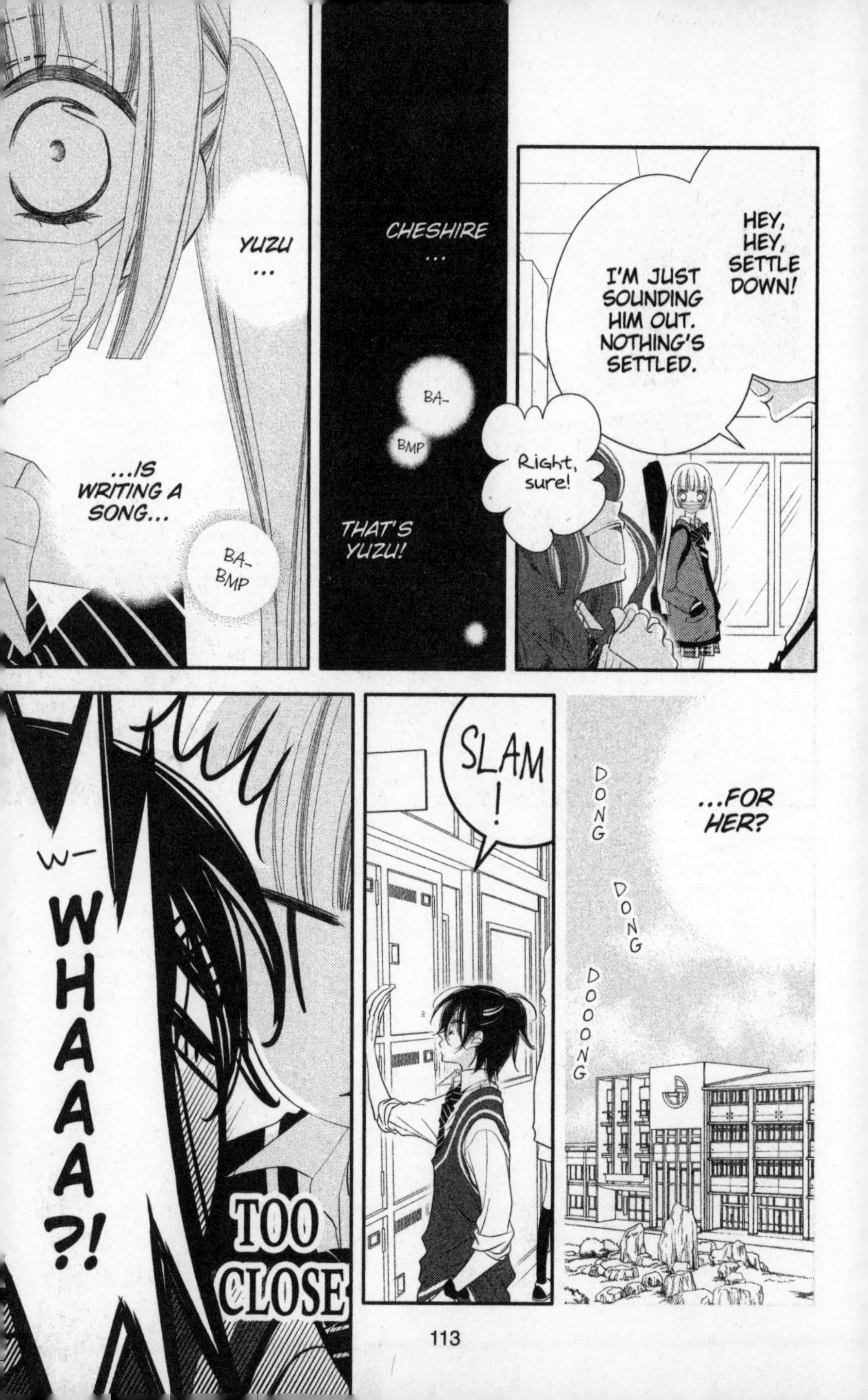
HEY, HEY, SETTLE DOWN!
I'M JUST SOUNDING HIM OUT. NOTHING'S SETTLED.
Right, sure!
CHESHIRE ...
BA- BMP
THAT'S YUZU!
YUZU ...
...IS WRITING A SONG...
BA- BMP
...FOR HER?
DONG DONG DOOOONG
SLAM!
W—
WHAAAA?!
TOO CLOSE

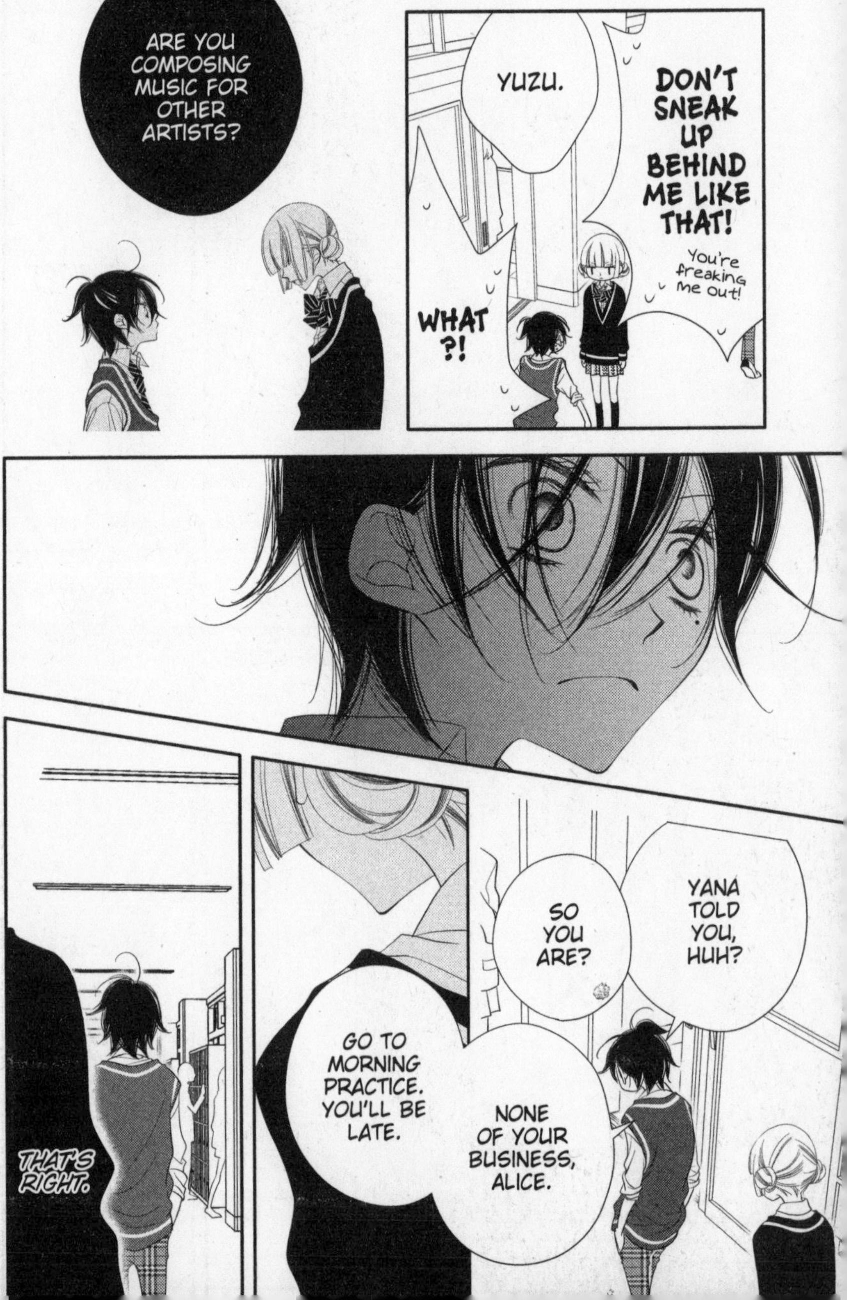
YUZU.
DON'T SNEAK UP BEHIND ME LIKE THAT!
You're freaking me out!
WHAT ?!
ARE YOU COMPOSING MUSIC FOR OTHER ARTISTS?
YANA TOLD YOU, HUH?
SO YOU ARE?
NONE OF YOUR BUSINESS, ALICE.
GO TO MORNING PRACTICE. YOU'LL BE LATE.
THAT'S RIGHT.

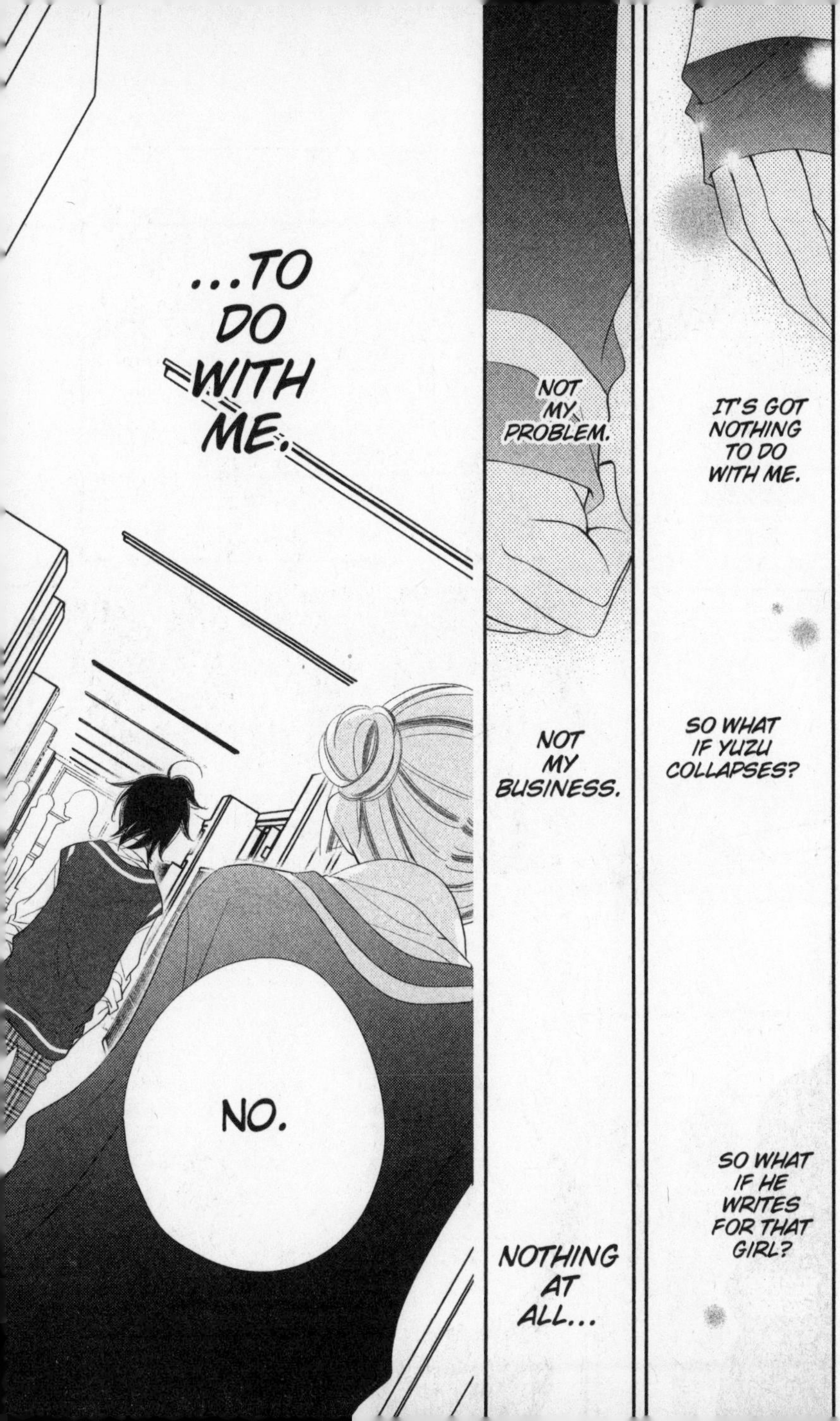
IT'S GOT NOTHING TO DO WITH ME.
SO WHAT IF YUZU COLLAPSES?
SO WHAT IF HE WRITES FOR THAT GIRL?
NOT MY PROBLEM.
NOT MY BUSINESS.
NOTHING AT ALL...
...TO DO WITH ME.
NO.

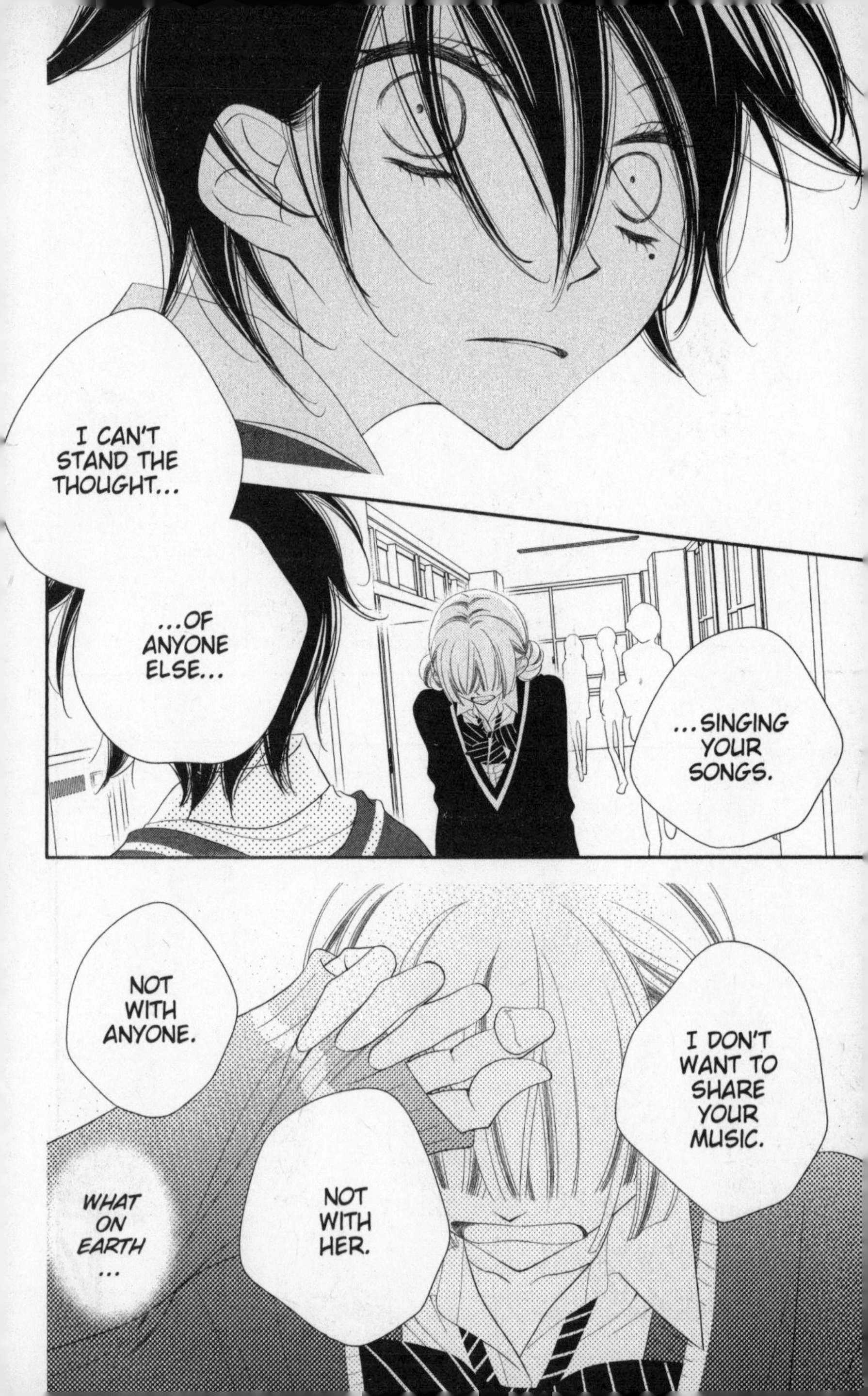
I CAN'T STAND THE THOUGHT...
...OF ANYONE ELSE...
...SINGING YOUR SONGS.
I DON'T WANT TO SHARE YOUR MUSIC.
NOT WITH ANYONE.
NOT WITH HER.
WHAT ON EARTH ...

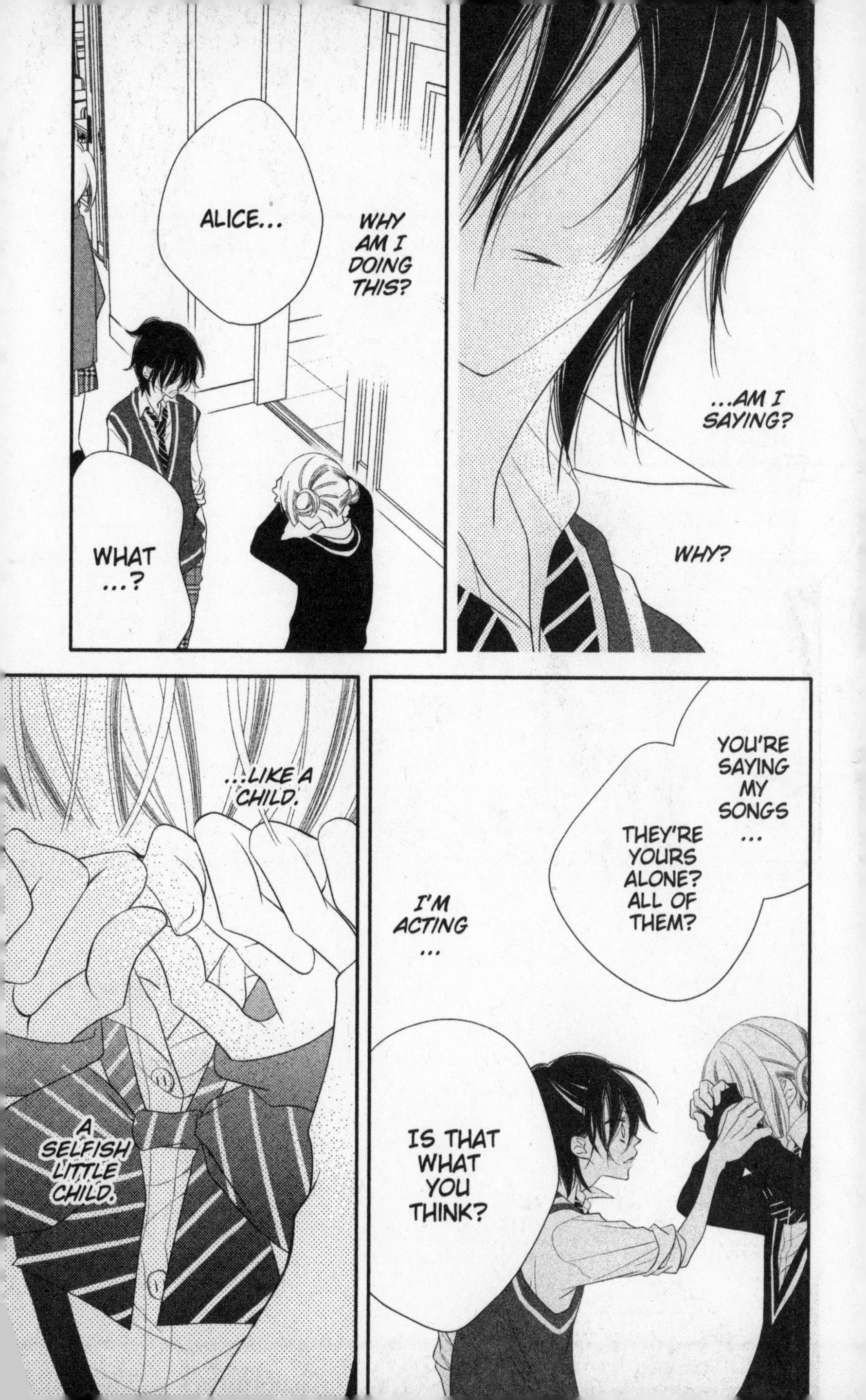
...AM I SAYING?
WHY?
ALICE...
WHY AM I DOING THIS?
WHAT ...?
YOU'RE SAYING MY SONGS ...
THEY'RE YOURS ALONE? ALL OF THEM?
I'M ACTING ...
IS THAT WHAT YOU THINK?
...LIKE A CHILD.
A SELFISH LITTLE CHILD.

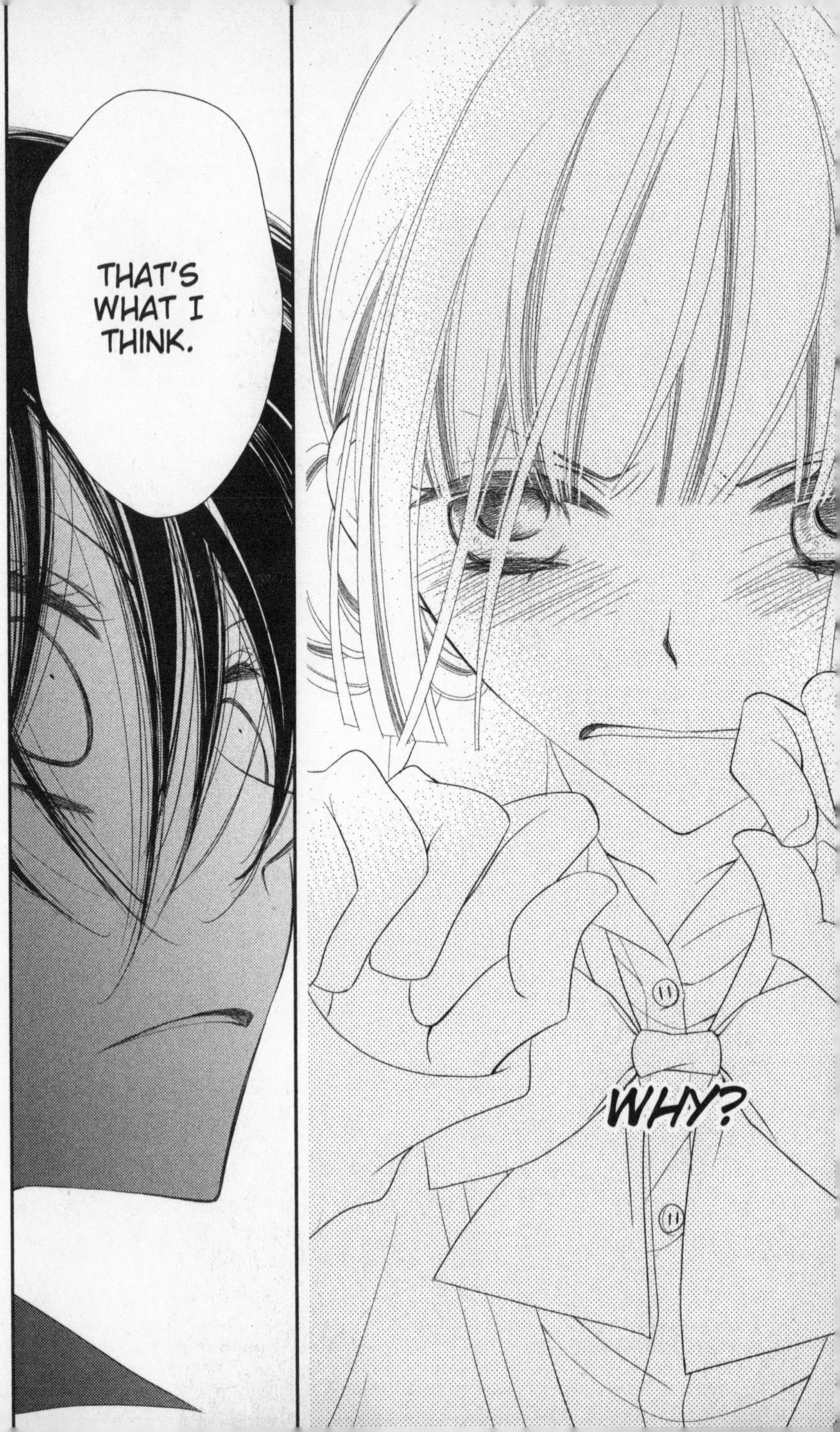
WHY?
THAT'S WHAT I THINK.

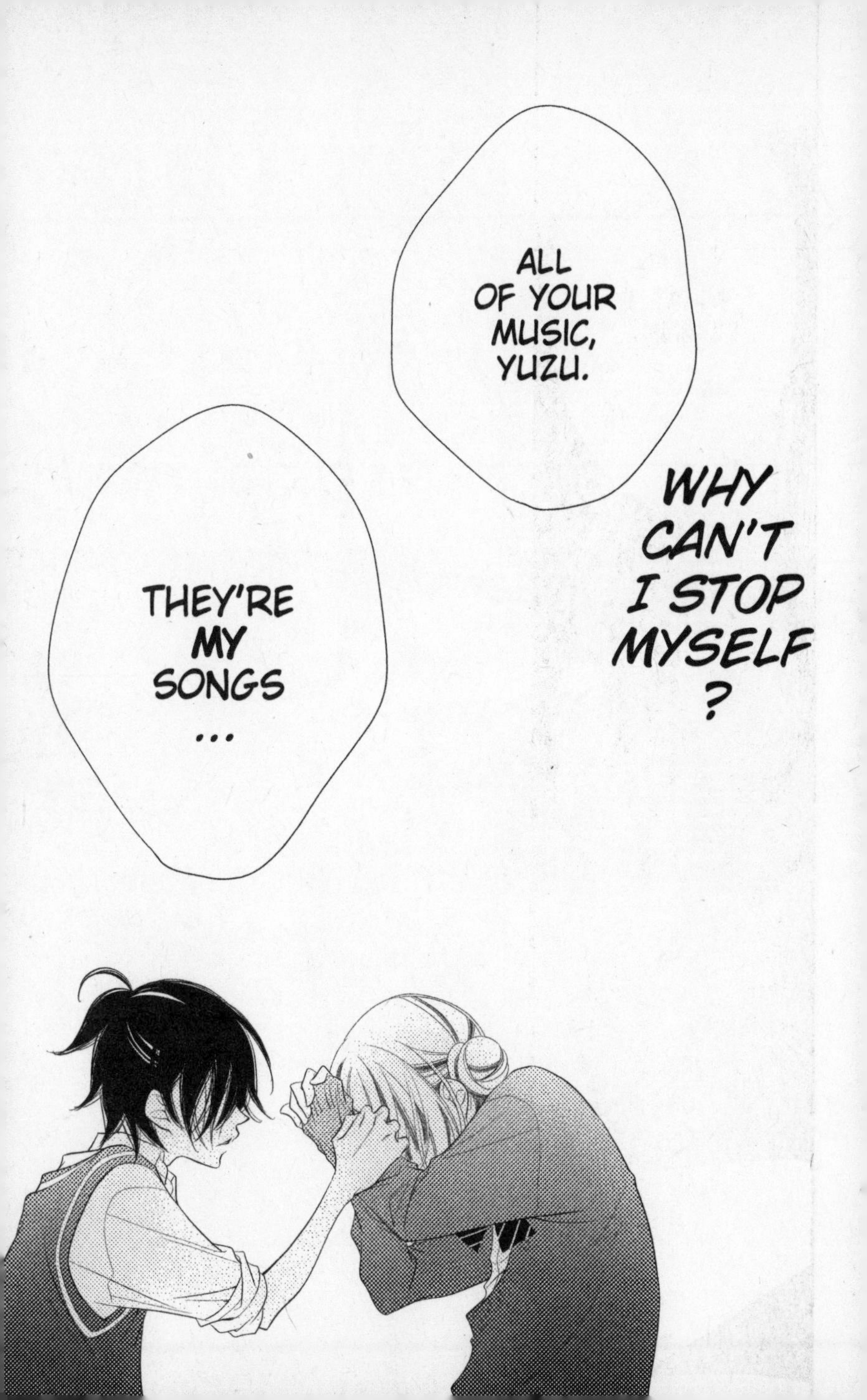
ALL OF YOUR MUSIC, YUZU.
THEY'RE MY SONGS ...
WHY CAN'T I STOP MYSELF ?

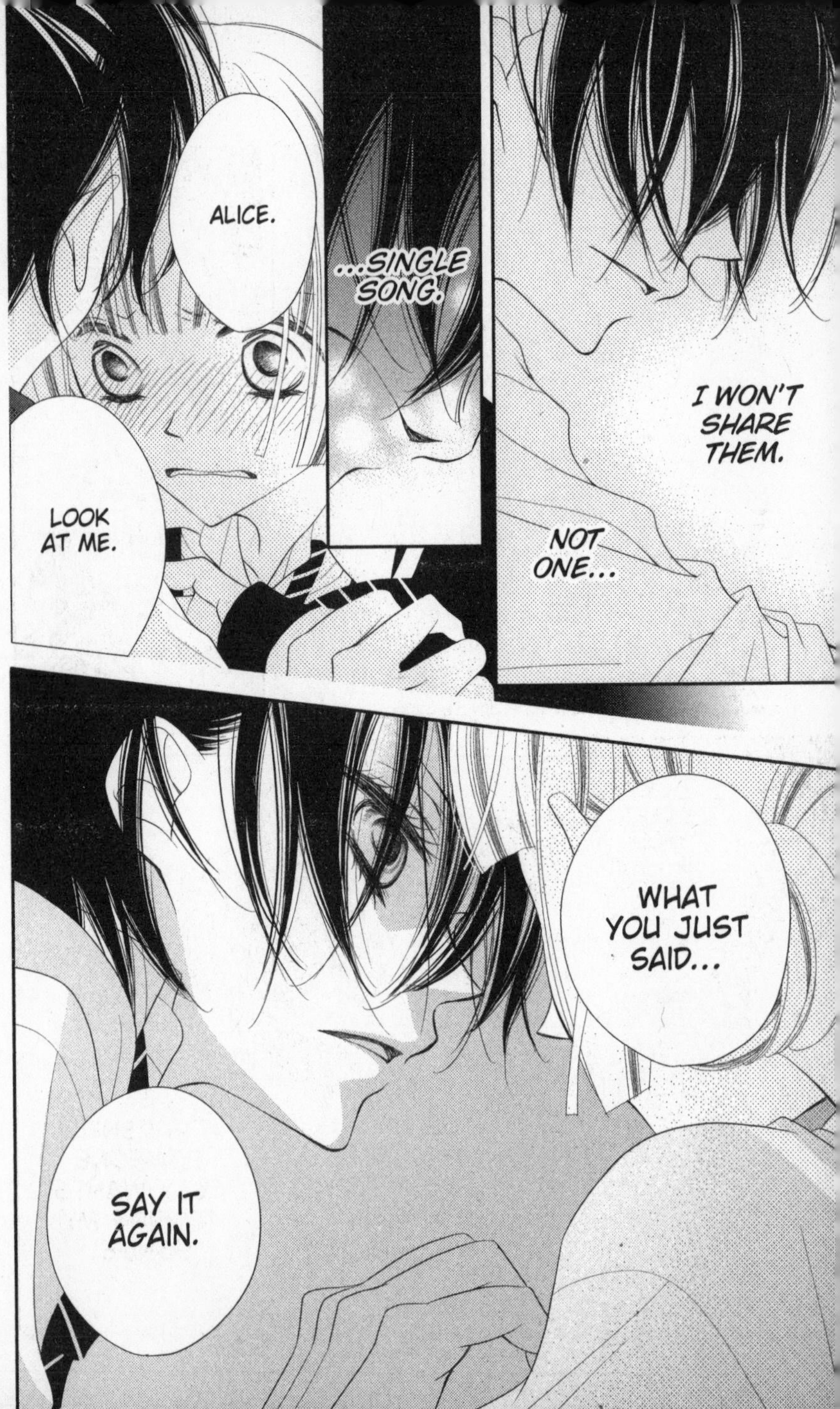
I WON'T SHARE THEM.
NOT ONE...
...SINGLE SONG.
ALICE.
LOOK AT ME.
WHAT YOU JUST SAID...
SAY IT AGAIN.

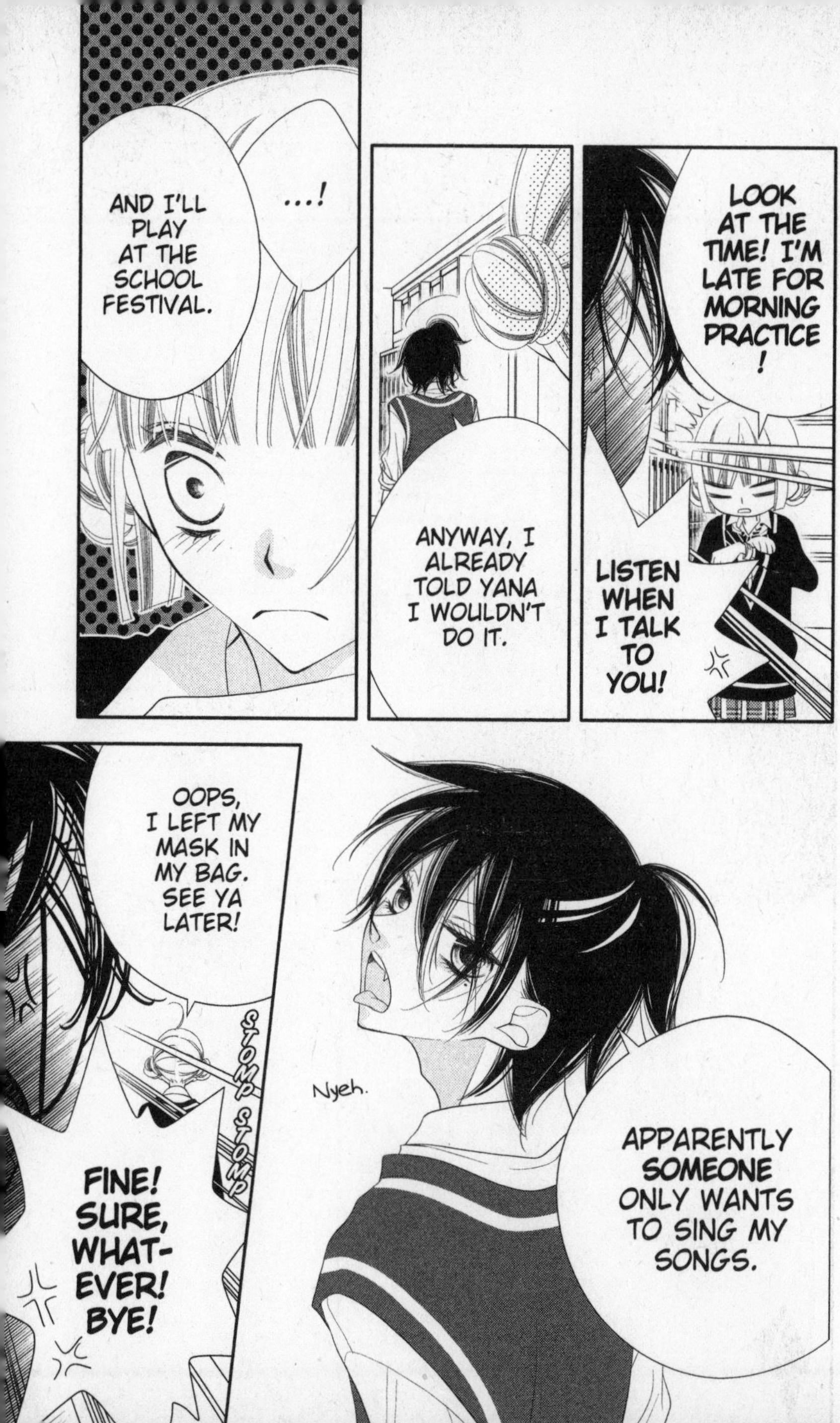
LOOK AT THE TIME! I'M LATE FOR MORNING PRACTICE!
LISTEN WHEN I TALK TO YOU!
ANYWAY, I ALREADY TOLD YANA I WOULDN'T DO IT.
...!
AND I'LL PLAY AT THE SCHOOL FESTIVAL.
APPARENTLY SOMEONE ONLY WANTS TO SING MY SONGS.
Nyeh.
OOPS, I LEFT MY MASK IN MY BAG. SEE YA LATER!
STOMP STOMP STOMP
FINE! SURE, WHAT-EVER! BYE!

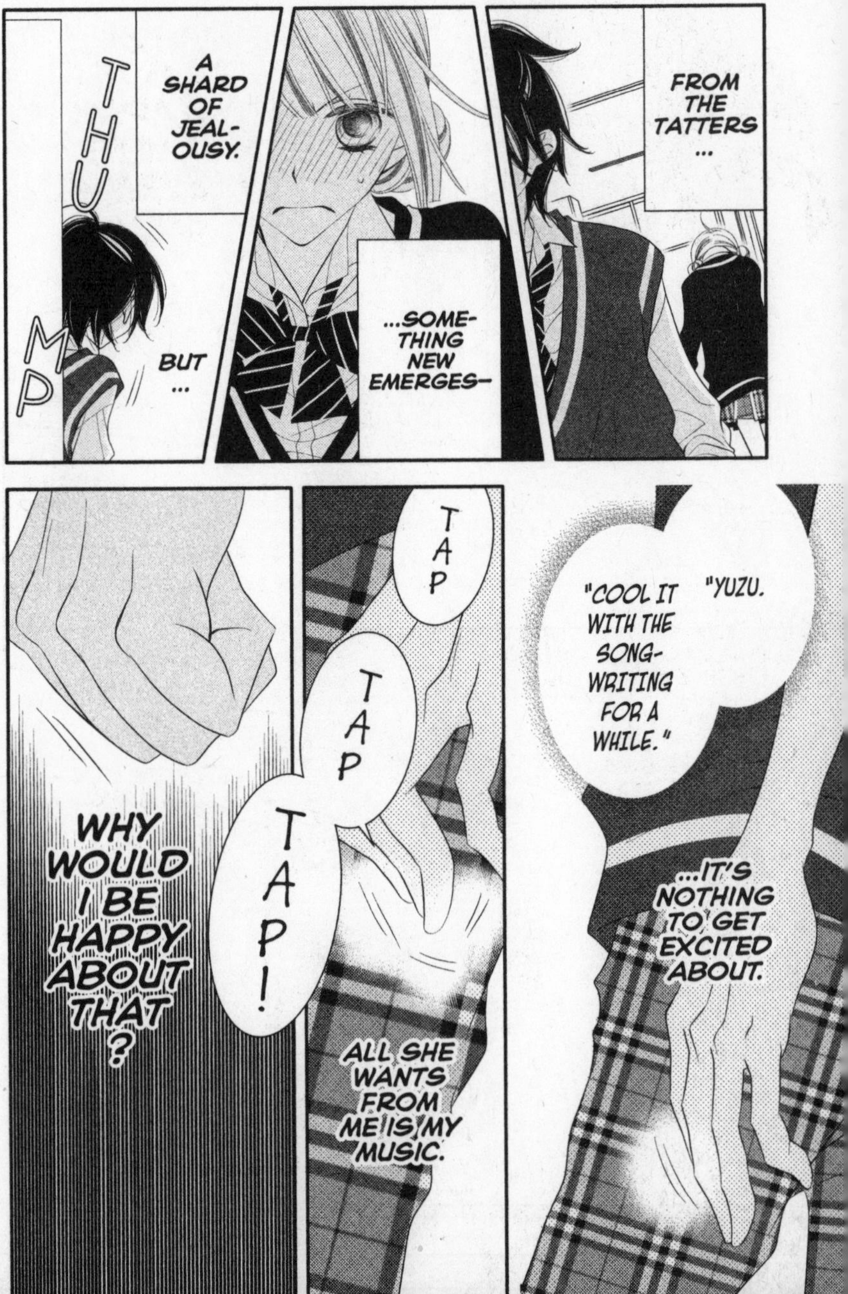
FROM THE TATTERS...
...SOMETHING NEW EMERGES—
A SHARD OF JEALOUSY.
BUT...
THUUMP
"YUZU.
"COOL IT WITH THE SONGWRITING FOR A WHILE."
...IT'S NOTHING TO GET EXCITED ABOUT.
TAP
TAP
TAP!
ALL SHE WANTS FROM ME IS MY MUSIC.
WHY WOULD I BE HAPPY ABOUT THAT?

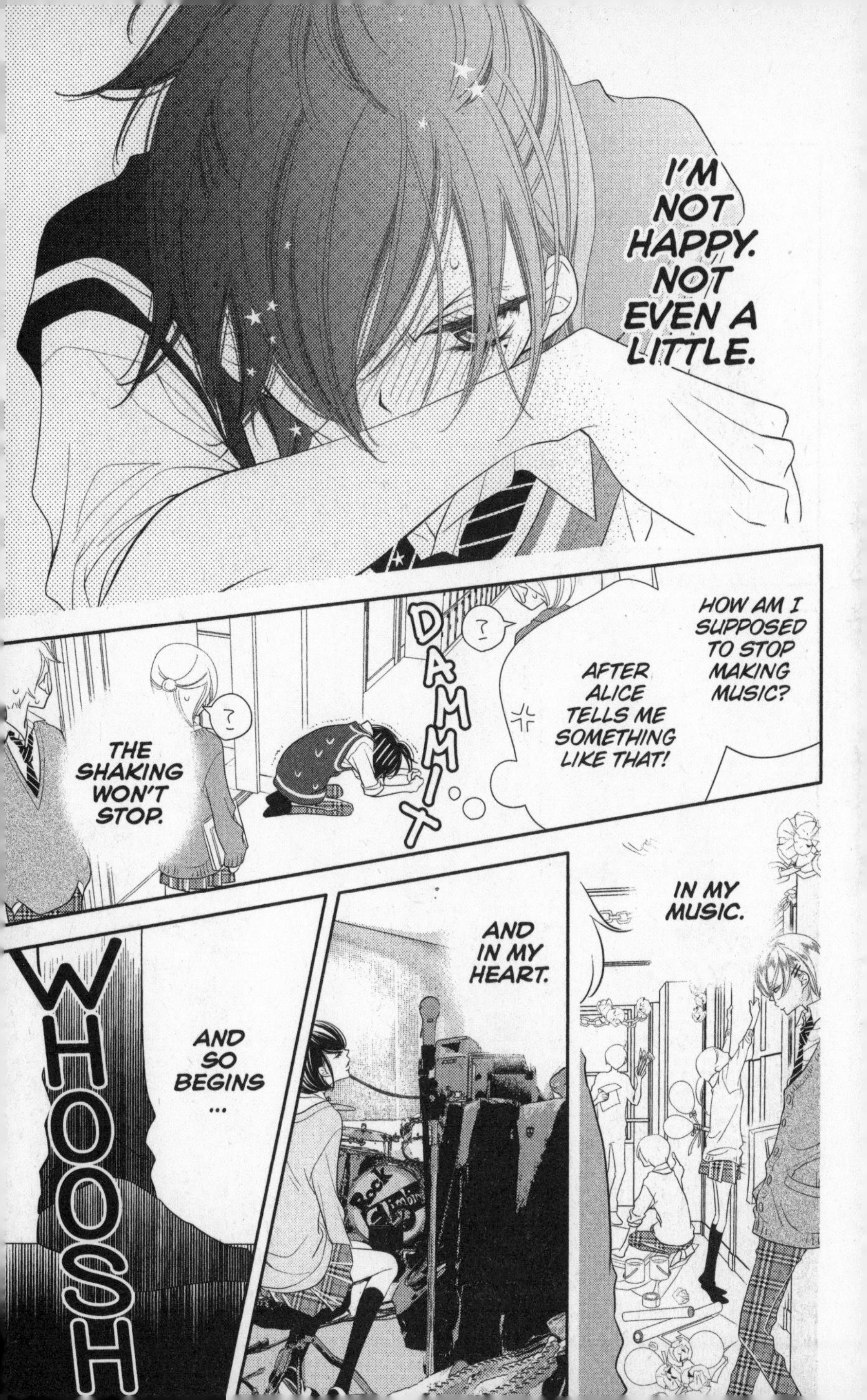
I'M NOT HAPPY. NOT EVEN A LITTLE.
HOW AM I SUPPOSED TO STOP MAKING MUSIC?
AFTER ALICE TELLS ME SOMETHING LIKE THAT!
?
DAMMIT
?
THE SHAKING WON'T STOP.
IN MY MUSIC.
AND IN MY HEART.
AND SO BEGINS ...
WHOOSH

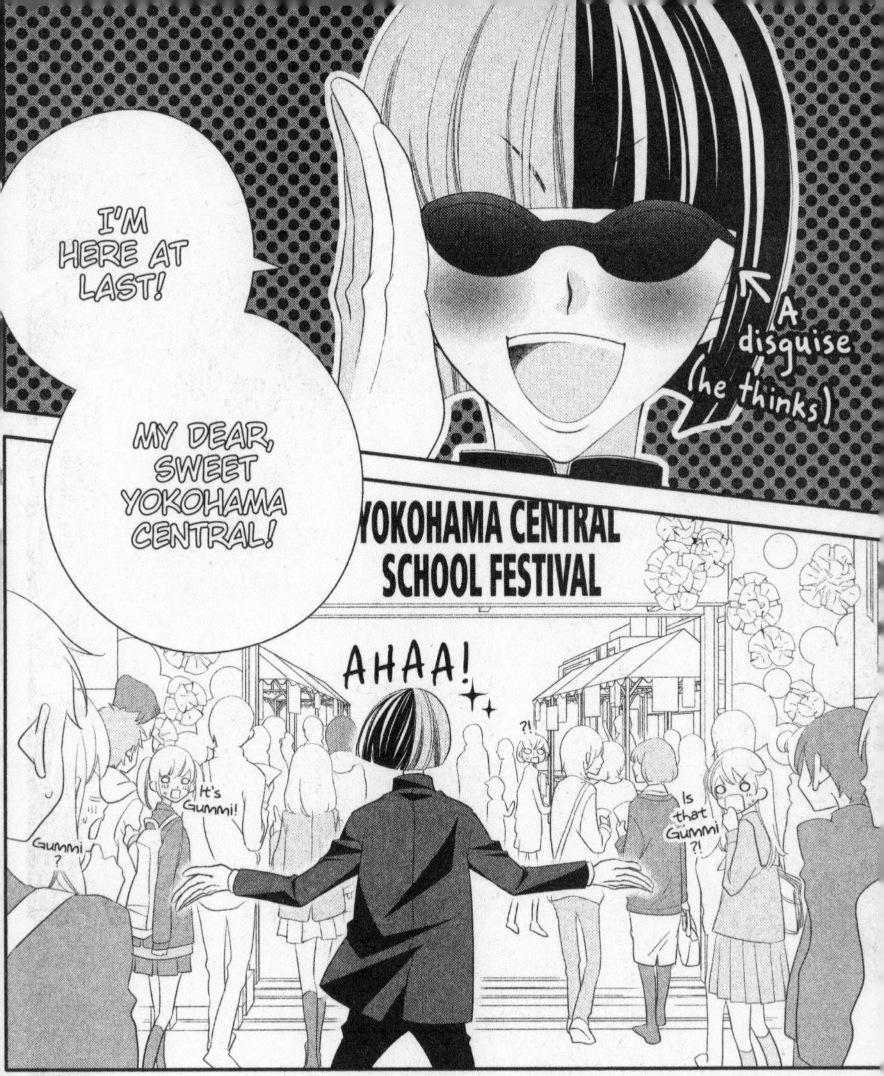
I'M HERE AT LAST!
MY DEAR, SWEET YOKOHAMA CENTRAL!
A disguise (he thinks)
YOKOHAMA CENTRAL SCHOOL FESTIVAL
AHAA!
Is that Gummi?!
?!
It's Gummi!
Gummi?

...OUR SCHOOL FESTIVAL.

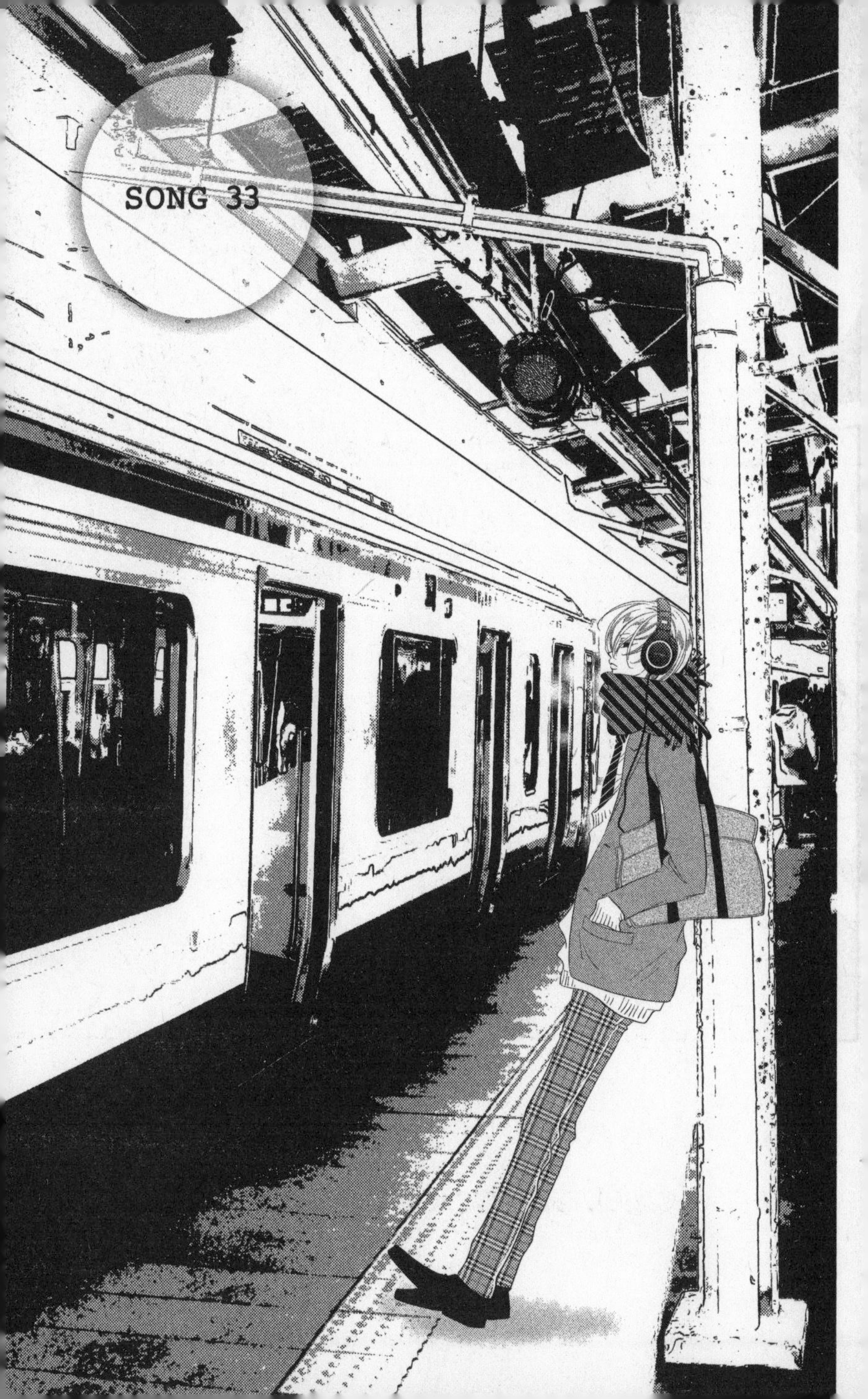
SONG 33

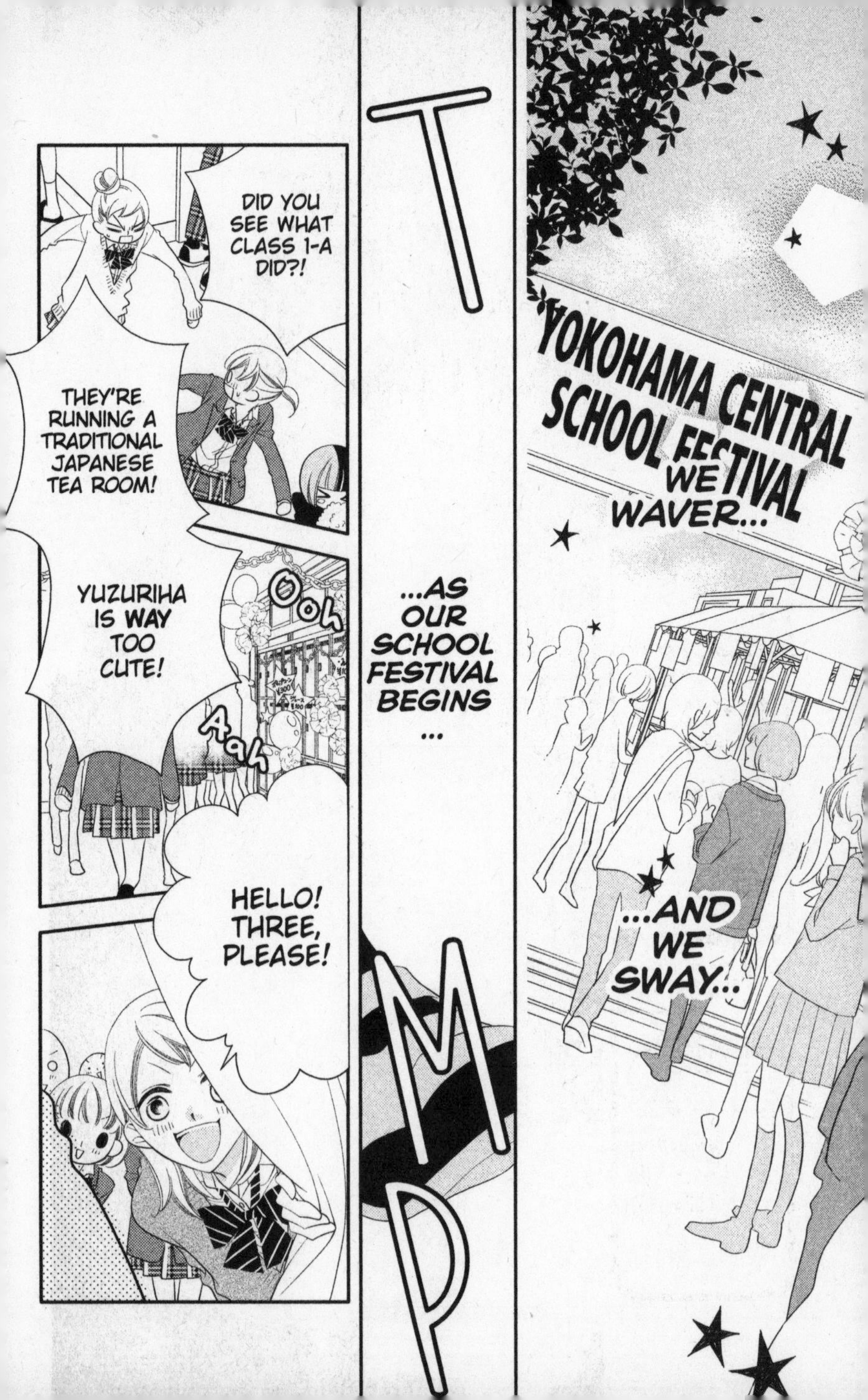
YOKOHAMA CENTRAL SCHOOL FESTIVAL
WE WAVER...
...AND WE SWAY...
TMP
...AS OUR SCHOOL FESTIVAL BEGINS...
DID YOU SEE WHAT CLASS 1-A DID?!
THEY'RE RUNNING A TRADITIONAL JAPANESE TEA ROOM!
Ooh
YUZURIHA IS WAY TOO CUTE!
Aah
HELLO! THREE, PLEASE!

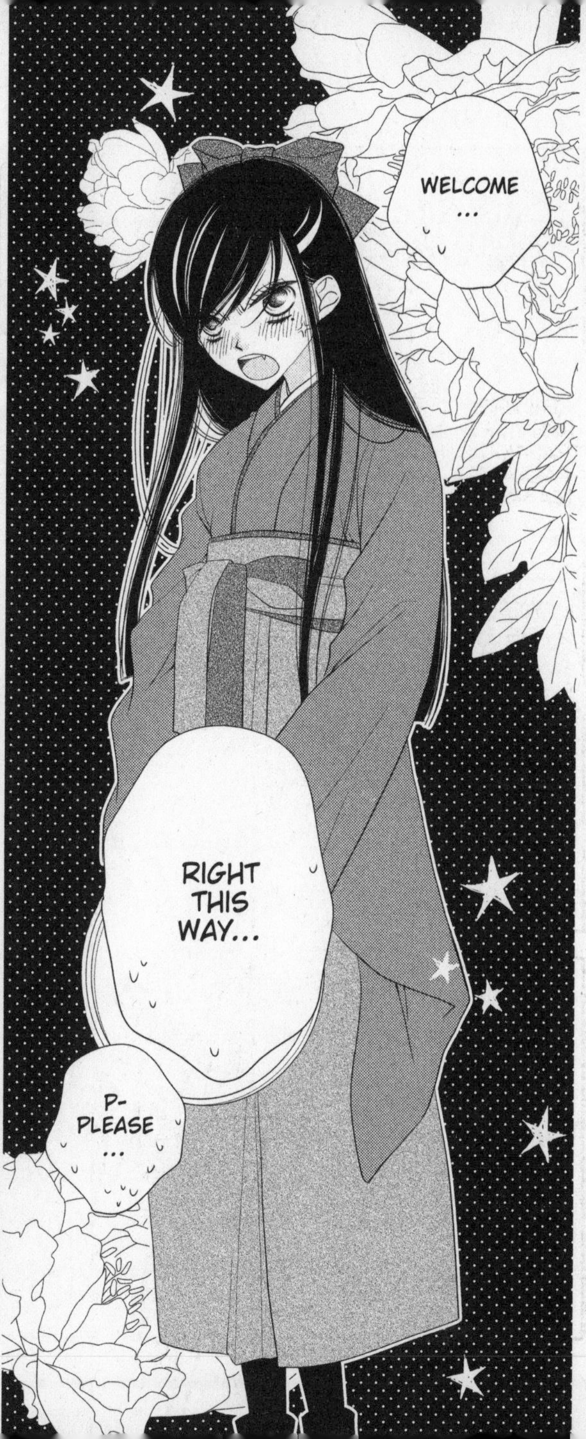
WELCOME ...
RIGHT THIS WAY...
P-PLEASE ...

5

Now that I've gone fully digital, my assistants have had to convert to digital as well.

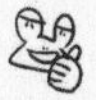

Now we just do all the sketch checking with screenshots using Dropbox It's so easy, but lately...

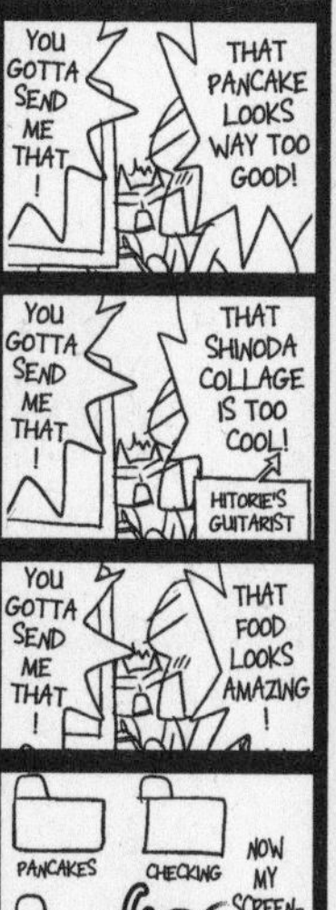
THAT PANCAKE LOOKS WAY TOO GOOD!
YOU GOTTA SEND ME THAT!
THAT SHINODA COLLAGE IS TOO COOL!
HITORIE'S GUITARIST
YOU GOTTA SEND ME THAT!
THAT FOOD LOOKS AMAZING!
YOU GOTTA SEND ME THAT!
NOW MY SCREEN-SHOT FOLDER LOOKS LIKE THIS.
PANCAKES
CHECKING
SHINODA
RECIPES
CHAOS

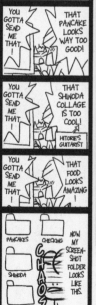

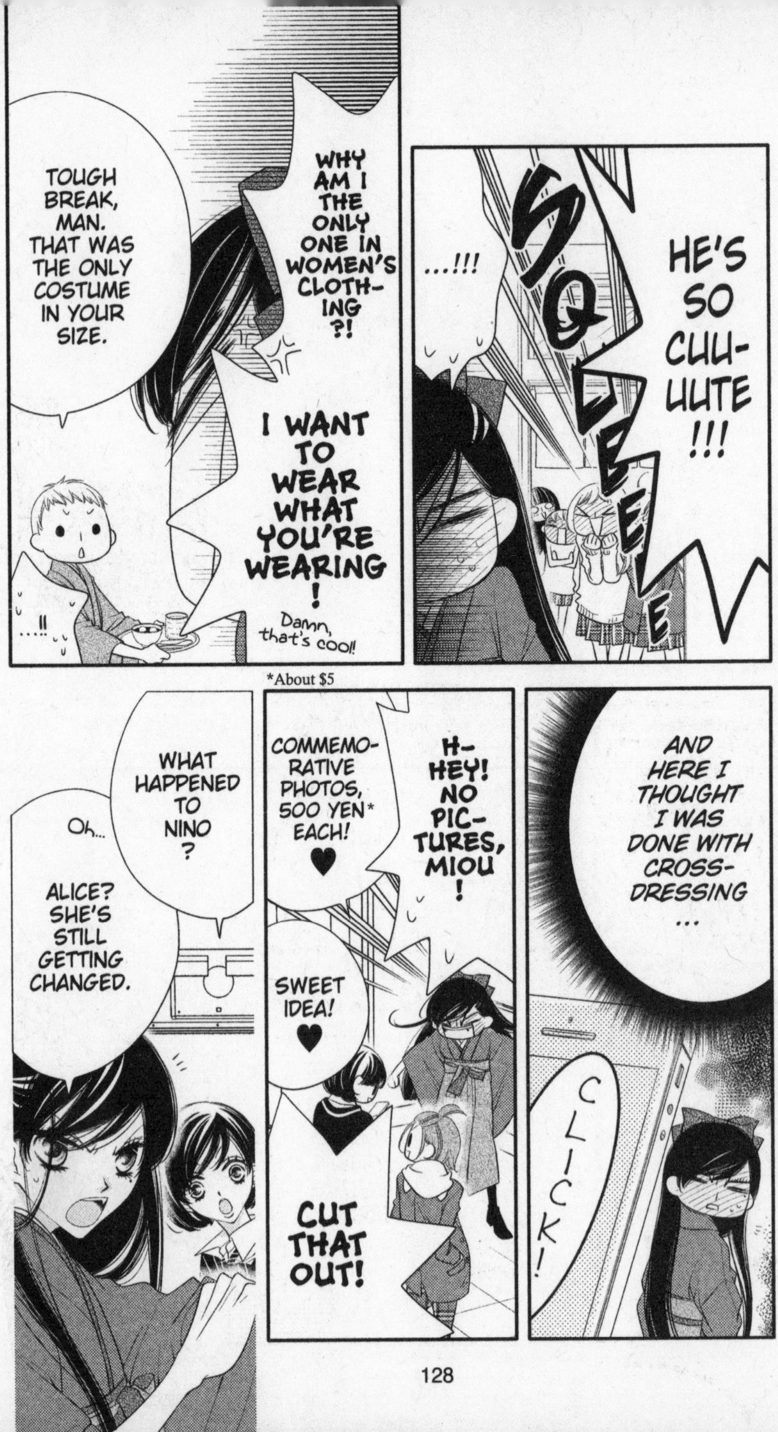
HE'S SO CUUUTE!!!
SQUEEE
...!!!
WHY AM I THE ONLY ONE IN WOMEN'S CLOTHING?!
TOUGH BREAK, MAN. THAT WAS THE ONLY COSTUME IN YOUR SIZE.
I WANT TO WEAR WHAT YOU'RE WEARING!
Damn, that's cool!
....!!
AND HERE I THOUGHT I WAS DONE WITH CROSS-DRESSING...
CLICK!
H-HEY! NO PICTURES, MIOU!
COMMEMORATIVE PHOTOS, 500 YEN* EACH! ♥
SWEET IDEA! ♥
CUT THAT OUT!
WHAT HAPPENED TO NINO?
Oh...
ALICE? SHE'S STILL GETTING CHANGED.

*About $5

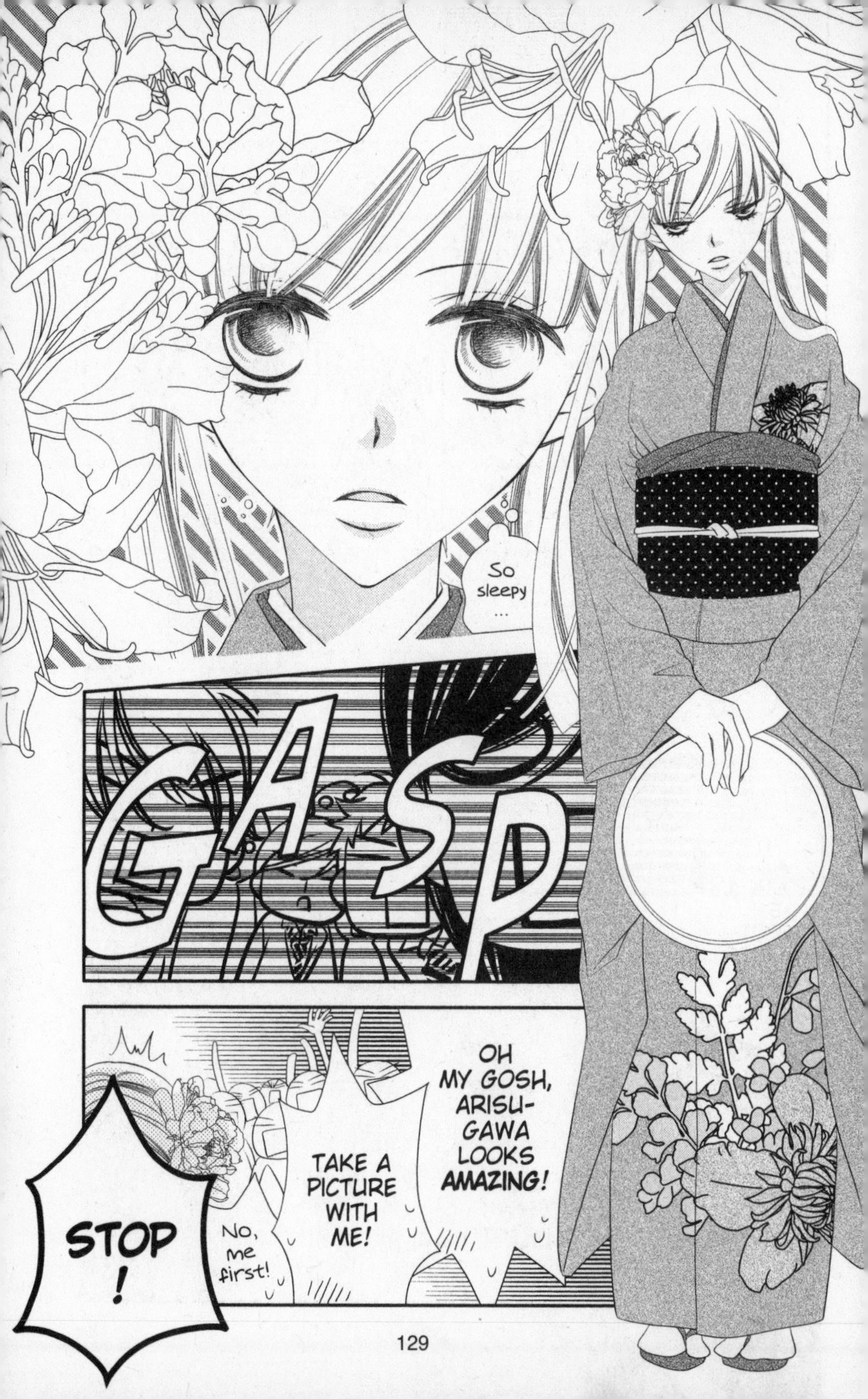
So sleepy ...
GASP
OH MY GOSH, ARISUGAWA LOOKS AMAZING!
TAKE A PICTURE WITH ME!
No, me first!
STOP!

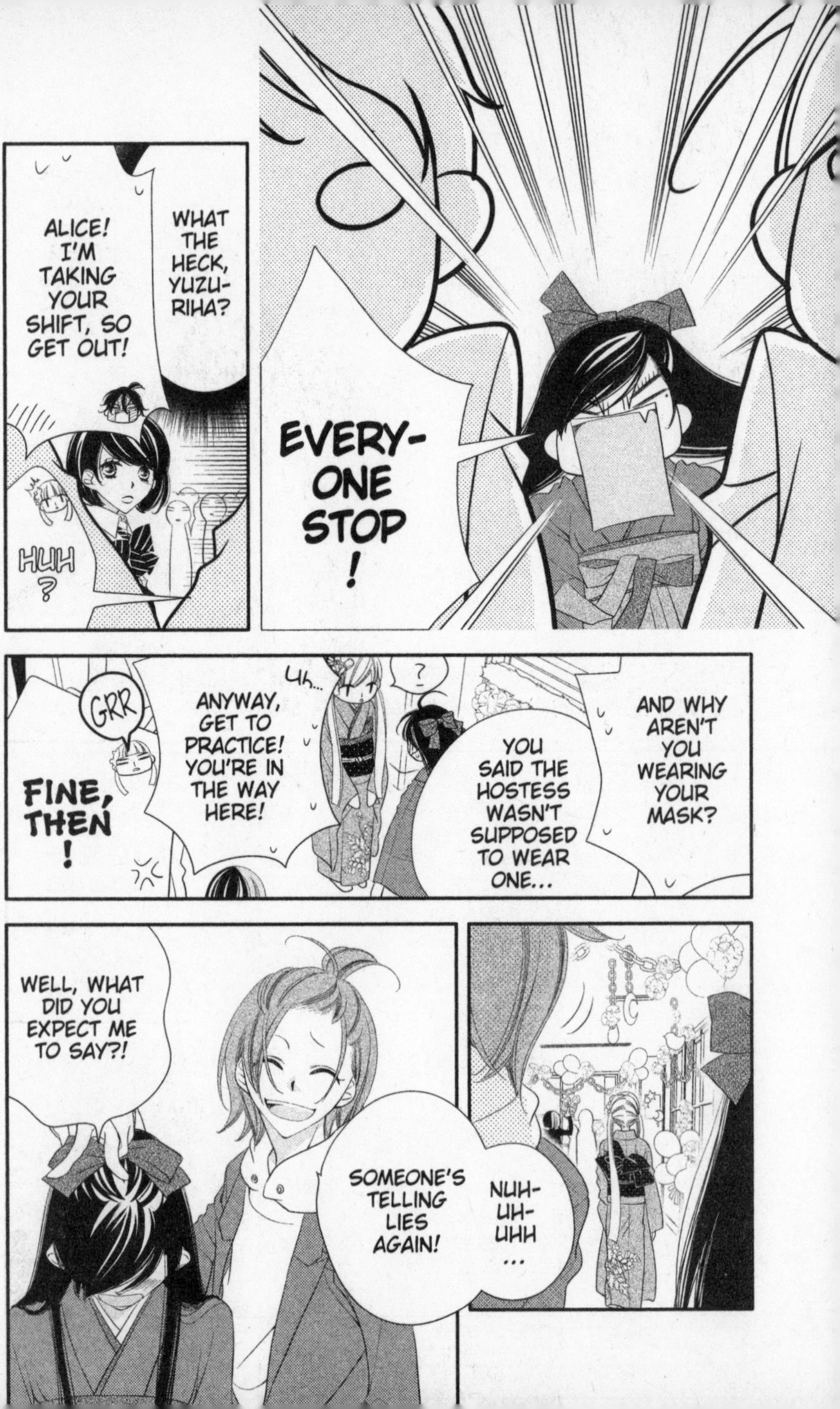
EVERY-ONE STOP!
WHAT THE HECK, YUZURIHA?
ALICE! I'M TAKING YOUR SHIFT, SO GET OUT!
HUH?
AND WHY AREN'T YOU WEARING YOUR MASK?
YOU SAID THE HOSTESS WASN'T SUPPOSED TO WEAR ONE...
?
Uh...
ANYWAY, GET TO PRACTICE! YOU'RE IN THE WAY HERE!
GRR
FINE, THEN!
NUH-UH-UHH...
SOMEONE'S TELLING LIES AGAIN!
WELL, WHAT DID YOU EXPECT ME TO SAY?!

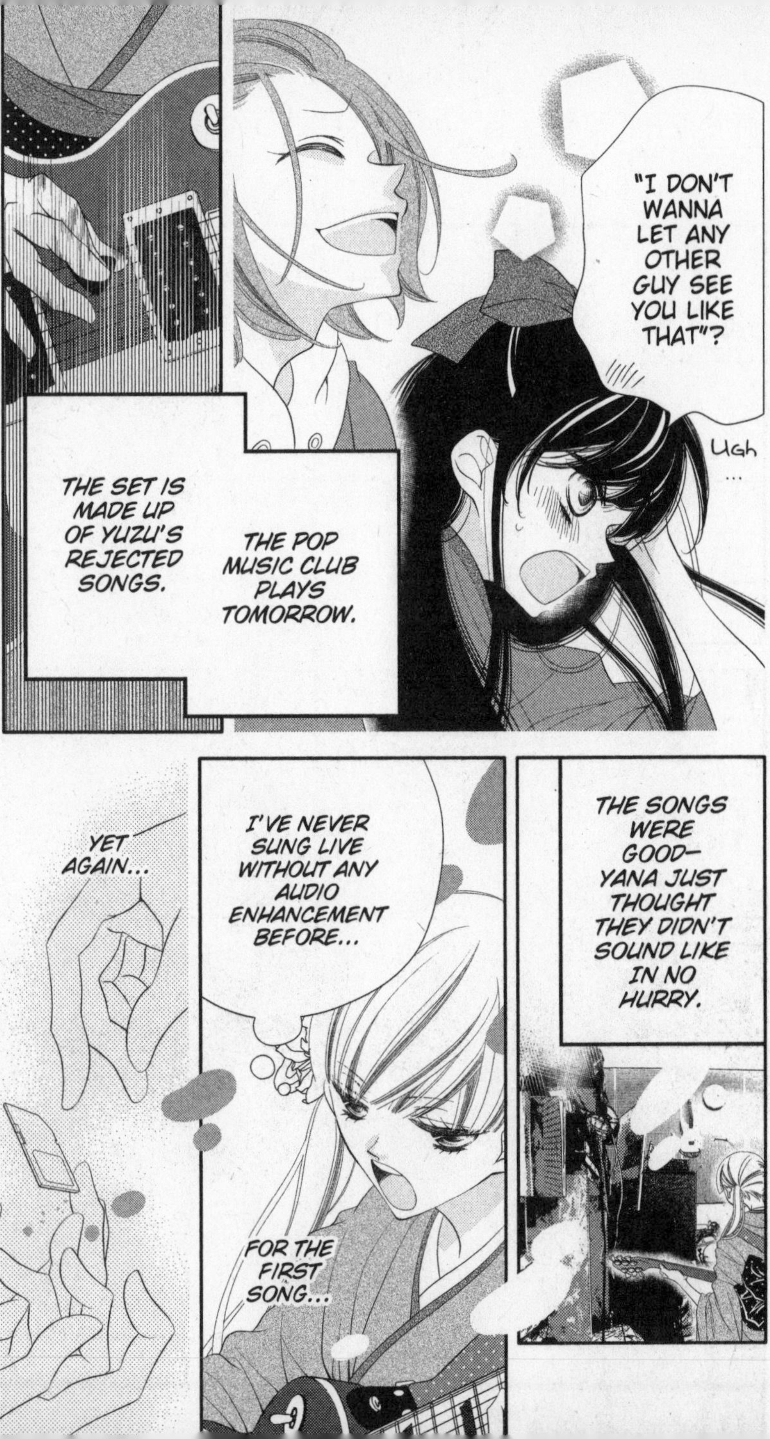
"I DON'T WANNA LET ANY OTHER GUY SEE YOU LIKE THAT"?
Ugh...
THE POP MUSIC CLUB PLAYS TOMORROW.
THE SET IS MADE UP OF YUZU'S REJECTED SONGS.
THE SONGS WERE GOOD— YANA JUST THOUGHT THEY DIDN'T SOUND LIKE IN NO HURRY.
I'VE NEVER SUNG LIVE WITHOUT ANY AUDIO ENHANCEMENT BEFORE...
FOR THE FIRST SONG...
YET AGAIN...

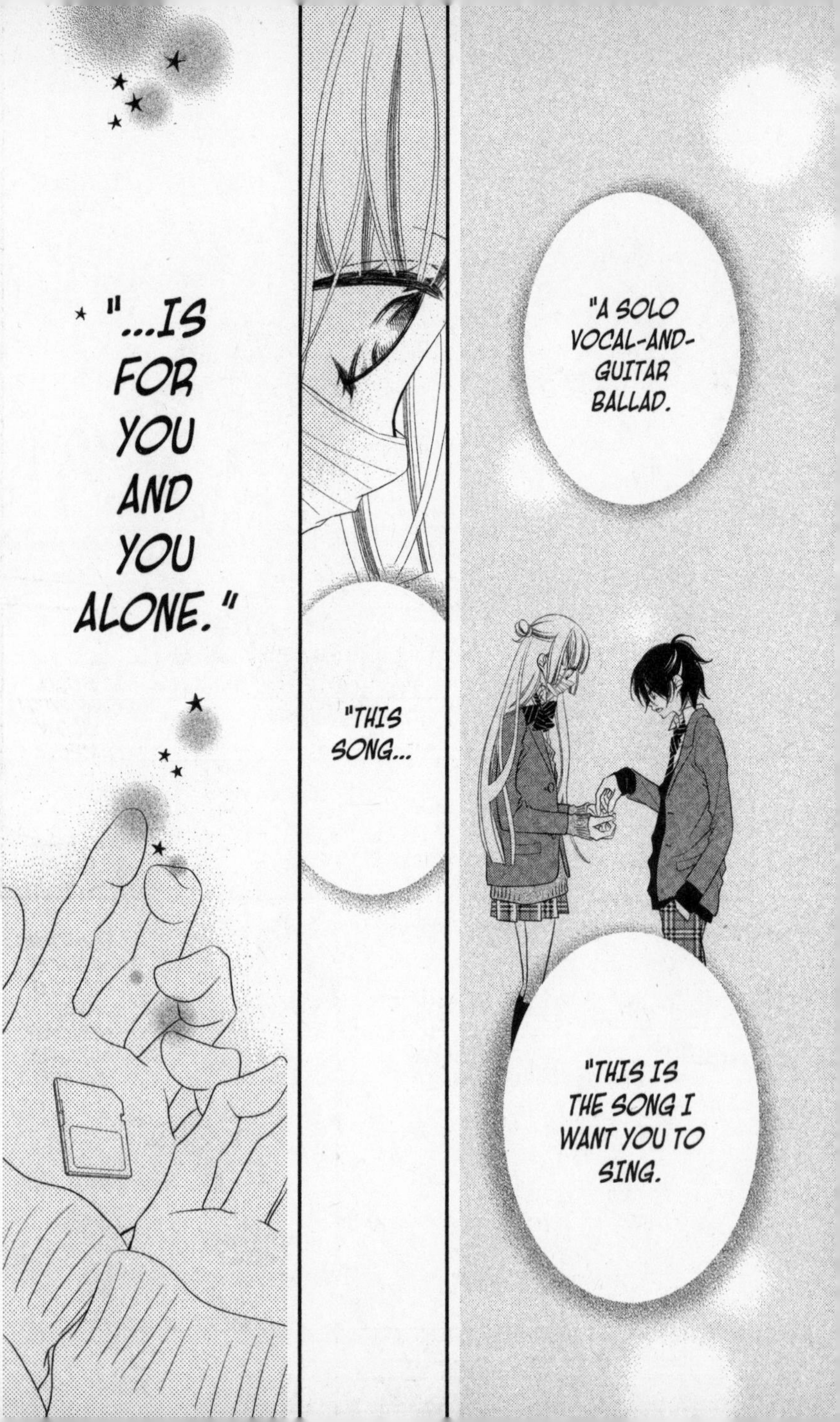
"A SOLO VOCAL-AND-GUITAR BALLAD.
"THIS IS THE SONG I WANT YOU TO SING.
"THIS SONG...
"...IS FOR YOU AND YOU ALONE."

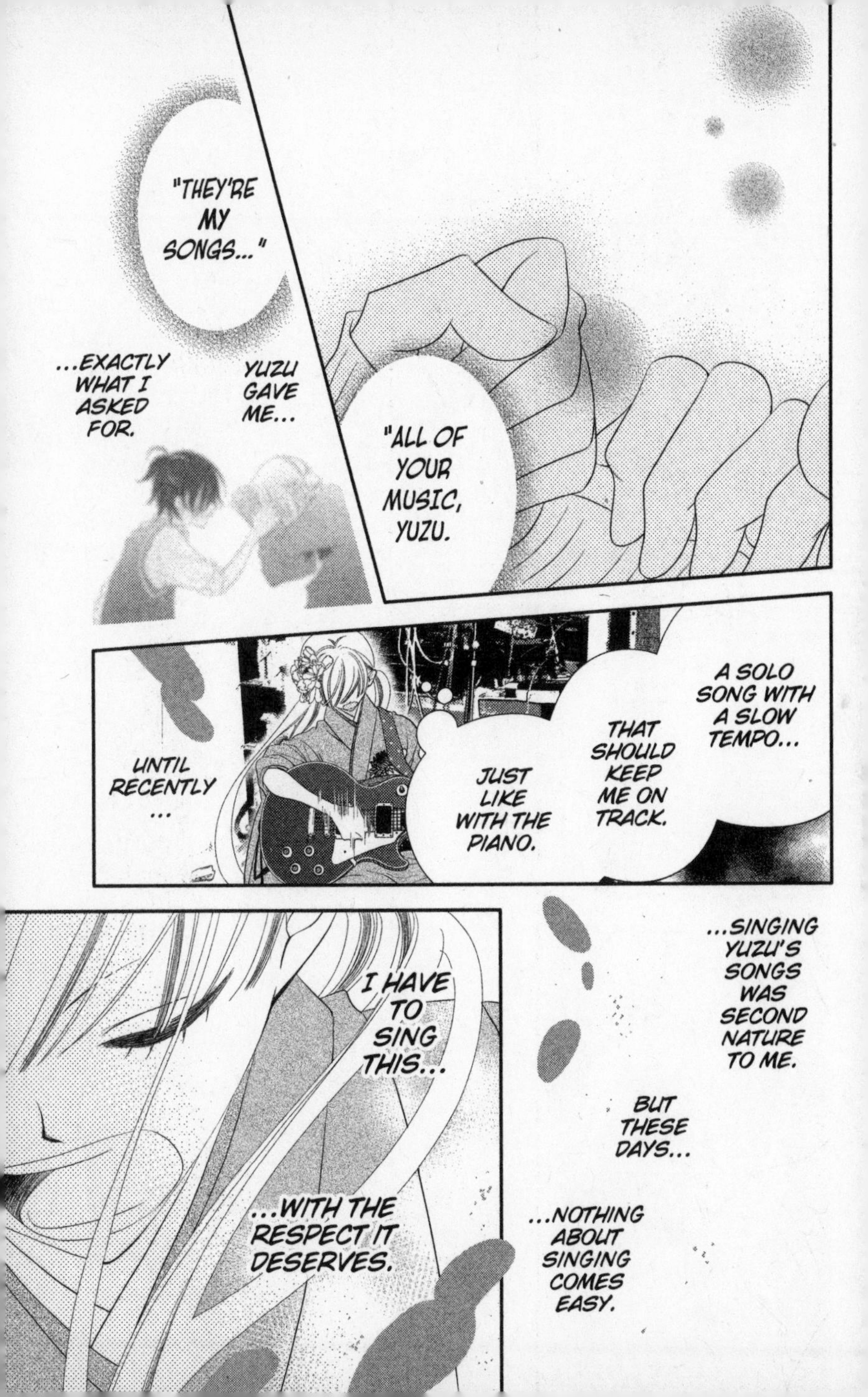
"ALL OF YOUR MUSIC, YUZU.
"THEY'RE MY SONGS..."
YUZU GAVE ME...
...EXACTLY WHAT I ASKED FOR.
A SOLO SONG WITH A SLOW TEMPO...
THAT SHOULD KEEP ME ON TRACK.
JUST LIKE WITH THE PIANO.
UNTIL RECENTLY...
...SINGING YUZU'S SONGS WAS SECOND NATURE TO ME.
BUT THESE DAYS...
...NOTHING ABOUT SINGING COMES EASY.
I HAVE TO SING THIS...
...WITH THE RESPECT IT DESERVES.

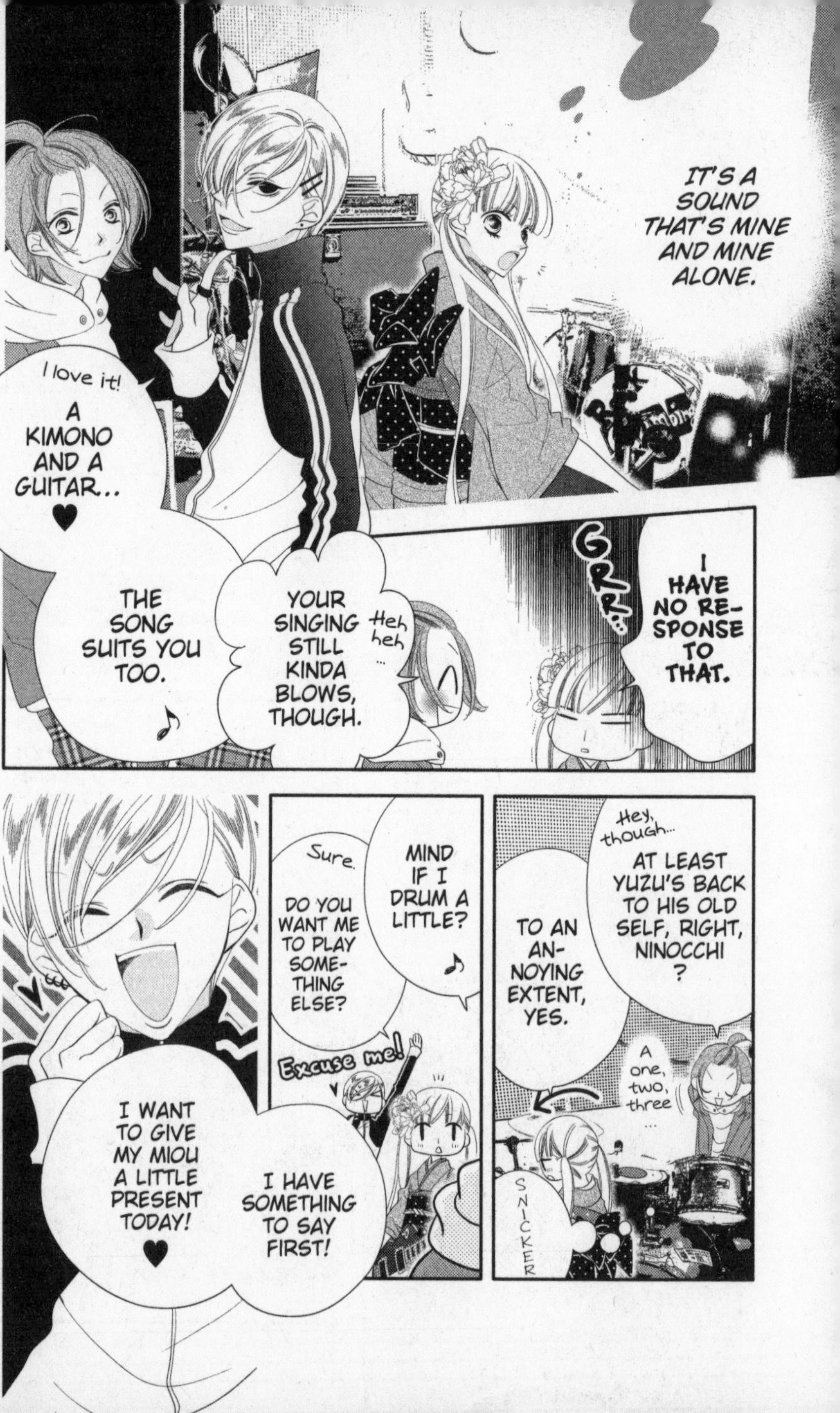

IT'S A SOUND THAT'S MINE AND MINE ALONE.
I love it!
A KIMONO AND A GUITAR... ♥
I HAVE NO RE-SPONSE TO THAT.
GRR...
Heh heh...
YOUR SINGING STILL KINDA BLOWS, THOUGH.
THE SONG SUITS YOU TOO. ♪
Hey, though...
AT LEAST YUZU'S BACK TO HIS OLD SELF, RIGHT, NINOCCHI?
TO AN AN-NOYING EXTENT, YES.
A one, two, three...
SNICKER
MIND IF I DRUM A LITTLE? ♪
Sure.
DO YOU WANT ME TO PLAY SOME-THING ELSE?
Excuse me!
I HAVE SOMETHING TO SAY FIRST!
I WANT TO GIVE MY MIOU A LITTLE PRESENT TODAY! ♥

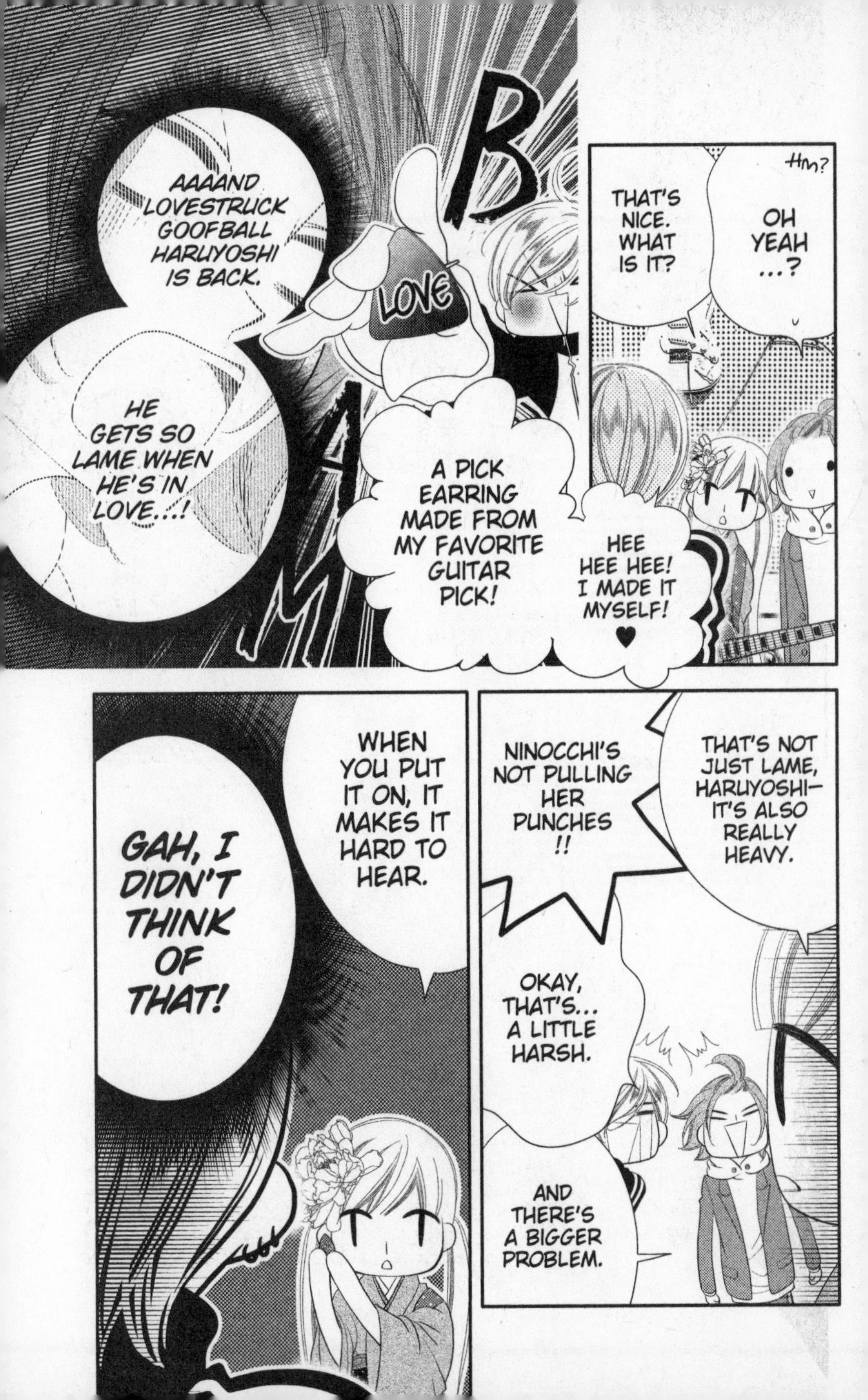
Hm?
OH YEAH ...?
THAT'S NICE. WHAT IS IT?
BAM
LOVE
A PICK EARRING MADE FROM MY FAVORITE GUITAR PICK!
HEE HEE HEE! I MADE IT MYSELF! ♥
AAAAND LOVESTRUCK GOOFBALL HARUYOSHI IS BACK.
HE GETS SO LAME WHEN HE'S IN LOVE...!
THAT'S NOT JUST LAME, HARUYOSHI— IT'S ALSO REALLY HEAVY.
NINOCCHI'S NOT PULLING HER PUNCHES !!
OKAY, THAT'S... A LITTLE HARSH.
AND THERE'S A BIGGER PROBLEM.
WHEN YOU PUT IT ON, IT MAKES IT HARD TO HEAR.
GAH, I DIDN'T THINK OF THAT!

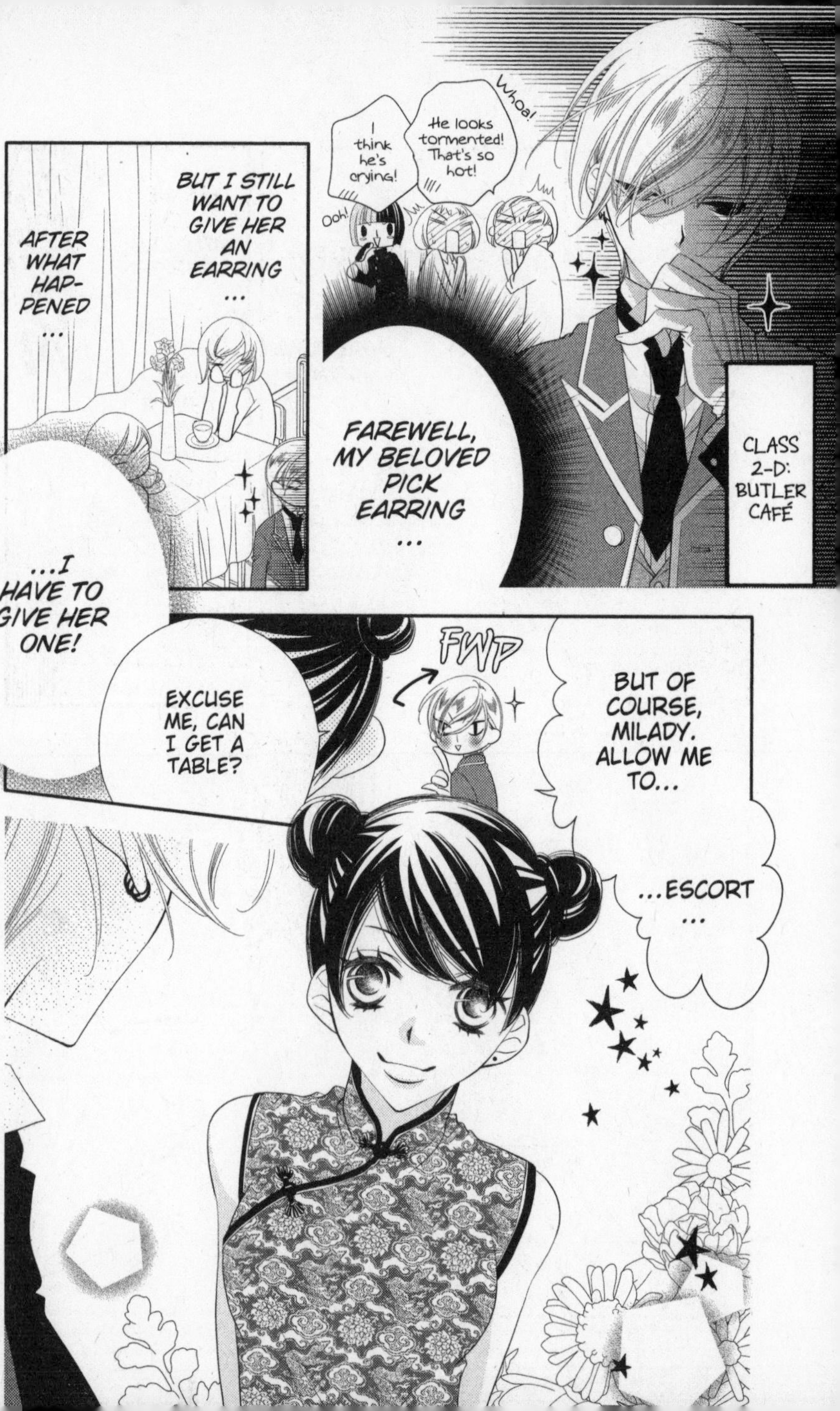
CLASS 2-D: BUTLER CAFÉ
Whoa!
He looks tormented! That's so hot!
I think he's crying!
Ooh!
FAREWELL, MY BELOVED PICK EARRING...
BUT I STILL WANT TO GIVE HER AN EARRING...
AFTER WHAT HAP-PENED...
...I HAVE TO GIVE HER ONE!
FWP
EXCUSE ME, CAN I GET A TABLE?
BUT OF COURSE, MILADY. ALLOW ME TO...
...ESCORT...

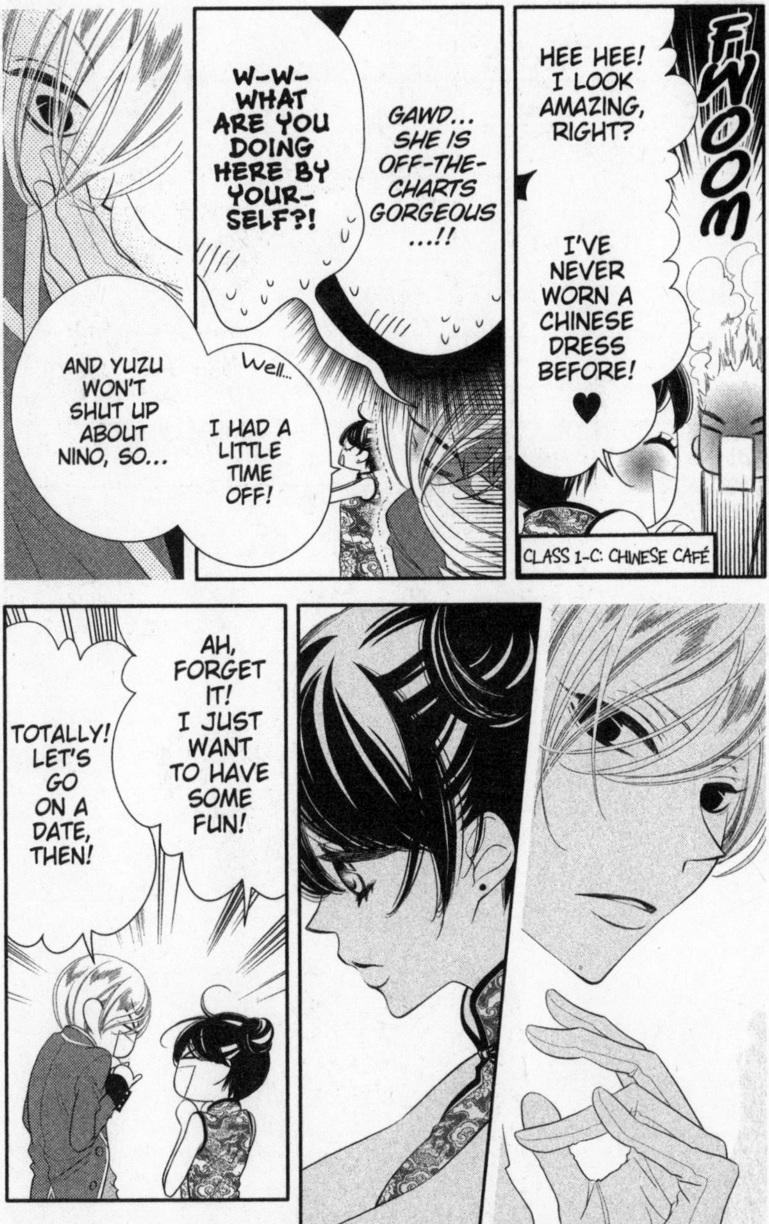
FWOOM
HEE HEE! I LOOK AMAZING, RIGHT?
I'VE NEVER WORN A CHINESE DRESS BEFORE! ♥
CLASS 1-C: CHINESE CAFÉ
GAWD... SHE IS OFF-THE-CHARTS GORGEOUS ...!!
W-W-WHAT ARE YOU DOING HERE BY YOURSELF?!
Well...
I HAD A LITTLE TIME OFF!
AND YUZU WON'T SHUT UP ABOUT NINO, SO...
AH, FORGET IT! I JUST WANT TO HAVE SOME FUN!
TOTALLY! LET'S GO ON A DATE, THEN!

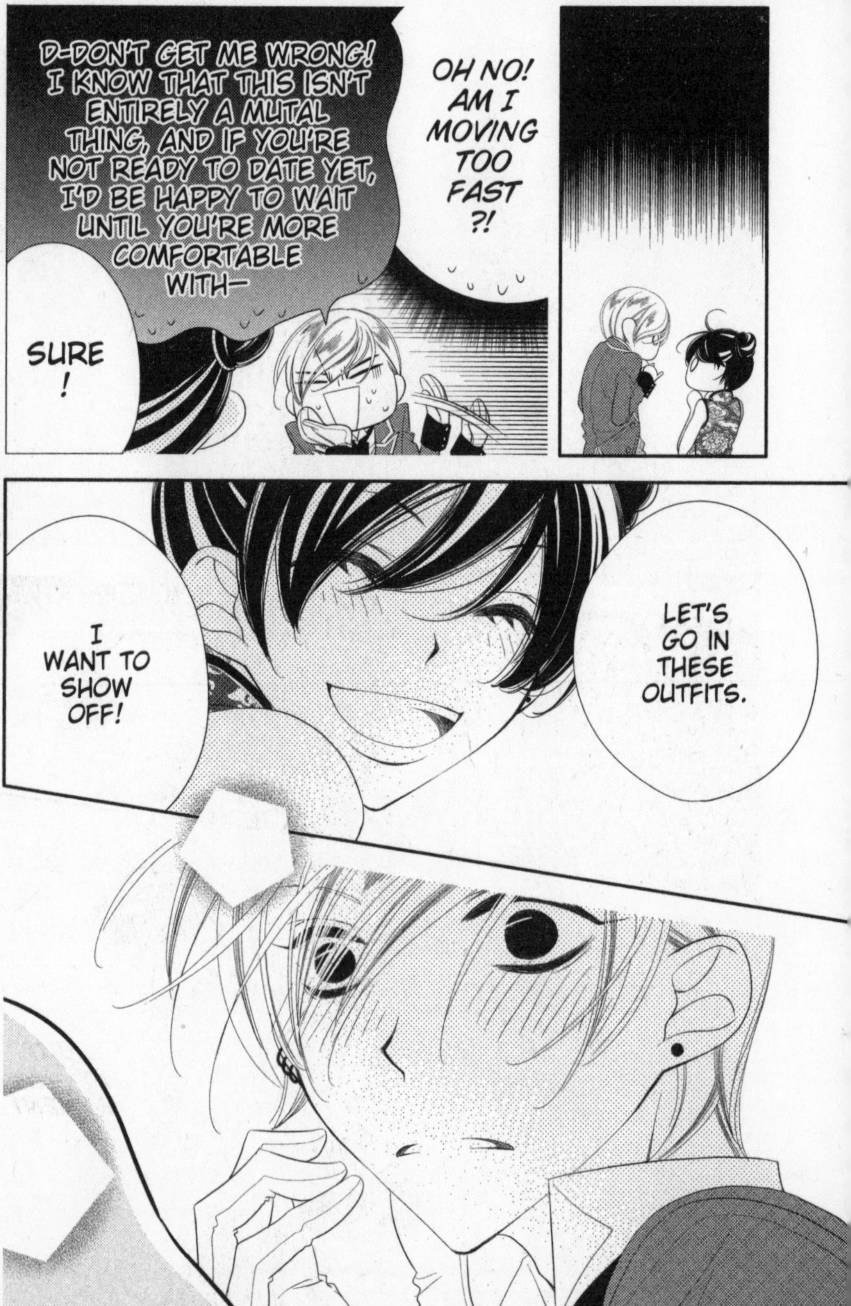
OH NO! AM I MOVING TOO FAST?!
D-DON'T GET ME WRONG! I KNOW THAT THIS ISN'T ENTIRELY A MUTAL THING, AND IF YOU'RE NOT READY TO DATE YET, I'D BE HAPPY TO WAIT UNTIL YOU'RE MORE COMFORTABLE WITH–
SURE!
LET'S GO IN THESE OUTFITS.
I WANT TO SHOW OFF!

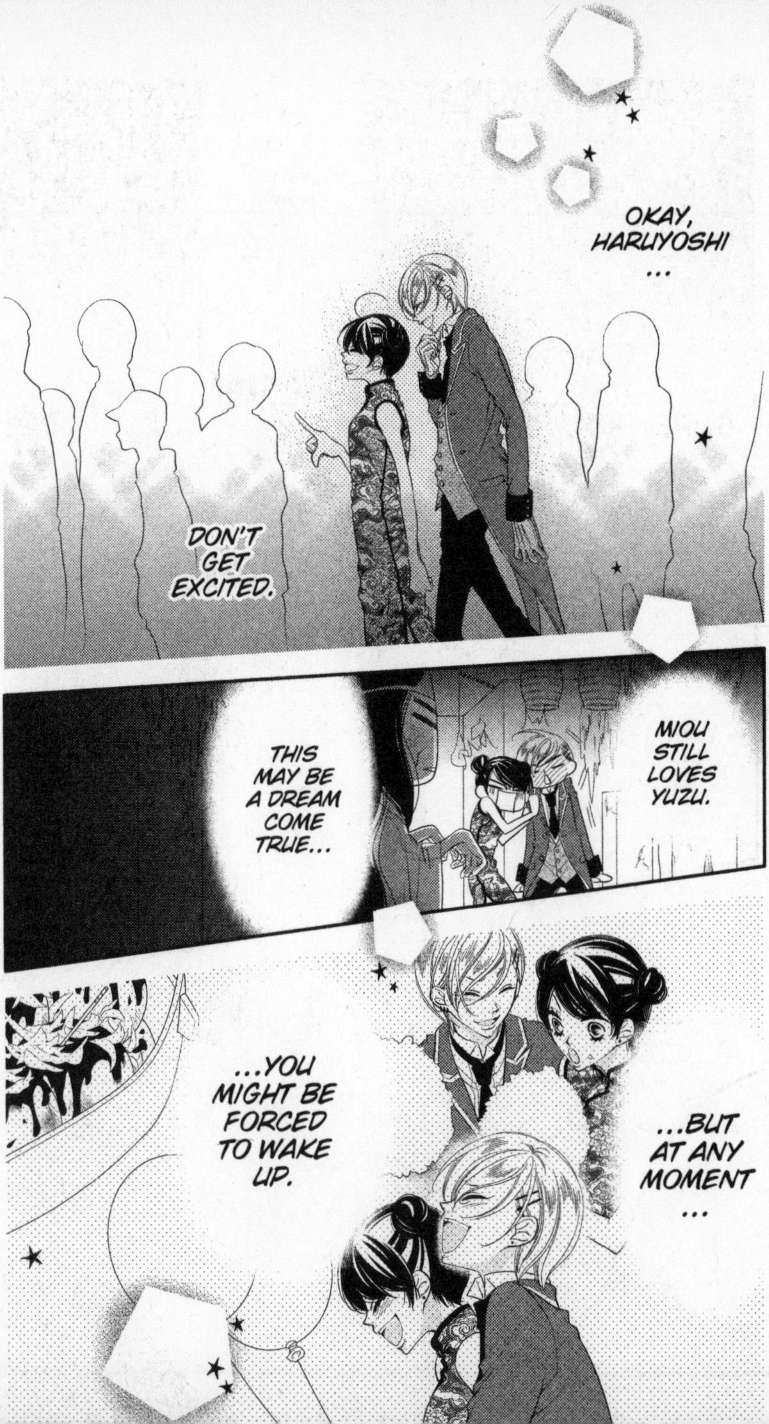
OKAY, HARUYOSHI ...
DON'T GET EXCITED.
MIOU STILL LOVES YUZU.
THIS MAY BE A DREAM COME TRUE...
...BUT AT ANY MOMENT ...
...YOU MIGHT BE FORCED TO WAKE UP.

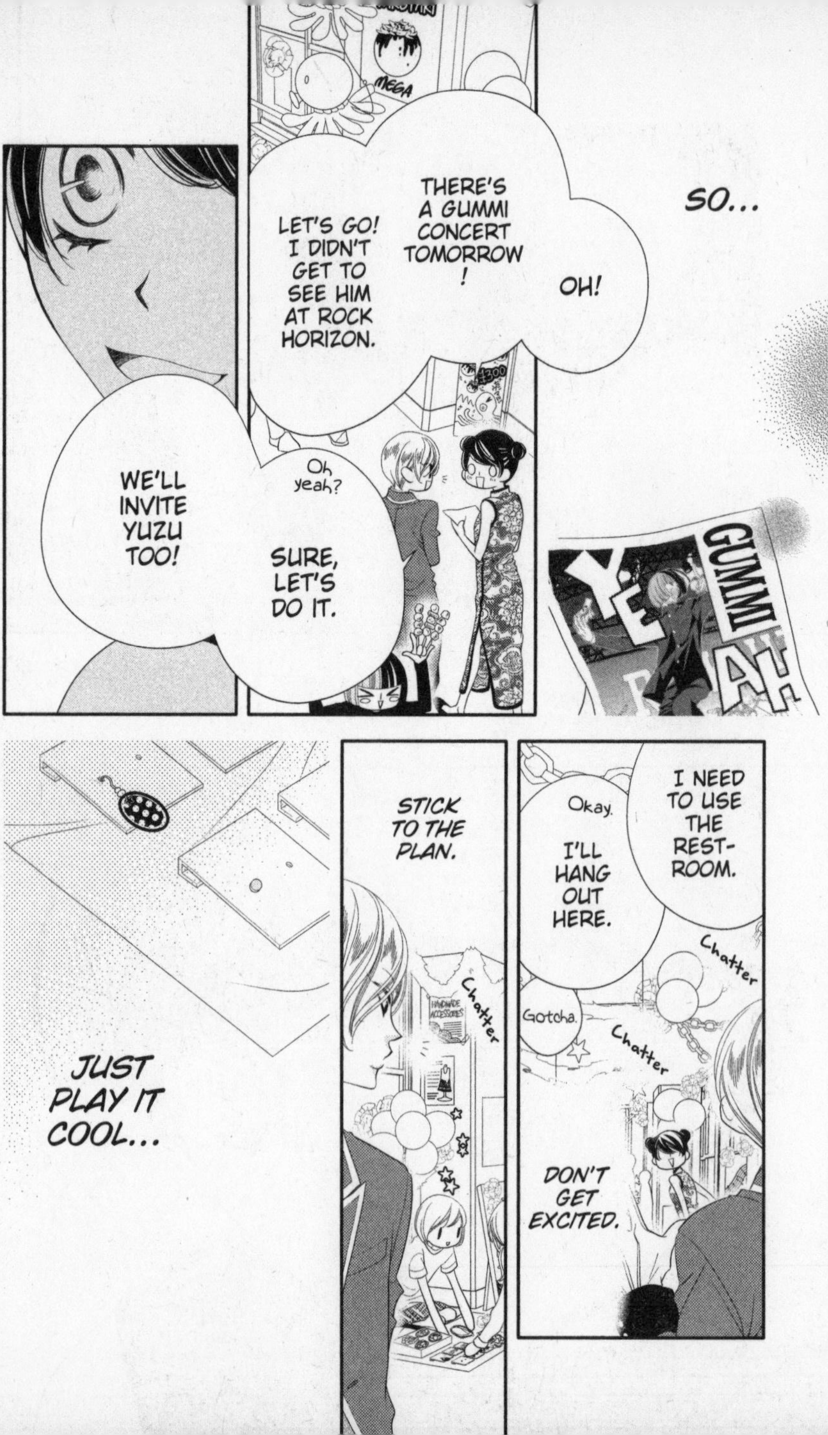

SO...
GUMMI
OH!
THERE'S A GUMMI CONCERT TOMORROW!
LET'S GO! I DIDN'T GET TO SEE HIM AT ROCK HORIZON.
MEGA
Oh yeah?
SURE, LET'S DO IT.
WE'LL INVITE YUZU TOO!
I NEED TO USE THE REST-ROOM.
Okay.
I'LL HANG OUT HERE.
Chatter
Gotcha.
Chatter
DON'T GET EXCITED.
STICK TO THE PLAN.
Chatter
HANDMADE ACCESSORIES
JUST PLAY IT COOL...

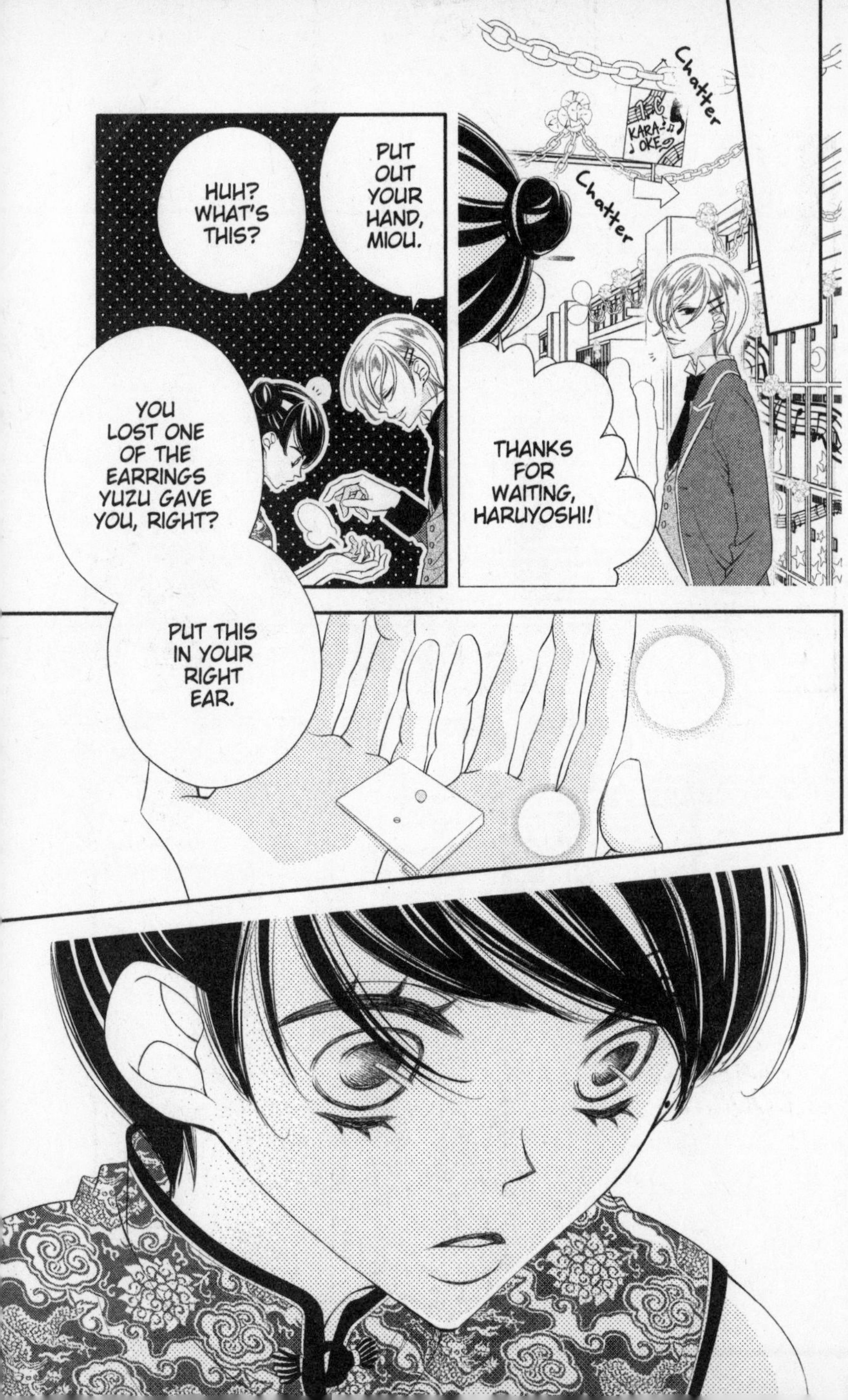
Chatter
KARA-OKE
Chatter
THANKS FOR WAITING, HARUYOSHI!
PUT OUT YOUR HAND, MIOU.
HUH? WHAT'S THIS?
YOU LOST ONE OF THE EARRINGS YUZU GAVE YOU, RIGHT?
PUT THIS IN YOUR RIGHT EAR.

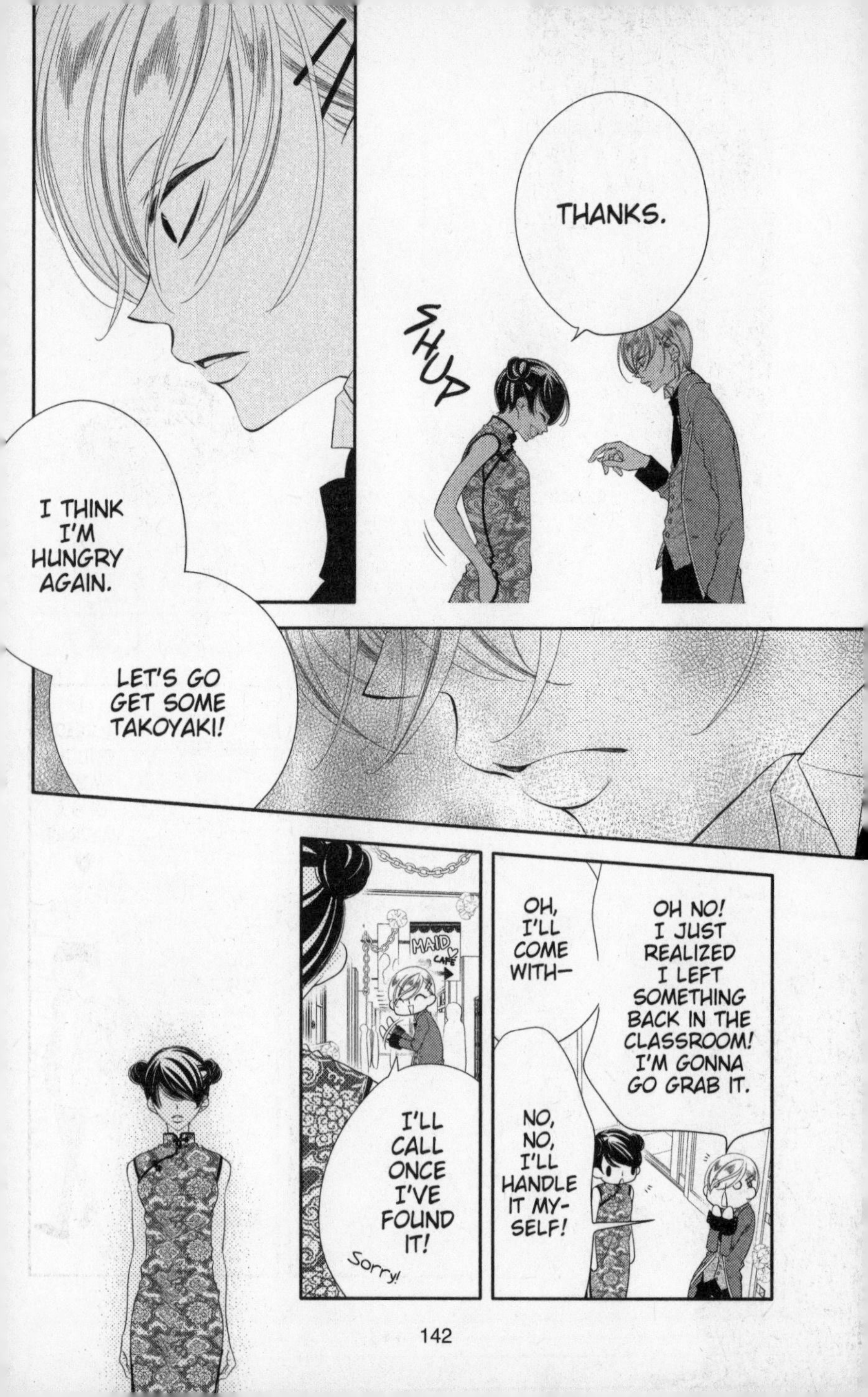
THANKS.
SHUP
I THINK I'M HUNGRY AGAIN.
LET'S GO GET SOME TAKOYAKI!
OH NO! I JUST REALIZED I LEFT SOMETHING BACK IN THE CLASSROOM! I'M GONNA GO GRAB IT.
OH, I'LL COME WITH—
NO, NO, I'LL HANDLE IT MY-SELF!
MAID CAFE
I'LL CALL ONCE I'VE FOUND IT!
Sorry!

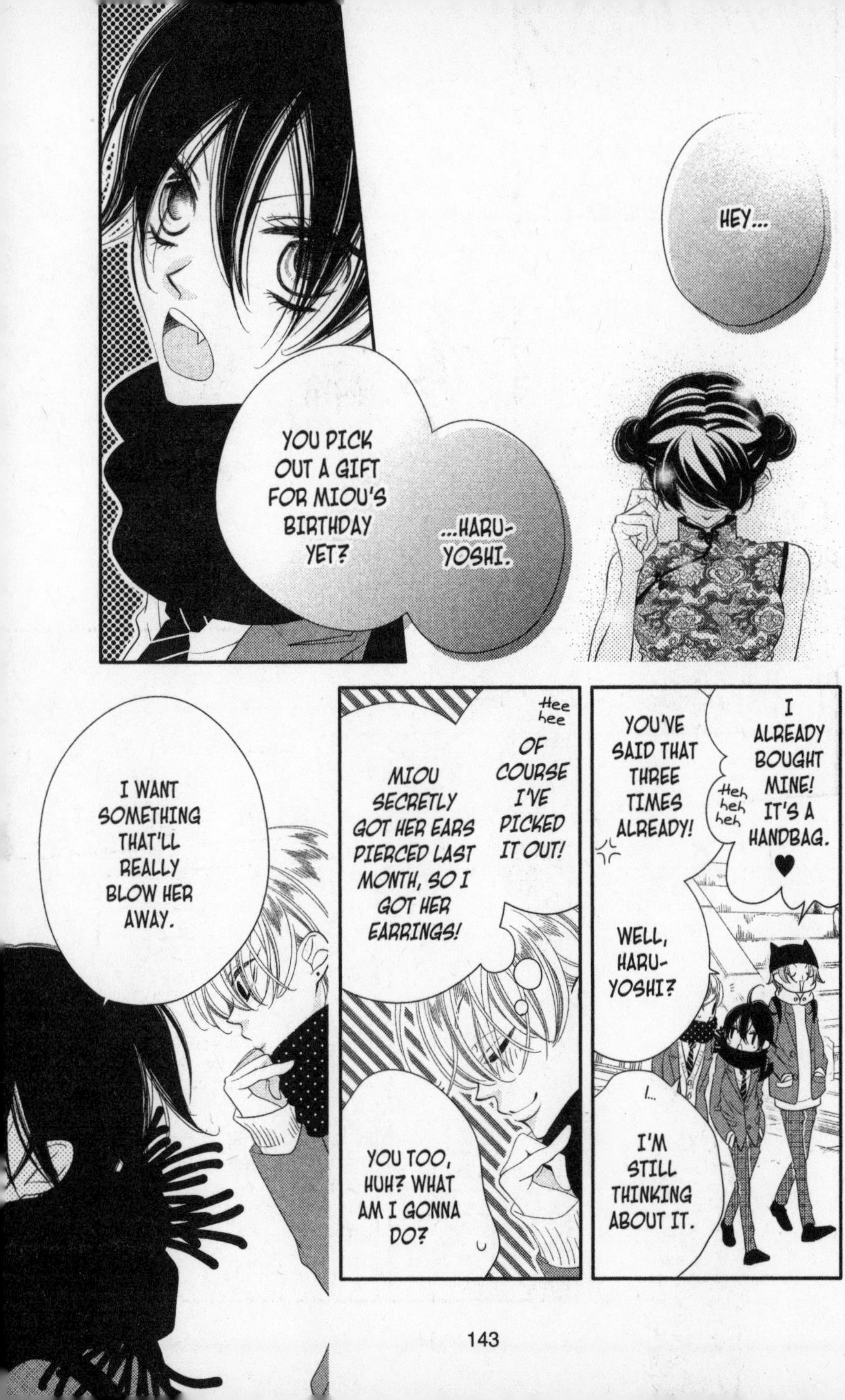
HEY...
...HARU-YOSHI.
YOU PICK OUT A GIFT FOR MIOU'S BIRTHDAY YET?
I ALREADY BOUGHT MINE! IT'S A HANDBAG. ♥
Heh heh heh
YOU'VE SAID THAT THREE TIMES ALREADY!
WELL, HARU-YOSHI?
I...
I'M STILL THINKING ABOUT IT.
Hee hee
OF COURSE I'VE PICKED IT OUT!
MIOU SECRETLY GOT HER EARS PIERCED LAST MONTH, SO I GOT HER EARRINGS!
YOU TOO, HUH? WHAT AM I GONNA DO?
I WANT SOMETHING THAT'LL REALLY BLOW HER AWAY.

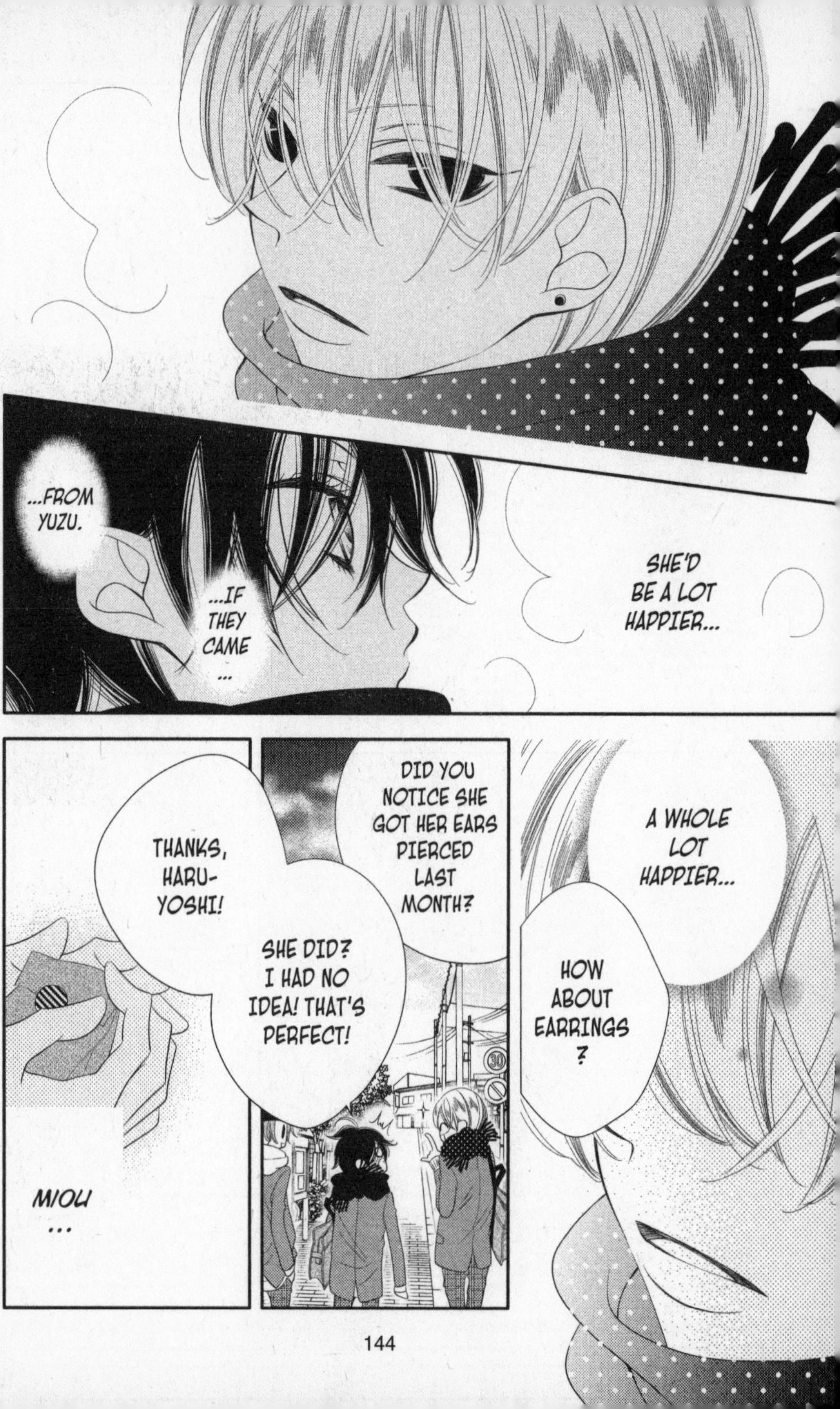
SHE'D BE A LOT HAPPIER...
...IF THEY CAME...
...FROM YUZU.
A WHOLE LOT HAPPIER...
HOW ABOUT EARRINGS?
DID YOU NOTICE SHE GOT HER EARS PIERCED LAST MONTH?
SHE DID? I HAD NO IDEA! THAT'S PERFECT!
THANKS, HARUYOSHI!
MIOU...

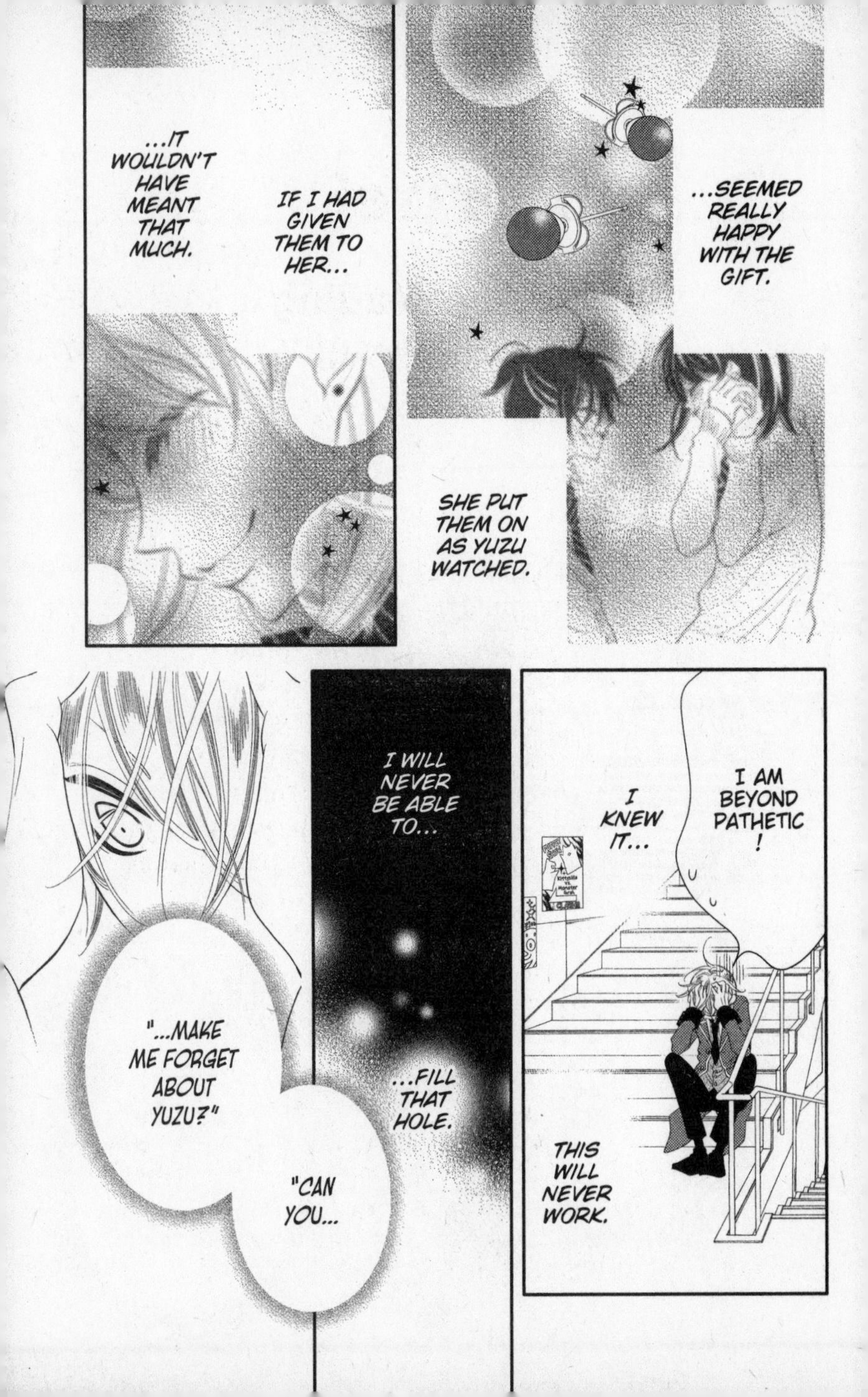
...SEEMED REALLY HAPPY WITH THE GIFT.
SHE PUT THEM ON AS YUZU WATCHED.
IF I HAD GIVEN THEM TO HER...
...IT WOULDN'T HAVE MEANT THAT MUCH.
I AM BEYOND PATHETIC!
I KNEW IT...
THIS WILL NEVER WORK.
I WILL NEVER BE ABLE TO...
...FILL THAT HOLE.
"CAN YOU...
"...MAKE ME FORGET ABOUT YUZU?"

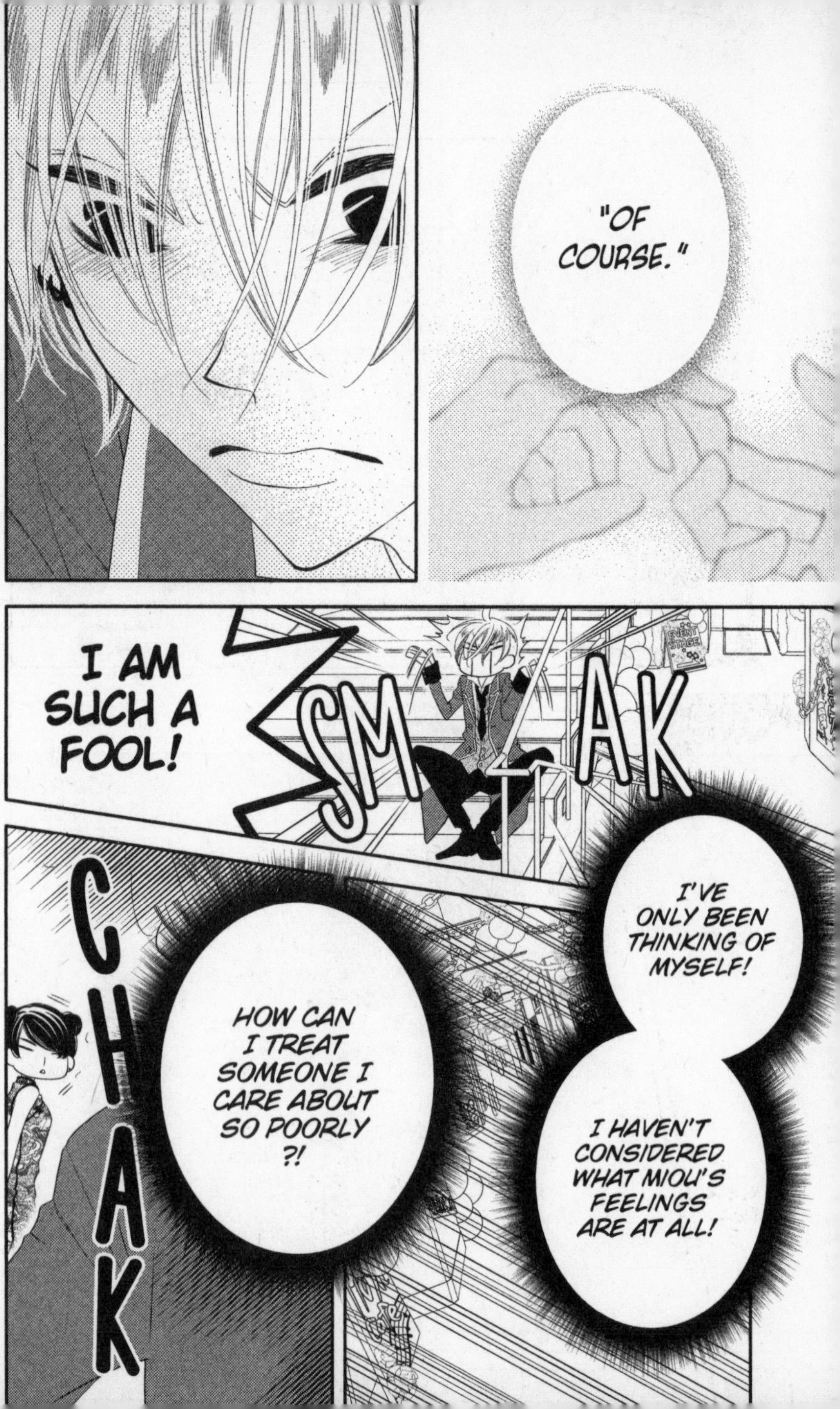
"OF COURSE."
I AM SUCH A FOOL!
SM AK
I'VE ONLY BEEN THINKING OF MYSELF!
I HAVEN'T CONSIDERED WHAT MIOU'S FEELINGS ARE AT ALL!
HOW CAN I TREAT SOMEONE I CARE ABOUT SO POORLY ?!
CHAK

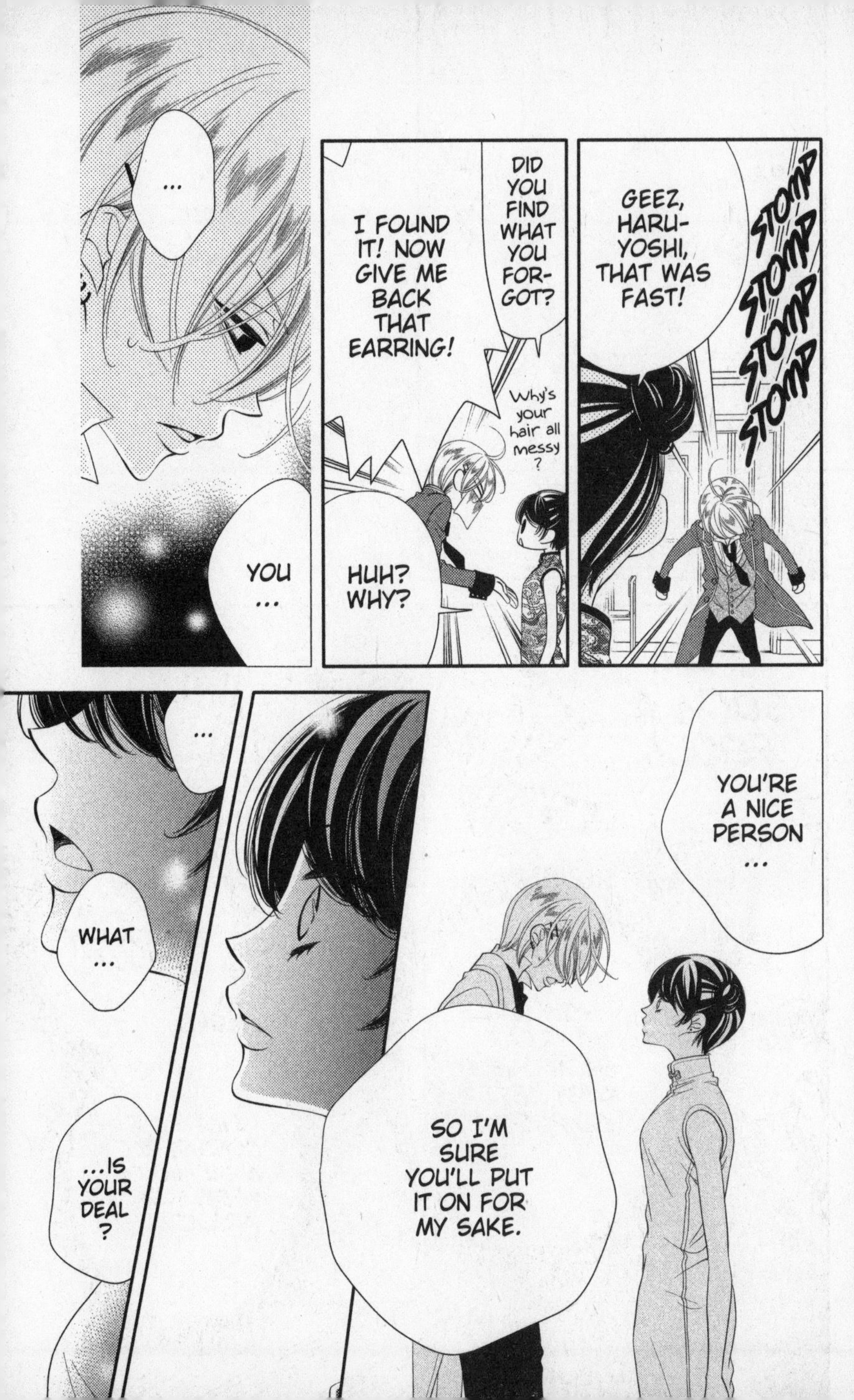
STOMP STOMP STOMP STOMP
GEEZ, HARU-YOSHI, THAT WAS FAST!
DID YOU FIND WHAT YOU FOR-GOT?
I FOUND IT! NOW GIVE ME BACK THAT EARRING!
Why's your hair all messy?
HUH? WHY?
...
YOU ...
YOU'RE A NICE PERSON ...
SO I'M SURE YOU'LL PUT IT ON FOR MY SAKE.
...
WHAT ...
...IS YOUR DEAL?

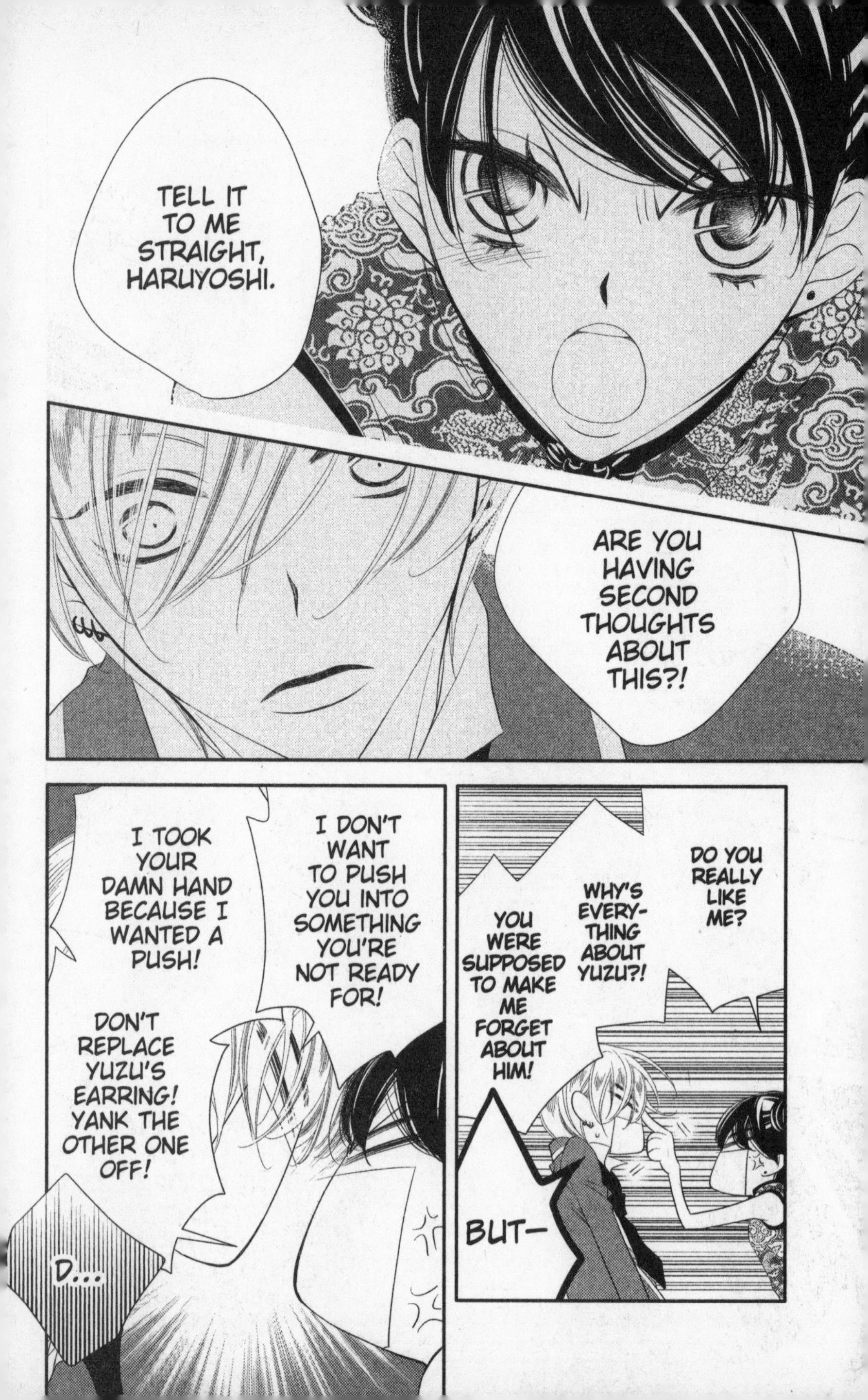
TELL IT TO ME STRAIGHT, HARUYOSHI.
ARE YOU HAVING SECOND THOUGHTS ABOUT THIS?!
DO YOU REALLY LIKE ME?
WHY'S EVERY-THING ABOUT YUZU?!
YOU WERE SUPPOSED TO MAKE ME FORGET ABOUT HIM!
BUT—
I DON'T WANT TO PUSH YOU INTO SOMETHING YOU'RE NOT READY FOR!
I TOOK YOUR DAMN HAND BECAUSE I WANTED A PUSH!
DON'T REPLACE YUZU'S EARRING! YANK THE OTHER ONE OFF!
D...

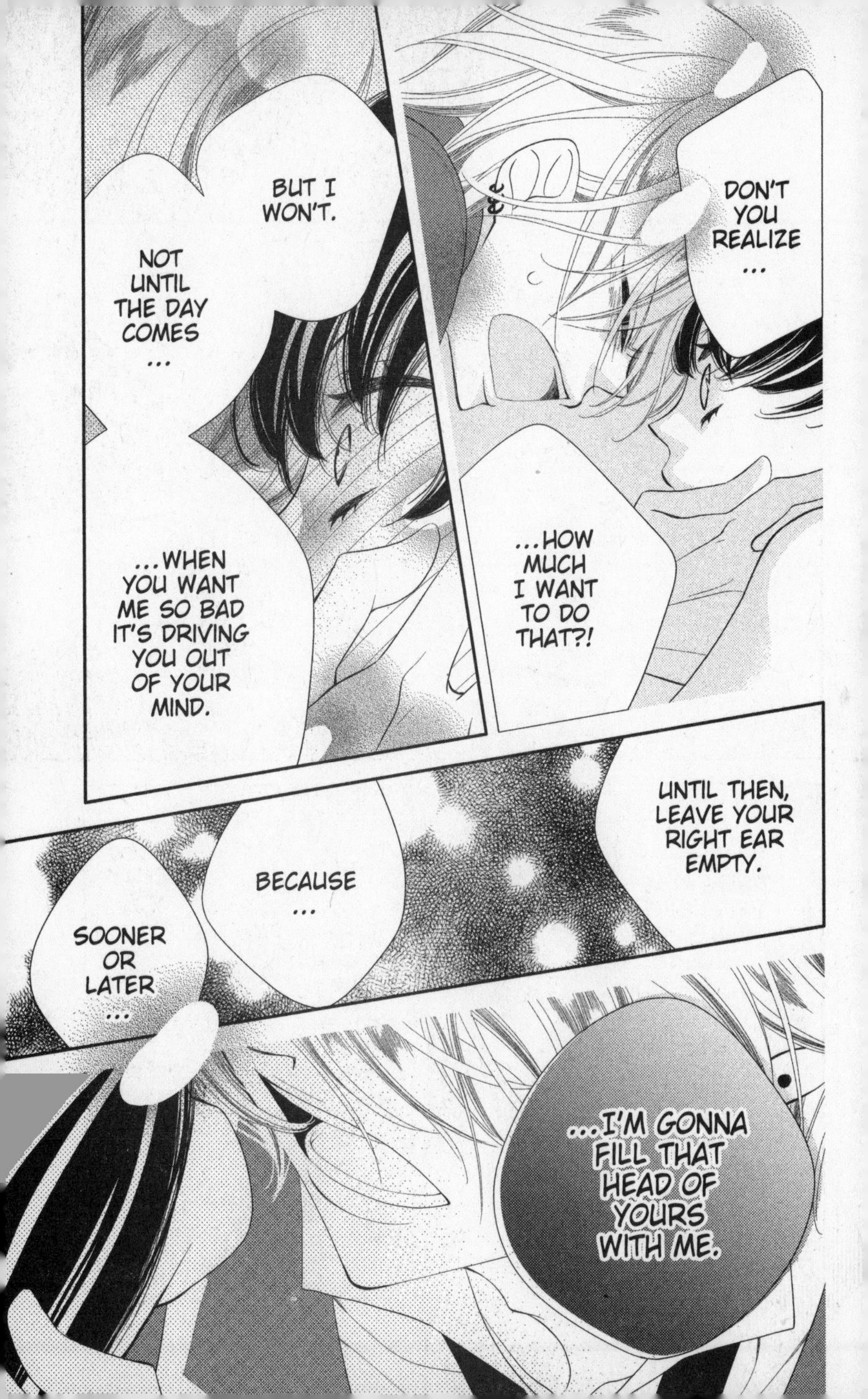
DON'T YOU REALIZE ...
...HOW MUCH I WANT TO DO THAT?!
BUT I WON'T.
NOT UNTIL THE DAY COMES ...
...WHEN YOU WANT ME SO BAD IT'S DRIVING YOU OUT OF YOUR MIND.
UNTIL THEN, LEAVE YOUR RIGHT EAR EMPTY.
BECAUSE ...
SOONER OR LATER ...
...I'M GONNA FILL THAT HEAD OF YOURS WITH ME.

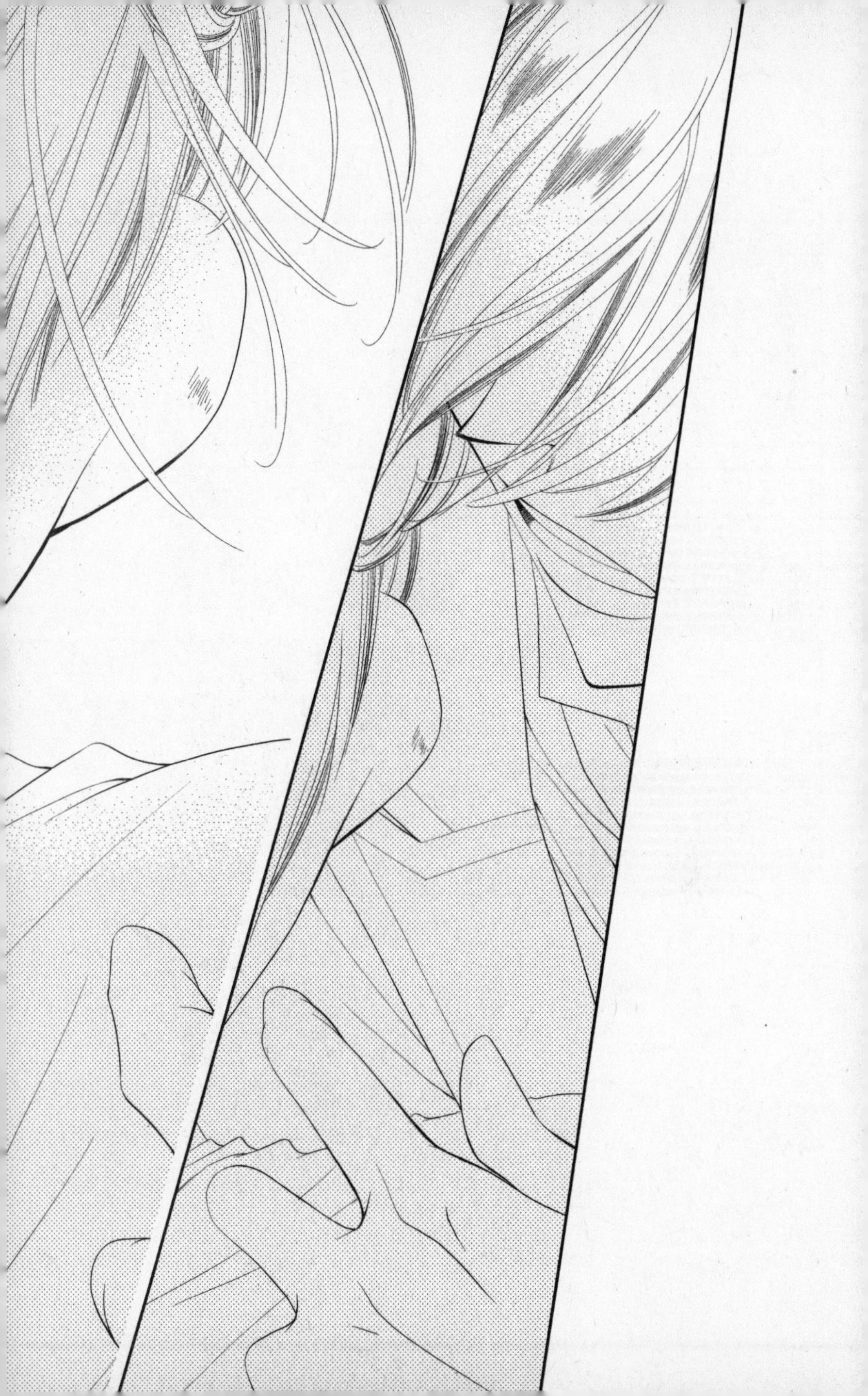

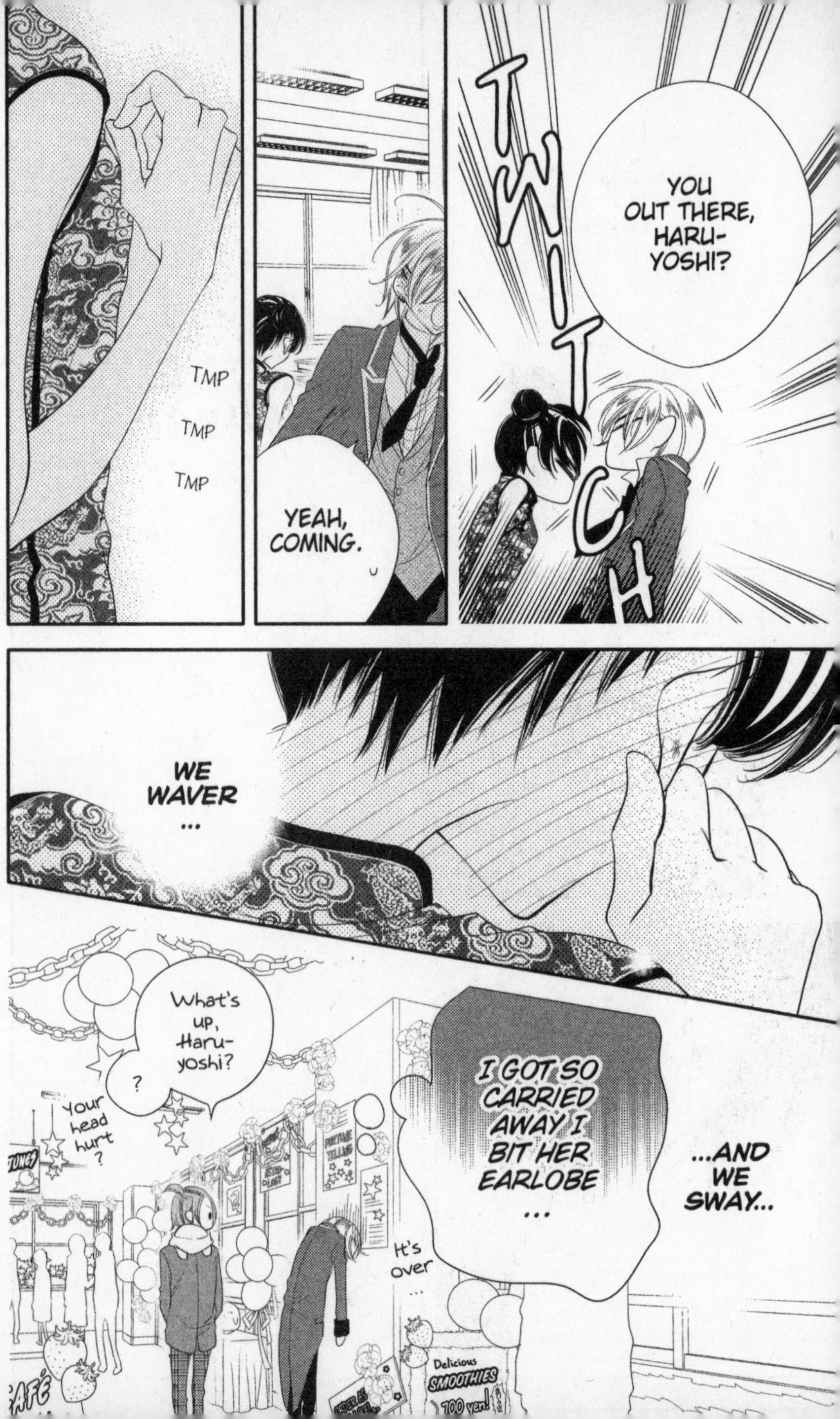
TWITCH
YOU OUT THERE, HARU-YOSHI?
YEAH, COMING.
TMP
TMP
TMP
WE WAVER ...
...AND WE SWAY...
I GOT SO CARRIED AWAY I BIT HER EARLOBE ...
What's up, Haru-yoshi?
?
Your head hurt?
It's over ...
FORTUNE TELLING
Delicious
SMOOTHIES
100 yen!
CAFÉ

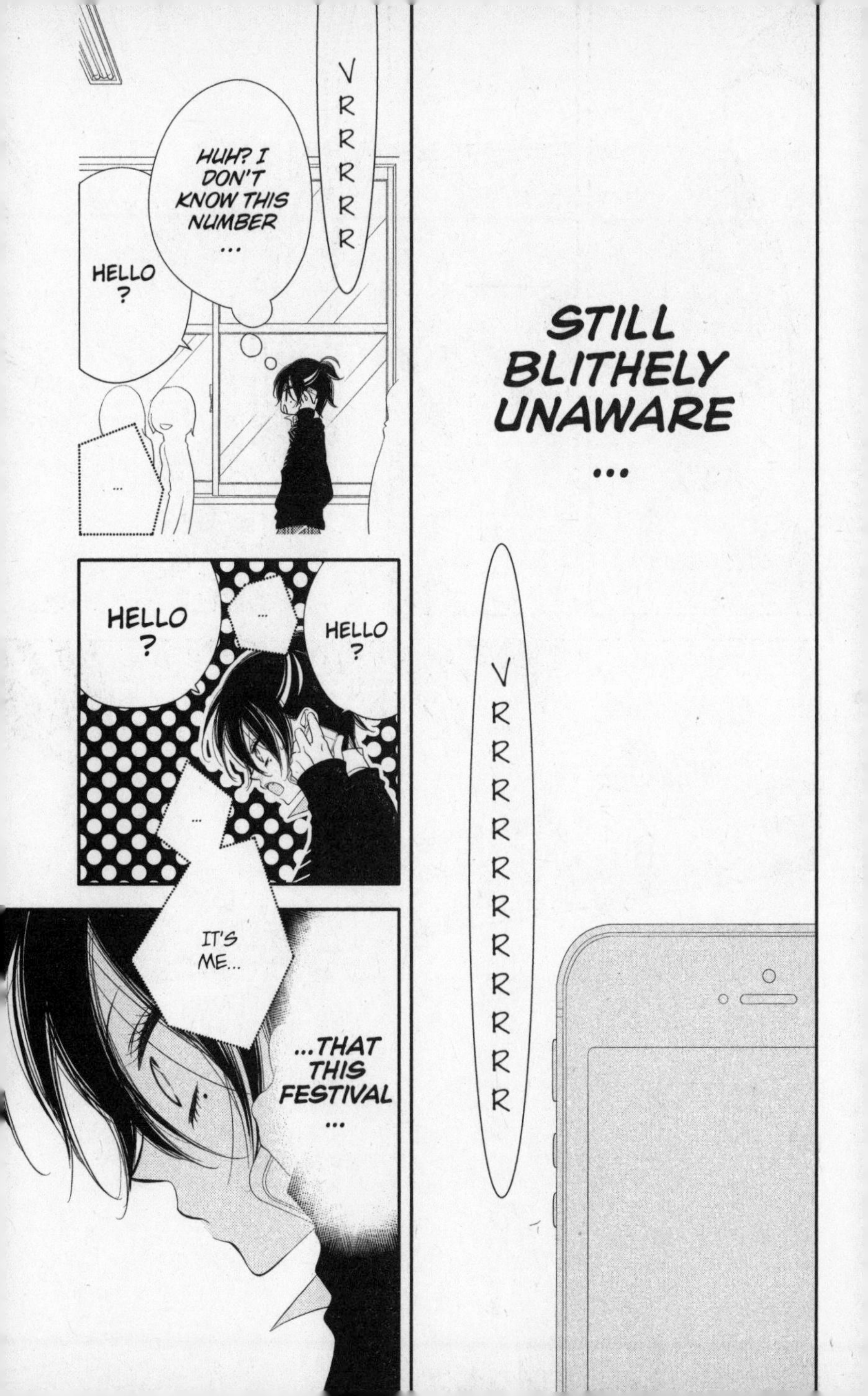
STILL BLITHELY UNAWARE ...
VRRRRRRRRRR
VRRRRR
HUH? I DON'T KNOW THIS NUMBER ...
HELLO ?
...
HELLO ?
...
HELLO ?
...
IT'S ME...
...THAT THIS FESTIVAL ...

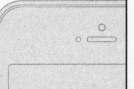

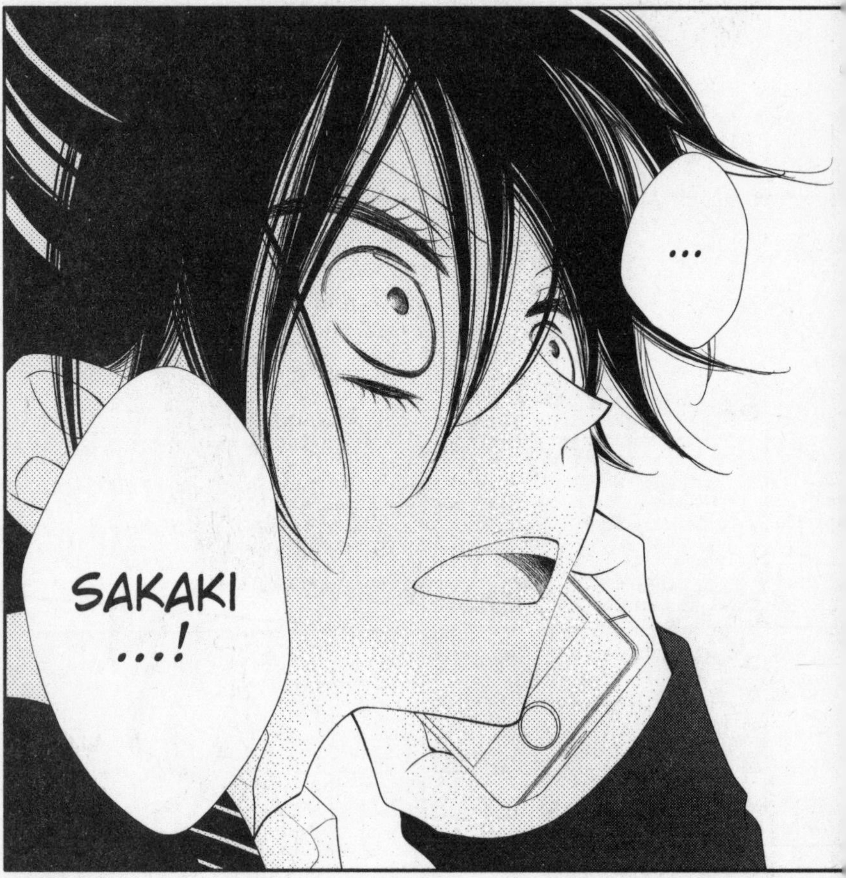
...
SAKAKI ...!

...WOULD REUNITE US ALL.

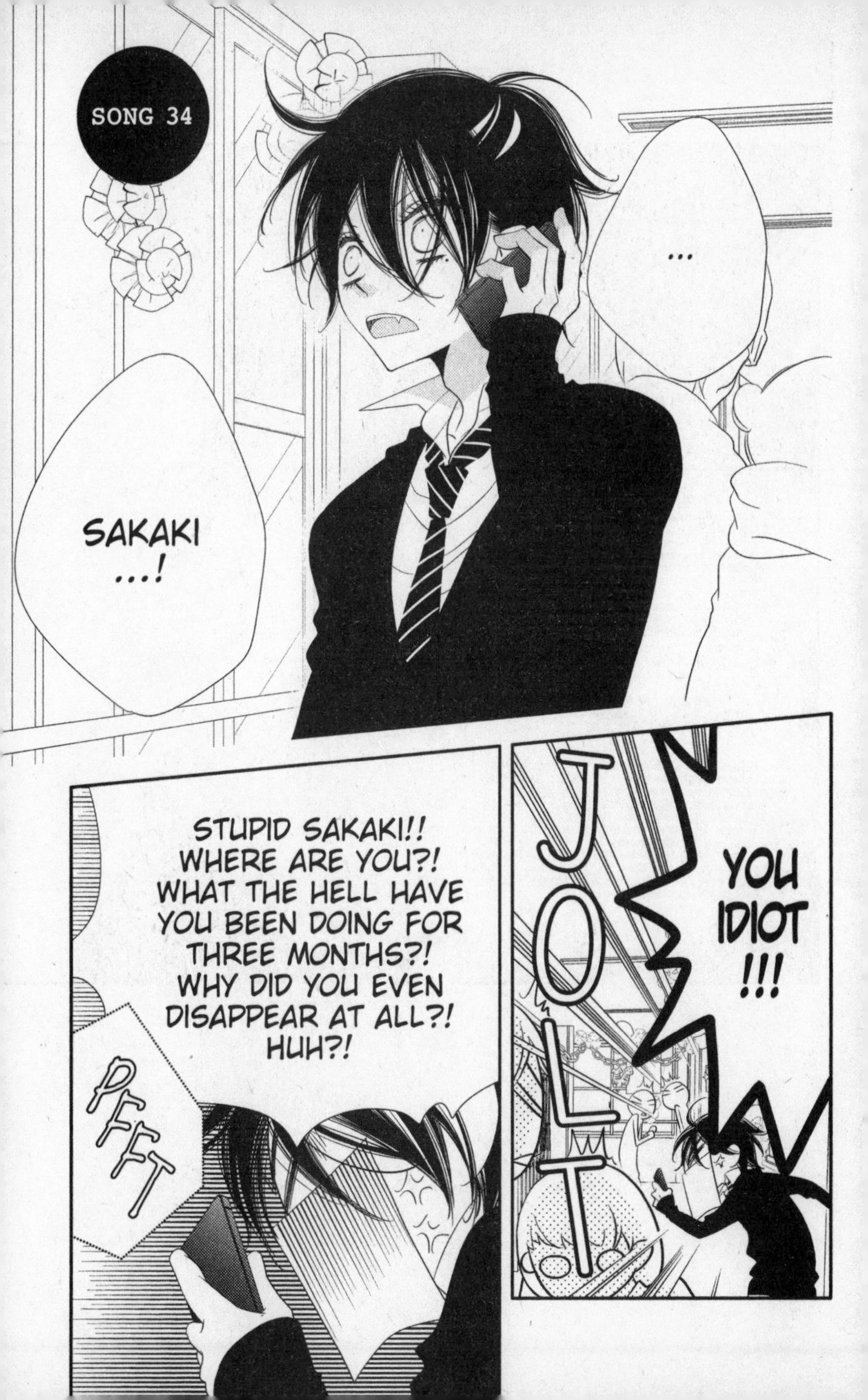
SONG 34
...
SAKAKI ...!
JOLT
YOU IDIOT !!!
STUPID SAKAKI!! WHERE ARE YOU?! WHAT THE HELL HAVE YOU BEEN DOING FOR THREE MONTHS?! WHY DID YOU EVEN DISAPPEAR AT ALL?! HUH?!
PFFT

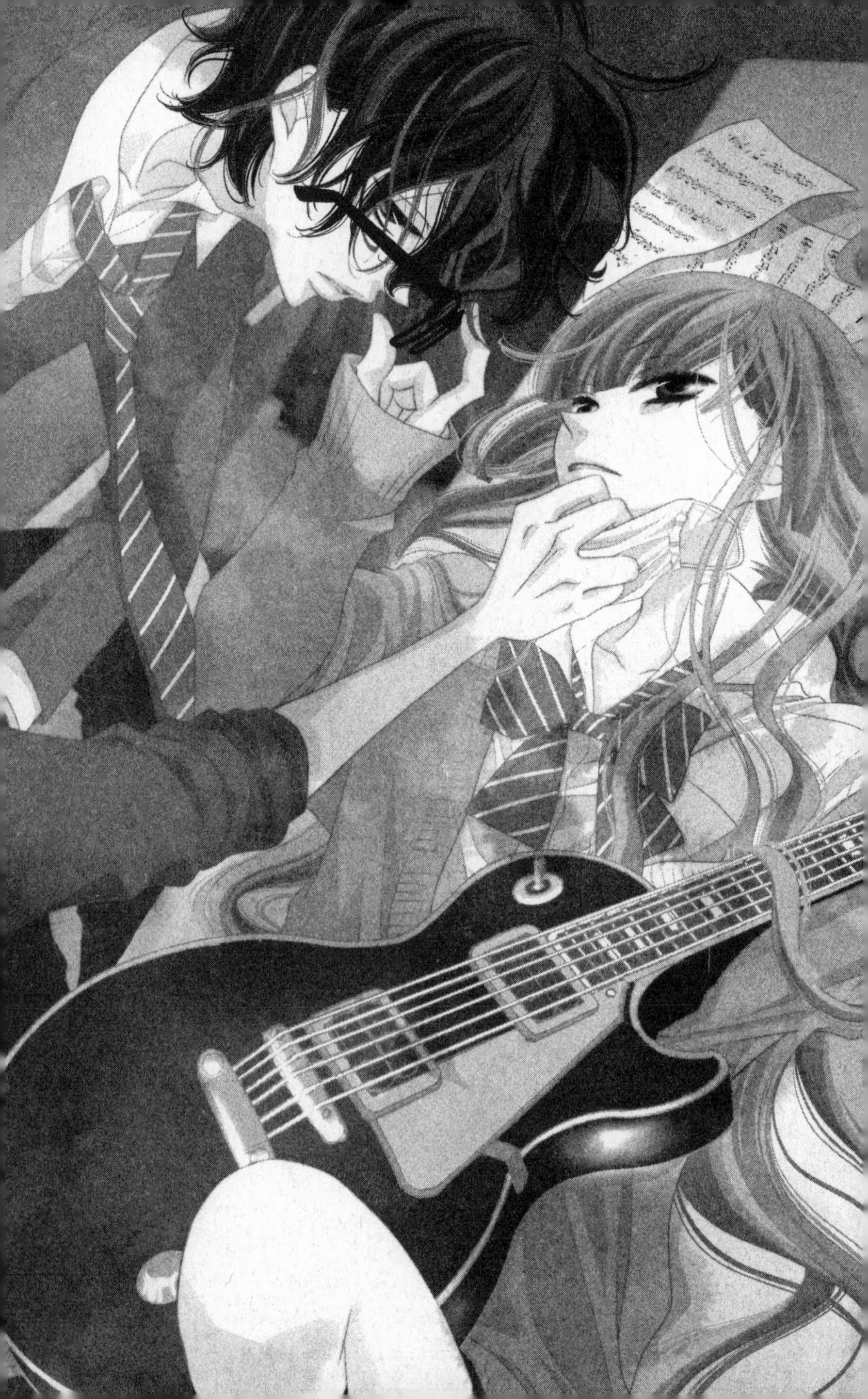

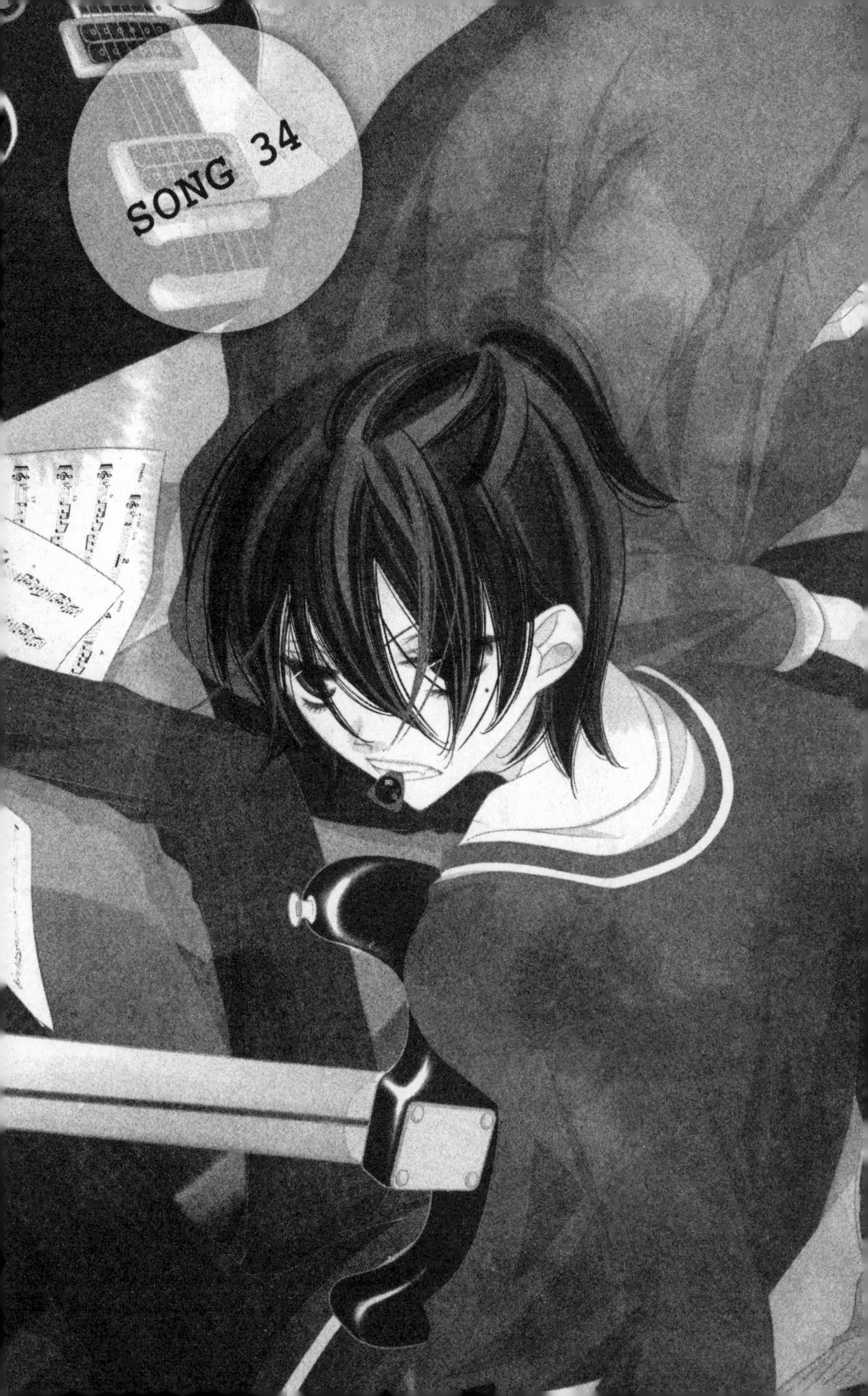
SONG 34

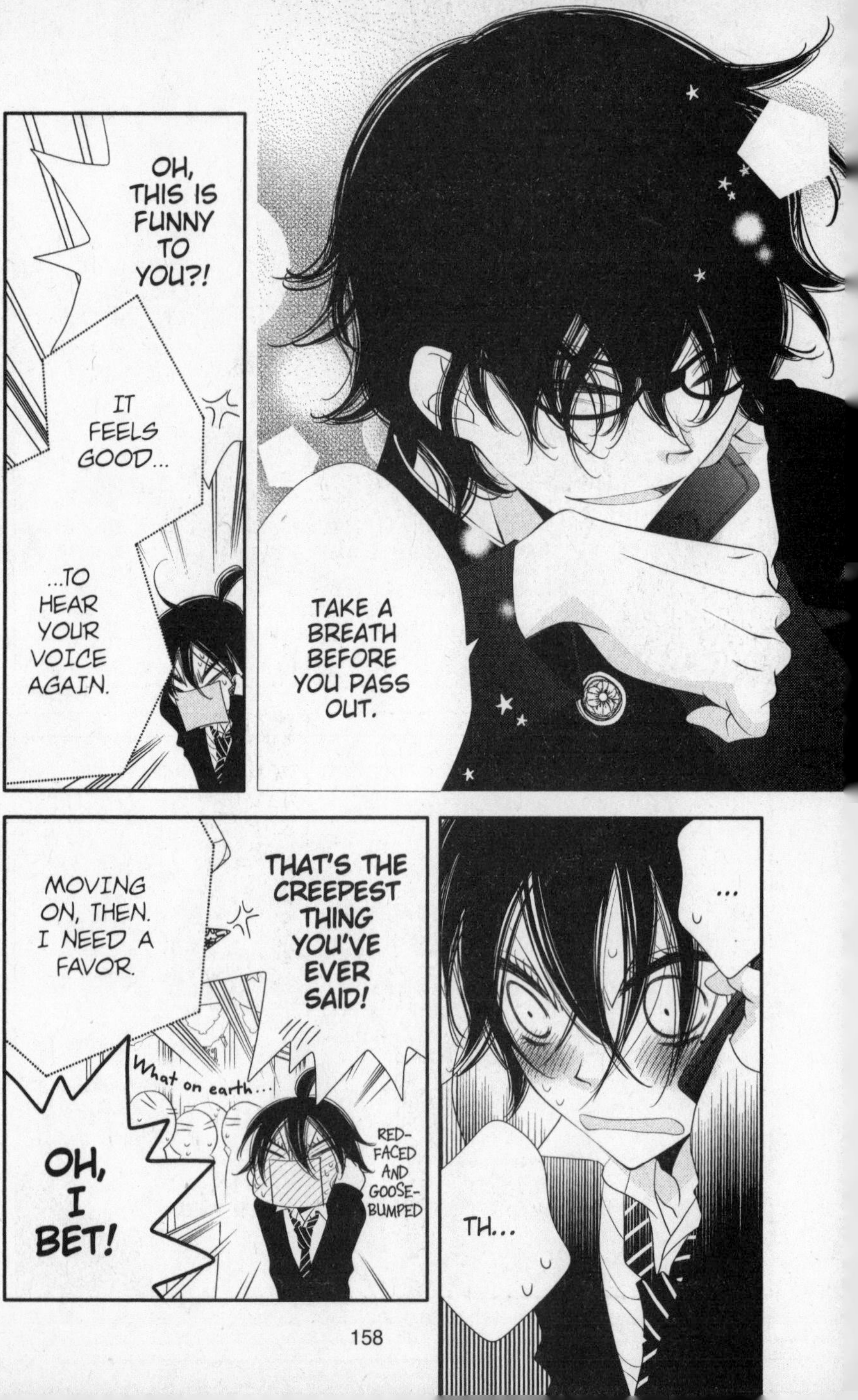
TAKE A BREATH BEFORE YOU PASS OUT.
OH, THIS IS FUNNY TO YOU?!
IT FEELS GOOD...
...TO HEAR YOUR VOICE AGAIN.
...
TH...
THAT'S THE CREEPEST THING YOU'VE EVER SAID!
MOVING ON, THEN. I NEED A FAVOR.
What on earth...
OH, I BET!
RED-FACED AND GOOSE-BUMPED

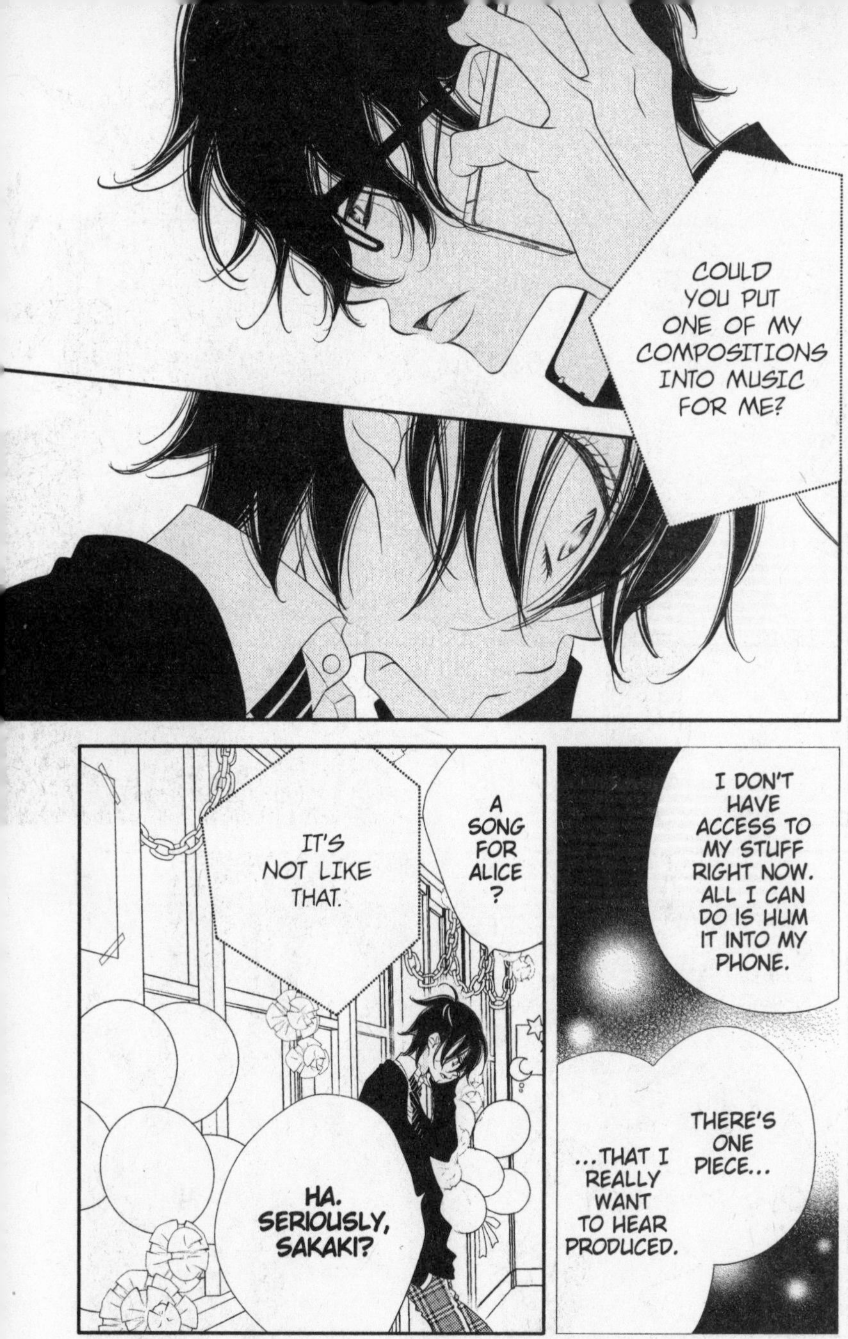
COULD YOU PUT ONE OF MY COMPOSITIONS INTO MUSIC FOR ME?
I DON'T HAVE ACCESS TO MY STUFF RIGHT NOW. ALL I CAN DO IS HUM IT INTO MY PHONE.
THERE'S ONE PIECE...
...THAT I REALLY WANT TO HEAR PRODUCED.
A SONG FOR ALICE?
IT'S NOT LIKE THAT.
HA. SERIOUSLY, SAKAKI?

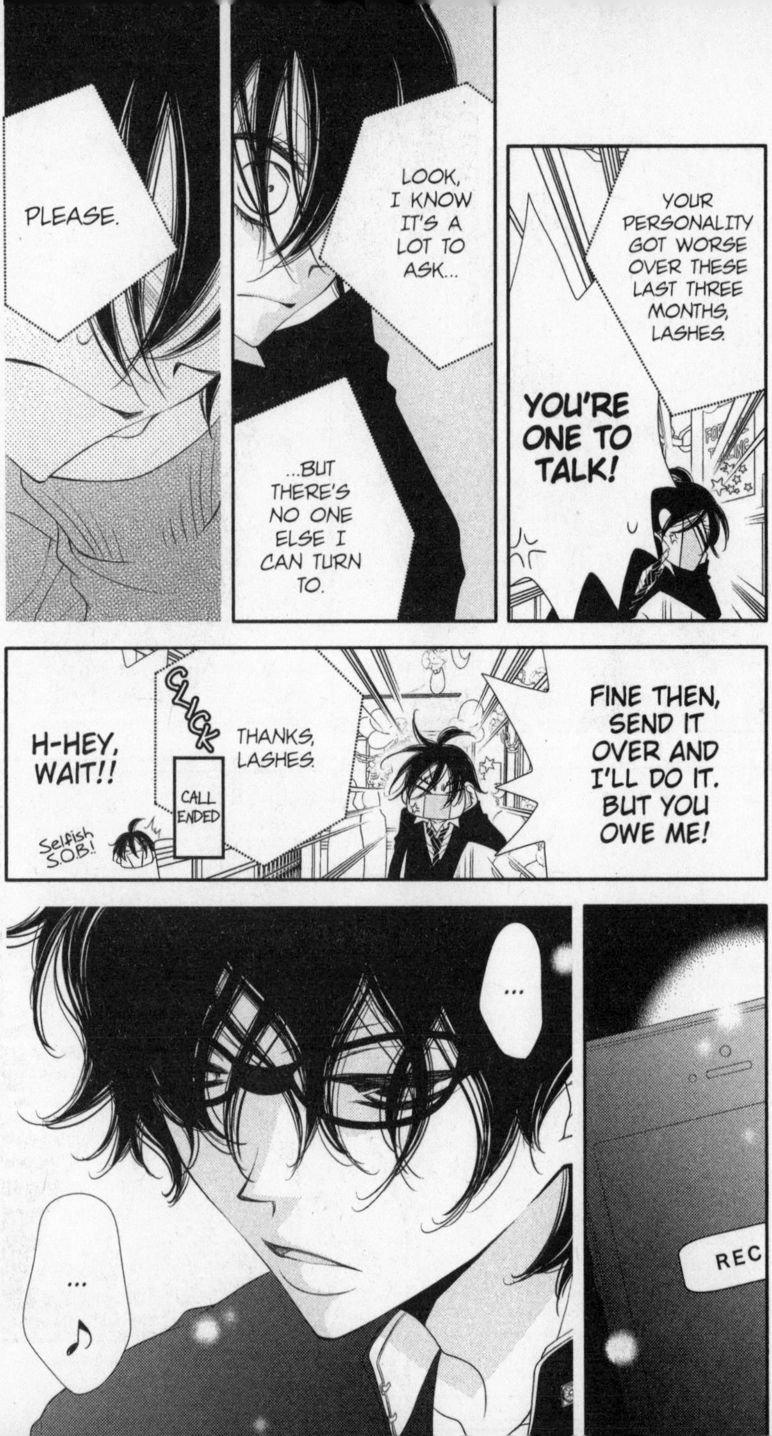
YOUR PERSONALITY GOT WORSE OVER THESE LAST THREE MONTHS, LASHES.
YOU'RE ONE TO TALK!
LOOK, I KNOW IT'S A LOT TO ASK...
...BUT THERE'S NO ONE ELSE I CAN TURN TO.
PLEASE.
FINE THEN, SEND IT OVER AND I'LL DO IT. BUT YOU OWE ME!
THANKS, LASHES.
CLICK
CALL ENDED
H-HEY, WAIT!!
Selfish S.O.B.!
REC
...
... ♪

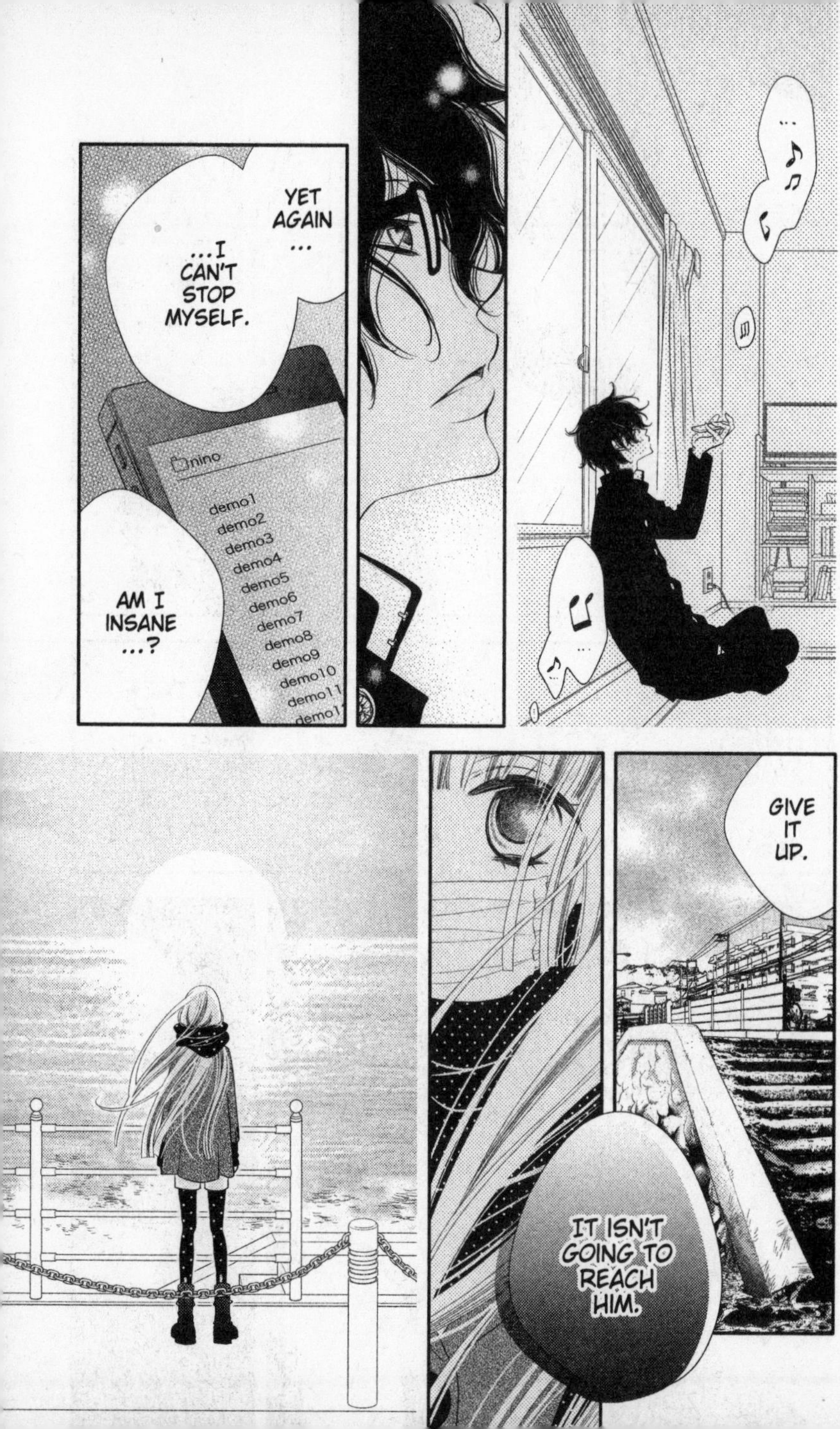
YET AGAIN ...
...I CAN'T STOP MYSELF.
nino
demo1
demo2
demo3
demo4
demo5
demo6
demo7
demo8
demo9
demo10
demo11
AM I INSANE ...?
GIVE IT UP.
IT ISN'T GOING TO REACH HIM.

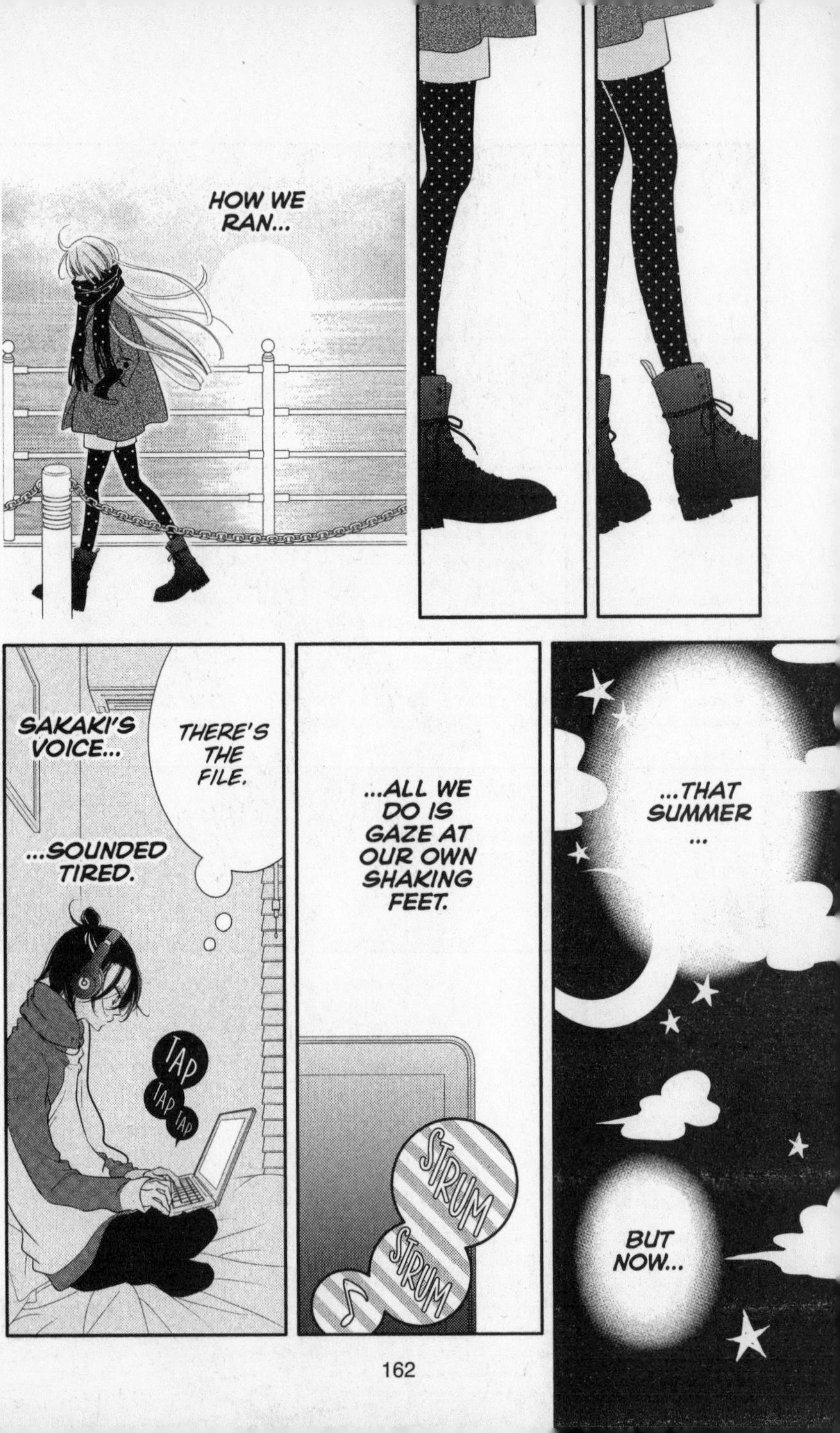
HOW WE RAN...
...THAT SUMMER ...
BUT NOW...
...ALL WE DO IS GAZE AT OUR OWN SHAKING FEET.
STRUM
STRUM
THERE'S THE FILE.
SAKAKI'S VOICE...
...SOUNDED TIRED.
TAP
TAP TAP

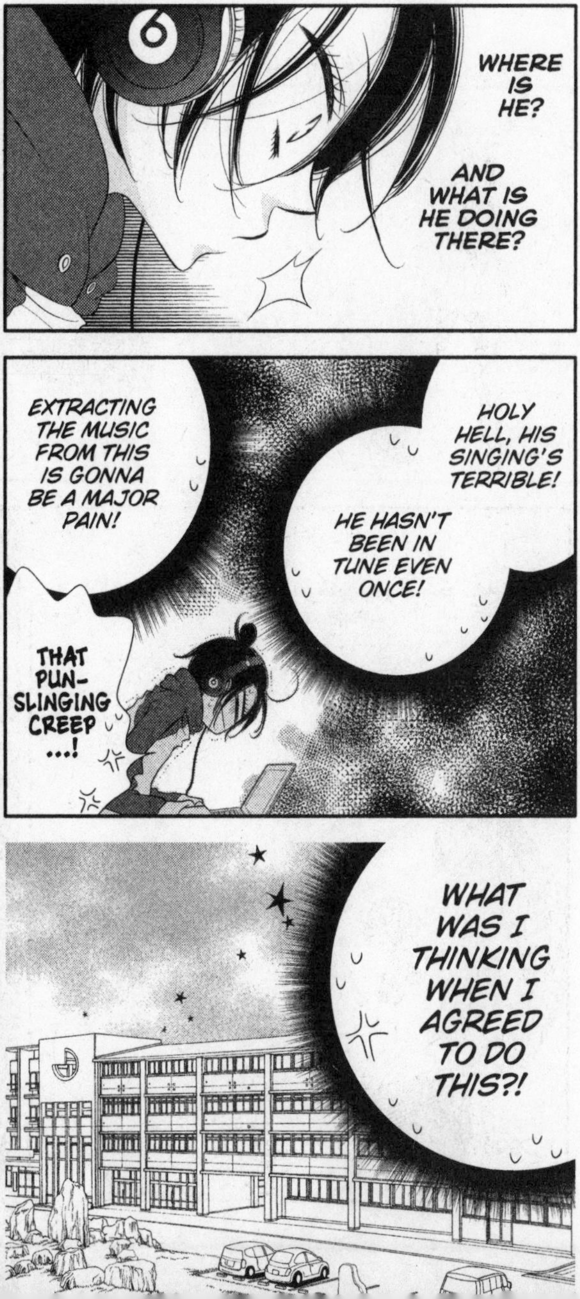
WHERE IS HE?
AND WHAT IS HE DOING THERE?
HOLY HELL, HIS SINGING'S TERRIBLE!
HE HASN'T BEEN IN TUNE EVEN ONCE!
EXTRACTING THE MUSIC FROM THIS IS GONNA BE A MAJOR PAIN!
THAT PUN-SLINGING CREEP ...!
WHAT WAS I THINKING WHEN I AGREED TO DO THIS?!

6

Well, how did you enjoy Anonymous Noise volume 6? Like Nino says, this volume is the "running start." Volume 7 will be the big Nino explosion. I can't wait for you to read it!

I hope to see you all again then! Farewell for now!

-Ryoko Fukuyama

7/17/2015

[SPECIAL THANKS]

MOSAGE

TAKAYUKI NAGASHIMA

KENJU NORO

MY FAMILY

MY FRIENDS

AND YOU!!

Ryoko Fukuyama
c/o Anonymous Noise Editor
VIZ Media
P.O. Box 77010
San Francisco, CA 94107

HP http://ryoconet/

@ryocoryocoryoco

http://facebook.com/ryocoryocoryoco/

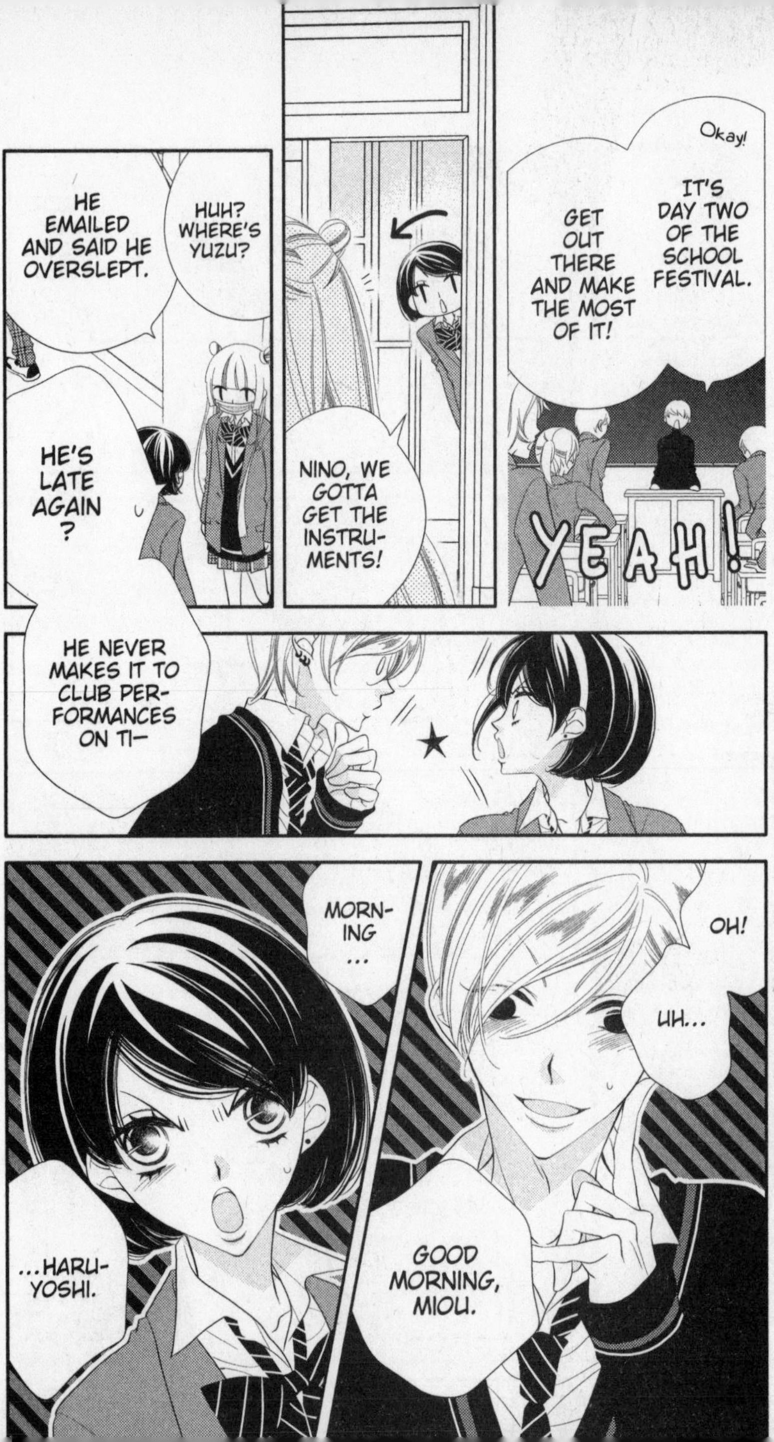
Okay!
IT'S DAY TWO OF THE SCHOOL FESTIVAL.
GET OUT THERE AND MAKE THE MOST OF IT!
YEAH!
NINO, WE GOTTA GET THE INSTRU-MENTS!
HUH? WHERE'S YUZU?
HE EMAILED AND SAID HE OVERSLEPT.
HE'S LATE AGAIN?
HE NEVER MAKES IT TO CLUB PER-FORMANCES ON TI—
OH!
UH...
GOOD MORNING, MIOU.
MORN-ING...
...HARU-YOSHI.

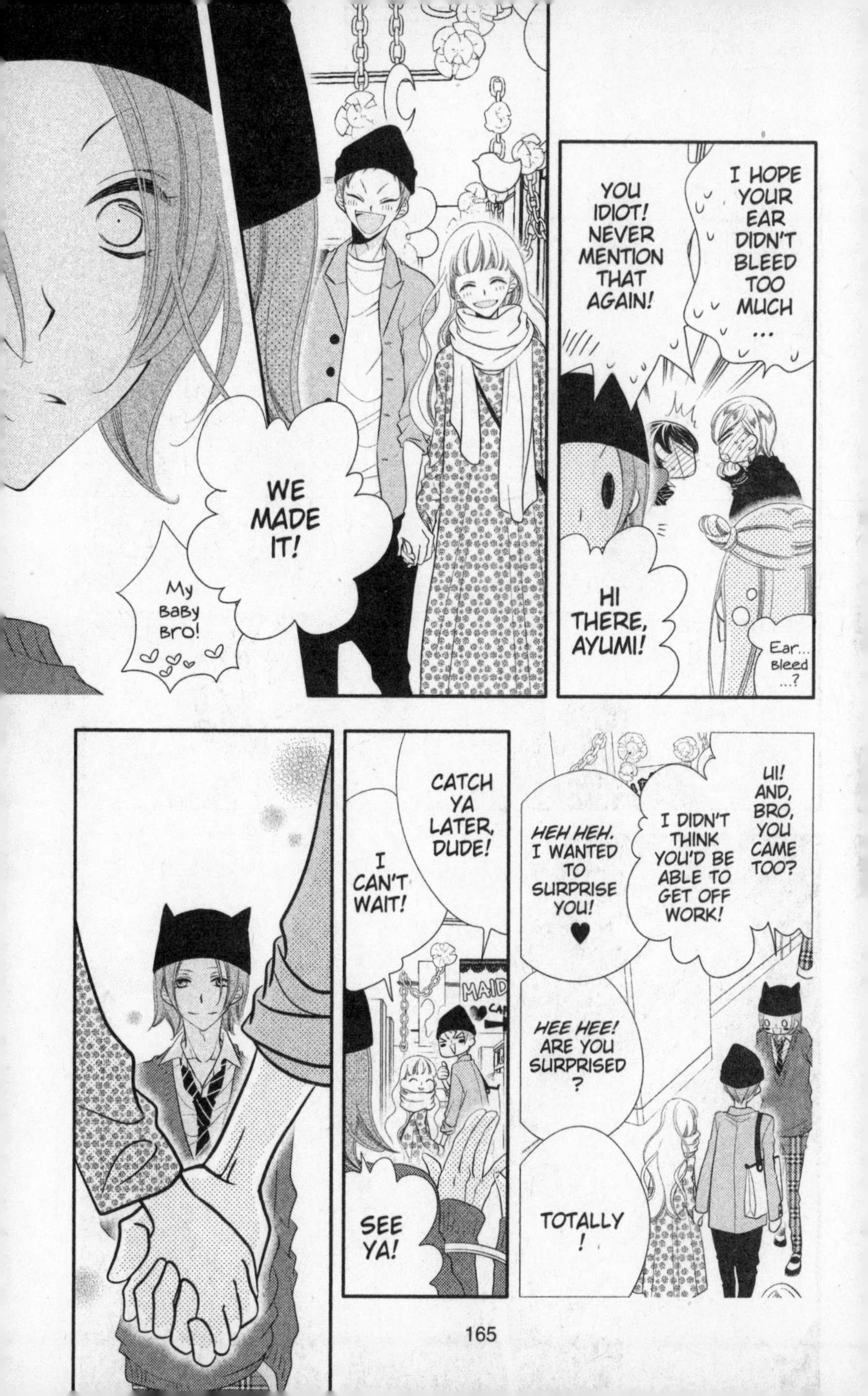
I HOPE YOUR EAR DIDN'T BLEED TOO MUCH ...
YOU IDIOT! NEVER MENTION THAT AGAIN!
Ear... Bleed ...?
HI THERE, AYUMI!
WE MADE IT!
My Baby Bro!
UI! AND, BRO, YOU CAME TOO?
I DIDN'T THINK YOU'D BE ABLE TO GET OFF WORK!
HEH HEH. I WANTED TO SURPRISE YOU! ♥
HEE HEE! ARE YOU SURPRISED ?
TOTALLY !
CATCH YA LATER, DUDE!
I CAN'T WAIT!
MAID CA
SEE YA!

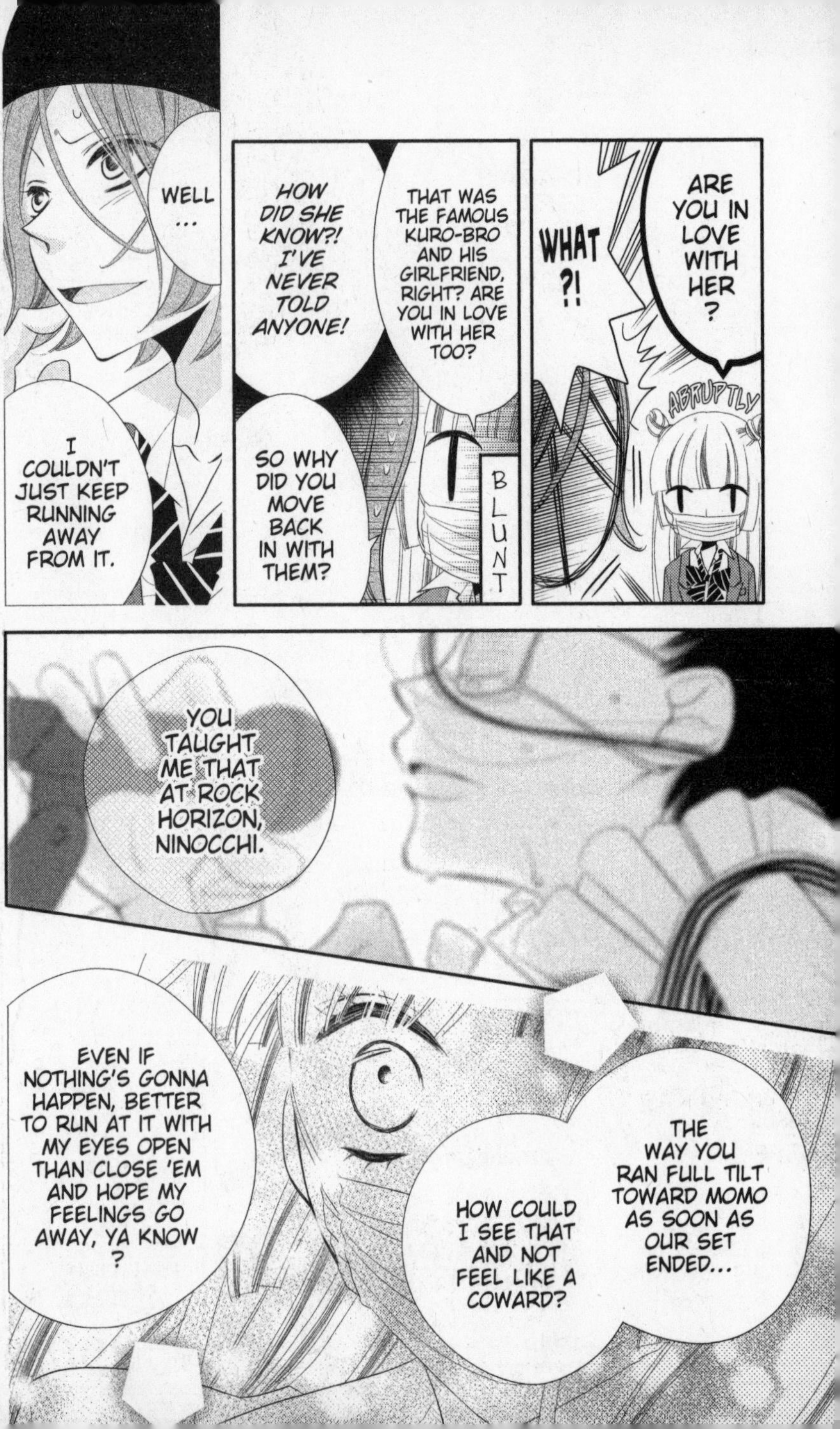
ARE YOU IN LOVE WITH HER?
WHAT?!
ABRUPTLY
THAT WAS THE FAMOUS KURO-BRO AND HIS GIRLFRIEND, RIGHT? ARE YOU IN LOVE WITH HER TOO?
HOW DID SHE KNOW?! I'VE NEVER TOLD ANYONE!
BLUNT
SO WHY DID YOU MOVE BACK IN WITH THEM?
WELL...
I COULDN'T JUST KEEP RUNNING AWAY FROM IT.
YOU TAUGHT ME THAT AT ROCK HORIZON, NINOCCHI.
THE WAY YOU RAN FULL TILT TOWARD MOMO AS SOON AS OUR SET ENDED...
HOW COULD I SEE THAT AND NOT FEEL LIKE A COWARD?
EVEN IF NOTHING'S GONNA HAPPEN, BETTER TO RUN AT IT WITH MY EYES OPEN THAN CLOSE 'EM AND HOPE MY FEELINGS GO AWAY, YA KNOW?

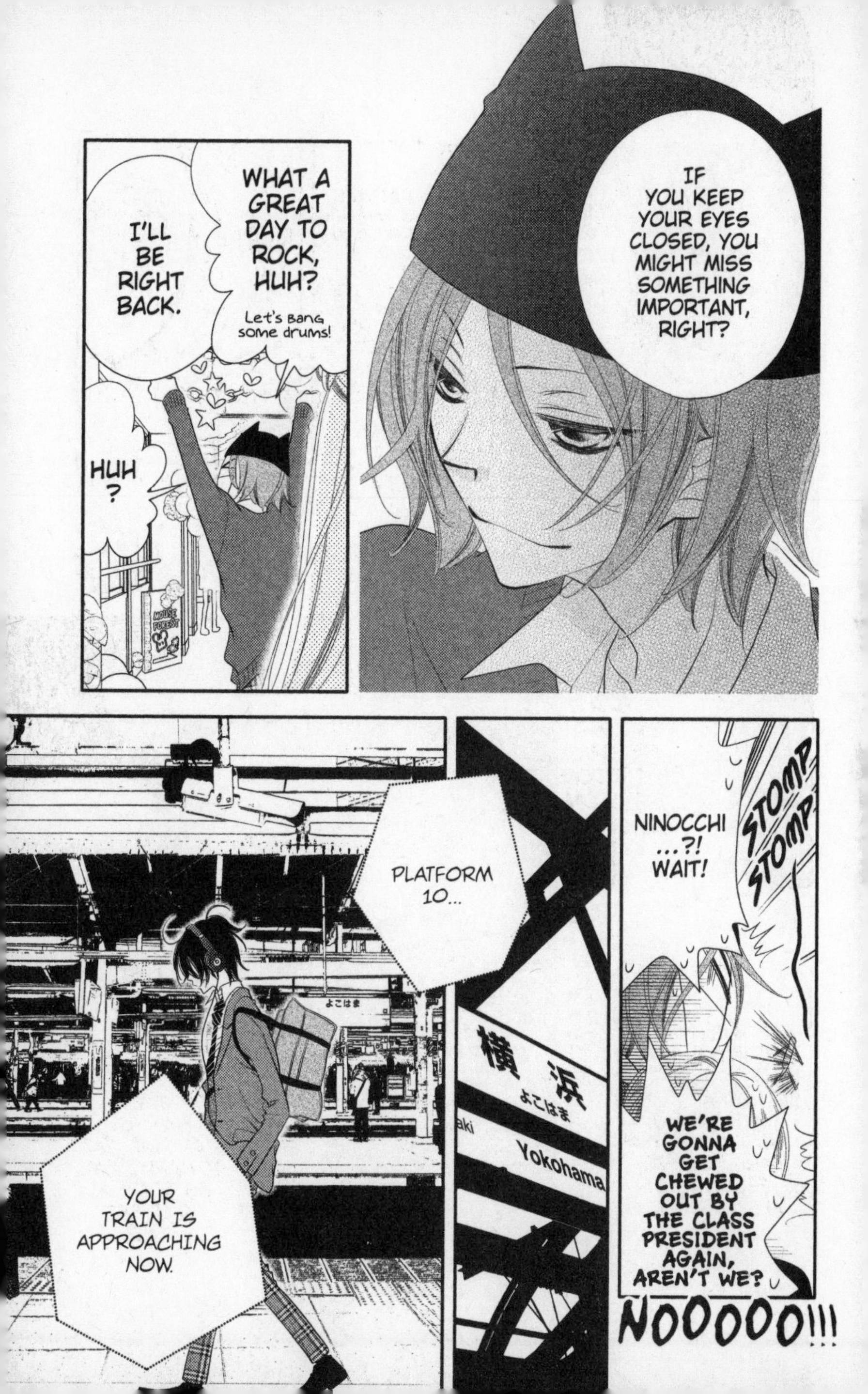
IF YOU KEEP YOUR EYES CLOSED, YOU MIGHT MISS SOMETHING IMPORTANT, RIGHT?
WHAT A GREAT DAY TO ROCK, HUH?
Let's bang some drums!
I'LL BE RIGHT BACK.
HUH ?
MOUSE FOREST
STOMP STOMP
NINOCCHI ...?! WAIT!
WE'RE GONNA GET CHEWED OUT BY THE CLASS PRESIDENT AGAIN, AREN'T WE?
NOOOOO!!!
横浜
よこはま
Yokohama
PLATFORM 10...
よこはま
YOUR TRAIN IS APPROACHING NOW.

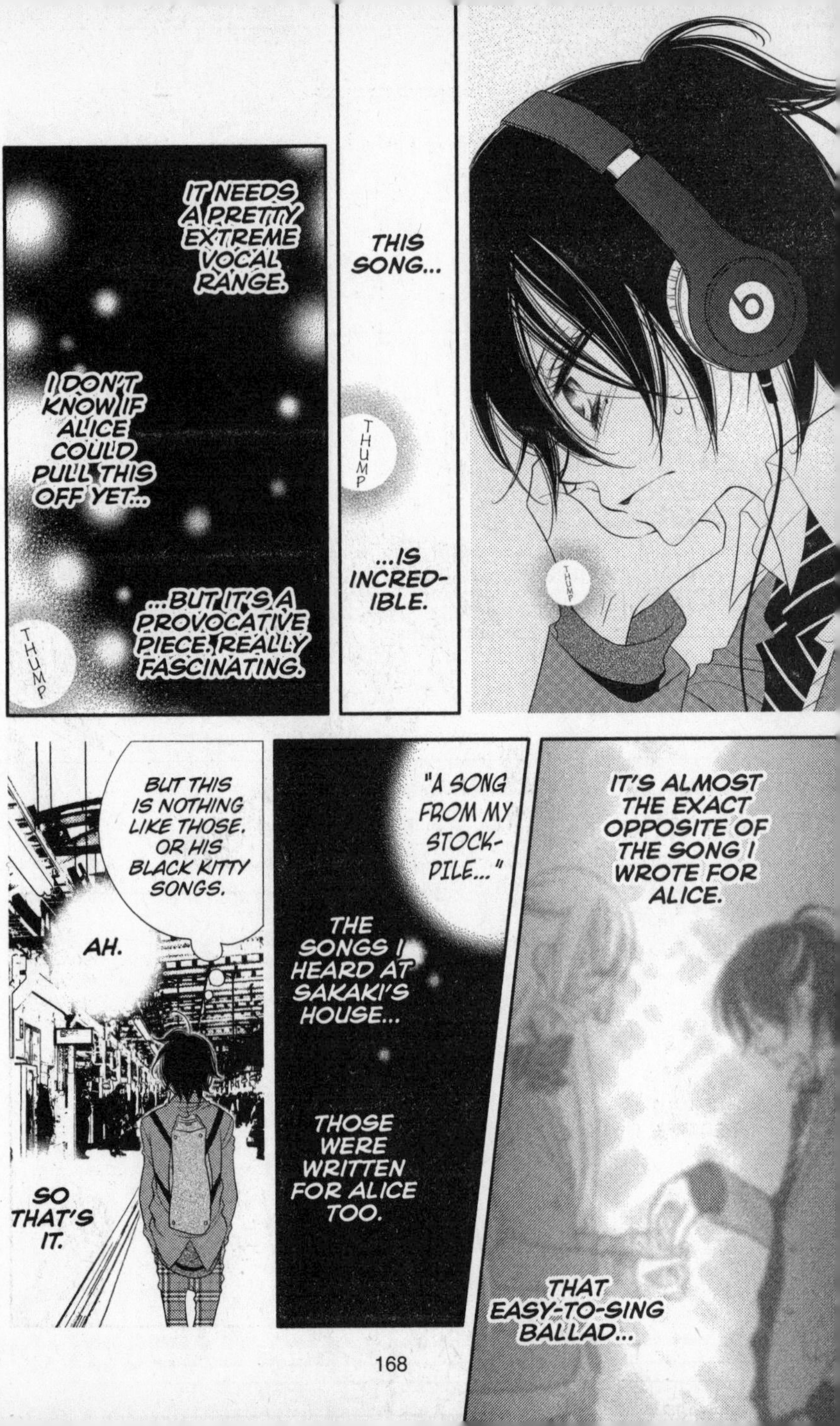
THUMP
THIS SONG...
THUMP
...IS INCREDIBLE.
IT NEEDS A PRETTY EXTREME VOCAL RANGE.
I DON'T KNOW IF ALICE COULD PULL THIS OFF YET...
...BUT IT'S A PROVOCATIVE PIECE. REALLY FASCINATING.
THUMP
IT'S ALMOST THE EXACT OPPOSITE OF THE SONG I WROTE FOR ALICE.
THAT EASY-TO-SING BALLAD...
"A SONG FROM MY STOCKPILE..."
THE SONGS I HEARD AT SAKAKI'S HOUSE...
THOSE WERE WRITTEN FOR ALICE TOO.
BUT THIS IS NOTHING LIKE THOSE. OR HIS BLACK KITTY SONGS.
AH.
SO THAT'S IT.

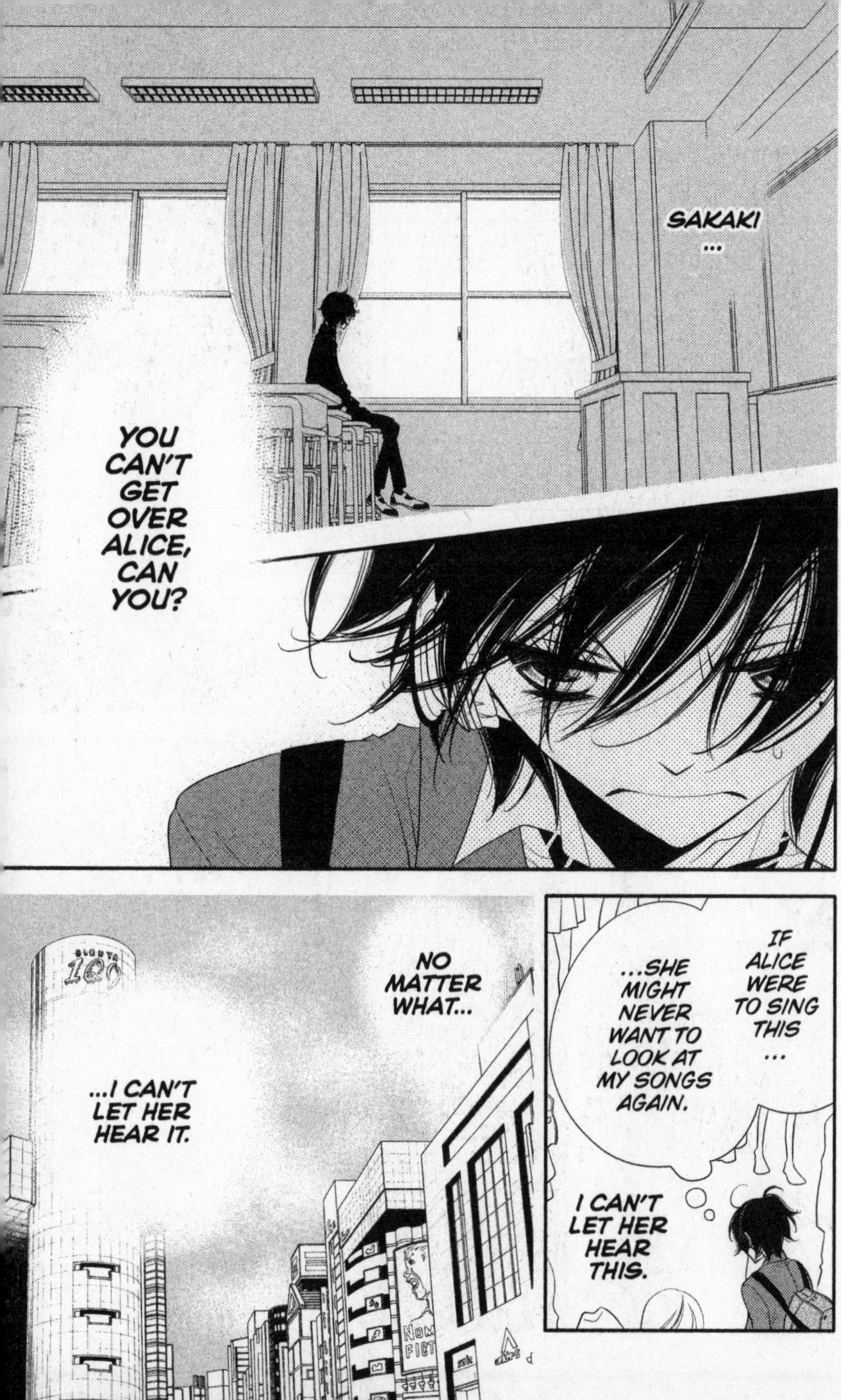
SAKAKI
...
YOU CAN'T GET OVER ALICE, CAN YOU?
IF ALICE WERE TO SING THIS
...
...SHE MIGHT NEVER WANT TO LOOK AT MY SONGS AGAIN.
I CAN'T LET HER HEAR THIS.
NO MATTER WHAT...
...I CAN'T LET HER HEAR IT.

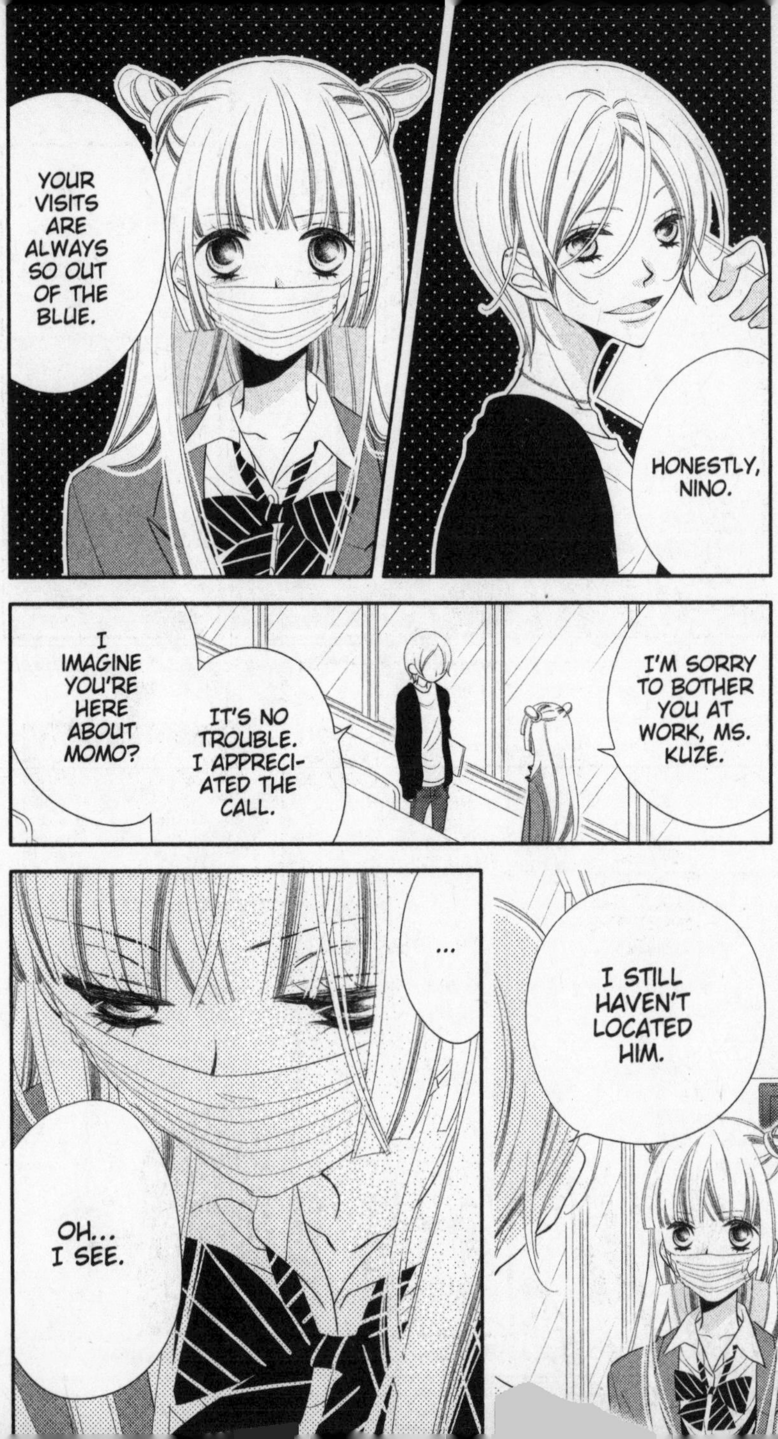
HONESTLY, NINO.
YOUR VISITS ARE ALWAYS SO OUT OF THE BLUE.
I'M SORRY TO BOTHER YOU AT WORK, MS. KUZE.
IT'S NO TROUBLE. I APPRECIATED THE CALL.
I IMAGINE YOU'RE HERE ABOUT MOMO?
I STILL HAVEN'T LOCATED HIM.
...
OH... I SEE.

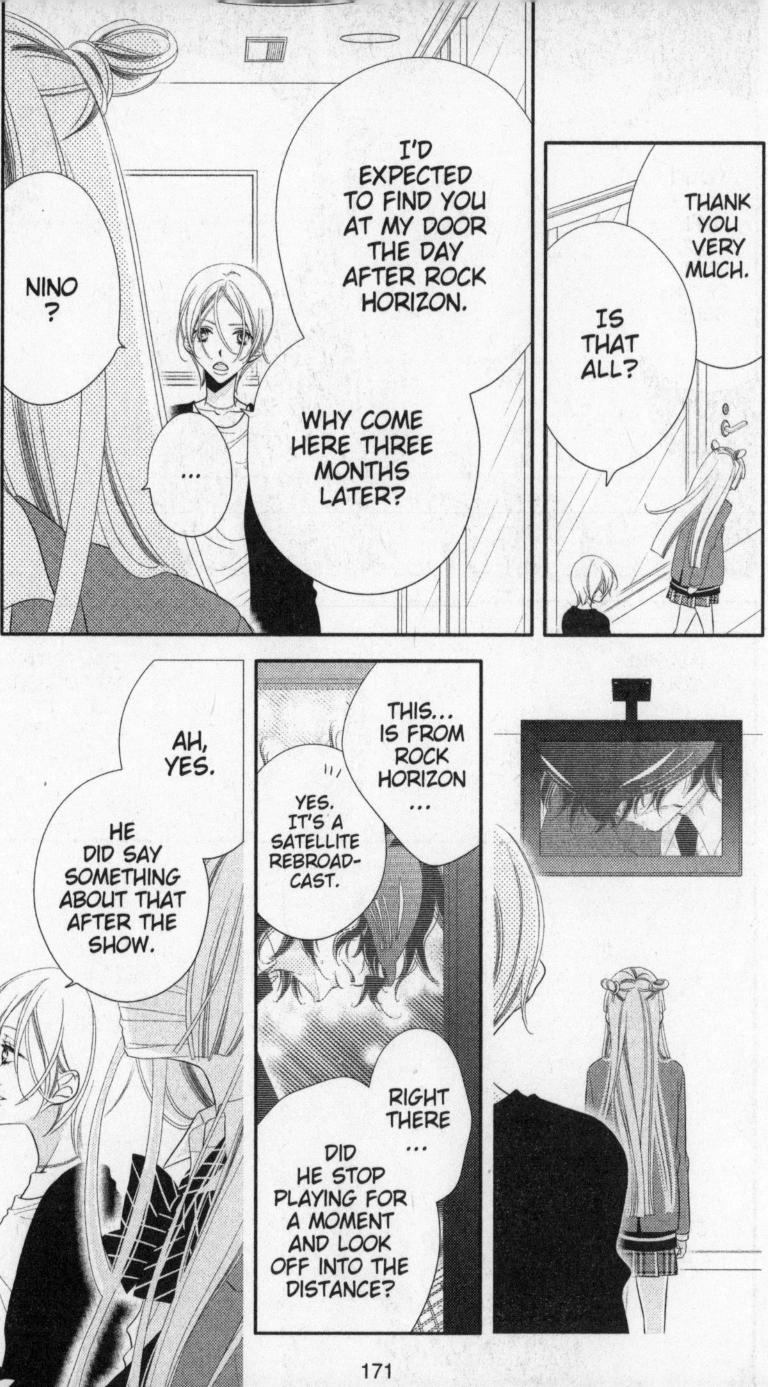
THANK YOU VERY MUCH.
IS THAT ALL?
I'D EXPECTED TO FIND YOU AT MY DOOR THE DAY AFTER ROCK HORIZON.
NINO?
WHY COME HERE THREE MONTHS LATER?
...
THIS... IS FROM ROCK HORIZON...
YES. IT'S A SATELLITE REBROAD-CAST.
RIGHT THERE...
DID HE STOP PLAYING FOR A MOMENT AND LOOK OFF INTO THE DISTANCE?
AH, YES.
HE DID SAY SOMETHING ABOUT THAT AFTER THE SHOW.

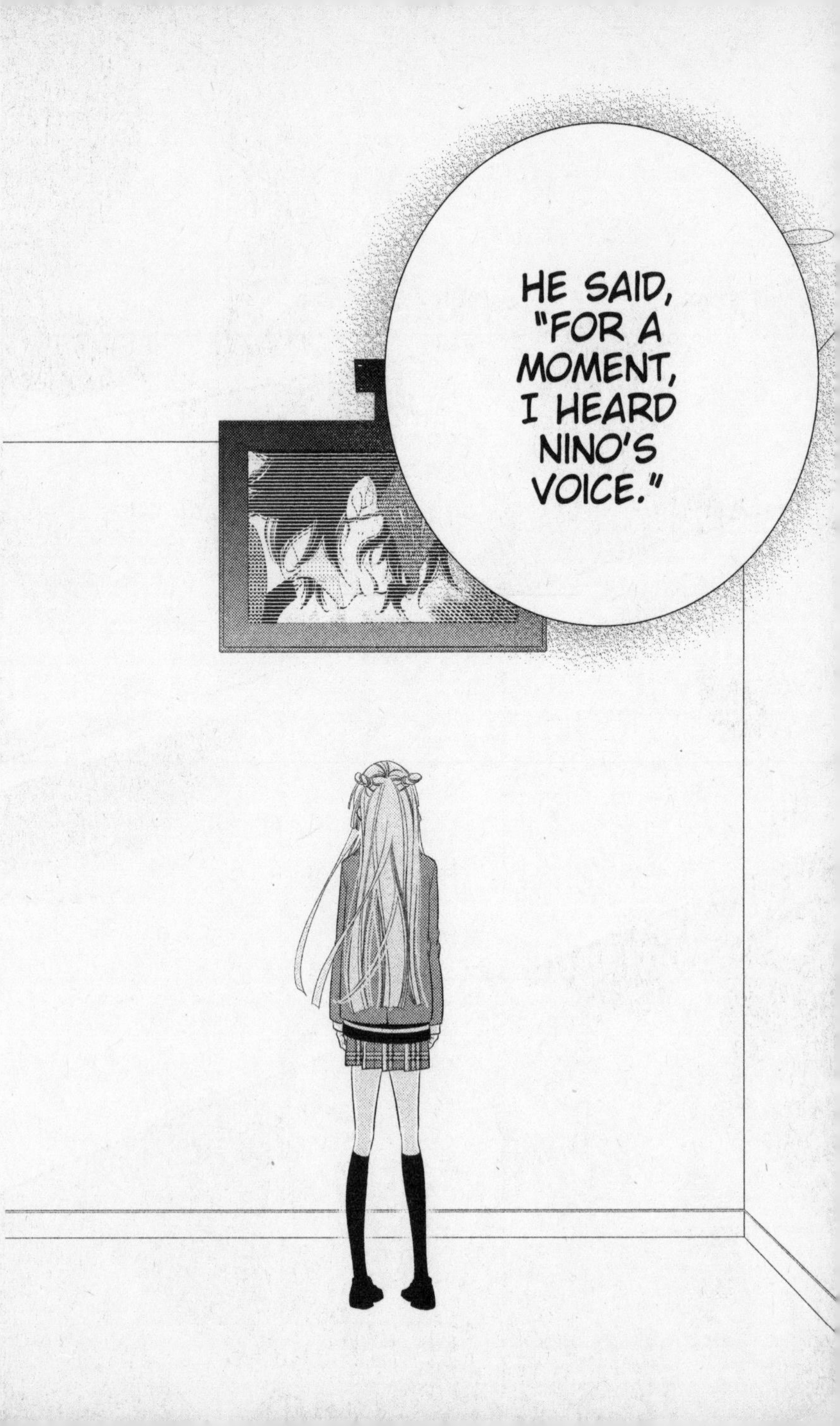
HE SAID, "FOR A MOMENT, I HEARD NINO'S VOICE."

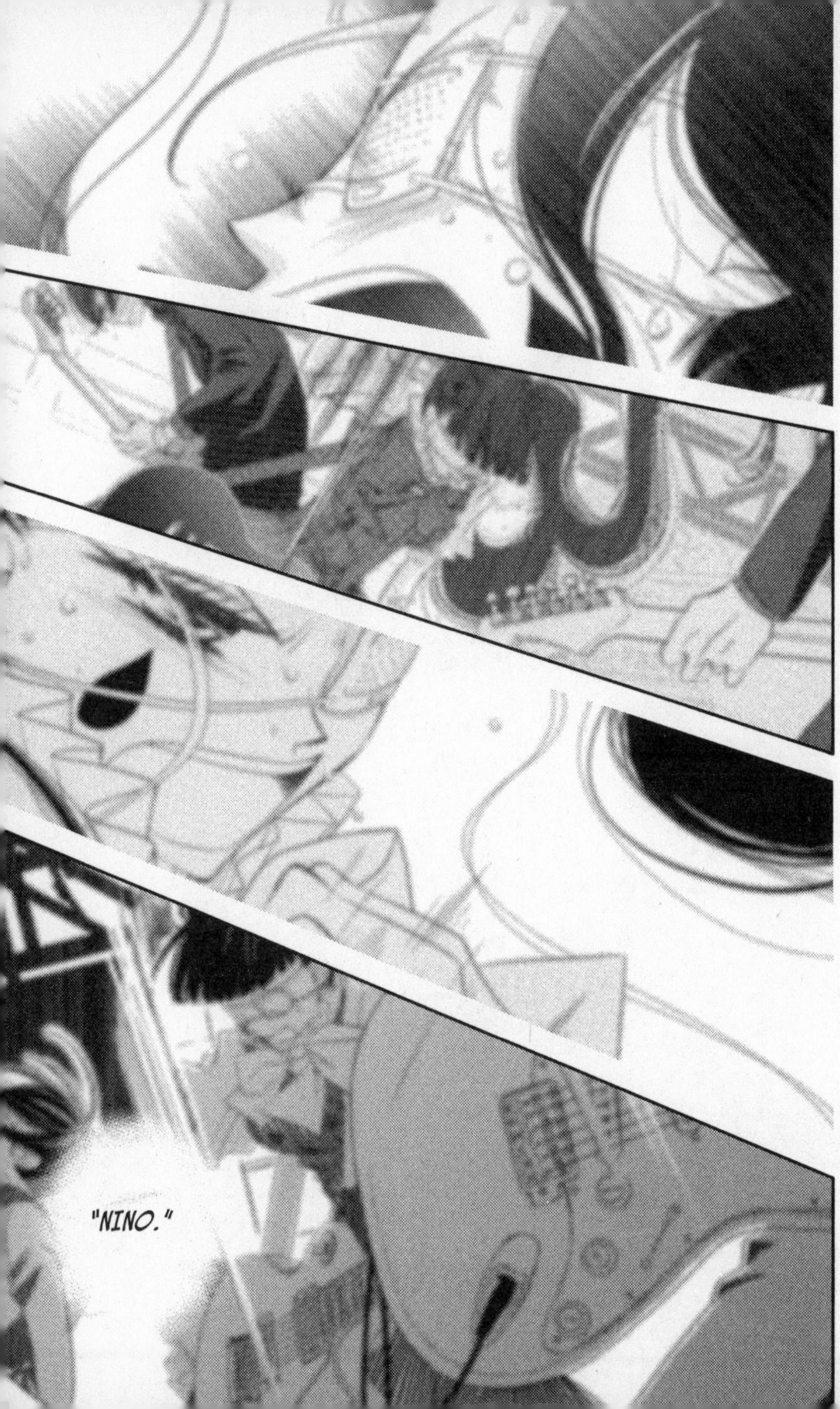
"NINO."

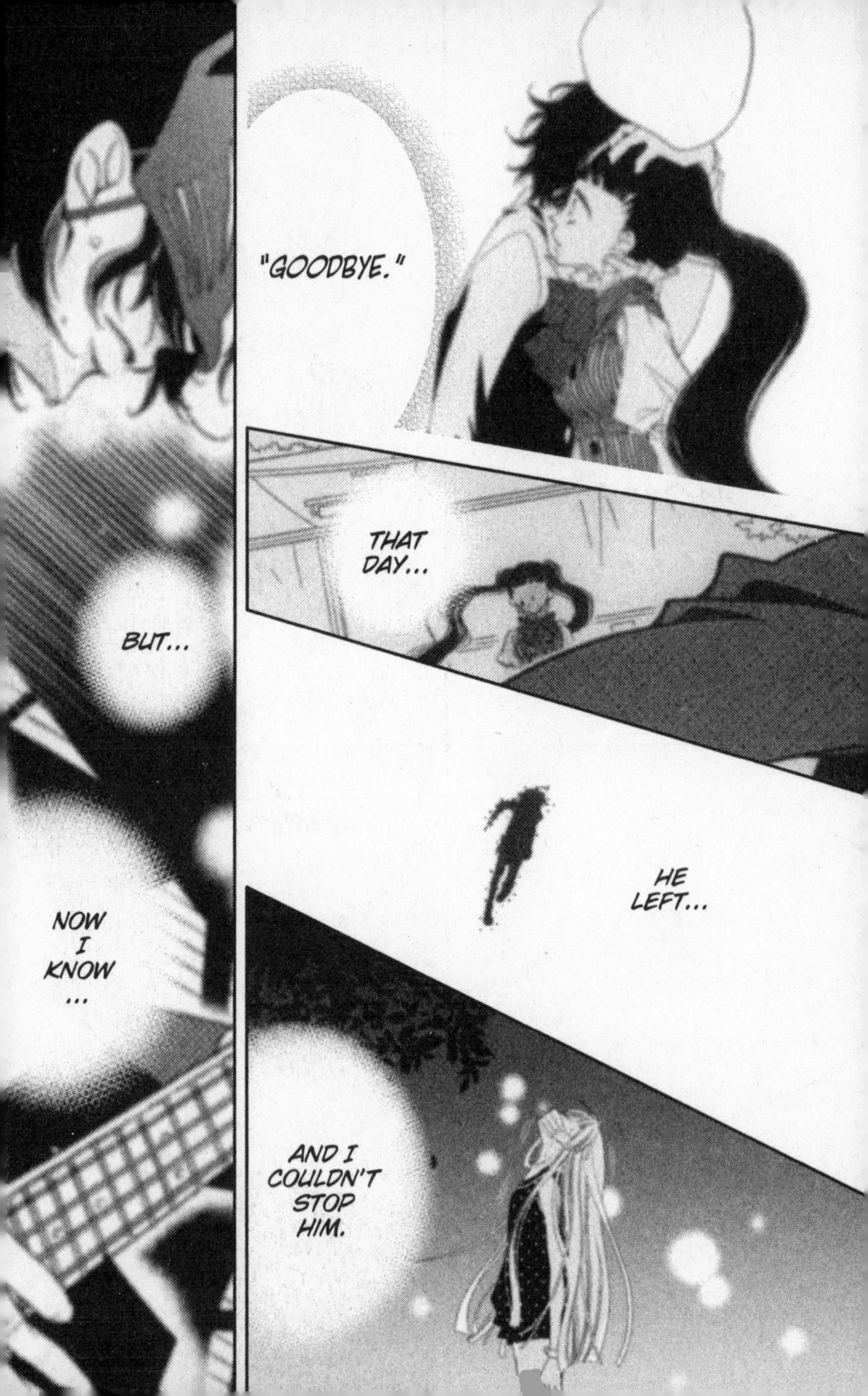
"GOODBYE."
THAT DAY...
HE LEFT...
AND I COULDN'T STOP HIM.
BUT...
NOW I KNOW ...

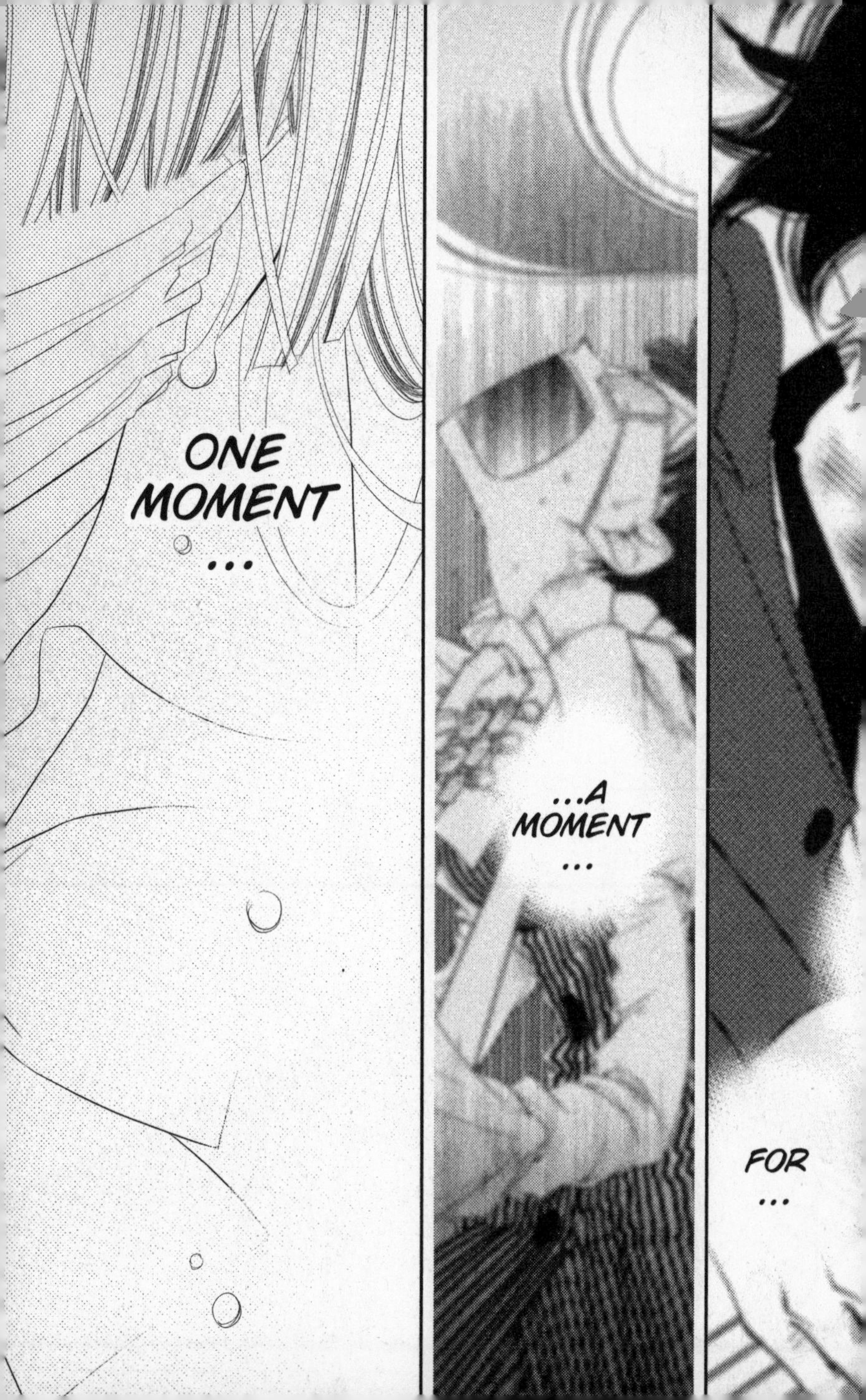
FOR ...
...A MOMENT ...
ONE MOMENT ...

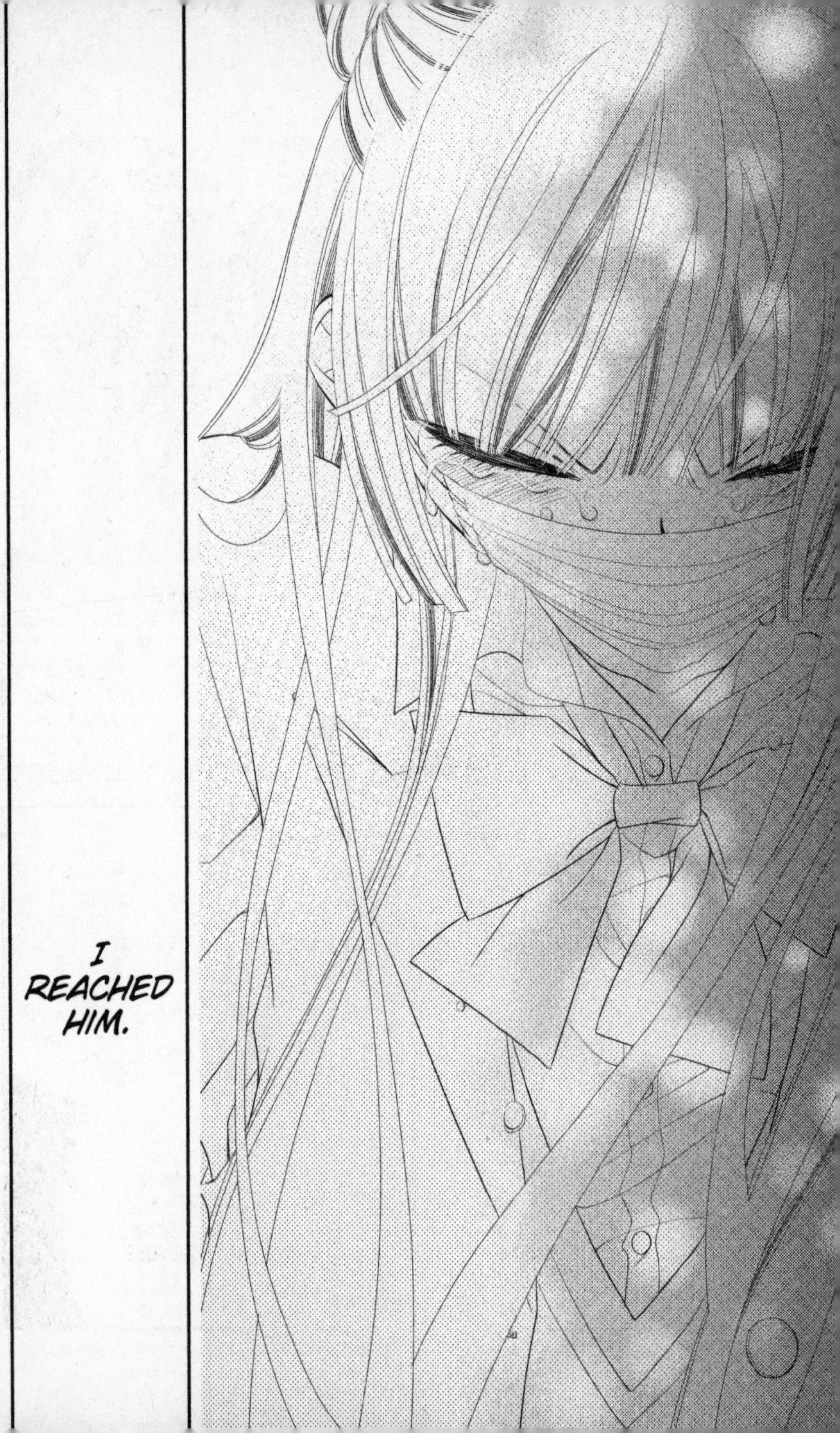
I REACHED HIM.

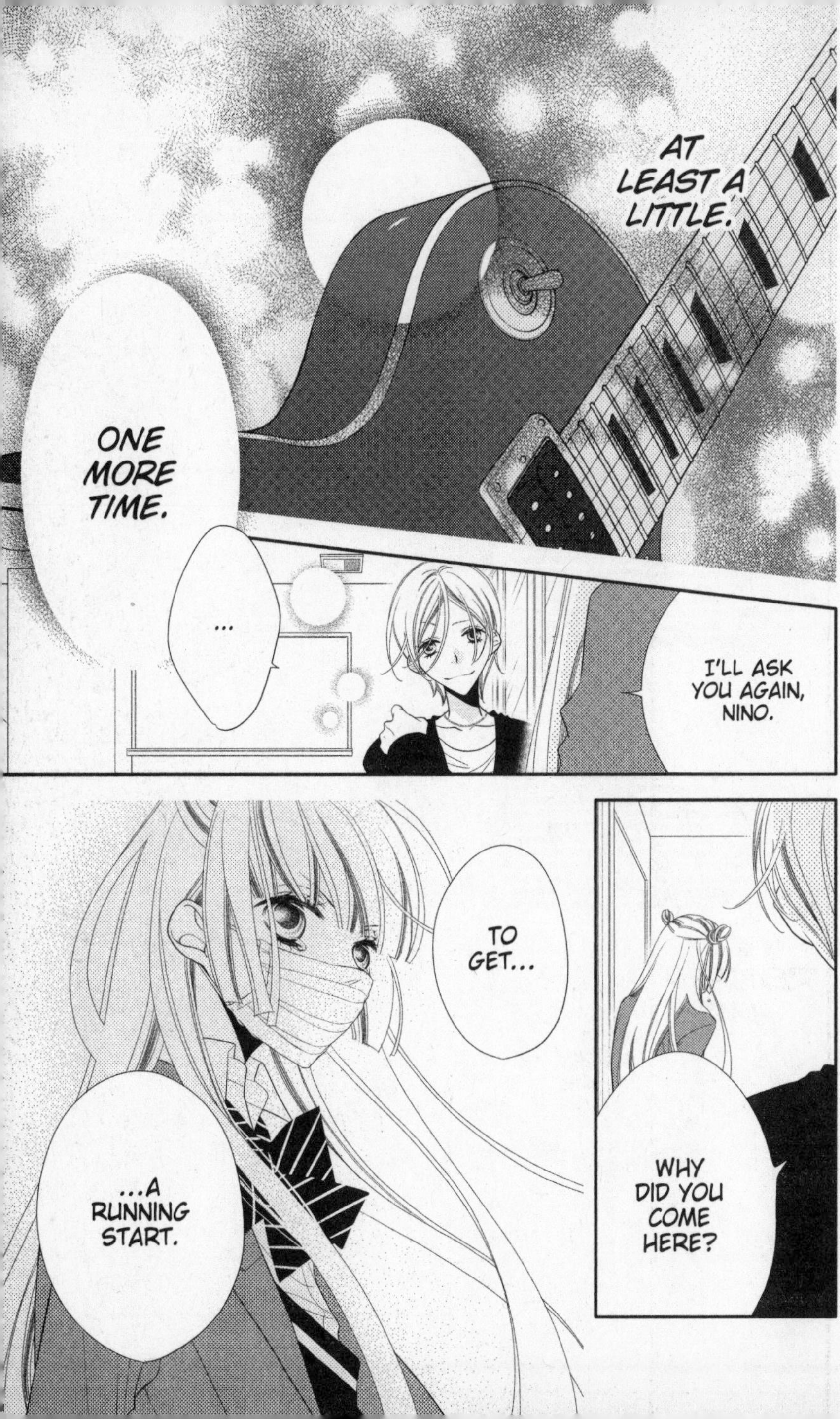
AT LEAST A LITTLE.
ONE MORE TIME.
I'LL ASK YOU AGAIN, NINO.
...
WHY DID YOU COME HERE?
TO GET...
...A RUNNING START.

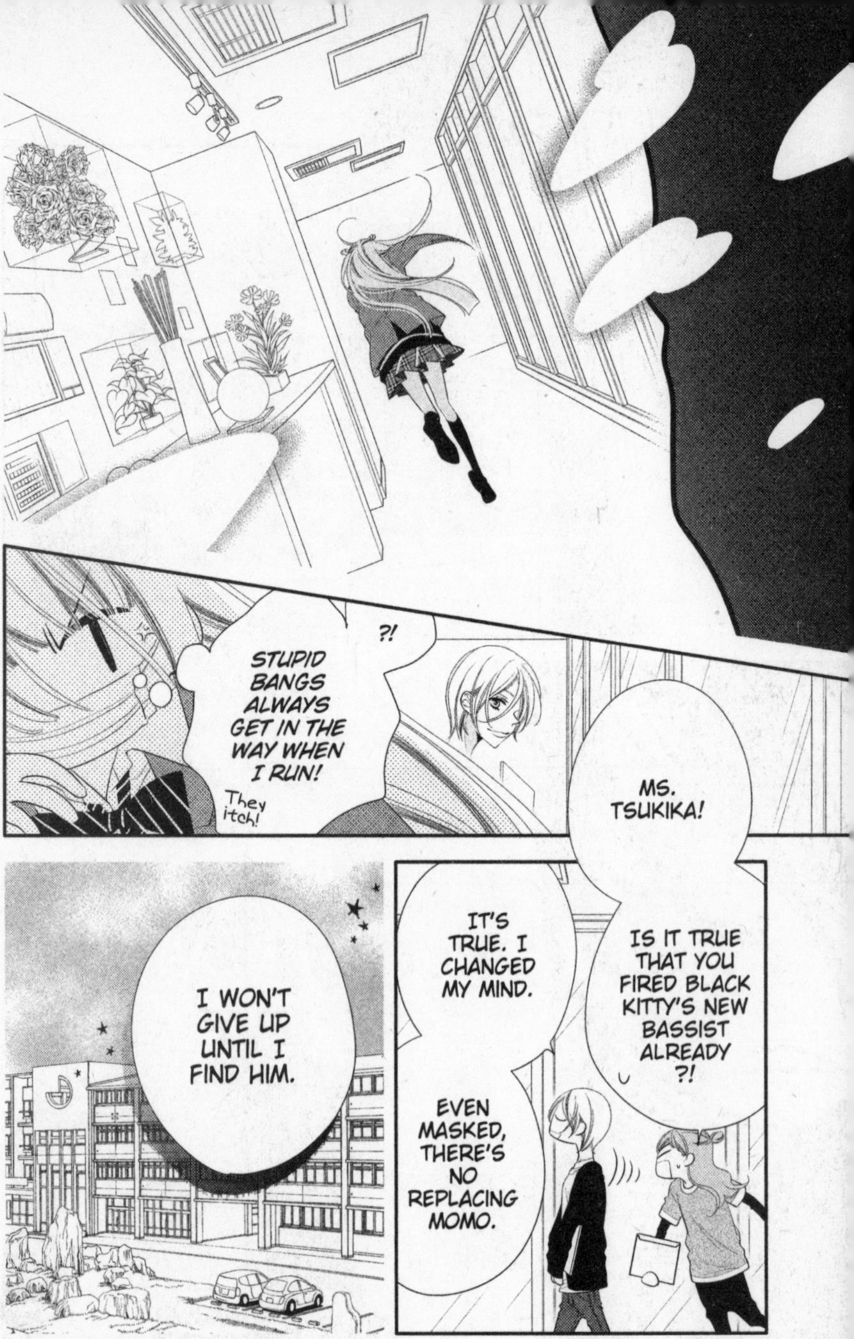
?!
STUPID BANGS ALWAYS GET IN THE WAY WHEN I RUN!
They itch!
MS. TSUKIKA!
IS IT TRUE THAT YOU FIRED BLACK KITTY'S NEW BASSIST ALREADY ?!
IT'S TRUE. I CHANGED MY MIND.
EVEN MASKED, THERE'S NO REPLACING MOMO.
I WON'T GIVE UP UNTIL I FIND HIM.

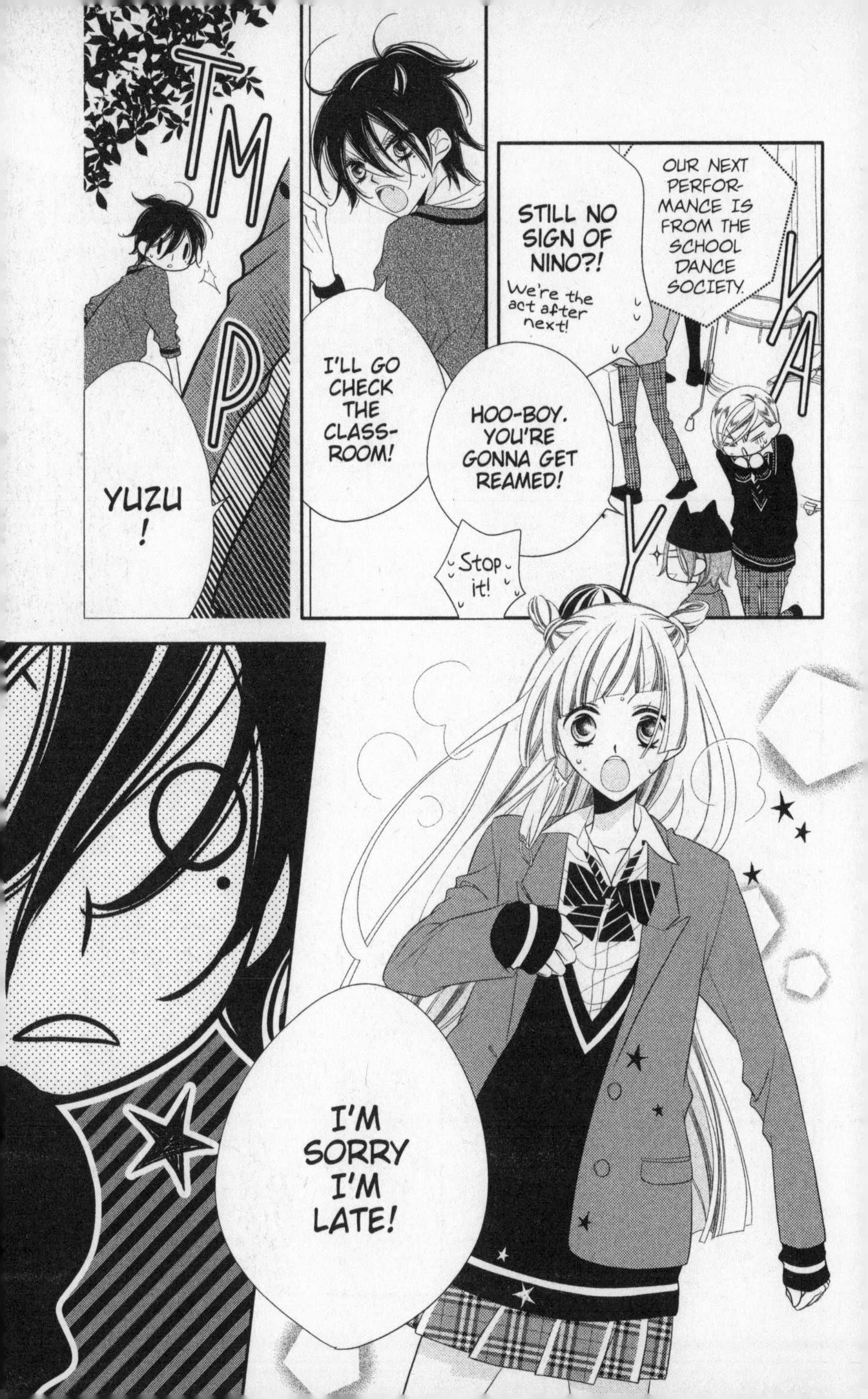
OUR NEXT PERFORMANCE IS FROM THE SCHOOL DANCE SOCIETY.
STILL NO SIGN OF NINO?!
We're the act after next!
YAY
HOO-BOY. YOU'RE GONNA GET REAMED!
Stop it!
I'LL GO CHECK THE CLASSROOM!
TMP
YUZU!
I'M SORRY I'M LATE!

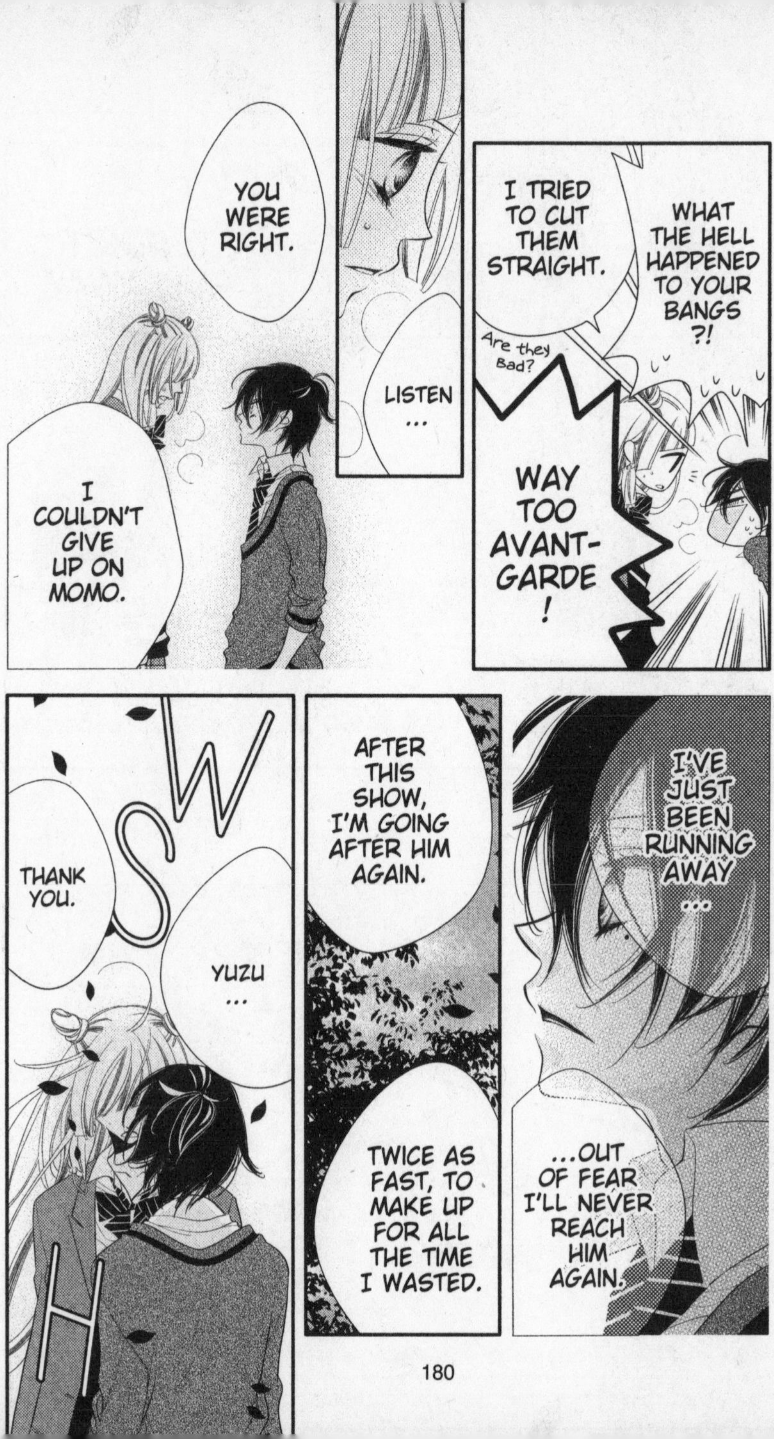
WHAT THE HELL HAPPENED TO YOUR BANGS ?!
I TRIED TO CUT THEM STRAIGHT.
Are they Bad?
WAY TOO AVANT-GARDE!
LISTEN...
YOU WERE RIGHT.
I COULDN'T GIVE UP ON MOMO.
I'VE JUST BEEN RUNNING AWAY...
...OUT OF FEAR I'LL NEVER REACH HIM AGAIN.
AFTER THIS SHOW, I'M GOING AFTER HIM AGAIN.
TWICE AS FAST, TO MAKE UP FOR ALL THE TIME I WASTED.
YUZU...
THANK YOU.
SW
H

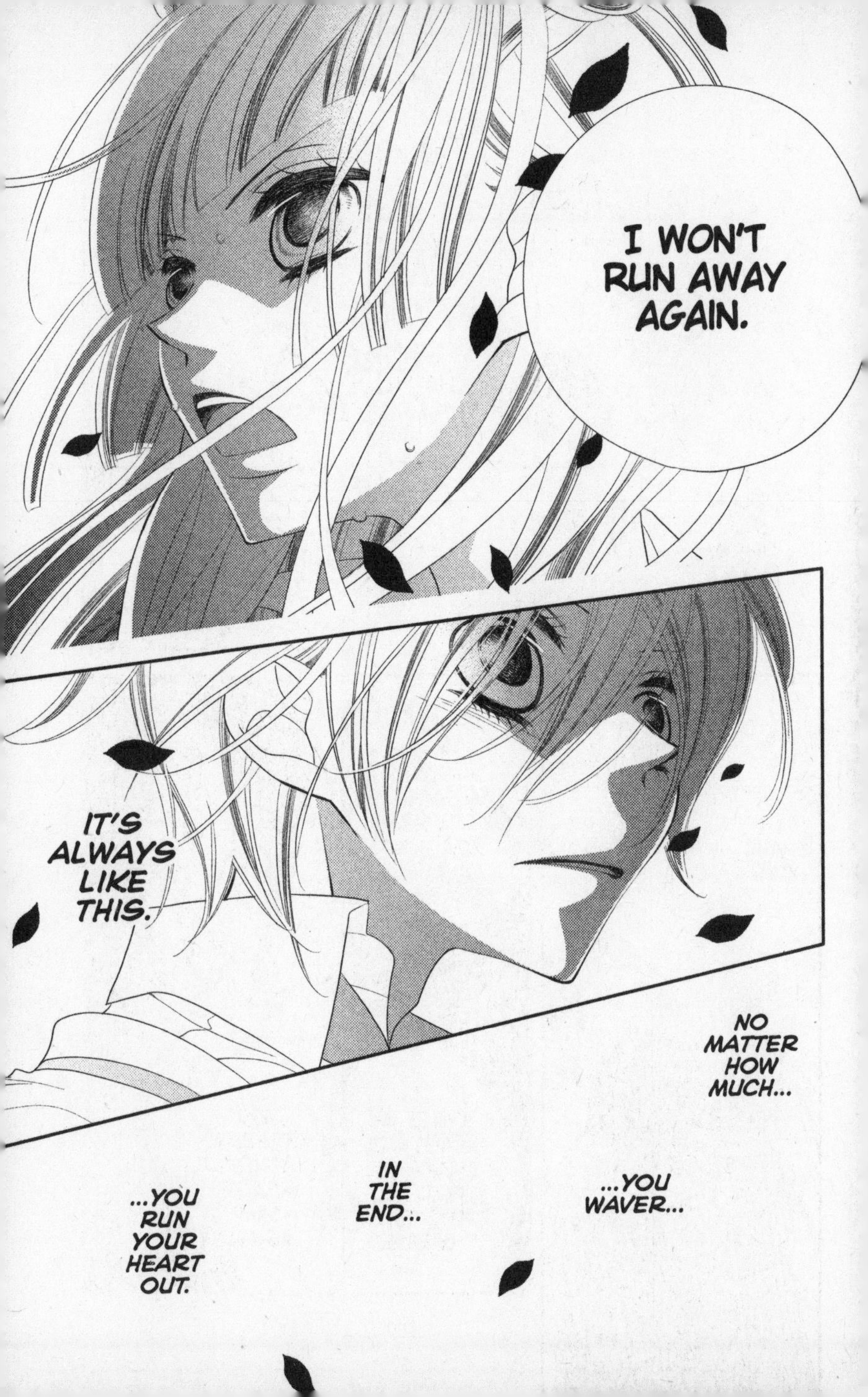
I WON'T RUN AWAY AGAIN.
IT'S ALWAYS LIKE THIS.
NO MATTER HOW MUCH...
...YOU WAVER...
IN THE END...
...YOU RUN YOUR HEART OUT.

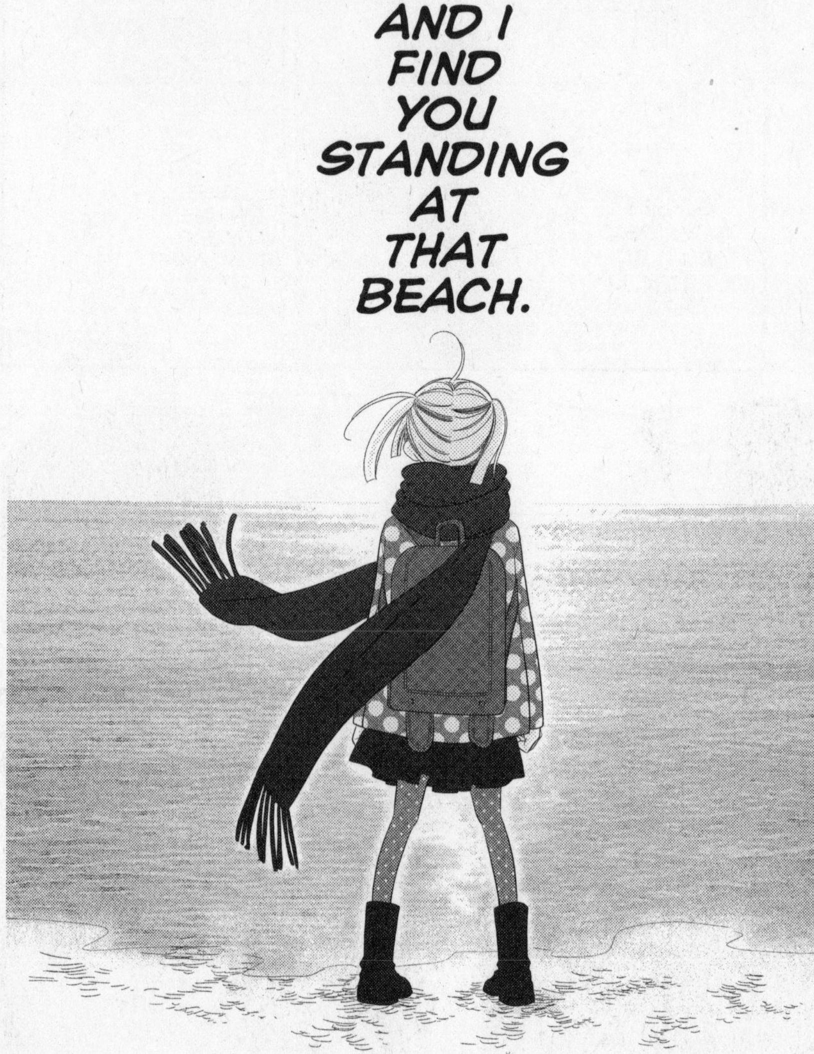
AND I FIND YOU STANDING AT THAT BEACH.

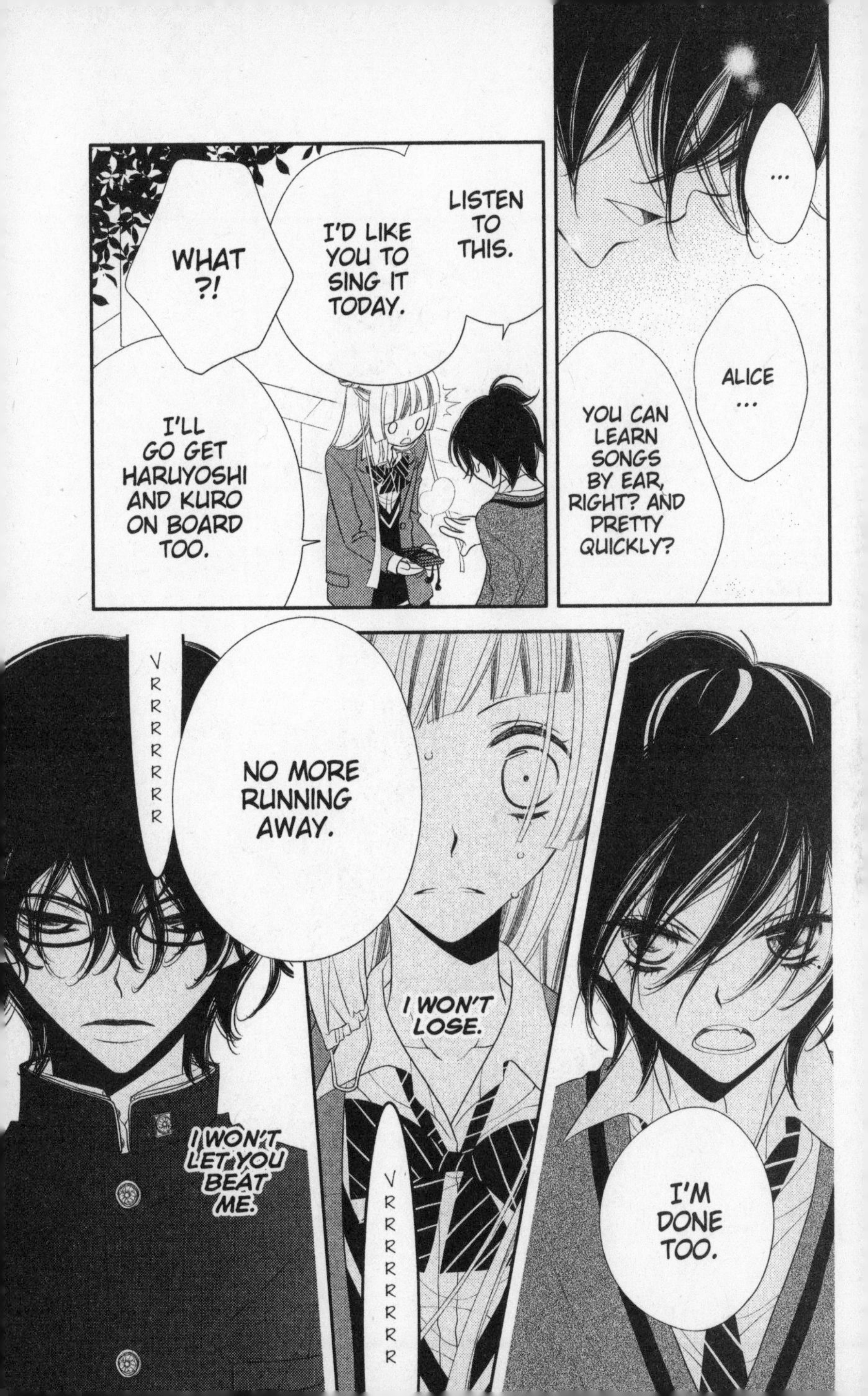
...
ALICE ...
YOU CAN LEARN SONGS BY EAR, RIGHT? AND PRETTY QUICKLY?
LISTEN TO THIS.
I'D LIKE YOU TO SING IT TODAY.
WHAT ?!
I'LL GO GET HARUYOSHI AND KURO ON BOARD TOO.
I'M DONE TOO.
VRRRRRRRR
I WON'T LOSE.
NO MORE RUNNING AWAY.
VRRRRRRR
I WON'T LET YOU BEAT ME.

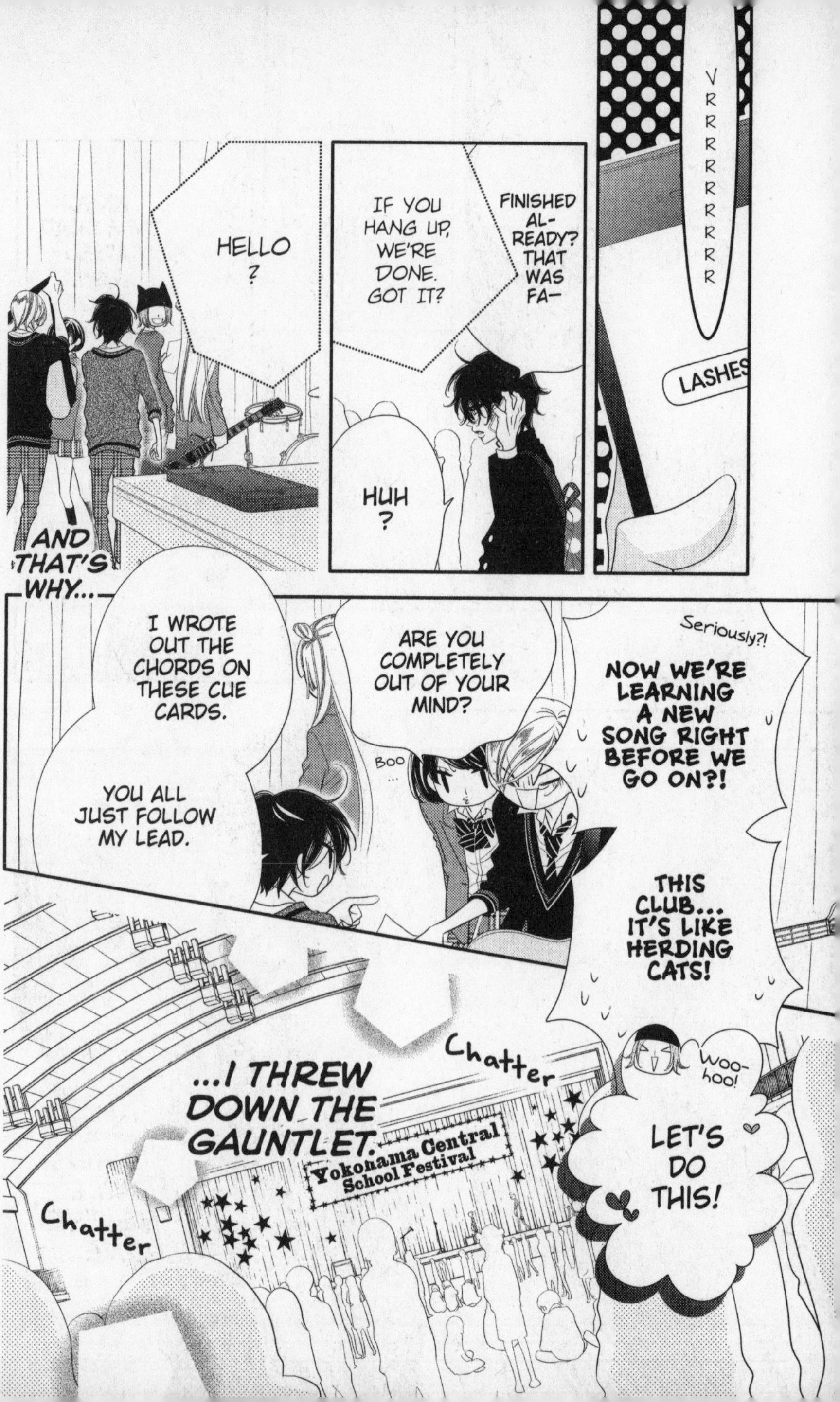
VRRRRRRRR
LASHES
FINISHED AL-READY? THAT WAS FA—
IF YOU HANG UP, WE'RE DONE. GOT IT?
HUH?
HELLO?
AND THAT'S WHY...
Seriously?!
NOW WE'RE LEARNING A NEW SONG RIGHT BEFORE WE GO ON?!
ARE YOU COMPLETELY OUT OF YOUR MIND?
I WROTE OUT THE CHORDS ON THESE CUE CARDS.
YOU ALL JUST FOLLOW MY LEAD.
BOO...
THIS CLUB... IT'S LIKE HERDING CATS!
Woo-hoo!
LET'S DO THIS!
Chatter
...I THREW DOWN THE GAUNTLET.
Yokohama Central School Festival
Chatter

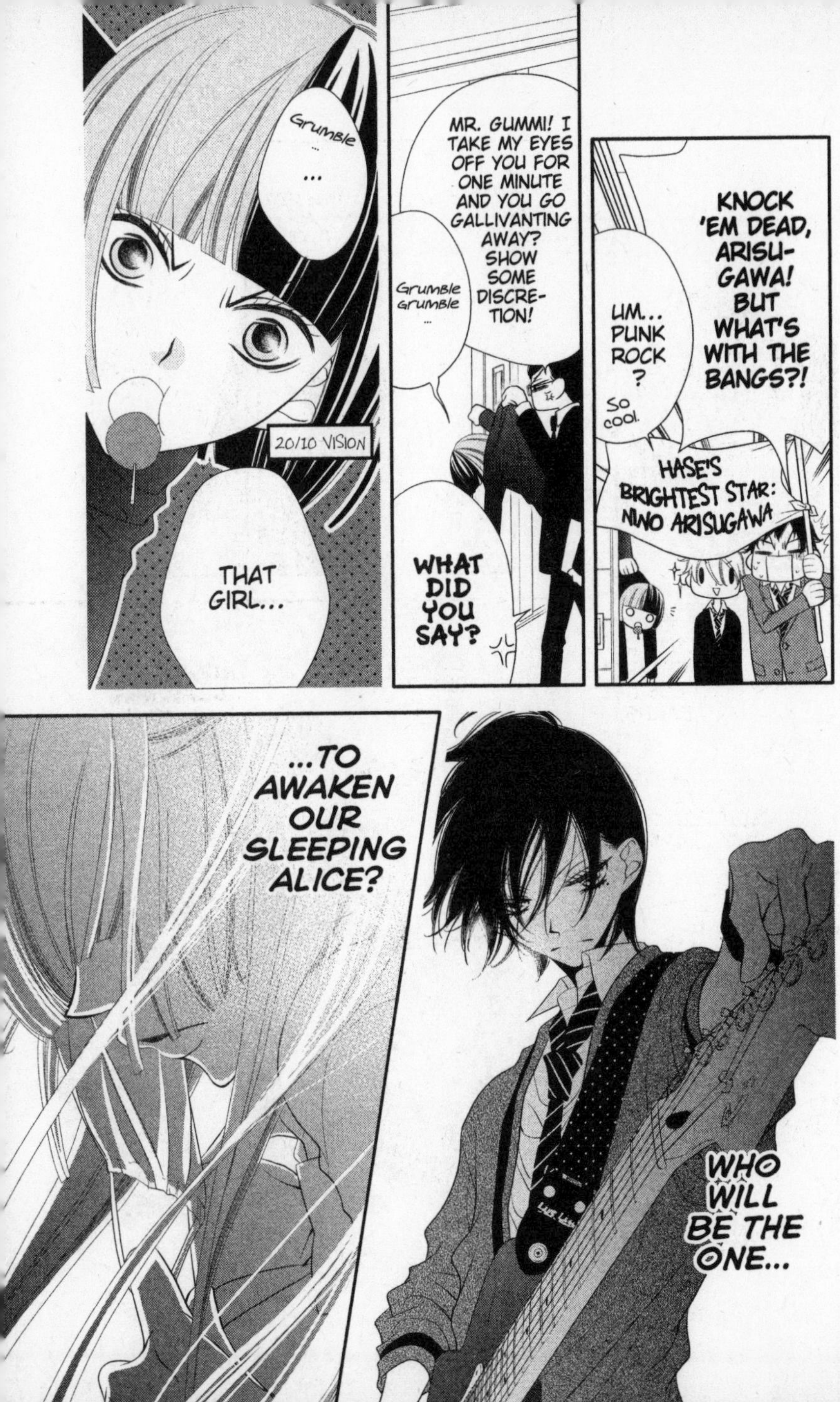
KNOCK 'EM DEAD, ARISUGAWA! BUT WHAT'S WITH THE BANGS?!
UM... PUNK ROCK?
So cool.
HASE'S BRIGHTEST STAR: NINO ARISUGAWA
MR. GUMMI! I TAKE MY EYES OFF YOU FOR ONE MINUTE AND YOU GO GALLIVANTING AWAY? SHOW SOME DISCRETION!
Grumble Grumble ...
WHAT DID YOU SAY?
Grumble ...
...
20/10 VISION
THAT GIRL...
WHO WILL BE THE ONE...
...TO AWAKEN OUR SLEEPING ALICE?

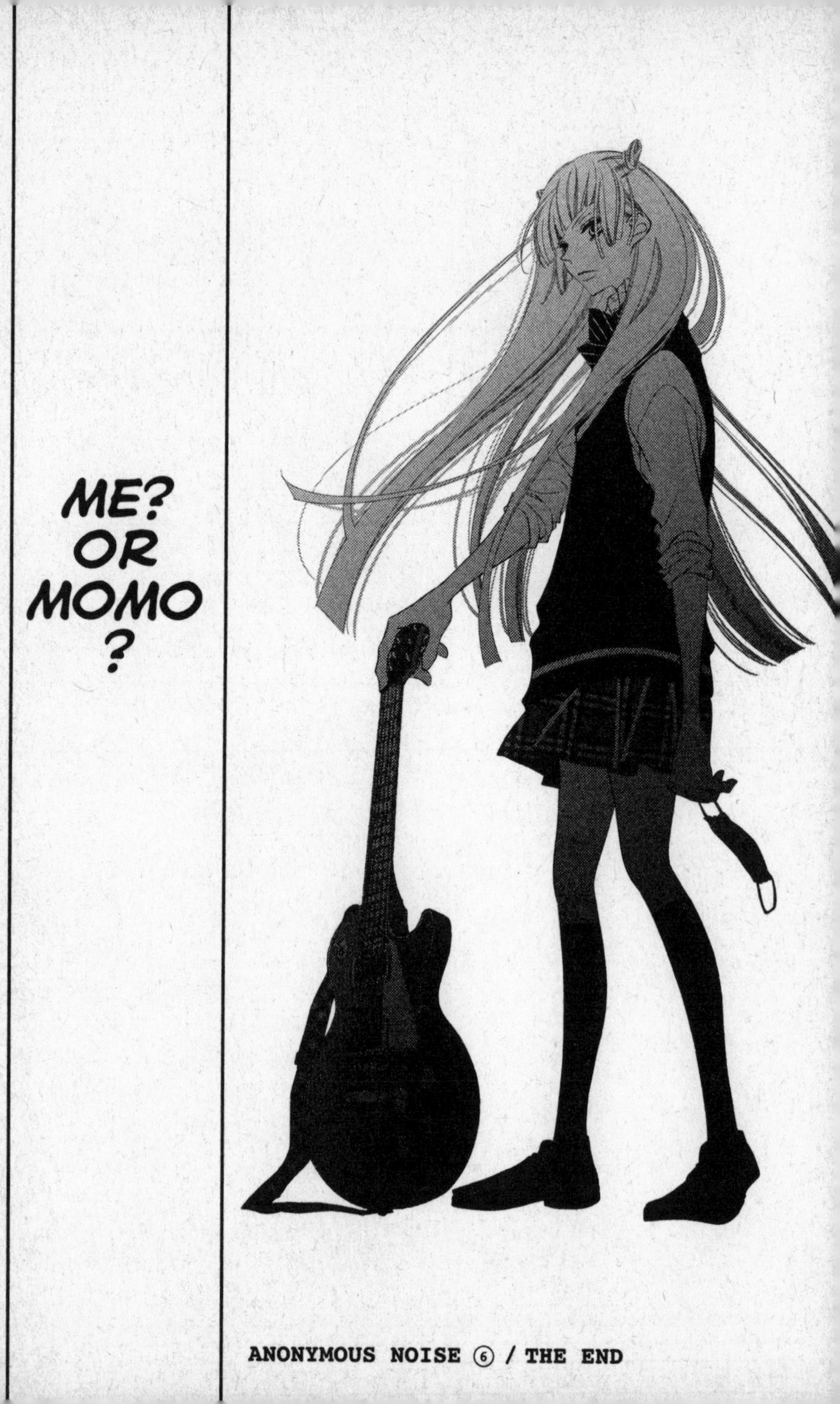
ANONYMOUS NOISE ⑥ / THE END
ME? OR MOMO ?

TO BE CONTINUED IN ANONYMOUS NOISE 7

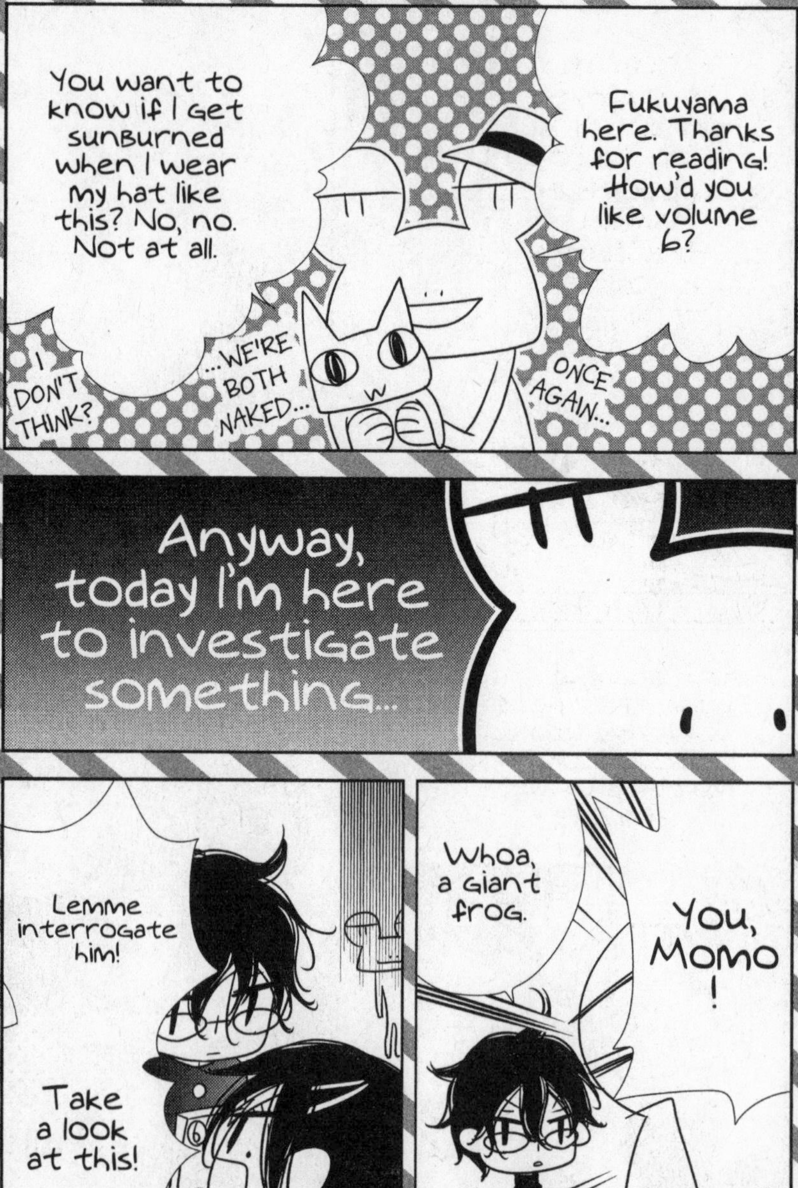
Fukuyama here. Thanks for reading! How'd you like volume 6?
You want to know if I get sunburned when I wear my hat like this? No, no. Not at all.
ONCE AGAIN...
...WE'RE BOTH NAKED...
I DON'T THINK?
Anyway, today I'm here to investigate something...
You, Momo!
Whoa, a giant frog.
YUCK.
Lemme interrogate him!
Take a look at this!

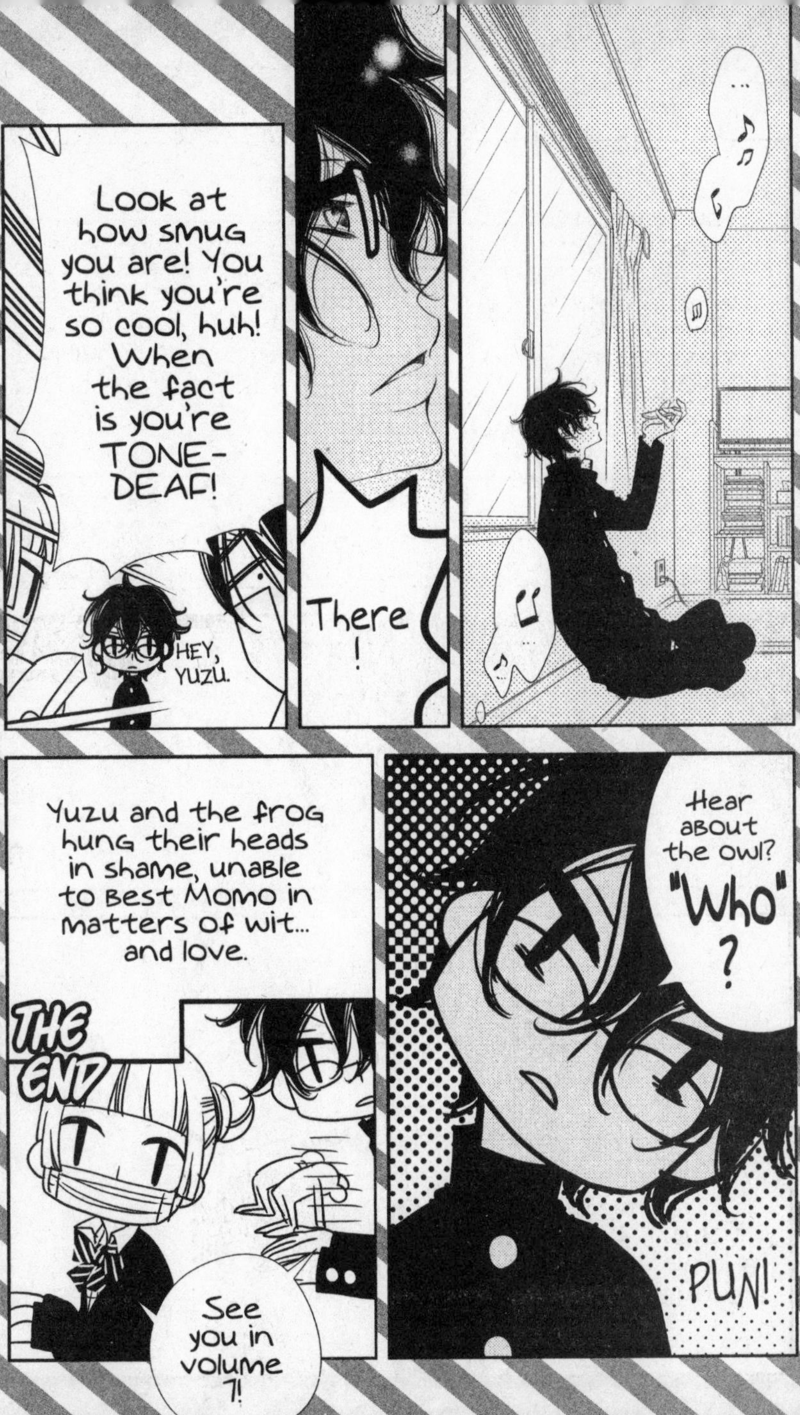
...
There!
Look at how smug you are! You think you're so cool, huh! When the fact is you're TONE-DEAF!
HEY, YUZU.
Hear about the owl? "Who"?
PUN!
Yuzu and the frog hung their heads in shame, unable to best Momo in matters of wit... and love.
THE END
See you in volume 7!

I think I get the biggest thrill out
of drawing the moments when my
characters are just about to launch
into a flying leap. I hope I'm
able to convey a taste of that
excitement to my readers!

- Ryoko Fukuyama

Born on January 5 in Wakayama Prefecture in
Japan, Ryoko Fukuyama debuted as a manga
artist after winning the Hakusensha Athena
Shinjin Taisho Prize from Hakusensha's *Hana to
Yume* magazine. She is also the author
of *Nosatsu Junkie. Anonymous Noise* was
adapted into an anime in 2017.

ANONYMOUS NOISE
Vol. 6
Shojo Beat Edition

STORY AND ART BY
RYOKO FUKUYAMA

English Translation & Adaptation/Casey Loe
Touch-Up Art & Lettering/Joanna Estep
Design/Yukiko Whitley
Editor/Amy Yu

Fukumenkei Noise by Ryoko Fukuyama
© Ryoko Fukuyama 2015
All rights reserved.
First published in Japan in 2015 by HAKUSENSHA, Inc., Tokyo.
English language translation rights arranged with HAKUSENSHA, Inc., Tokyo.

Printed in Canada

Published by VIZ Media, LLC
P.O. Box 77010
San Francisco, CA 94107

10 9 8 7 6 5 4 3 2 1
First printing, January 2018

www.viz.com   www.shojobeat.com

Surprise!

You may be reading the wrong way!

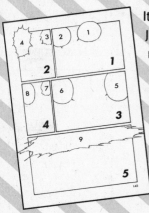

It's true: In keeping with the original Japanese comic format, this book reads from right to left—so action, sound effects and word balloons are completely reversed. This preserves the orientation of the original artwork—plus, it's fun! Check out the diagram shown here to get the hang of things, and then turn to the other side of the book to get started!